COMPETITION, INNOVATION AND TRADE

World Scientific Studies in International Economics

(ISSN: 1793-3641)

World Scientific Studies in International Economics includes works dealing with the theory, empirical analysis, and evaluation of international economic policies and institutions, with topics covering international macroeconomics and finance, international trade theory and policy, as well as international legal and political economy. Monographs and edited volumes will comprise the core of the publications.

Vol. 75 *Competition, Innovation and Trade*
edited by Larry D. Qiu (Lingnan University, Hong Kong)

Vol. 74 *Understanding the Implications of Trade and Financial Market Integration for Business Cycles*
edited by Mario J. Crucini (Vanderbilt University, USA)

Vol. 73 *The International Economics of Wine*
edited by Kym Anderson (University of Adelaide, Australia & Australian National University, Australia)

Vol. 72 *Foreign Direct Investment*
by Bruce A. Blonigen (University of Oregon, USA & National Bureau of Economic Research, USA)

Vol. 71 *Offshoring: Causes and Consequences at the Firm and Worker Level*
edited by Holger Görg (Kiel Institute for the World Economy, Germany) & Aoife Hanley (Kiel Institute for the World Economy, Germany)

Vol. 70 *Policy Externalities and International Trade Agreements*
by Nuno Limão (University of Maryland, USA)

Vol. 69 *Economic Analysis of the Rules and Regulations of the World Trade Organization*
edited by Kamal Saggi (Vanderbilt University, USA)

Vol. 68 *International Trade, Capital Flows and Economic Development*
edited by Francisco L. Rivera-Batiz (Columbia University, USA) & Luis A. Rivera-Batiz (University of Puerto Rico, USA)

Vol. 67 *Megaregionalism 2.0: Trade and Innovation within Global Networks*
edited by Dieter Ernst (East-West Center, USA & The Centre for International Governance Innovation/CIGI, Canada) & Michael G. Plummer (The Johns Hopkins University, SAIS, Italy)

The complete list of the published volumes in the series can be found at
https://www.worldscientific.com/series/wssie

75 World Scientific Studies in International Economics

COMPETITION, INNOVATION AND TRADE

Editor

Larry D. Qiu

Lingnan University, Hong Kong

World Scientific

NEW JERSEY • LONDON • SINGAPORE • BEIJING • SHANGHAI • HONG KONG • TAIPEI • CHENNAI • TOKYO

Published by

World Scientific Publishing Co. Pte. Ltd.
5 Toh Tuck Link, Singapore 596224
USA office: 27 Warren Street, Suite 401-402, Hackensack, NJ 07601
UK office: 57 Shelton Street, Covent Garden, London WC2H 9HE

Library of Congress Cataloging-in-Publication Data
Names: Qiu, Larry D., editor.
Title: Competition, innovation and trade / editor, Larry D. Qiu, Lingnan University, Hong Kong.
Description: New Jersey : World Scientific, 2020. | Series: World scientific studies in international economics, 1793-3641 ; vol. 75 | Includes bibliographical references and Index.
Identifiers: LCCN 2020010596 | ISBN 9789811203985 (hardcover)
Subjects: LCSH: Technological innovations--Economic aspects. | International trade. | Competition. | Economic development.
Classification: LCC HC79.T4 C658 2020 | DDC 338.6/048--dc23
LC record available at https://lccn.loc.gov/2020010596

British Library Cataloguing-in-Publication Data
A catalogue record for this book is available from the British Library.

For any available supplementary material, please visit
https://www.worldscientific.com/worldscibooks/10.1142/11374#t=suppl

Desk Editors: Balamurugan Rajendran/Yulin Jiang

Typeset by Stallion Press
Email: enquiries@stallionpress.com

Preface

Economic growth and development crucially depend on innovation and international trade. While innovation enhances production efficiency (by improving technologies) and consumer welfare (by introducing new products and services), international trade enables resources to be used efficiently at the global level (by specialization and comparative advantages) and benefits consumers (due to increased competition and product varieties).

Both innovation and international trade are familiar topics of economic research. Numerous journal articles and books have been written on these topics, mostly separately. Existing literature has advanced our understanding of these two issues and informed business and policy decisions. Several scholars have even been awarded Nobel Prize in Economics for their path-breaking contributions to these topics. Nonetheless, innovation and international trade have become even more important in contemporary society. The world has been changing rapidly. As a result, new issues related to innovation and international trade emerge from time to time. Traditional wisdom may not be able to fully explain the reality and new ideas need to come up for us to help make a better world by taking advantage of innovation and international trade.

The objective of this book is to present to the readers a collection of my research papers related to innovation and international trade. It aims at giving the readers different perspectives on these two topics. The book contains several articles on the theory of innovation and international trade, as well as several papers on empirical investigations of these two topics. Some of the papers are about innovation or international trade only (and separately), while some of them contain both issues within the same framework to explore their interplay. Although some of the research studies were done more than a decade ago, some are very recent works. The differences in these works are not about the time dimension but rather the different types of questions being addressed. I would like to thank my co-authors for teaching me and working with me in those research projects.

The book consists of two parts. The first part mainly focuses on innovation and the second part focuses on international trade.

Part 1 contains six chapters under the title "R&D, Innovations and IPR Policy". Chapter 1, titled "On the Dynamic Efficiency of Bertrand and Cournot Equilibria" (*Journal of Economic Theory*, 1997), contributes to the famous debate in the industrial organization literature on the comparison between Cournot (or quantity) competition and Bertrand (or price) competition. The debate had almost concluded (prior to 1997) that Bertrand competition is more efficient than Cournot competition from a social welfare point of view because the former results in low equilibrium prices. I introduce innovation to the debate. I show that when firms conduct research and development (R&D) to reduce production cost, firms have stronger incentives to invest in R&D under Cournot competition than Bertrand competition. As a result, it is possible that the traditional belief is wrong, and Cournot competition is more efficient, from a dynamic point of view. An important implication of this research is that when we consider innovation, some existing results could be reversed.

Chapter 2, titled "Policy on International R&D Cooperation: Subsidy or Tax?" (*European Economic Review*, 1998), studies R&D policies. In the market, firms normally do not invest sufficiently from a social welfare point of view because of the positive externalities of R&D investment. This observation calls for government intervention, and specifically, R&D subsidization. What should be the government policy on R&D investment if domestic firms are in competition with foreign firms in the international market? Traditional results have shown that each country's government has strong incentive to subsidize R&D to strengthen a domestic firm's competitive advantage in the market. This is the so-called strategic aspect of R&D policy. However, rivalry firms sometimes are not contesting on the R&D front even though they compete in the product market. There are often two types of R&D cooperations: collaboration and coordination. When firms cooperate in R&D, they share their R&D outcomes. When firms coordinate in R&D, they try to reduce or even eliminate the competition between themselves. The question is as follows: how should the governments change their R&D policies in each of these two situations? I (with my co-author Zhigang Tao) prove that R&D subsidy is still an optimal policy for each country's government in the case of R&D coordination and, more strikingly, the subsidies are larger for higher degrees of coordination; but in the case of R&D collaboration, both R&D subsidy and tax are possible. This research shows that analyzing government policy becomes more complicated in a global setting because firms may take various types of corporations.

With regard to innovation policies, perhaps the most important one is intellectual property rights (IPR) protection. The next three chapters focus on IPR protection. Everyone agrees that IPR protection is necessary and important for innovation. The difficult question is about the level of protection. Is a 15-year protection too short? Is a 20-year protection too long? In Chapter 3, "The North's Intellectual Property Rights Standard for the South?" (*Journal of International Economics*, 2003), I (and my co-author Edwin Lai) try to answer the famous question, which is, whether the developing countries should adopt the IPR standard of the developed countries. To this end, we build a multi-sectoral North–South trade model to compare the Nash equilibrium IPR protection standard of the South (the developing countries) with that of the North (the developed countries). Naturally, because the South and North are different in many aspects including innovation capability, the South naturally adopts a weaker standard than the North. More importantly, we argue that both regions can gain from an agreement that requires the South to harmonize its IPR standards with those of the North, and the North to liberalize its traditional goods market in return. This demonstrates the merits of multi-sectoral negotiations in the World Trade Organization (WTO) and the former General Agreement on Tariffs and Trade (GATT).

Chapter 4, titled "Entry, Reputation and Intellectual Property Rights Enforcement" (*Canadian Journal of Economics*, 2014), examines how IPR protection in developing countries affects multinational firms' entry decision. I (with my co-author Jiahua Che and Wen Zhou) argue that facing with imitation under weak IPR enforcement in a developing country, a multinational firm is concerned about its product's reputation and may choose to partly withhold its entry into the country. We show that holding constant a multinational's incentive to innovate, better IPR enforcement encourages entry but reduces social welfare. The multinational's incentive to innovate may be inversely U-shaped in the strength of IPR enforcement.

While the first four chapters are theoretic analyses of R&D and related policies, the next two chapters present some empirical evidence. Chapter 5, titled "Does the Protection of Foreign Intellectual Property Rights Stimulate Innovation in the US?" (*Review of International Economics*, 2010), investigates the effect of IPR protection on innovation activities. Although standard theories suggest that patent protection helps stimulate innovative activities, indeed existing empirical studies do not generate conclusive results. In this chapter, I (with my co-author Huayang Yu) examine the impacts of foreign patent reforms on innovation in the US, using data on successful patent applications in the US over 33 years and major IPR reforms in 21 countries, in addition to the patent reforms in the US and the TRIPS Agreement of the WTO. Interestingly, we find that very large (such as the TRIPS Agreement) and only very large IPR reforms can have significant impacts on the aggregate innovation in the US. In particular, the effects of strengthening patent protection by individual countries are not significant. An interesting implication of this finding is that the US market is already sufficiently large/profitable to provide innovation incentives in the US, and therefore, further strengthening foreign patent protection simply increases the US innovators' rent, but not their innovation.

Chapter 6, titled "Intermediate Input Imports and Innovations: Evidence from Chinese Firms' Patent Filings" (*Journal of International Economics*, 2016), turns to innovation in China. Although China is still similar to other developing countries in many dimensions including imitation and weak IPR enforcement, China has become one of the most important countries in innovation in recent years. Why and how do Chinese firms increase their R&D investment and patent application so fast? How does trade liberalization affect Chinese firms' innovation incentives? While the first question is very big and general, the second question is more specific. There are various types of trade liberalization, and in this chapter, I (with my co-author Qing Liu) investigate the effects of intermediate input tariff reduction on the innovation activities of domestic firms, which belongs to the second question just mentioned. Our focus is interesting because input tariff reduction has two differing effects on the innovation decision of a firm: it may promote innovation because the cost of innovation activities decreases, but it may also result in a decrease in innovation because foreign technologies become cheaper. Using Chinese firm-level data from 1998 to 2007, which feature a drastic input tariff cut in 2002 because of China's WTO accession, we find that input tariff cut results in *less* innovation undertaken by Chinese firms. In this chapter, I also provide a theoretical framework to generate insights to the empirical findings.

Part 2 titled "International Trade and Trade Policy" contains five chapters on international trade in general and protection in particular. It starts with Chapter 7 "Optimal Strategic Trade Policy under Asymmetric Information" (*Journal of International Economics*, 1994). In the 1980s, one stream of research which received a lot of interest is strategic trade policy. Strategic trade policy is about trade policy in oligopolistic industries which alters large firms' strategic behavior. It was believed that some countries, for example Japan, use such policies to help domestic firms take advantages in international competition. One criticism on strategic trade policy is that the government often lacks information of the market and therefore is unlikely to design appropriate policies. In this chapter, I examine one type of information problem: the government does not know the cost of the domestic firm but the firm knows. I explore how an optimal policy should be designed and looks like under asymmetric information.

The next two chapters explore how business practices may act like a protection. Chapter 8 is titled "Keiretsu and Relationship-Specific Investment: A Barrier to Trade?" (*International Economic Review*, 2001). It is generally believed that it is very difficult for multinationals to enter the Japanese market and for foreign firms to compete (via export) in the Japanese market. However, Japan is not very special among developed countries in terms of trade policies such as tariffs and import quota. It is believed that some business practices in Japan may be viewed as a kind of protection, but there was no serious research on this topic. In this chapter, I (with my co-author Barbara Spencer, who is one of the pioneers of strategic trade policy) develop a model of informal procurement within Japanese keiretsu, which is a unique Japanese business network, in the automobile industry. Within keiretsu, parts-suppliers make relationship-specific investments that benefit the automaker, and thus, the automaker is willing to buy those domestic parts with a higher price than the imported parts. Thus, we argue that keiretsu practice looks like a barrier to trade but is efficiency improving.

Chapter 9, titled "Keiretsu and Relationship-Specific Investment: Implications for Market-Opening Trade Policy" (*Journal of International Economics*, 2002), applies the keiretsu model introduced in Chapter 8 to analyze the effects of trade policies. Specifically, I (again with the same co-author Barbara Spencer) consider the implications of relationship-specific investment within keiretsu for policies aimed at opening the Japanese market for intermediate goods, such as auto-parts. Two types of policies are studied, one being voluntary import expansion (VIE) and the other being voluntary export restriction (VER). The analysis shows which type of policy is preferred by which country.

If keiretsu, analyzed in the previous two chapters, is very unique to Japan, technical barriers to trade (TBT) are very common among all countries. The last two chapters of this book focus on TBT. Chapter 10 asks the following question: "How Do Technical Barriers to Trade Influence Trade?" (*Review of International Economics*, 2012). TBT is a type of non-tariff barrier and it includes standards and technical regulations. TBT is relatively new, but has become more and more important. TBT has been introduced for a range of reasons (for example, for environmental protection, safety, national security and consumer information) and varies from country to country in terms of its magnitude and product coverage. In this chapter, I (with my co-author Xiaohua Bao) empirically estimate the trade effects of TBT based on all TBT notifications from 105 WTO countries during 1995–2008. We find that a country's TBT notifications decrease other countries' probability of exporting, but increase their export volumes. The result can be explained by the TBT's differential effects on the fixed and variable cost of export and consumer confidence. We also find that the effects are different, depending on the nature of the importing and exporting countries.

The last chapter, Chapter 11 titled "Do Technical Barriers to Trade Promote or Restrict Trade? Evidence from China" (*Asia-Pacific Journal of Accounting & Economics*, 2010), focuses on TBT in China in order to have a more detailed analysis. I (with co-author Xiaohua Bao) argue that in contrast to most other trade measures, TBT have both trade promotion and trade restriction effects. In this chapter, we construct a TBT database from 1998 to 2006 to examine the influence of TBT imposed by China on the country's imports. One result is interesting: when using frequency index as a measure of TBT, we find that TBT are trade restrictive: a one-unit increase in TBT will decrease the import value by about 0.8%. However, when using coverage ratio as a measure, we find that a one-unit increase in TBT will increase the import value by about 0.2%.

As I pointed out at the beginning, innovation and international trade are key to economic growth and development. Despite the existence of the huge literature, continuous investigations on these topics are still very (even more) important because the world is changing every day. If this book can help enhance your understanding of these topics, or stimulate your further research, or change your business decisions, I will consider it a great success.

Larry D. Qiu
Sydney S.W. Leong Chair Professor of Economics
Lingnan University, Hong Kong

About the Editor

Larry D. Qiu received a PhD degree (in 1993) in economics from the University of British Columbia. He was a professor in Hong Kong University of Science and Technology and Chung Hon-Dak Professor (in Economic Development) at the University of Hong Kong (HKU). He is currently Sydney S.W. Leong Chair Professor of Economics, Head of Department of Economics, Lingnan University, Hong Kong. He was a president of Hong Kong Economic Association and founding President of China Trade Research Group. His teachings and research focus on international trade, foreign direct investment, research and development, and industrial organization.

Contents

Part I

R&D, Innovations and IPR Policy

Chapter 1

On the Dynamic Efficiency of Bertrand and Cournot Equilibria*

Abstract

This paper compares Bertrand and Cournot equilibria in a differentiated duopoly with research and development (R&D) competition. Cournot competition is shown to induce more R&D effort than Bertrand competition. However, the price is lower and output is higher in Bertrand than in Cournot competition. Furthermore, the Bertrand equilibrium is more efficient than the Cournot equilibrium if either R&D productivity is low, spillovers are weak, or products are very different. If R&D productivity is high, spillovers are strong and goods are close substitutes, the Bertrand equilibrium becomes *less* efficient than the Cournot equilibrium.

1. Introduction

It is well understood that (i) equilibrium prices are lower and outputs are higher in Bertrand (price) competition than in Cournot (quantity) competition, and (ii) the Bertrand equilibrium is more efficient than the Cournot equilibrium, in terms of greater consumer surplus and welfare (see Singh and Vives, 1984; Cheng, 1985; Vives, 1985). These traditional results are obtained under the assumption that firms face the *same* demand and cost structure in both types of competition. To make the comparison meaningful, such a static assumption seems reasonable and desirable. However, this

*This chapter is reproduced from *Journal of Economic Theory*, 75(1), 213–229, 1997, with permission from Elsevier.

assumption may not be innocuous because firms often compete against each other by investing in research and development (R&D) to improve in product quality (in the case of product R&D) and/or to reduce production cost (in the case of process R&D). As a result, the structure of market demand and cost of production may change. In such a *dynamic* environment, if R&D investments are different in Bertrand and Cournot competition, the post-innovation demand and cost structures will be different even though they were identical before the R&D competition. The ensuing important question is whether the traditional result still holds will be affected in any way.

The present study focuses on cost-reducing R&D and reexamines the relative efficiency of Cournot and Bertrand equilibria. The case for cost-reducing R&D is of particular interest. As I shall show, firms invest more in R&D in Cournot competition than in Bertrand competition. With lower pre-competition production costs in Cournot competition, do the firms still charge lower prices and produce more in Bertrand competition? Even if the answer is yes, it does not always yield the traditional welfare results since the cost of production is now larger in Bertrand than in Cournot competition. In other words, if the market with Bertrand competition enjoys higher *static* efficiency, will it necessarily lead to higher *dynamic* efficiency?

In Section 2, the basic model is introduced. It augments the Singh and Vives (1984) model by including R&D investment. I then derive the equilibrium when the market is characterized by a Cournot game. In Section 3, the same exercise is repeated using a Bertrand game. In Sections 4 and 5, I show that although firms conduct more R&D and therefore have lower post-innovation costs in Cournot competition,[1] they still charge higher prices, produce less, and generate a smaller consumer surplus than in Bertrand competition. If R&D productivity is low, or spillovers are weak, or goods are not close substitutes, the Bertrand equilibrium is shown to be more efficient, in terms

[1] Brander and Spencer (1983) analyze R&D incentives in a Cournot and Okuno-Fujiwara and Suzumura (1974) examine them in a Bertrand model. Bester and Petrakis (1993) have also compared R6D incentives in Bertrand and Cournot competition but reach different conclusions. An explanation will be given in Section 4.

of a larger total surplus, than the Cournot equilibrium; but the opposite holds when R&D productivity is high, spillovers are strong and product differentiation is low.

2. The Basic Model and Cournot Equilibrium

Consider a non-cooperative two-stage game with two firms producing differentiated goods. In the first stage (R&D stage), each firm independently undertakes cost-reducing R&D. In the second stage (market stage), both firms produce and sell their products to the market. I first consider Cournot (quantity) competition in this section. The case of Bertrand (price) competition is relegated to the next section.

Following Singh and Vives (1984), I assume that the representative consumer's utility function is $(q_1, q_2) = \alpha(q_1 + q_2) - \frac{1}{2}(q_1^2 + 2\gamma q_1 q_2 + q_2^2)$, where q_i is the quantity of the good produced by firm $i, \alpha > 0$, and $\gamma \in (0, 1)$. The degree of product differentiation decreases with the parameter γ. The resulting market demands are linear and given by

$$p_i = \alpha - q_i - \gamma q_j, \quad i, j = 1, 2, \ i \neq j. \tag{1}$$

The two firms start with the same constant marginal cost ($< \alpha$). If only firm does R&D, then by spending $V(x_i)$ on R&D it can lower its marginal cost by x_i. It is commonly assumed that R&D investment has diminishing returns and that the R&D expenditure function is quadratic (e.g. d'Aspremont and Jacquemin, 1988): $V(x_i) = \frac{1}{2}vx_i^2$, where the parameter v relates to the efficiency or productivity of the R&D technology (higher v means lower efficiency). Assume

Al: $v > \alpha/c$.

It will be shown below that Al guarantees positive post-innovation costs of production in both price and quantity competition. Al is also needed for the second-order and stability conditions. To understand Al, note that if the demand is very strong (i.e. α is large) and the pre-innovation cost of production c is not too high, then the R&D technology should not be too efficient or otherwise the firms will invest a lot in R&D, resulting in zero or even negative post-innovation costs, which is unrealistic.

To model the spillover effects of R&D, I assume that the firms' marginal costs are

$$c_i = c - x_i - \theta x_j, \quad i, j = 1, 2, \quad \text{and} \quad i \neq j,$$

should they spend $V(x_i)$ and $V(x_i)$ on R&D, respectively. The parameter $\theta \in [0, 1]$ captures the extent of spillovers.

I use the backward induction approach to derive sub-game perfect equilibria. Let π_i denote firm i's market profit (profit excluding R&D costs). Then given any first-stage R&D outcome (x_1, x_2), $\pi_i(q_1, q_2; x_1, x_2) = p_i q_i - (c - x_i - \theta x_j)q_i$. The firms choose output to maximize their respective market profits and the Cournot–Nash equilibrium is

$$q_i^*(x_1, x_2) = \frac{1}{4 - \gamma^2}[(\alpha - c)(2 - \gamma) + (2 - \theta\gamma)x_i + (2\theta - \gamma)x_j]. \quad (2)$$

I now turn to the R&D stage. Each firm chooses an R&D level to maximize its overall profit, $\Pi_i(x_1, x_2) = \pi_i(q_1^*, q_2^*; x_1, x_2) - \frac{1}{2}vx_i^2$. The (symmetric) equilibrium R&D level of each firm is[2]

$$x_C = \frac{2(2 - \theta\gamma)(\alpha - c)}{\Delta_c}, \quad (3)$$

where $\Delta_c \equiv v(2 + \gamma)(4 - \gamma^2) - 2(2 - \theta\gamma)(1 + \theta)$. It is straightforward to verify the following lemma (the proof is omitted).

Lemma 1. *For all θ and γ, Al is sufficient but not necessary for $v(4 - \gamma^2)^2 - 2(2 - \theta\gamma)^2 > 0$ (the second-order condition) and $c > 0$ (the stability condition); Al is both necessary and sufficient for $c - (1 + \theta)x_C > 0$ (positive post-innovation costs).*

Substituting x_C into (1) and (2) gives the (symmetric) equilibrium output and price:

$$q_C = \frac{1}{\Delta_c} v(\alpha - c)(4 - \gamma^2) \quad \text{and} \quad p_C = \alpha - (1 + \gamma)q_C. \quad (4)$$

[2] The second-order and the Routh–Hurwitz stability conditions are, respectively,

$$\frac{\partial^2 \Pi_i}{\partial x_i^2} < 0 \quad \text{and} \quad \frac{\partial^2 \Pi_1}{\partial x_1^2}\frac{\partial^2 \Pi_2}{\partial x_2^2} - \frac{\partial^2 \Pi_1}{\partial x_2 \partial x_1}\frac{\partial^2 \Pi_2}{\partial x_1 \partial x_{12}} > 0.$$

Finally, I obtain the equilibrium consumer surplus $[CS = U(q_1, q_2) - p_1 q_1 - p_2 q_2]$, producer profits $(\Pi = \Pi_1 + \Pi_2)$, and welfare (total surplus) in Cournot competition as follows:

$$CS_C = (1+\gamma)q_C^2, \quad \Pi_C = 2q_C^2 - vx_C^2, \tag{5}$$

$$\begin{aligned} W_C &= CS_C + \Pi_C \\ &= \frac{1}{\Delta_C^2} v(\alpha - c)^2[v(3+\gamma)(4-\gamma^2)^2 - 4(2-\theta\gamma)^2]. \end{aligned} \tag{6}$$

3. Bertrand Equilibrium

Suppose now that the product market involves Bertrand competition. Rewrite (1) as

$$q_i = \frac{1}{1-\gamma^2}[\alpha(1-\gamma) - p_i + \gamma p_j], \quad i, j = 1, 2, \quad i \neq j. \tag{7}$$

Given any first-stage R&D outcome (x_1, x_2), firm i in the market stage chooses p_i to maximize its market profit. The resulting Bertrand–Nash equilibrium is

$$p_i^*(x_1, x_2) = \frac{1}{4-\gamma^2}[(2+\gamma)(\alpha - \alpha\gamma + c) - (2+\theta\gamma)x_i - (2\theta+\gamma)x_j]. \tag{8}$$

In the R&D stage, each firm chooses its R&D level to maximize its overall profit. In the (symmetric) equilibrium, both firms choose

$$x_B = \frac{2}{\Delta_B}(\alpha - c)(2 - \theta\gamma - \gamma^2), \tag{9}$$

where $\Delta_B \equiv v(1+\gamma)(2-\gamma)(4-\gamma^2) - 2(1+\theta)(2-\theta\gamma-\gamma^2)$.

It is now possible to check the following lemma (the proof is straightforward and omitted).

Lemma 2. *For all θ and γ, A1 is sufficient but not necessary for $\Delta_B > 0$ (the stability condition), and it is both necessary and sufficient for $c - (1+\theta)x_B > 0$ (positive post-innovation costs). If $\theta = 1$, the second-order condition for optimal x_B is $v(1+\gamma)(2-\gamma)^2 - 2(1-\gamma) > 0$, which is ensured by A1; but if $\theta \neq 1$, the second-order* *condition is*

$$v > \frac{2(2-\theta\gamma-\gamma^2)^2}{(1-\gamma^2)(4-\gamma^2)^2}, \tag{10}$$

and A1 is no longer sufficient to ensure (10) *for all* γ *and* θ.

A brief discussion of Lemma 2 regarding the second-order condition is in order. According to (10), if θ is not equal to 1 and γ is very close to one, v must be large in order to satisfy the second-order condition for an interior solution of optimal R&D. When the two goods are close substitutes, competition is fierce as both firms cut prices to seize market shares. The ability of the firms to lower prices, however, is limited by their marginal costs. Suppose v is small, i.e. it is not too costly to do R&D. In this case, a firm is always willing to invest a lot to create a cost advantage over its rival so as to win the price war. That means, v has to be large to avoid a corner solution which results from an extremely large R&D investment. When $\theta = 1$, such a restriction on v is not needed. With perfect spillovers, no pre-competition cost advantages could occur and so this motive of R&D investment goes away. In fact, as γ approaches one, x_B becomes zero $\theta = 1$ [see (9)].

Using (9) in (7) and (8), I obtain the market equilibrium:

$$\begin{aligned} p_B &= \frac{1}{\Delta_B}[v(\alpha-\alpha\gamma+c)(1+\gamma)(4-\gamma^2) - 2\alpha(1+\theta)(2-\theta\gamma-\gamma^2)], \\ q_B &= \frac{1}{\Delta_B}v(\alpha-c)(4-\gamma^2). \end{aligned} \tag{11}$$

Finally, I calculate the equilibrium consumer surplus, producer profits, and welfare (total surplus) in Bertrand competition:

$$CS_B = (1+\gamma)q_B^2, \quad \Pi_B = 2(1-\gamma^2)q_B^2 - vx_B^2, \tag{12}$$

$$\begin{aligned} W_B = CS_B + \Pi_B &= \frac{1}{\Delta_B^2}v(\alpha-c)^2 \\ &\quad \times [v(3+\gamma-2\gamma^2)(4-\gamma^2)^2 - 4(2-\theta\gamma-\gamma^2)^2]. \end{aligned} \tag{13}$$

4. Comparison I: R&D Incentives

Before comparing the two equilibria, I first derive the socially optimal (or the first-best) allocation as a benchmark. The social planner's problem is[3]

$$\underset{x_1,x_2,q_1,q_2}{\text{Max}}, W_S = U(q_1, q_2) - \sum_{i=1}^{2}(c - x_i - \theta x_j)q_i - \frac{1}{2}v\sum_{i=1}^{2} x_i^2.$$

Assume

A2: $v > 4\alpha/c$.

This assumption is necessary and sufficient for the optimal post-innovation costs to be positive and is sufficient but not necessary to ensure the second-order condition for the social planner's problem.

It is easily verified that the social planner's optimal decision is symmetric and given by

$$x_i = x_S = \frac{(1+\theta)(\alpha - c)}{(1+\gamma)v - (1+\theta)^2} \quad \text{and}$$
$$q_i = q_S = \frac{(\alpha - c)v}{(1+\gamma)v - (1+\theta)^2}. \tag{14}$$

I am now in a position to address several important questions. Would the firms invest more in R&D when the product market involves Cournot competition than when it involves Bertrand competition? How are these investment levels compared to the first-best levels? What are the comparisons between the Bertrand and Cournot outputs and prices when the pre-competition production costs are endogenously determined by the first-stage R&D efforts? These are the questions that beg for answers. A simple and direct

[3]In general, the degree of cross-firm R&D spillover is jointly determined by many factors including the nature of technologies, the legal framework, and the information control of the firms. I consider the case in which even the social planner cannot affect θ.

comparison based on (3), (9), and (14) immediately yields the following proposition.

Proposition 1. *For any given* $\gamma \in (0,1)$ *and* $\theta \in [0,1]$, $x_S > x_C > x_B$ *under A2 and* (10).

In words, Proposition 1 states that the firms always invest more in R&D if the product market involves Cournot competition than if it involves Bertrand competition, but in both cases they invest less than the social optimum. The key to the understanding of this result is to carefully examine the factors that induce the firms to undertake R&D and their interactions in different competition modes. Even with general demand and R&D cost functions, I can decompose each firm's R&D effect into four parts (see Appendix for derivation). In Cournot competition,

$$\begin{aligned}\frac{\partial \Pi_i}{\partial x_i} &= \left[-\frac{1}{\Psi_C}\frac{\partial \pi_i}{\partial q_j}\frac{\partial^2 \pi_i}{\partial q_i^2}\theta\right] + \left[\frac{1}{\Psi_C}\frac{\partial \pi_i}{\partial q_j}\frac{\partial^2 \pi_j}{\partial q_i \partial q_j}\right] + q_i + [-V_i'(x_i)] \\ &= \underbrace{\text{spillover effect}}_{(-)} + \underbrace{\text{strategic effect}}_{(+)} + \underbrace{\text{size effect}}_{(+)} + \underbrace{\text{cost effect}}_{(-)}\end{aligned}$$

In Bertrand competition,

$$\begin{aligned}\frac{\partial \Pi_i}{\partial x_i} &= \left[-\frac{1}{\Psi_B}\frac{\partial \pi_i}{\partial p_j}\frac{\partial^2 \pi_i}{\partial p_i^2}\frac{\partial q_j}{\partial p_j}\theta\right] + \left[\frac{1}{\Psi_B}\frac{\partial \pi_i}{\partial p_j}\frac{\partial^2 \pi_j}{\partial p_i \partial p_j}\frac{\partial q_i}{\partial p_i}\right] \\ &\quad + q_i + [-V_i'(x_i)] \\ &= \underbrace{\text{spillover effect}}_{(-)} + \underbrace{\text{strategic effect}}_{(+)} + \underbrace{\text{size effect}}_{(+)} + \underbrace{\text{cost effect}}_{(-)}\end{aligned}$$

First, the firm's R&D lowers the unit cost of production. For a given cost reduction, *ceteris paribus*, the more it produces, the more it benefits. Thus, the size effect is always positive (i.e. it gives the firm incentives to do R&D) in both Cournot and Bertrand competition. Second, the firm's R&D also lowers its rival's cost, which in turn is detrimental to the R&D-taking firm. Because of this, the spillover eect is always negative (i.e. it gives the firm disincentives to do R&D) in both Cournot and Bertrand competition. Third, R&D activity is costly, implying that the cost effect is negative in both types of competition. Finally, the firm's R&D lowers its production cost and so affects the rival firm's output or price decision. This is the strategic effect and, unlike the other effects, is positive in Cournot competition but negative in Bertrand competition. In the Cournot case, by doing more R&D and thereby lowering its cost, the firm is tougher in the market and thus discourages its rival's sale, which in turn benefits itself.[4] In contrast, in the Bertrand case, the firm's R&D lowers its cost and induces its rival to cut price, which in turn hurts itself.[5]

In the central planning case, both the spillover and strategic effects are internalized. The spillover effect becomes positive and the strategic effect vanishes.[6] Table 1.1 summarizes the above discussion.

Based on Proposition 2 to be stated below, the size effect is strongest in the central planning case and weakest in the Cournot case. This, together with Table 1.1, clearly shows that $x_S > x_B$. Other comparisons hinge on the relative importance of the three effects that gives rise to the ranking reported in Proposition 1.[7]

It is worth pointing out that while I obtain a unique R&D investment ranking for all possible values of θ and γ, Bester and Petrakis (1993), who do not consider spillovers, show that all types of rankings are possible, depending on γ and the degree of cost reduction. To understand the differences, it suffices to discuss just one of their results, $x_C < x_B$ for a large γ (and of course $= 0$) and compare it with Proposition 1. Recall that Bester and Petrakis allow only one of the two firms to invest in R&D. The innovating firm ends up enjoying of a large cost advantage over its competitor, which

Table 1.1. Decomposition of R&D incentives.

	Spillover effect	Strategic effect	Size effect
Central planning	+	nil	+
Cournot	−	+	+
Bertrand	−	−	+

[4]This positive strategic effect leads to over-investment in the absence of spillovers (see Brander and Spencer, 1985).

[5]This negative strategic effect leads to under-investment in the absence of spillovers (see Okuno-Fujiwara and Suzumura, 1974).

[6]This is because $\partial x_S/\partial\theta > 0$ from (14).

[7]For more detailed discussions on these three effects, see Qiu (1995a) and (1995b).

results in different market shares of the R&D firm and the non-R&D firm. This asymmetry helps the R&D firm but hurts the non-R&D firm. As a result, the R&D firm's output in this asymmetry case substantially exceeds that in the symmetric case. In other words, the size effect is much stronger in the model of Bester and Petrakis (1993) (the asymmetric case) than in the present one (the symmetric case), and it may become sufficiently strong to dominate the strategic effect. When the size effect prevails and products are alike, a firm will have incentives to do more R&D in Bertrand competition than in Cournot competition. This follows because a Bertrand firm always produces more (see Proposition 2) and thus faces a stronger size effect than a Cournot firm. The R&D game in the present model, in contrast, is symmetric. Both firms conduct R&D and the amounts of cost reduction are optimally chosen by each firm in a non-cooperative manner. If pre-innovation conditions are symmetric between the two firms, the post-innovation equilibrium is also symmetric. Therefore, the size effect is less important than that in Bester and Petrakis (1993).

I now turn to the quantity and price comparison. Directly comparing (4), (5), (11), (12), and (14) establishes the following proposition.

Proposition 2. *For any given* $\gamma \in (0, 1)$ *and* $\theta \in [0, 1]$, $q_S > q_B > q_C$, $p_B < p_C$ *under A2 and* (10). *Consequently,* $CS_B > CS_C$ *under the same conditions.*

Propositions 1 and 2 together convey a *new message*: Although Cournot firms make more R&D investments and therefore have lower costs than Bertrand firms, the Bertrand firms still charge lower prices and produce more than the Cournot firms. However, greater outputs and lower prices do not ensure larger total surplus as costs of production in Bertrand competition are higher than those in Cournot competition. This warrants a careful scrutiny of the efficiency issue which is the focus of the next section.

5. Comparison II: Welfare and Efficiency

Obviously, welfare is highest in the case of social planning. However, the rankings of the Cournot and Bertrand equilibria are not so clear. These rankings will be investigated first for the case of perfect spillovers and then respectively for cases with no spillovers and partial spillovers [i.e. $\theta \in (0,1)$].

For $\theta = 1$, the welfare functions in Cournot competition can be simplified to

$$W_{C1} = \frac{v(\alpha - c)^2}{\Delta_{C1}^2}[v(3+\gamma)(2+\gamma)^2 - 4],$$

where $\Delta_{C1} \equiv v(2+\gamma)^2 - 4$, and in Bertrand competition to

$$W_{B1} = \frac{v(\alpha - c)^2}{\Delta_{B1}^2}[v(1+\gamma)(3-2\gamma)(2-\gamma)^2 - 4(1-\gamma)^2],$$

where $\Delta_{B1} \equiv v(1+\gamma)(2-\gamma)^2 - 4(1-\gamma)$. Note that when v is large, R&D investment will be small in both types of competition. Consider the more interesting case wherein R&D could be large. Succinctly, assume that Al is not too restrictive for v in the sense that

A3: $v^* \equiv (32 + 4\sqrt{55})/9 > \alpha/c$.

Proposition 3. *Suppose that $\theta = 1$, and both A1 and A3 hold.*

(i) *If $v \geq v^*$, then $W_{B1} > W_{C1} \forall \gamma \in (0,1)$; and*
(ii) *if $v < v^*$, then there exists $\overline{\gamma}(v) \in (0,1)$ such that*

$$W_{B1} - W_{C1} \begin{cases} > 0 & \forall \gamma < \overline{\gamma}(v) \\ = 0 & if\ \gamma = \overline{\gamma}(v) \\ < 0 & \forall \gamma > \overline{\gamma}(v). \end{cases}$$

Proof: See Appendix. □

The main message contained in Proposition 3 is that the Bertrand equilibrium does not always have higher dynamic efficiency than the Cournot equilibrium.[8] This is in contrast to the traditional result. The underlying intuition is as follows. It is well known (Singh and Vives, 1984) that, in the absence of R&D investment, consumer surplus is larger in the Bertrand equilibrium, but the Bertrand profits are lower. Given the opportunity to reduce pre-competition

[8]For example, it can be easily checked that if $\alpha = 4$, $c = 1$, $v = 5(< v^*)$, $\theta = 1$ and $\gamma = 0.9$, then both A1 and A3 hold, and $W_{B1} = 5.0279 < W_{C1} = 6.27266$.

production cost, Proposition 1 shows that Cournot firms do more R&D than Bertrand firms, but due to spillovers, even the Cournot firms do not over-invest. Thus, both consumers and producers benefit from R&D and they benefit more in Cournot competition. However, if R&D is very costly [case (i) of Proposition 3], even Cournot firms will only do minimal amounts of R&D. That means, the extra social benefit from R&D in Cournot competition no longer outweighs the static efficiency of Bertrand competition. As a result, the traditional result remains valid. If, however, the R&D cost is moderate [case (ii) of Proposition 3], it is possible that the cost discrepancy between Cournot and Bertrand firms is large enough to generate sufficiently high dynamic efficiency in Cournot competition to dominate the static efficiency of Bertrand competition, especially for closely substitutable goods.

The above discussion also implies that the traditional result should continue to hold in the absence of spillovers. This is stated in Proposition 4 and proved in the appendix.

Proposition 4. *Suppose that* $\theta = 0$. *Then,* $W_B > W_C$ *for all* γ *so long as* $A1$ *and* (10) *are satisfied.*

Proof: See Appendix. □

Propositions 3 and 4 indicate that in the efficiency comparison, the degrees of spillover and product differentiation play a very critical role. Our final proposition (Proposition 5) concludes that the traditional result holds for small θ or γ, and the opposite result holds for large θ and γ. The explanation for this claim is as follows. Although spillovers adversely affect individual firms' incentives to invest in R&D, they enhance welfare from the social point of view.[9] Since firms do more R&D in Cournot than in Bertrand competition, the welfare increase from a larger spillover is greater in Cournot than in Bertrand competition. Thus, for given v and γ, it is more likely that the Cournot equilibrium has greater efficiency than the Bertrand equilibrium as θ increases, and it is less likely that the Cournot equilibrium gives larger welfare as θ decreases.

[9]To see this, simply apply the envelope theorem to W_S.

Proposition 5. *Suppose that $\theta \in (0,1)$, and both A1 and A3 hold. Also suppose that for any given $\theta \in (0,1)$, inequality* (10) *holds and in particular v^* satisfies* (10). *Then, given γ, either*

(i) $W_B > W_C$, $\forall v$ *and* θ, *or*
(ii) *there exists a unique $\bar{v}(\gamma)(> 1)$ such that*
   (a) $W_B > W_C$, $\forall v \geq \bar{v}(\gamma)$ *and* $\in (0,1)$, *and*
   (b) *for $v < \bar{v}(\gamma)$, there exists $\overline{\theta}(v) \in (0,1)$ such that*

$$W_B - W_C \begin{cases} > 0 & \forall\theta < \overline{\theta}(v) \\ = 0 & if\ \theta = \overline{\theta}(v) \\ < 0 & \forall\theta > \overline{\theta}(v). \end{cases}$$

Furthermore, for γ close to 0, *outcome (i) prevails. For γ close to* 1, *outcome* (ii) *prevails.*

Proof: See Appendix. □

6. Concluding Remarks

The main finding of the present study is that, in contrast to the conventional wisdom, the Cournot equilibrium can be more efficient than the Bertrand equilibrium. First, when R&D is not too costly, firms in Cournot competition invest much more in R&D and thus have much lower production costs than they do in Bertrand competition. Second, when spillovers are sufficiently high, the resulting welfare increase from more R&D investment is drastic.

Except in the case of perfect spillovers, the strongest condition imposed for most of the results to hold is condition (10), which ensures interior solutions of optimal R&D investment. It might be of interest to carry out further study on the corner-solution equilibrium once condition (10) is relaxed.

Government intervention in R&D investment, especially for the type of R&D with strong spillovers, is a world-wide common practice. When R&D investment is controlled through either subsidization or taxation, will the welfare superiority of Bertrand competition be reinstated? Elsewhere (Qiu, 1995b), I have shown that in the case of Cournot competition, R&D subsidy is optimal, i.e. subsidy is preferred to laissez faire and tax. Since underinvestment is more serious in Bertrand competition than in Cournot competition as evident from Proposition 1, a larger subsidy is required in Bertrand competition. If that is the case, the R&D differential between Cournot and Bertrand competition would be reduced. Recall that a larger R&D investment in Cournot competition is the reason for the welfare of Cournot competition being higher than that of Bertrand competition. Also note that the subsidy per se is simply a transfer from the government to the firms, and so it is cancelled out in the welfare function (it does affect the equilibrium welfare though). Therefore, the possibility that the Cournot equilibrium dominates the Bertrand equilibrium in welfare term would be lower in the presence of government intervention than laissez faire. Whether the Cournot equilibrium can dominate the Bertrand equilibrium with government intervention deserves a closer scrutiny.

Appendix

A. *Decomposition of R&D incentives*

Consider general market demand $p_i = p_i(q_1, q_2)$, $\partial p_i/\partial q_j < 0$, and R&D cost $V_i(x_i)$, $V_i' > V_i'' > 0$. The first-order conditions for Cournot–Nash outputs are

$$\frac{\partial \pi_i}{\partial q_i} = p_i + q_i \frac{\partial p_i}{\partial q_i} - (c - x_i - \theta x_j) = 0.$$

Assume that both the second-order conditions and the stability condition are satisfied, i.e.

$$\frac{\partial^2 \pi_i}{\partial q_i^2} \leq 0, \quad \Psi_C \equiv \frac{\partial^2 \pi_1}{\partial q_1^2}\frac{\partial^2 \pi_2}{\partial q_2^2} - \frac{\partial^2 \pi_1}{\partial q_2 \partial q_1}\frac{\partial^2 \pi_2}{\partial q_1 \partial q_2} > 0.$$

Differentiating the first-order conditions with respect to x_i yields

$$\begin{pmatrix} \partial^2 \pi_i/\partial q_i^2 & \partial^2 \pi_i/\partial q_j \partial q_i \\ \partial^2 \pi_j/\partial q_i \partial q_j & \partial^2 \pi_j/\partial q_j^2 \end{pmatrix} \begin{pmatrix} \partial q_i/\partial x_i \\ \partial q_j/\partial x_i \end{pmatrix} = \begin{pmatrix} -1 \\ -\theta \end{pmatrix},$$

from which I obtain

$$\frac{\partial q_j}{\partial x_i} = \frac{1}{\Psi_C}\left(\frac{\partial^2 \pi_j}{\partial q_i \partial q_j} - \frac{\partial^2 \pi_i}{\partial q_i^2}\theta\right).$$

Note also $\partial\pi_i/\partial q_j = q_i(\partial p_i/\partial q_j) < 0$ for substitute products and $\pi_i/\partial x_i = q_i > 0$. Thus,

$$\begin{aligned}\frac{\partial\Pi_i}{\partial x_i} &= \frac{\partial\pi_i}{\partial q_j}\frac{\partial q_j}{\partial x_i} + \frac{\partial\pi_i}{\partial x_i} - V_i^0(x_i)\\ &= \left[-\frac{1}{\Psi_C}\frac{\partial\pi_i}{\partial q_j}\frac{\partial^2\pi_i}{\partial q_i^2}\theta\right] + \left[\frac{1}{\Psi_C}\frac{\partial\pi_i}{\partial q_j}\frac{\partial^2\pi_j}{\partial q_i\partial q_j}\right] + q_i + [-V_i'(x_i)]\\ &= \underbrace{\text{spillover effect}}_{(-)} + \underbrace{\text{strategic effect}}_{(+)} + \underbrace{\text{size effect}}_{(+)} + \underbrace{\text{cost effect}}_{(-)}\end{aligned}$$

Derivation of the decomposition for Bertrand competition is similar and hence I omit it.

B. *Proof of Proposition 3*

$$W_{B1} - W_{C1} = \frac{v(\alpha-c)^2}{\Delta_{B1}^2\Delta_{C1}^2}F(v;\gamma),$$

where $F(v;\gamma) \equiv [v(3+\gamma-2\gamma^2)(2-\gamma)^2 - 4(1-\gamma)^2]\Delta_{C1}^2 - [v(3+\gamma)(2+\gamma)^2 - 4]\Delta_{B1}^2$.

Define $(v;\gamma) = F(v;\gamma)/(v\gamma^2)$. It follows that $(W_{B1} - W_{C1}) = sign(G)$.

Simplification and term collection yield $G(v;\gamma) = 16g_1 - 8g_2v + g_3v^2$, where $g_1 = (1+\gamma)(4-2\gamma-\gamma^2) > 0$, $g_2 = 16+8\gamma-8\gamma^2-2\gamma^3+\gamma^4+\gamma^5 > 0$, and $g_3 = (1+\gamma)(4-\gamma^2)^2(4-2\gamma-\gamma^2) > 0$. Since the second derivative is positive ($G_{vv} = 2g_3 > 0$), G is strictly convex in v. Moreover, $g_2^2 - g_1g_3 > 0$ for all $\gamma \in (0,1)$. Thus, given any γ, there exist two real solutions to $G = 0$, which are

$$v_1^*(\gamma) = \frac{4}{g_3}(g_2 - \sqrt{g_2^2 - g_1g_3}) \quad \text{and} \quad v_2^*(\gamma) = \frac{4}{g_3}\left(g_2 + \sqrt{g_2^2 - g_1g_3}\right).$$

With the help of Mathematica (Wolfram, 1991), it can be shown that $v_1^*(\cdot)$ is a decreasing function with $v_1^*(1) = (32 - 4\sqrt{55})/9$, and $v_2^*(\cdot)$ is an increasing function with $v_2^*(1) = (32+4\sqrt{55})/9$. Moreover, $v_1^*(0) = v_2^*(0) = 1$. The above analysis leads to Figure 1.1. By making use of the figure with the focus on $v_2^*(\cdot)$ as required by Al and noting $G(v_2^*(\overline{\gamma});\overline{\gamma}) = 0$, the rest of the proof is straightforward.

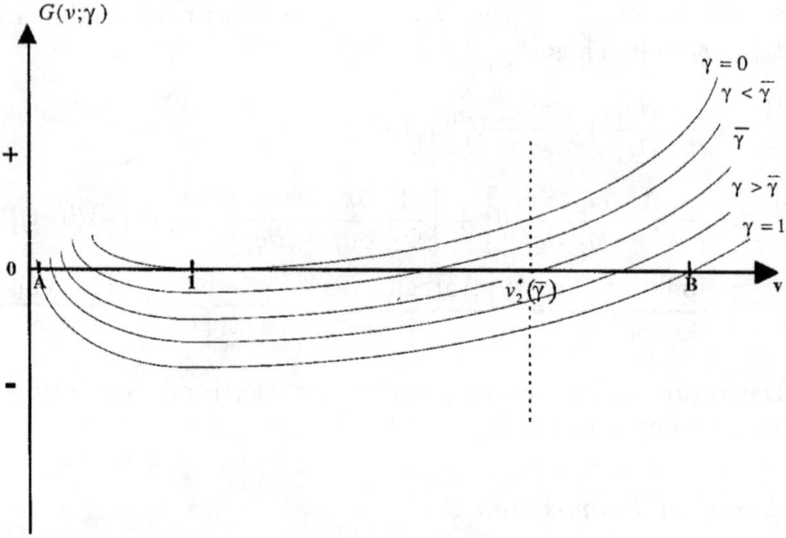

$A = v_1^*(1) = \left(32 - 4\sqrt{55}\right)/9$

$B = v_2^*(1) = \left(32 + 4\sqrt{55}\right)/9$

$\text{sign}\left(W_{B1} - W_{C1}\right) = \text{sign}(G)$

Figure 1.1. Welfare Comparison 1.

C. *Proof of Proposition 4*

Part I. Although I only need to consider $\theta = 0$ in this proof, it proves useful to examine $\theta \in [0, 1)$ now. Following the proof of Proposition 3 and based on (6) and (13), I calculate

$$W_B - W_C = \frac{v(\alpha - c)^2}{\Delta_B^2 \Delta_C^2} F(v; \gamma, \theta),$$

where

$$\begin{aligned} F(v; \gamma, \theta) \equiv\ & [v(3 + \gamma - 2\gamma^2)(4 - \gamma^2)^2 - 4(2 - \theta\gamma - \gamma^2)^2]\Delta_C^2 \\ & - [v(3 + \gamma)(4 - \gamma^2)^2 - 4(2 - \theta\gamma)^2]\Delta_B^2. \end{aligned}$$

Define $G(v; \gamma, \theta) = F(v; \gamma, \theta)/[v\gamma^2(4 - \gamma^2)]$. It follows that $(W_B - W_C) = \text{sign}(G)$. After collecting terms, I obtain

$$G(v; \gamma, \theta) = 4(1 + \theta)^2 g_1 - 4(1 + \theta) g_2 v + g_3 v^2,$$

where

$$g_1 = 16 + 8\theta\gamma - 8(2 - \theta + \theta^2)\gamma^2 - 2\theta(1 + 2\theta)\gamma^3 + (3 - 2\theta + 2\theta^2)\gamma^4 + \gamma^5,$$
$$g_2 = 64 + 16(1 + \theta)\gamma - 16(5 - 2\theta)\gamma^2 - 16\gamma^3 + 4(7 - 4\theta)\gamma^4 + (7 - \theta)\gamma^5 - (3 - 2\theta)\gamma^6 - \gamma^7,$$
$$g_3 = 256 + 128\gamma - 384\gamma^2 - 160\gamma^3 + 192\gamma^4 + 72\gamma^5 - 40\gamma^6 - 14\gamma^7 + 3\gamma^8 + \gamma^9 > 0.$$

Since $G_{vv} > 0$, G is strictly convex in v. Note, $g_2^2 - g_1 g_3 > 0$ for all $\gamma \in (0, 1)$ and $\theta \in [0, 1)$. Thus, given any γ and θ, there exist two real solutions to $G = 0$. As in the proof of Proposition 3, I only need to consider the high-value solution, i.e.

$$v_2^*(\gamma, \theta) = 2(1 + \theta)(g_2 + \sqrt{g_2^2 - g_1 g_3})/g_3.$$

Part II. Now let's concentrate on $\theta = 0$. It can be shown that $v_2^*(\gamma, 0)$ is increasing in γ and $v_2^*(1, 0) = 2/3$. Thus, if we draw a family of $(v; \gamma, 0)$, they will be similar to those in Figure 1.1 except that $B = 2/3 < 1$. Since $v > 1$ by Al, $G > 0$ for all γ. The result follows.

D. *Proof of Proposition 5*

Continue from Part I of Proposition 4's proof. First, g_3 is not a function of θ, $\partial g_2/\partial\theta = \gamma(16 + 32\gamma - 16\gamma^3 - \gamma^4 + 2\gamma^5) > 0$, and $\partial(g_2^2 - g_1 g_3)/\partial\theta = 2\gamma^2(4 - \gamma^2)^2[48(1+3\theta) + 32(1+6\theta)\gamma - 56(1+\theta)\gamma^2 - 32(1+4\theta)\gamma^3 + (19+\theta)\gamma^4 + 2(5+14\theta)\gamma^5 - (1-2\theta)\gamma^6 - (1+2\theta)\gamma^7] > 0$. Thus, for all $\in (0, 1)$, $\partial v_2^*(\gamma, \theta) = \partial\theta > 0$. This property allows us to draw a family of G on various θs (for a given γ), as shown in Figure 1.2.

Second, calculate $v_2^*(\gamma, 1)$ for the given γ. Either $v = v_2^*(\gamma, 1)$ satisfies both Al and (10) or it violates at least one of the conditions. In the latter case, all $v = v_2^*(\gamma, \theta)$ will violate at least Al or (10). It follows that for v satisfying Al and (10), $G > 0$, $\forall\theta \in (0, 1)$ (using Figure 1.2 and the argument similar to that used in the proof of Proposition 4). In the former case, using Figure 1.2 and

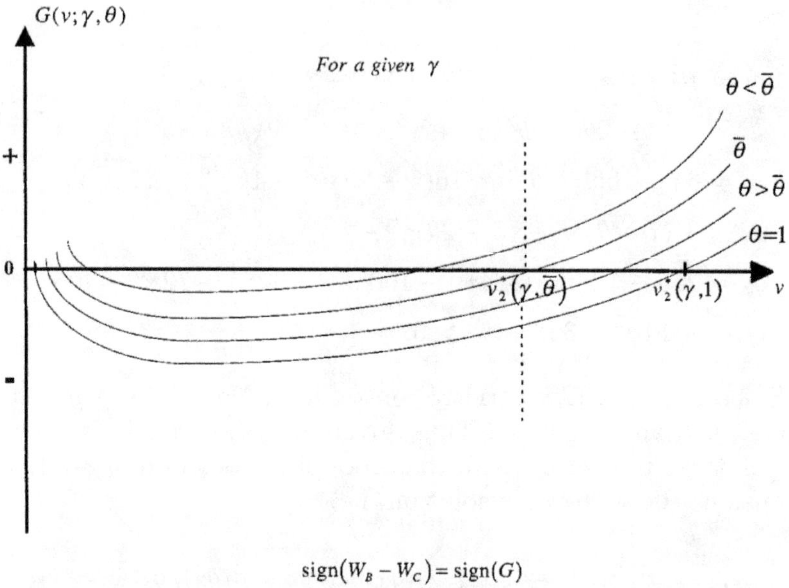

Figure 1.2. Welfare Comparison 2.

the arguments similar to those used in the proof of Proposition 3, we know that outcome (ii) is the result.

Third, consider the case of large γ. Recall $v_2^*(1,1) = v^*$ and $\partial v_2^*(\gamma,1)/\partial\gamma > 0$. The continuity property of $v_2^*(\gamma,\theta)$ ensures the following: for any given $\varepsilon > 0$, $v^* - \varepsilon < v_2^*(\gamma,\theta) < v^*$ as long as both γ and θ are sufficiently close to 1. Thus, for large γ, $v_2^*(\gamma,1)$ satisfies both Al and (10), and hence outcome (ii) obtains.

Finally, consider the case of small γ. Recall $v_2^*(0,1) = 1$. Thus, given any small $\varepsilon > 0$, there exists γ_ε such that $v_2^*(\gamma,1) < 1+\varepsilon$, $\forall\gamma \le \gamma_\varepsilon$. As Al implies $v > 1$, by choosing ε appropriately, $v = v_2^*(\gamma,1)$ will violate Al and thus outcome (i) obtains.

References

Bester, H. and E. Petrakis, 1993. The incentives for cost reduction in a differentiated industry. *International Journal of Industrial Organization* 11, 519–534.

Brander, J. and B. Spencer, 1983. Strategic commitment with R&D: The symmetric case. *Bell Journal of Economics* 14, 225–235.

Cheng, L., 1985. Comparing Bertrand and Cournot equilibria: A geometric approach. *Rand Journal of Economics* 16(1), 146–147.

d'Aspremont, C. and A. Jacquemin, 1988. Cooperative and noncooperative R&D in duopoly with spillovers. *American Economic Review* 78(5), 1133–1137.

Okuno-Fujiwara, M. and K. Suzumura, 1987. Strategic cost-reduction investment and economic welfare, (CARESS) Working Paper 87-05, University of Pennsylvania Center for Analytic Research in Economics and the Social Sciences.

Qiu, L., 1995a. R&D incentives and product differentiation: Cournot vs Bertrand competition, Working Paper, The Hong Kong University of Science and Technology.

Qiu, L., 1995b. R&D Incentives in a differentiated duopoly with spillovers, Working Paper, The Hong Kong University of Science and Technology.

Singh, N. and X. Vives, 1984. Price and quantity competition in a differentiated duopoly. *Rand Journal of Economics* 15(4), 546–554.

Wolfram, S., 1991. *Mathematica: A System for Doing Mathematics by Computer*, 2nd edition, Addison-Wesley Publishing Company.

Vives, X., 1985. On the efficiency of Bertrand and Cournot equilibria with product differentiation. *Journal of Economic Theory* 36(1), 166–175.

Chapter 2

Policy on International R&D Cooperation: Subsidy or Tax?*

Abstract

In this paper we derive the non-cooperative, optimal policy towards international R&D cooperation. Two types of R&D cooperation are considered: collaboration and coordination. When firms cooperate, the familiar strategic behavior, which prevails in R&D competition, is reduced, or eliminated, or even completely reversed. However, we prove that R&D subsidy is still an optimal policy for individual governments in the case of R&D coordination and, more strikingly, the subsidies are larger for higher degrees of coordination. Government policies do not help the firms to commit. In the case of R&D collaboration, both R&D subsidy and tax are possible. With linear demands, however, tax is never optimal; moreover, we show that the optimal policy is subsidy regardless of the strategic nature (substitute or complement) of the strategy variables, a result that contradicts the traditional wisdom.

1. Introduction

The number of agreements on international research and development (R&D) cooperation has been increasing at an unprecedented rate. A survey article by Chesnais (1988) contains much information on various forms of R&D cooperation in a wide range of industries.

*This chapter is reproduced from *European Economic Review*, 42, 1727–1750, 1998, with permission from Elsevier.

For example, it reports from the FOR (Italy) data that between 1982 and 1985 there were 1061 inter-firm agreements in high technology industries, where the product markets are characterized by imperfect competition. Among those agreements, a large portion were for R&D cooperation, and more than half were for international cooperation.[1] Government support for both domestic and international R&D cooperation, including public investment, subsidy, and antitrust law modification, has also become more frequent.[2]

It is not only evident that governments often assist their domestic producers via trade and industrial policies when the latter are competing with foreign rivals in markets characterized by imperfect competition, but also clear that theories have provided justification for such policy interventions. Export subsidies can be used to shift rents strategically between rival firms;[3] however, such outright subsidies on exports are strictly forbidden by the World Trade Organization (WTO). In contrast, subsidizing domestic R&D is allowed by the WTO[4] and, as demonstrated by Spencer and Brander (1983), via an R&D policy a government can achieve the same strategic outcomes otherwise obtained under direct export subsidies. While Spencer and Brander, and all subsequent studies, have provided useful insights on subsidies to domestic firms participating in *international R&D competition*, it remains unclear what would be a "good" policy towards *international R&D cooperation*. The present study addresses this issue and is motivated by the following two questions. First, should a government subsidize the domestic firm's R&D activity when the firm cooperates with its foreign rival? The answer to this question would test the robustness of the

---

[1]See also Murphy (1991) for a list of international R&D cooperation involving at least one American firm. Even rival firms competing in the same final product markets may cooperate in A&D investment. For example, IBM and Toshiba formed a research joint venture, named Display Technologies Inc., to develop liquid crystal color displays, which will be used to produce their final products (see 'Such good friends with IBM', *Fortune* Oct. 4, 1993.)

[2]It was estimated that Airbus benefited from public subsidies totalling US$2.5 billion during 1968–1982 (Krugman, 1984).

[3]See Brander (1995) for the most recent survey of the strategic trade literature.

[4]In the most recent GATT talk, the Uruguay Round, the scope for R&D subsidies was substantially widened (Cline, 1995).

Spencer–Brander-type strategic R&D subsidy to R&D cooperation. The second question concerns the magnitude of subsidies: if a subsidy is optimal then is it larger for cooperative R&D or for non-cooperative R&D?

Our analysis is built upon two existing sets of literature. One is the strategic trade literature, which focuses on how governments can alter the market games played by firms of various countries in favor of their domestic firms through trade and/or R&D policies. The other is the cooperative R&D literature, which justifies cooperative R&D in a variety of settings and investigates the effects of this cooperation. In terms of analysis, the former literature has a dominant model of Spencer and Brander (1983), while the latter has at least two popular models of cooperative R&D.

To focus on the effect of international R&D cooperation on strategic government policy, we choose a model that differs from Spencer and Brander only in the assumption about R&D competition and cooperation. In particular, as in Spencer and Brander, we consider deterministic cost-reducing R&D; but unlike Spencer and Brander, who consider only competition of firms in R&D, we consider two possible types of R&D cooperation between a domestic firm and a foreign firm. In the first type of R&D cooperation, the two firms share the benefit of their R&D investments (see Katz, 1986; Veugelers and Kesteloot, 1994). Specifically, each firm's marginal cost of production depends on both its own and its counterpart's R&D investments.[5] In the second type of R&D cooperation, the two firms coordinate to reduce R&D overinvestment (see d'Aspremont and Jacquemin, 1988; Kamien *et al.*, 1992; Suzumura, 1992).

Specifically, each firm chooses its R&D investment to maximize a weighted sum of both its own and its counterpart's profits. To distinguish these two types of cooperation, we refer to the first type as R&D collaboration and the second type as R&D coordination. We are already familiar with the rationale for a government R&D subsidy

[5]International R&D spillover is the focus of Coe and Helpman (1995). They show that a country's total factor productivity depends not only on the domestic R&D stock but also on its trade partners' R&D stock. R&D spillover could be a natural and inevitable result of economic interaction or it could also be a chosen outcome by various parties that conduct R&D. By spillover in this study, we refer to the latter type.

when the domestic firm and the foreign firm make the cost-reducing R&D investment in a competing fashion. Each firm has two motives for R&D investments: (1) to raise its profit directly by lowering the cost of production (profit motive), and (2) to raise its profit indirectly by discouraging its rival's production (strategic motive). This latter motive leads to R&D overinvestment. An R&D subsidy by the domestic government enhances the firm's cost advantage through discouraging the foreign rival's R&D investment, which in turn enables the domestic firm to snatch a larger market share at the expense of the foreign firm.

If the domestic and foreign firms engage in R&D collaboration (i.e., the first type of R&D cooperation), each firm still has two (profit and strategic) motives for R&D investment. However, the strategic motive could be either positive or negative depending on the degree of R&D collaboration. Consider the case of full collaboration, namely, each firm's R&D investment reduces by the same amount its own and its counterpart's marginal costs of production. In this case, by committing to a higher R&D investment, a firm cannot gain a cost advantage over its counterpart. As a result, no market share will be shifted by any government R&D subsidy. This seems to indicate that there will be no role for government R&D subsidy to shift profits in the firms' interest. However, we show that, under reasonable conditions, the governments still have the unilateral incentives to subsidize their firms' R&D. Furthermore, we show that, in a specific version of the model, the government R&D subsidies first decrease and then increase with respect to the degree of international R&D collaboration.

If the domestic and foreign firms engage in R&D coordination (i.e., the second type of R&D cooperation), each firm has a new motive for R&D investment. Specifically, coordinating firms are not totally selfish in the sense that they care not only for their individual profits but also for the counterparts' profits. Thus, each firm has the incentive to reduce its R&D investment so as to mitigate the negative effect on its counterpart's profit (the coordination motive).[6]

[6]Overinvestment is harmful to producers, but not to consumers. This type of coordination could be viewed and is often criticized as collusion (see Brodley, 1990; Jorde and Teece, 1990; Shapiro and Willig, 1990).

This works in the opposite direction of the strategic motive. Hence, depending on the degree of R&D coordination, either the strategic motive or the coordination motive could dominate, leading to, respectively, R&D overinvestment or underinvestment. In the case of full coordination, the firms' strategic motive is dominated by their coordination motive, and firms have incentive to underinvest in R&D. This seems to indicate that there will be no role for government R&D subsidy to shift profits in the firms' interest. Surprisingly, we find that individual governments still have unilateral incentives to subsidize their firms' R&D. In a specific version of the model, we further show that the government R&D subsidies are increasing with respect to the degree of international R&D coordination.

While unilateral R&D subsidies may still be optimal for international R&D cooperation, the rationales are quite different from that of the existing strategic trade literature. In the absence of R&D cooperation, the foreign firm's R&D investment adversely affects the domestic firm's profit, but an R&D subsidy to the domestic firm discourages the foreign firm's R&D investment. Together, these two effects provide the rationale for government R&D subsidies. On the contrary, in the case of international R&D collaboration, thanks to the induced R&D spillovers, the foreign firm's R&D investment may positively affect the domestic firm's profit, while a domestic R&D subsidy may encourage the foreign firm's R&D activity. Nevertheless, these effects also call for R&D subsidies.

In the case of international R&D coordination, the effects are similar to the R&D competition case in that an R&D subsidy lowers the foreign firm's R&D investment, which in turn raises the domestic firm's profit. But underinvestment occurs, in the sense that each firm undertakes less R&D investment than that would maximize its profit. This leaves room for additional R&D subsidies. In addition to the above discussed different rationales for government policies, from the analysis and results of the present study, we identify two departures from the existing strategic trade literature.[7] First, the literature has stressed that the role of a government's strategic policy is to help its firm to commit to certain action (e.g., larger output or higher price).

[7]The following two points can be found in Brander and Spencer (1985) and Eaton and Grossman (1986).

In the case of R&D coordination, however, we show that the R&D subsidy drives the subsidized firm's action to the opposite direction of its commitment (i.e., underinvestment). The second departure is about the relationship between the type of strategic policy and the strategic nature of the strategy variables. It is generally concluded that the optimal policy is a subsidy (a tax) for strategic substitutes (complements). In contrast, we, in the case of R&D collaboration, are able to derive the result that an R&D subsidy is optimal even when R&D investments are strategic complements.

The plan of the paper is as follows. Section 2 focuses on R&D collaboration, while Section 3 focuses on R&D coordination. In each case, we analyze the interaction between firms, that between governments, and that between governments and firms. In particular, we analyze the firms' incentive to make R&D investments and the governments' R&D policies. The relation between the government R&D policies and the degree of international R&D collaboration/coordination is addressed in the specific versions of the models. The paper concludes in Section 4.

2. R&D Collaboration

2.1. *The model*

The model is similar to Spencer and Brander (1983) except that we consider R&D collaboration. There are two firms located in two different countries. The firms produce homogeneous products and compete in a third country's market by setting quantity (Cournot competition). Demand for the product follows a general inverse demand function:

$$p = p(q_1 + q_2), \quad p' < 0,$$

where q_1 and q_2 are firms 1 and 2's outputs, respectively, and p is the product price.

Before making output decisions, the firms invest in R&D to lower their respective production costs. Moreover, the firms may engage in R&D collaboration. Specifically, the firms share the benefits of their R&D investments in that firm i's marginal cost of production depends on its own R&D investment (x_i) and firm j's investment (x_j), or,

$$MC_i = C - c(x_i) - \lambda_R c(x_j),$$

where C is large enough such that MC_i is positive, c is increasing and concave, and $\lambda_R \in [0, 1]$ capturing all possible degrees of R&D collaboration. Note that the two firms have identical technology to begin with and are equally efficient in R&D activities.[8]

Finally, the government in each country has an R&D policy towards its firm's R&D activity. As in the current strategic trade literature, we consider R&D tax or subsidy proportional to the firm's R&D expenditure.

Firms collaborate in R&D by setting, through negotiation, the spillover parameter λ_R. Although how λ_R is set is an important issue, it is not in the interest of this paper. In this study, λ_R is exogenously given, allowing us to focus on our central question, i.e., how government policy responds to R&D collaboration.

2.2. *A three stage game*

We describe the interaction between the firms and governments using a non-cooperative, three-stage game. In the first stage, the governments simultaneously announce their R&D subsidy (tax if negative) rates, s_1 and s_2. In the second stage, each firm chooses its R&D level knowing its spillovers to the other firm. Finally, in the third stage, the firms compete in the product market by setting quantities. To obtain a subgame perfect equilibrium, this multi-stage game is solved by backward induction.

Given (x, s), where $x = (x_1, x_2)$ and $s = (s_1, s_2)$, firm i in the last stage chooses q_i to maximize its profit:

$$\pi_i = [p(q_i + q_j) - MC_i]q_i - x_i(1 - s_i).$$

The following two first-order conditions,

$$\frac{\partial \pi_i}{\partial q_i} = p'q_i + p - MC_i = 0, \quad i = 1, 2, \tag{1}$$

[8]When identical, the two firms have the most to gain from R&D collaboration, as neither can beat the other without suffering badly. In addition, this assumption makes our analysis much simpler.

determine the Cournot–Nash equilibrium output and profits, denoted by

$$q_1^*(x, \lambda_R), \quad q_2^*(x, \lambda_R), \quad \pi_1^*(x, s_1, \lambda_R), \quad \pi_2^*(x, s_2, \lambda_R),$$

and the welfare, which is defined as the firm's profit net of subsidy payment and denoted by

$$\begin{aligned} W_1^*(x, s_1, \lambda_R) &= \pi_1^*(x, s_1, \lambda_R) - s_1 x_1, \\ W_2^*(x, s_2, \lambda_R) &= \pi_2^*(x, s_2, \lambda_R) - s_2 x_2. \end{aligned}$$

Let $a_{ij} \equiv \partial^2 \pi_i / \partial q_j \partial q_i$. Then $a_{ii} < 0$ by the second-order conditions to the above profit maximization, and $a_{ij} < 0$ for $i \neq j$ because of strategic substitution. Moreover, we impose the stability condition $\Delta_1 \equiv a_{11}a_{22} - a_{12}a_{21} > 0$. In the second stage, given s, firm i chooses x_i to maximize its profit: $\pi_i^*(x, s_i, \lambda_R) = [p(q_i^* + q_j^*) - (C - c(x_i) - \lambda_R c(x_j))]q_i^* - x_i(1 - s_i)$.

The following two first-order conditions,

$$\frac{\partial \pi_i^*}{\partial x_i} = \left[p'(q_i^* + q_j^*) \frac{\partial q_j^*}{\partial x_i} + c'(x_i) \right] q_{1-}^*(1 - s_i) = 0,$$

$$i, j = 1, 2 \quad \text{and} \quad i \neq j, \tag{2}$$

jointly determine the firms' optimal R&D investments and the resulting profits, denoted by

$$x_i^*(s, \lambda_R), \pi_i^{**}(s, \lambda_R).$$

Let $b_{ij} \equiv \partial^2 \pi_i^* / \partial x_j \partial x_i$. Assume that both the second-order and the stability conditions are satisfied, i.e.,

$$b_{ii} < 0 \quad \text{and} \quad \Delta_2 \equiv b_{11}b_{22} - b_{12}b_{21} > 0. \tag{3}$$

The sign of b_{ij} is indeterminant. By definition, x_1^* and x_2^* are strategic substitutes if $b_{ij} < 0$ and strategic complements if $b_{ij} > 0$.

Finally (in the first stage), each government selects a subsidy rate (unrestricted in sign), knowing its effects on the subsequent two stages of the game, to maximize its country's welfare:

$$W_i^{**}(s,\lambda_R) = \pi_i^{**}(s,\lambda_R) - s_i x_i^*(s,\lambda_R).$$

Let $s_i^*(\lambda_R)$ denote the optimal subsidy rates, which are simultaneously determined by the following first-order conditions:

$$\frac{\partial W_i^{**}}{\partial s_i} = \frac{\partial \pi_i^{**}}{\partial s_i} - x_i^* - S_i \frac{\partial x_i^*}{\partial s_i} = 0, \quad i = 1, 2. \tag{4}$$

As with the other two stages' optimization problems, we assume the satisfaction of the second-order and stability conditions:

$$e_{ii} < 0, \Delta_3 \equiv e_{11}e_{22} - e_{12}e_{21} > 0,$$

where $e_{ij} \equiv \partial^2 W_i^{**}/\partial s_j \partial s_i$ and $i, j = 1, 2$.

2.3. *Comparative statics results*

Having described the three-stage game, we now examine how government R&D policy affects R&D activities and how they, in turn, affect the market outcomes. We look at the latter effect first. Partially differentiating Eq. (1) with respect to x_1 yields

$$\begin{pmatrix} a_{11} & a_{12} \\ a_{21} & a_{22} \end{pmatrix} \begin{pmatrix} \partial q_1^*/\partial x_1 \\ \partial q_2^*/\partial x_1 \end{pmatrix} = \begin{pmatrix} -c'(x_1) \\ -\lambda_R c'(x_1) \end{pmatrix}.$$

By differentiating Eq. (1) with respect to x_2 we can also obtain a similar equation system. Solving these two equation systems, we get

$$\frac{\partial q_i^*}{\partial x_i} = \frac{1}{\Delta_1}(-a_{jj} + \lambda_R a_{ij})c'(x_i) \text{ and } \frac{\partial q_i^*}{\partial x_j} = \frac{1}{\Delta_1}(a_{ij} - \lambda_R a_{jj})c'(x_j). \tag{5}$$

For $\lambda_R = 0$, we have $\partial q_i^*/\partial x_i = -a_{jj}c'(x_i)/\Delta_1 > 0$ and $\partial q_i^*/\partial x_j = a_{ij}c'(x_j)/\Delta_1 < 0$. However, for $\lambda_R = 1$, we have $\partial q_i^*/\partial x_i = (a_{ij} - a_{jj})c'(x_i)/\Delta_1$ and $\partial q_i^*/\partial x_j = (a_{ij} - a_{jj})c'(x_j)/\Delta_1$, both of which are positive under the symmetric setting (namely, $a_{11} = a_{22}$, $a_{12} = a_{21}$, and $\Delta_1 > 0$ implies $a_{ij} - a_{jj} > 0$). Intuitively as x_i increases, both firms' marginal costs are reduced. For $\lambda_R < 1$, the reduction of firm i's marginal cost is greater than that of firm j's; however, the difference is smaller when λ_R gets larger. Lowering one's marginal cost tends to raise one's output and lower the rival's output. Thus, with a small λ_R one's own effect dominates the spillover effect and so an increase in x_i leads to higher q_i^* and lower q_j^*. When λ_R is large, the spillover effect becomes strong, and so both firms' marginal costs become so low that both q_i^* and q_j^* are higher.

Next, we examine the policy implications for R&D activities. Differentiating Eq. (2) with respect to s_1 gives

$$\begin{pmatrix} b_{11} & b_{12} \\ b_{21} & b_{22} \end{pmatrix} \begin{pmatrix} \partial x_1^*/\partial s_1 \\ \partial x_2^*/\partial s_1 \end{pmatrix} = \begin{pmatrix} -1 \\ 0 \end{pmatrix}.$$

Similar equations can be obtained by differentiating Eq. (2) with respect to s_2 Solving these two equation systems, we get

$$\frac{\partial x_i^*}{\partial s_i} = -\frac{b_{jj}}{\Delta_2} > 0 \quad \text{and} \quad \frac{\partial x_j^*}{\partial s_i} = -\frac{b_{ji}}{\Delta_2}. \tag{6}$$

It is clear that the sign of $\partial x_j^*/\partial s_i$ is the same as that of b_{ji}. The intuition is as follows. First, s_i always raises x_i. Second, an increase in x_i lowers x_j for strategic substitutes and raises x_j for strategic complements. Thus, whether s_i raises or reduces x_j completely depends on the strategic nature of x_i and x_j (captured by b_{ji}).

In summary, while government i's R&D subsidy raises its firm's R&D investment, it may not reduce the rival firm's R&D investment. Moreover, by investing in R&D, firm i may not be able to restrict its rival firm's output.

2.4. *R&D incentives*

It is established in the strategic trade literature that firms have strategic motive to overinvest in R&D, and, consequently, governments subsidize their firms to enhance further their strategic motive. Thus, in order to analyze government R&D policy in the presence of R&D collaboration, we first examine the firms' incentives for R&D investment. Recall that $\partial \pi_i/\partial q_i = 0$ by Eq. (1) and so

$$\frac{\partial \pi_i^*}{\partial x_i} = \underbrace{\frac{\partial \pi_i}{\partial x_i}}_{\text{profit motive}} + \underbrace{\frac{\partial \pi_i \partial q^* j}{\partial q_j \partial x_i}}_{\text{strategic motive}}. \tag{7}$$

Thus, a firm has both the profit and strategic motives for R&D investment. The former comes from the fact that R&D investment allows the firm to raise its profit by lowering the production cost. The latter is that the firm's R&D investment indirectly affects its profit through its influence on its rival's output. In the existing strategic trade literature, it has been known that the strategic motive is always positive and because of that, overinvestment occurs.[9] However, in the presence of R&D collaboration, the strategic motive could be either positive or negative. Specifically, the sign of the strategic motive is the same as that of $\partial q_j^*/\partial x_i$, which depends on λ_R as shown in Section 2.3. When λ_R is small $\partial q_j^*/\partial x_i$ is negative and firm i overinvests in R&D; when λ_R is large, $\partial q_j^*/\partial x_i$ is positive and firm i underinvests in R&D.

2.5. *R&D policy*

We have just shown that, in the presence of R&D collaboration, firms may no longer have the strategic motive to overinvest in R&D. The ensuing question is: would the governments still have the unilateral interests to subsidize their firms' R&D when the latter engage in R&D collaboration?

Recall that the equilibrium R&D subsidies (or taxes) are determined by Eq. (4). Note that

$$\frac{\partial \pi_i^{**}}{\partial s_i} = \frac{\partial \pi_i^*}{\partial x_i}\frac{\partial x_i^*}{\partial s_i} + \frac{\partial \pi_i^*}{\partial x_j}\frac{\partial x_j^*}{\partial s_i} + \frac{\partial \pi_i^*}{\partial s_i}, \tag{8}$$

where the first term on the right-hand side is zero by Eq. (2) and the third term is x_i^* by the envelope theorem. Substituting Eq. (8) into Eq. (4), we have

$$s_i^* \frac{\partial x_i^*}{\partial s_i} = \frac{\partial \pi_i^*}{\partial x_j}\frac{\partial x_j^*}{\partial s_i}. \tag{9}$$

Eqs. (6) and (9) together imply that the sign of s_i^* coincides with that of $(\partial \pi_i^*/\partial x_j)(\partial x_j^*/\partial s_i)$. In the absence of international R&D collaboration, higher s_i leads to lower x_j^* (i.e., $\partial x_j^*/\partial s_i < 0$) and higher x_j leads to lower π_i^* (i.e., $\partial n_i^*/\partial x_j < 0$), altogether implying

[9] See Spencer and Brander (1983) for more detailed discussions.

$s_i^* > 0$. However, in the presence of R&D collaboration, the signs of $\partial x_j^*/\partial s_i$ and $\partial \pi_i^*/\partial x_j$ depend on λ_R and other factors. From $\pi_i^*(x, s_i, \lambda_R)$ we have

$$\frac{\partial \pi_i^*}{\partial x_j} = \frac{\partial \pi_i}{\partial q_j}\frac{\partial q_j^*}{\partial x_j} + \frac{\partial \pi_i}{\partial x_j} = \left[p'\frac{\partial q_j^*}{\partial x_j} + \lambda_R c'(x_j)\right] q_i^*. \tag{10}$$

x_j affects π_i^* negatively, as it decreases the market price through inducing higher q_j^*. The first term in the square bracket of Eq. (10) captures this effect. However, in the presence of R&D collaboration, x_j could also affect π_i^* positively through indirectly reducing firm i's marginal cost. The second term captures this effect. Depending on the relative magnitude of these two terms, $\partial n_i^*/\partial x_j$ could be either positive or negative.

On the other hand, the sign of $\partial x_j^*/\partial s_i$ is determined by b_{ji}. When λ_R is small x_1 and x_2 are strategic substitutes and b_{ji} is negative; when λ_R is large, x_1 and x_2 are strategic complements and b_{ji} is positive. Overall, we have:

Proposition 1. *In the case of international R&D collaboration, (i) when λ_R is small enough, governments subsidize R&D investments; (ii) when λ_R is large enough, governments may or may not subsidize R&D investments.*

As in the existing strategic trade literature, the only role played by a government's R&D policy is to help its firm commit to overinvestment or underinvestment, according to the strategic motive. That is, a government will subsidize or tax its firm's R&D if by doing so it could affect the rival firm's R&D investment in such a way that its own firm's profit will increase. In the absence of international R&D collaboration, a subsidy does the job, as higher s_i leads to lower x_j^* and higher x_j leads to lower π_i^*. However, in the presence of international R&D collaboration, the strategic incentive does not necessarily call for government R&D subsidies. When it does, the rationale is different: first, higher s_i leads to higher x_j^* (i.e., $\partial x_j^*/\partial s_i > 0$) and second, higher x_j leads to higher π_i^* (i.e., $\partial \pi_i^*/\partial x_j > 0$), both of which are made possible by the induced R&D spillovers.

2.6. *Degree of government policy*

We have shown in the preceding subsection the possibility of both subsidy and tax on international R&D collaboration. It is this subsection's purpose to give an example that emphasizes the case for subsidy and from which we can examine how the government subsidy responds to the changing degree of collaboration. In particular, would the governments subsidize more or less as λ_R becomes larger?

To serve the above purpose, we assume that demand and cost functions take the following *forms*:[10]

$$p = a - (q_1 + q_2) \quad \text{and} \quad c(x_i) = \sqrt{\frac{X_i}{\beta}}, \tag{11}$$

where parameters a and β are positive, $\alpha \equiv a - C > 0$, and C is sufficiently large so that MC_i is non-negative for all relevant x_i and x_j Let $y_i \equiv \sqrt{x_i/\beta}$. Then, choosing y_i is equivalent to choosing x_i in each firm's R&D decision. In Appendix A, we will show that the optimal R&D responses are

$$y_i = \frac{(2-\lambda_R)[\alpha - (1-2\lambda_R)y_j]}{9\beta(1-s_i) - (2-\lambda_R)^2}, \tag{12}$$

where the denominator is positive as required by the second-order condition in this stage's maximization. Thus,

$$\frac{\partial y_i}{\partial y_j} \begin{cases} < 0 \text{ if } \lambda_R < 1/2, \\ = 0 \text{ if } \lambda_R = 1/2, \\ > 0 \text{ if } \lambda_R > 1/2. \end{cases}$$

The strategic nature between x_i and x_j changes from substitute to complement when λ_R increases from below half to above half.

The following lemma gives the necessary and sufficient condition for the existence of a symmetric equilibrium and characterizes the non-cooperative government R&D policy.

[10]This model is similar to the one used by d'Aspremont and Jacquemin (1988) except we include government policy. Notice that our qualitative result does not change if the slope of the demand curve is a constant b rather than the specific case, i.e., $b = 1$.

Lemma 1. *The model as specified by Eq. (11) has a unique solution to the optimal government policy if and only if $\beta \geq 1$. Specifically, the equilibrium R&D subsidy by each government is*

$$s^* = \frac{1}{6\beta}(3\beta - 1 + \lambda_R^2 - \sqrt{(1-\lambda_R^2)^2 - 2(5 - 8\lambda_R + 5\lambda_R^2)\beta + 9\beta^2}); \tag{13}$$

and the equilibrium R&D investment by each firm is

$$x^* = \frac{(2-\lambda_R)^2\alpha^2\beta}{[9\beta(1-s^*) - (1+\lambda_R)(2-\lambda_R)]^2}. \tag{14}$$

Proof: See Appendix A.1. □

In this specific model the governments always subsidize their firms' R&D except when $\lambda_R = \frac{1}{2}$ at which there will be no tax or subsidy.

Proposition 2. *In the case of international R&D collaboration, $s^* \geq 0$ for all $\lambda_R \in [0,1]$. Moreover, the optimal R&D subsidy rate, s^* (given in Eq. (13)), is decreasing in λ_R for $\lambda_R < \frac{1}{2}(ds^*/d\lambda_R < 0)$ but increasing in λ_R for $\lambda_R > \frac{1}{2}(ds^*/d\lambda_R > 0)$. At $\lambda_R = \frac{1}{2} s^* = 0$ and $ds^*/d\lambda_R = 0$.*

Proof: See Appendix A.2. □

It is worth noting that when $\lambda_R > \frac{1}{2}$, x_i and x_j become strategic complements, but the governments still subsidize their firms' R&D investments. This contradicts the general conclusion about export subsidy /*tax*: subsidize (tax) when the competing variables are strategic substitutes (complements).[11]

3. R&D Coordination

3.1. *The model*

In this section, we analyze the policy implication of another popular model of R&D cooperation, namely, R&D coordination, pioneered by d'Aspremont and Jacquemin (1988). The setup differs from that

[11]See Eaton and Grossman (1986).

of Section 2.1 in two ways. First, in the production stage, firm i's marginal cost of production depends only on its own R&D investment and is denoted by $MC_i = C - c(x_i)$. Second, in the investment stage, firm i chooses x_i to maximize $(\pi_i + \lambda_F \pi_j)$, where $\lambda_F \in [0, 1]$, capturing all possible degrees of R&D coordination.[12] In the extreme case of full coordination (when $\lambda_F = 1$), each firm chooses its investment level to maximize their joint profits.

3.2. *A three-stage game*

For simplicity of exposition, we will keep the same notations as in Section 2 when there is no need for change. In the third stage, for given (x, s), the equilibrium production levels, q_1^* and q_2^*, are determined by Eq. (1) except with $MC_i = C - c(x_i)$. We define a_{ij} as in Section 2 and make the same assumptions. In the second stage, firm i chooses x_i to maximize $(\pi_i^* + \lambda_F \pi_j^*)$. The following first-order conditions determine the equilibrium R&D investments:

$$\frac{\partial \pi_i^*}{\partial x_i} + \lambda_F \frac{\partial \pi_j^*}{\partial x_i} = 0. \tag{2a}$$

Let $\tilde{\pi} \equiv (\pi_i^* + \lambda_F \pi_j^*)$, $b_{ii} \equiv \partial^2 \tilde{\pi} / \partial x_i^2$, $b_{ij} \equiv \partial^2 \tilde{\pi} / \partial x_j \partial x_i$. We make the same assumptions about b_{ij} as in Section 2 Furthermore, in this section, the firms' R&D investments are always strategic substitutes, which implies $b_{ij} < 0$. Finally, the equilibrium R&D subsidies (or taxes) are determined by Eq. (4). Notation e_{ij} is retained and the same assumptions about e_{ij} are made as in Section 2.

3.3. *Comparative statics results*

Following the analysis in Section 2.3, we can probe the effect of firms' R&D investments on the product market competition. Without the induced R&D spillover of Section 2, the effect becomes unambiguous. Specifically,

$$\frac{\partial q_i^*}{\partial x_i} = -\frac{1}{\Delta_1} a_{jj} c'(x_i) > 0 \quad \text{and} \quad \frac{\partial q_i^*}{\partial x_j} = \frac{1}{\Delta_1} a_{ij} c'(x_j) < 0. \tag{5a}$$

---

[12] For this approach, see papers by d'Aspremont and Jacquemin (1988), Kamien *et al.* (1992), and Suzumura (1992). They only consider $\lambda_F = 1$, however.

Intuitively, with higher R&D investment, firm i gains a cost advantage over firm j, resulting in higher q_i^* and lower q_j^* The effect of government R&D policy on the firms' R&D investments can be shown to be the same in formulation as that of Section 2 What is different is that $b_{ij} < 0$ in this section whereas the sign of b_{ij} depends on λ_R in Section 2.

Thus, we have

$$\frac{\partial x_i^*}{\partial s_i} = -\frac{b_{jj}}{\Delta_2} > 0 \quad \text{and} \quad \frac{\partial x_j^*}{\partial s_i} = \frac{b_{ji}}{\Delta_2} < 0. \tag{6a}$$

In summary, government i's subsidy raises firm i's R&D investment and reduces firm j's investment, which subsequently improves firm i's competitiveness in the market.

3.4. *R&D incentives*

Following the analysis in Section 2.4, we decompose

$$\frac{\partial \tilde{\pi}}{\partial x_i} = \frac{\partial(\pi_i + \lambda_F \pi_j)}{\partial x_i} + \frac{\partial(\pi_i + \lambda_F \pi_j)}{\partial q_i}\frac{\partial q_i^*}{\partial x_i} + \frac{\partial(\pi_i + \lambda_F \pi_j)}{\partial q_j}\frac{\partial q_j^*}{\partial x_i}.$$

Using the market stage first-order conditions and the fact that π_j is not a direct function of x_i, we can simplify the above equation as

$$\frac{\partial \tilde{\pi}}{\partial x_i} = \underbrace{\frac{\partial \pi_i}{\partial x_i}}_{\text{profit motive}} + \underbrace{\frac{\partial \pi_i \partial q_j^*}{\partial q_j \partial x_i}}_{\text{strategic motive}} + \lambda_F \underbrace{\frac{\partial \pi_j \partial q_i^*}{\partial q_i \partial x_i}}_{\text{coordination motive}}. \tag{7a}$$

Thus, when firms engage in R&D coordination ($\lambda_F > 0$) , there are three motives for R&D investment. The first two are the familiar profit and strategic motives. For the R&D coordination considered in this section, the strategic motive is always positive (by Eq. (5a)). This is in contrast to the results in Section 2. The third term on the right-hand side of Eq. (7a) represents a new motive, which we call the coordination motive. Intuitively, when firm i increases its R&D investment x_i, it decreases firm j's profit (by Eq. (5a)). As firm i cares about firm j's profit, its R&D incentive is diminished.

The coordination motive to underinvest in R&D is at odds with the strategic motive to overinvest in R&D, which can be better illustrated in the symmetric equilibrium. In the symmetric case (i.e., $s_1 = s_2$) we have $a_{11} = a_{22}$ and $a_{12} = a_{21}$, which implies $\partial\pi_i/\partial q_j = \partial\pi_j/\partial q_i$ and $a_{jj}/a_{ji} > 1$; by Eq. (5a), we also have $\partial q_i^*/\partial x_i = -(a_{jj}/a_{ji})\partial q_j^*/\partial x_i$. The net effect of these two motives can be simplified and signed:

$$\underbrace{\frac{\partial\pi_j\partial q_i^*}{\partial q_i\partial x_i}}_{\text{strategic motive}} + \lambda_F \underbrace{\frac{\partial\pi_j\partial q_i^*}{\partial q_i\partial X_i}}_{\text{coordination motive}}$$

$$= \left(1 - \lambda_F\frac{a_{jj}}{a_{ji}}\right)\frac{\partial\pi_i}{\partial q_j}\frac{\partial q_j^*}{\partial X_i}\begin{cases} > 0 \text{ for } \lambda_F = 0 \\ < 0 \text{ for } \lambda_F = 1. \end{cases} \tag{15}$$

For a sufficiently small λ_F, the strategic motive dominates the coordination motive, and firm i has incentive to overinvest in R&D. For a sufficiently large λ_F the coordination motive dominates the strategic motive, and firm i has incentive to underinvest in R&D. Thus, similar to the case of R&D collaboration, firms may underinvest or overinvest in R&D depending on the degree of R&D coordination.

3.5. *R&D policy*

As in Section 2.5, the equilibrium R&D subsidies (or taxes) are determined by equation system given by Eq. (4). By Eq. (8), we can simplify Eq. (4) as

$$s_i^*\frac{\partial x_i^*}{\partial s_i} = \frac{\partial\pi_i^*}{\partial x_i}\frac{\partial x_i^*}{\partial s_i} + \frac{\partial\pi_i^*}{\partial x_j}\frac{\partial x_j^*}{\partial s_i}. \tag{9a}$$

Compared with Eq. (9) of Section 2, Eq. (9a) has an additional term, $(\partial n_i^*/\partial x_i)(\partial x_i^*/\partial s_i)$. The reason that this term does not show up in Section 2.5 is simple. Under the R&D cooperation of Section 2, firm i chooses x_i to maximize π_i^* and thus this term is equal to zero by the first-order condition.

Moreover, we can show

$$\frac{\partial\pi_j^*}{\partial x_i} = \frac{\partial\pi_j}{\partial q_i}\frac{\partial q_i^*}{\partial x_i} + \frac{\partial\pi_j}{\partial q_j}\frac{\partial q_j^*}{\partial x_i} + \frac{\partial\pi_j}{\partial x_i} = p'q_j^*\frac{\partial q_i^*}{\partial x_i} < 0,$$

which implies by Eq. (2a) that $\partial\pi_i^*/\partial x_i > 0$. By Eq. (6a), both terms on the right-hand side of Eq. (9a) are positive. We have

Proposition 3. *With international R&D coordination, governments always subsidize R&D investments. That is, $s_i^* > 0$ for all λ_F.*

There are two reasons for the governments to subsidize their firms' R&D investments. First, the foreign firm's R&D investment adversely affects the domestic firm's profit (i.e., $\partial\pi_i^*/\partial x_j < 0$), and a government's R&D subsidy to the domestic firm discourages the foreign firm's R&D investment (i.e., $\partial x_j^*/\partial s_i < 0$). The combined effect (the second term on the right-hand side of Eq. (9a)) is the familiar strategic incentive for R&D policies. For the R&D coordination considered in this section, the strategic incentive always leads to R&D subsidies. This is similar to those studies in the literature, but is in contrast to the case of the R&D collaboration considered in Section 2.

Second, when firms engage in R&D coordination, they undertake fewer investments than those that would maximize their own respective profits (this is because $\partial\pi_i^*/\partial x_i > 0$ at the equilibrium x_i^*). This allows a government's R&D subsidy to raise the domestic firm's profit directly by encouraging the firm's R&D investment (namely, $(\partial\pi_i^*/\partial x_i)(\partial x_i^*/\partial s_i)$ — the first term on the right-hand side of Eq. (9a) — is positive). Note that the first term is equal to zero when the domestic firm chooses the R&D level to maximize its own profit (namely, $\partial\pi_i^*/\partial x_i = 0$) as in the R&D competition case and in the R&D collaboration discussed in Section 2.

In R&D coordination, a firm has an incentive to lower R&D investment, but the government wishes to change the firm's behavior by providing R&D subsidies to the firm. Thus, the governments' policies do not help their firms to commit. This is a new message for the literature.

3.6. *Coordination at the government level*

From the discussion following Proposition 3, it seems that the governments' incentives for R&D subsidies are partly due to the fact that the governments do not have coordination as their firms do. To investigate the robustness of Proposition 3, we examine the case of government coordination in this subsection.

Suppose now that in the first stage, government 1 chooses s_1 to maximize $\overline{W}$ while government 2 chooses s_2 to maximize $\overline{W}$, where $\overline{W}$ is defined as $\overline{W} = W_i^{**} + \lambda_G W_j^{**}$, $i \neq j$. Here $\lambda_G \in [0, 1]$, capturing all possible degrees of government coordination. Accordingly, the two first-order conditions that jointly determine the optimal policies become

$$\frac{\partial \overline{W}}{\partial s_i} = \frac{\partial (W_i^{**} + \lambda_G W_j^{**})}{\partial s_i} = 0, \tag{4a}$$

which can be rearranged to get

$$s_i \frac{\partial x_i^*}{\partial s_i} + \lambda_G s_j \frac{\partial x_j^*}{\partial s_i} = \frac{\partial (\pi_i^* + \lambda_G \pi_j^*)}{\partial x_i} \frac{\partial x_i^*}{\partial s_i} + \frac{\partial (\pi_i^* + \lambda_G \pi_j^*)}{\partial x_j} \frac{\partial x_j^*}{\partial s_i}.$$

The above equation can be further simplified using Eqs. (2a) and (6a):

$$\left(s_i - s_j \lambda_G \frac{b_{ji}}{b_{jj}} \right) \frac{\partial x_i^*}{\partial s_i} = \left(\frac{\lambda_F - \lambda_G}{\lambda_F} \right) \frac{\partial \pi_i^*}{\partial x_i} \frac{\partial \pi_i^*}{\partial s_i} + (1 - \lambda_G \lambda_F) \frac{\partial \pi_i^*}{\partial x_j} \frac{\partial x_j^*}{\partial s_i}. \tag{9b}$$

Let us examine the right-hand side of Eq. (9b) to explain the governments' policy incentives. When the governments coordinate in setting R&D policies (i.e., $\lambda_G > 0$), they care about not only their own welfare but also their rival's welfare. It follows that, though the firms still underinvest in R&D, the governments have less incentive to subsidize their firms' R&D. In particular, when the governments coordinate more than their firms do (i.e., $\lambda_G > \lambda_F$), they instead have incentive to tax their firms' R&D. The first term on the right-hand side of Eq. (9b) indicates this. Specifically,

$$\left(\frac{\lambda_F - \lambda_G}{\lambda_F} \right) \frac{\partial \pi_i^*}{\partial x_i} \frac{\partial \pi_i^*}{\partial s_i} \begin{cases} > 0 \text{ for } \lambda_G < \lambda_F, \\ = 0 \text{ for } \lambda_G = \lambda_F, \\ < 0 \text{ for } \lambda_G > \lambda_F. \end{cases} \tag{16}$$

On the other hand, the governments' strategic incentive to shift profits (the second term on the right-hand side of Eq. (9b)) remains so long as the governments are not fully coordinate ($\lambda_G \neq 1$). This is the case even when the firms fully coordinate in R&D (i.e., $\lambda_F = 1$). Thus, we have

Proposition 4. *In the absence of full coordination at the government level, i.e.,* $\lambda_G < 1$, *the optimal government R&D policy is to subsidize so long as the governments do not cooperate more than the firms do. More precisely,* $s^* > 0$ *if* $\lambda_G \leq \lambda_F$ *and* $\lambda_G \neq 1$.

Proof: See Appendix A.3. □

The full coordination case, $\lambda_G = 1$, deserves further scrutiny. When $\lambda_G = 1$, the first term on the right-hand side of Eq. (9b) is non-positive while the second term is non-negative. However, we can show that the first term dominates the second term unless the firms also have full coordination (i.e., $\lambda_F = 1$) in which case the two terms cancel out each other.

Proposition 5. *Fully coordinating governments should tax R&D unless their firms are also fully cooperating in R&D activities. With full coordination at both governmental and firm levels, the optimal policy is laissez faire. More precisely, the optimal R&D policies are*

$$s^* \begin{cases} = 0 \ for \ \lambda_F = \lambda_G = 1, \\ < 0 \ for \ \lambda_F < \lambda_G = 1. \end{cases}$$

Proof: See Appendix A.4. □

3.7. *Degree of government policy*

Similar to Section 2.6, here we examine the relationship between the degree of R&D coordination and that of R&D subsidy. In this section, we return to our basic framework of Section 3.1 (i.e., no policy coordination). As in Section 2.6, assume linear demand and the specific function $c(x_i)$ as in Eq. (11). The following lemma gives the necessary and sufficient condition for the existence of a symmetric equilibrium and characterizes the non-cooperative government R&D policy.

Lemma 2. *The model as specified by Eq. (11) has a unique solution to the optimal government policy if and only if* $\beta \geq 2.96$. *Specifically,* *the equilibrium R&D subsidy by each government is*

$$s^* = \frac{1}{12\beta}(-2 + 6\beta + 3\lambda_F\beta - \sqrt{4 - 4(10 - \lambda_F - 2\lambda_F^2)\beta + 9(2 - \lambda_F)^2\beta^2}); \quad (17)$$

and the equilibrium R&D investment by each firm is

$$x^* = \frac{(2 - \lambda_F)^2\alpha^2\beta}{(\lambda_F - 2 + 9\beta - 9\beta s^*)^2}. \quad (18)$$

Proof: See Appendix A.5. □

Furthermore, we can derive the following property of the equilibrium subsidy.

Proposition 6. *The optimal R&D subsidy rate, s^* (given in Eq.* (17)), *is increasing in λ_F, i.e., $ds^*/d\lambda_F > 0$.*

Proof: See Appendix A.6. □

4. Conclusions

It has become increasingly prevalent that rival firms of different countries engage in R&D cooperation. This presents challenges to the existing strategic trade literature, which focuses on government R&D policies for firms engaging in international R&D competition. This paper investigates the role of strategic government policies, if there is any, in the presence of international R&D cooperation.

In the absence of R&D cooperation, firms have incentive to overinvest in R&D, which is then further enhanced by their governments' R&D subsidies. However, under the two types of R&D cooperation (i.e., R&D collaboration and R&D coordination as we call them in this paper), firms may have incentives to overinvest or underinvest in R&D depending on the degree of R&D cooperation. Furthermore, we show that governments may still have the unilateral incentives to subsidize their firms' R&D though the rationales for such government R&D subsidies are quite different from those in the existing literature.

We have also pointed out the two departures of the present study from the existing strategic trade literature. First, optimal government policies may not necessarily reinforce the firms' commitments. Second, subsidies could be still optimal when the strategy variables are strategic complements.

The present analysis is by no means complete. While we have investigated government R&D policies using two popular models of international R&D cooperation, it is interesting to probe the robustness of our main results to other forms of R&D cooperation. In addition, while R&D subsidies or taxes are important policy tools, governments can also use R&D cooperation policies — i.e., whether to allow R&D cooperation — as a tool. Only by addressing these two extensions, can unambiguous policy suggestions be obtained.

Acknowledgements

We would like to thank Leonard Cheng, Stephen Chiu, Brian Copeland, Sugata Marjit, and particularly, Elhanan Helpman (Ed.) and the anonymous referee for very helpful suggestion and comments. We also benefit from presentation in the workshop of HKUST and the WEA International Pacific Rim Conference held in 1996 (Hong Kong).

Appendix A

A.1. *Proof of Lemma 1*

Due to linearity of the demand, the equilibrium outputs and profits in the third stage can be easily calculated,

$$q_i^* = \frac{1}{3}[\alpha + (2 - \lambda_R)y_i - (1 - 2\lambda_R)y_j],$$

$$\pi_i^* = \frac{1}{9}[\alpha + (2 - \lambda_R)y_i - (1 - \lambda_R)y_j]^2 - (1 - s_i)\beta y_i^2, i \neq j.$$

In the second stage, the firms maximize their individual profits by choice of x_i, which is equivalent to the corresponding profit maximization by choice of y_i. In what follows, we choose the latter to simplify our expressions. From the first-order conditions, we can compute the firms' second stage reaction functions, which are given in Eq. (12). Thus, the second-stage equilibrium is

$$y_i^* = \frac{(2-\lambda_R)[9(1-s_j)\beta - 3(2-\lambda_R)(1-\lambda_R)]\alpha}{\begin{array}{c}[9(1-s_1)\beta-(2-\lambda_R)^2][9(1-s_2)\beta-(2-\lambda_R)^2]\\ -(2-\lambda_R)^2(1-2\lambda_R)^2\end{array}} i \neq j.$$

Turning to the first stage, government i chooses s_i to maximize its country's welfare, which is given by

$$W_i^{**}(s_1, s_2) = \frac{1}{9}(\alpha + (2-\lambda_R)y_i^* - (1-2\lambda_R)y_j^*)^2 - \beta y_i^{*2}, i \neq j.$$

To simplify the analysis, let us suppose that government i chooses $t_i \equiv (1-s_i)$ rather than s_i to maximize its welfare. The two ways are clearly equivalent. We first derive the first-order conditions. Suppose the equilibrium exists. Then, for symmetry, the two optimal subsidy rates are equal, i.e., $s^* = s_1^* = s_2^*$, which means $t^* = t_1^* = t_2^*$ and

$$y^* = y_1^* = y_2^* = \frac{(2-\lambda_R)\alpha}{9\beta t^* - (2-\lambda_R)(1+\lambda_R)}. \quad \text{(A.1)}$$

Thus, using these symmetric results in the first-order conditions we can simplify them to

$$9\beta t^{*2} - 3(1+3\beta-\lambda_F^2)t^* + (2-\lambda_R)^2 = 0.$$

There are two solutions to the above equation, one of which being

$$t^* = \frac{1}{6\beta}[1+3\beta-\lambda_R^2+\sqrt{9\beta^2-2(5-8\lambda_R+5\lambda_R^2)\beta+(1-\lambda_R^2)^2}]. \quad \text{(A.2)}$$

It is straightforward to verify that $t^* \in (0,1)$. Thus, Eq. (13) follows. Eq. (A.1) also gives rise to Eq. (14). The other solution has the same expression as Eq. (A.2) except the plus sign in front of the square root is replaced with a minus sign. But this latter solution minimizes rather than maximizes the welfare and therefore we delete it.

It remains to show the existence of a unique equilibrium. To guarantee real-value solutions in Eq. (A.2), we require

$$f(\lambda_R, \beta) \equiv 9\beta^2 - 2(5 - 8\lambda_R + 5\lambda_R^2)\beta + (1 - \lambda_R^2)^2 \geq 0.$$

Note that, given any λ_R, there exist two real-value solutions to $f(\lambda_R, \beta) = 0$:

$$\beta_1(\lambda_R) = \frac{1}{9}[5 - 8\lambda_R + 5\lambda_R^2 - 2(2 - \lambda_R)|1 - 2\lambda_R|],$$

$$\beta_2(\lambda_R) = \frac{1}{9}[5 - 8\lambda_R + 5\lambda_R^2 + 2(2 - \lambda_R)|1 - 2\lambda_R|].$$

Note also that $f(\lambda_R, \beta)$ is convex in β. Thus, the necessary and sufficient condition for $f(\lambda_R, \beta) \geq 0$ for all λ_R is $\beta \geq \beta^* \equiv$ max $\beta_2(\lambda_R) = \beta_2(0) = 1$.

In fact, the inequality, $f(\lambda_R, \beta) \geq 0 \forall \lambda_R$, also holds for all $\beta \leq \min_{\lambda_R \in [0,1]} \beta_1(\lambda_R) = \frac{1}{4}$. However, we eliminate this range of β because these values violate the stability condition to the second stage optimization. Note that the stability condition for optimal y_i requires $\beta > \frac{4}{9}$ in the case of no subsidy and no spillovers.

A.2. *Proof of Proposition 2*

It is straightforward to show $s^* \geq 0$ for all $\lambda_R \in [0, 1]$. We now check the monotonicity of s^*

Step 1: Note from Eq. (13) that $n(\partial s/\partial \lambda_R) = sign(\partial s_a/\partial \lambda_R)$, where

$$s_a \equiv \lambda_R^2 - \sqrt{(3\beta + 1 - \lambda_R)^2 - 4\beta(2 - \lambda_R)^2}.$$

By calculation, we further obtain $sign(\partial s_a/\partial \lambda_R) = sign(s_b)$ where

$$s_b \equiv \lambda_R \sqrt{(3\beta + 1 - \lambda_R)^2 - 4\beta(2 - \lambda_R)^2} + 5\beta\lambda_R + \lambda_R - \lambda_R^3 - 4\beta.$$

Step 2: $\partial s_b/\partial \lambda_R = (5\beta + 1 - 3\lambda_R^2) + s_c/\sqrt{(3\beta + 1 - \lambda_R)^2 - 4\beta(2 - \lambda_R)^2}$, where $s_c \equiv (3\beta + 1 - \lambda_R^2)^2 - 4\beta(2 - \lambda_R)^2 - 2\lambda_R^2(3\beta + 1 - \lambda_R^2) + 4\beta\lambda_R(2 - \lambda_R)$. First, the first term in bracket is positive since $\beta \geq 1$. Second, by rearrangement, we obtain $s_c = (9\beta - 1)(\beta - 1) + 20\beta\lambda_R(1 - \lambda_R) + 4\lambda_R(\beta - \lambda_R) + 3\lambda_R^4 \geq 0$. Moreover, $s_b = 0$ when $\lambda_R = \frac{1}{2}$ Combining steps 1 and 2, we conclude that $s_b < 0$ when $\lambda_R < \frac{1}{2}$ and $s_b > 0$ when $\lambda_R > \frac{1}{2}$. The conclusion in the proposition then follows.

A.3. *Proof of Proposition 4*

The above analysis shows that the right-hand side of Eq. (9b) is positive under the conditions of Proposition 3, In the symmetric equilibrium, we have $s_i = s_j$ By Eq. (3), we also have $b_{jj} - \lambda_G b_{ji} \leq b_{jj} - b_{ji} < 0$, which implies $(1 - \lambda_G b_{ji}/b_{jj}) > 0$. Proposition 3 follows immediately.

A.4. *Proof of Proposition 5*

The case for $\lambda_F = \lambda_G = 1$ has been proven in the analysis leading to Proposition 3. For symmetric equilibrium, $\partial\pi_i^*/\partial x_i = \partial n_j^*/\partial x_j$. By Eqs. (2a) and (6a), respectively, we also have:

$$\frac{\partial\pi_i^*}{\partial x_j} = -\frac{1}{\lambda_F}\frac{\partial\pi_j^*}{\partial x_j} \quad \text{and} \quad \frac{\partial \mathrm{x}_j^*}{\partial_i} = -\frac{b_{ji}}{b_{jj}}\frac{\partial \mathrm{x}_i^*}{\partial_i}.$$

Thus, the right-hand side of Eq. (9b) can be simplified as

$$-\frac{(1-\lambda_F)}{\lambda_F}\left(1 - \frac{b_{ji}}{b_{jj}}\right)\frac{\partial\pi_i^*}{\partial x_i}\frac{\partial \mathrm{x}_i^*}{\partial s_i} < 0.$$

Thus, $s^* < 0$.

A.5. *Proof of Lemma 2*

Due to linearity of the demand, the equilibrium outputs and profits in the third stage can be easily calculated,

$$q_i^* = \frac{1}{3}(\alpha + 2y_i - y_j), \pi_i^* = \frac{1}{9}(\alpha + 2y_i - y_j)^2 - (1 - s_i)\beta y_i^2, i \neq j.$$

In the second stage, depending on whether they compete or cooperate in R&D investment, the firms maximize their individual or joint profits by choice of x_i which is equivalent to the corresponding profit maximization by choice of y_i. In what follows, we choose the latter to simplify our expressions. From the first-order conditions, we can compute the firms' second-stage optimal decisions:

$$y_i^* = \frac{3(2-\lambda_F)[3(1-s_j)\beta - 2 - \lambda_F]\alpha}{[9(1-s_1)\beta - 4 - \lambda_F][9(1-s_2)\beta - 4 - \lambda_F)] - 4(1+\lambda_F)^2}, i \neq j.$$

Turning to the first stage, government i chooses t_i to maximize its country's welfare, which is given by

$$W_i^{**}(s_1, s_2) = \frac{1}{9}(\alpha + 2y_i^* - y_j^*)^2 - \beta y_i^{*2}, i \neq j.$$

Then, the first-order conditions are, for $i \neq j$

$$\begin{aligned}(\alpha + 2y_i^* - y_j^*)&[(2-\lambda_F)\alpha - (4+\lambda_F - 9\beta t_j)(2y_i^* - y_j^*)] \\ &+ 9\beta(4+\lambda_F - 9\beta t_j)y_i^{*2} = 0. \qquad \text{(A.3)}\end{aligned}$$

Suppose the equilibrium exists. Then, for symmetry, the two optimal subsidy rates are equal, i.e., $s^* = s_1^* = s_2^*$, which means $t^* = t_1^* = t_2^*$ and

$$y^* = y_1^* = y_2^* = \frac{(2-\lambda_F)\alpha}{\lambda_F - 2 + 9\beta t^*}. \qquad \text{(A.4)}$$

Thus, the first-order conditions, Eq. (A.3), can be simplified to

$$18\beta t^{*2} - 3(2 + 6\beta - 3\lambda_F\beta)t^* + (8 - 2\lambda_F - \lambda_F^2) = 0.$$

There are two solutions to the above equation, one of which being

$$\begin{aligned}t^* = \frac{1}{12\beta}&[(2+6\beta - 3\lambda_F\beta) \\ &+ \sqrt{4 - 4(10 - \lambda_F - 2\lambda_F^2)\beta + 9(2-\lambda_F)^2\beta^2}]. \qquad \text{(A.5)}\end{aligned}$$

It is straightforward to verify that $t^* \in (0, 1)$. Thus, Eq. (17) follows. Eq. (A.4) also gives rise to Eq. (18). The other solution has the same expression as Eq. (A.5) except the plus sign in front of the square root is replaced with a minus sign. But this latter solution minimizes rather than maximizes the welfare and therefore we delete it.

It remains to show the existence of a unique equilibrium. To guarantee real-value solutions in Eq. (A.5), we require

$$f(\lambda_F, \beta) \equiv 4 - 4(10 - \lambda_F - 2\lambda_F^2)\beta + 9(2 - \lambda_F)^2\beta^2 \geq 0. \quad \text{(A.6)}$$

Note that, given any λ_F, there exist two real-value solutions to $f(\lambda_F, \beta) = 0$:

$$\beta_1(\lambda_F) = \frac{2(5 + 2\lambda_F) - 4\sqrt{(1 + \lambda_F)(4 + \lambda_F)}}{9(2 - \lambda_F)},$$

$$\beta_2(\lambda_F) = \frac{2(5 + 2\lambda_F) + 4\sqrt{(1 + \lambda_F)(4 + \lambda_F)}}{9(2 - \lambda_F)}.$$

Note also that $f(\lambda_F, \beta)$ is convex in β. Thus, the necessary and sufficient condition for $f(\lambda_F, \beta) \geq 0$ for all λ_F is

$$\beta \geq \beta^* \equiv \max \beta_2(\lambda_F) = \frac{14 + 4\sqrt{10}}{9} \approx 2.96.$$

In fact, the inequality, $f(\lambda_F, \beta) \geq 0 \forall \lambda_F$, also holds for all $\beta \leq \min_{\lambda_F \in [0,1]} \beta_1(\lambda_F) = \frac{1}{9}$. However, we eliminate this range of β because these values violate the stability condition to the second-stage optimization. For stable second-stage equilibrium, β must be greater than $\frac{2}{3}$. One can obtain this critical value from expression given by Eq. (6) of Henriques (1990), who discusses the stability conditions in a model similar to ours.

A.6. *Proof of Proposition 6*

It can be easily verified that $f(\lambda_F, \beta)$ as defined by Eq. (A.6) is a strictly decreasing function of λ_F for any given $\beta \geq \beta^*$. Thus, from Eq. (A.5), t^* clearly decreases in λ_F. Therefore,

$$\text{sign}\left(\frac{ds^*}{d\lambda_F}\right) = -\text{sign}\left(\frac{dt^*}{d\lambda_F}\right) = +.$$

References

Brander, J., 1995. Strategic trade policy. In: Grossman, G., Rogoff, K. (Eds.), *Handbook of International Economics*, vol. III, North-Holland, Amsterdam.

Brander, J. and Spencer, B., 1985. Export subsidies and market share rivalry. *Journal of International Economics* 18, 83–100.

Brodley, J.F., 1990. Antitrust law and innovation cooperation. *Journal of Economic Perspectives* 4, 97–112.

Chesnais, Γ., 1988. Technical co-operation agreements between firms. STI Review (Organisation for Economic Co-operation and Development, Paris), pp. 51–121.

Cline, W.R., 1995. Evaluating the Uruguay Round. *World Economy* 18, 1–23.

Coe, D.T. and Helpman, E., 1995. International R&D spillovers. *European Economic Review* 39, 859–887.

d'Aspremont, C. and Jacquemin, A., 1988. Cooperative and noncooperative R&D in duopoly with spillovers. *American Economic Review* 78, 1133–1137.

Eaton, J. and Grossman, G., 1986. Optimal trade and industrial policy under oligopoly. *Quarterly Journal of Economics* 101, 383–406.

Henriques, I., 1990. Cooperative and noncooperative R&D with spillovers: Comment. *American Economic Review* 80, 638–640.

Jorde, T.M. and Teece, D.J., 1990. Innovation and cooperation: Implications for competition and antitrust. *Journal of Economic Perspectives* 4, 75–96.

Kamien, M., Muller, E. and Zang, I., 1992. Research joint ventures and R&D cartels. *American Economic Review* 82, 1293–1306.

Katz, M., 1986. An analysis of cooperative research and development. *Rand Journal of Economics* 17, 527–543.

Krugman, P., 1984. The U.S. response to foreign industrial targeting. Brooking's Paper on Economic Activity, 74–121.

Murphy, W.J., 1991. R&D Cooperation Among Marketplace Competitors. Quorum Books, New York.

Shapiro, C. and Willig, R.D., 1990. On the antitrust treatment of production joint ventures. *Journal of Economic Perspectives* 4, 113–130.

Spencer, B. and Brander, J., 1983. International R&D rivalry and industrial strategy. *Review of Economic Studies L*, 707–722.

Suzumura, K., 1992. Cooperative and noncooperative R&D in an oligopoly with spillovers. *American Economic Review* 82, 1307–1320.

Veugelers, R. and Kesteloot, K., 1994. On the design of stable joint ventures. *European Economic Review* 38, 1799–1815.

Chapter 3

The North's Intellectual Property Rights Standard for the South?*

Abstract

We build a multi-sectoral North-South trade model to analyze international intellectual property rights (IPR) protection. By comparing the Nash equilibrium IPR protection standard of the South (the developing countries) with that of the North (the developed countries), we find that the former is naturally weaker than the latter. Moreover, we show that both regions can gain from an agreement that requires the South to harmonize its IPR standards with those of the North, and the North to liberalize its traditional goods market. This demonstrates the merits of multi-sectoral negotiations in the GATT/WTO.

1. Introduction

One important breakthrough of the Uruguay Round of the General Agreement on Tariffs and Trade (GATT) is the signing of the Agreement on Trade-Related Aspects of Intellectual Property Rights (the TRIPS Agreement), which stipulates that all members adopt a set of universal minimum standards on intellectual property rights (IPR) protection.[1] According to many observers (e.g., Reichman, 1995), most of the terms of the agreement are based on the prevailing

*This chapter is reproduced from *Journal of International Economics*, 59, 183–209, 2003, with permission from Elsevier.

[1]See UNCTAD (1997) and Maskus (1998, 2000) for more about the TRIPS Agreement and related issues.

standards in developed countries (the North) at the time of the negotiation. The major consequence is that developing countries (the South) have to strengthen substantially the legal protection of IPR. Based on this observation, it is often argued that the agreement 'forces' the South to harmonize its IPR standards with those of the North.

The TRIPS Agreement has raised several questions. For example, has the South been doing too little to protect IPR (from the South's and the global welfare points of view)? What are the welfare consequences, for the South, the North and the world, from strengthening IPR protection in the South? From the global welfare point of view, does the South protect too much if it adopts the North's IPR standard? How can we make the TRIPS Agreement compatible with the South's incentive? Answers to these questions would help us address other important issues as well. For example, if raising the South's IPR standard improves the world's welfare, then the TRIPS can potentially make all regions better off. This paper deals with the above questions and issues.

We build a model with two regions in the world, the North and the South, which trade two types of goods, differentiated products and traditional products. Innovation and imitation are carried out in the differentiated-products sectors of both regions. We assume that the North and the South adopted their respective Nash equilibrium IPR standards before the TRIPS was put in place, and the TRIPS Agreement requires both regions to adopt the pre-TRIPS IPR standard of the North as a minimum standard. The cost-benefit analysis we adopt is not fundamentally different from Nordhaus's (1969) classical work in which he calculates the optimal patent length. Like his analysis, our optimal IPR protection strikes an optimal balance between the gains from increased R&D efforts and the deadweight losses resulting from the prolonged monopoly power of the innovators. Based on our analysis, we find that the South's equilibrium IPR standard is naturally not as strong as that of the North. Moreover, it is globally welfare-improving for the South to raise its IPR standard to harmonize with the North's pre-TRIPS level. The major effects of the TRIPS are: the South's consumers lose by paying higher prices, the North's producers gain higher profits, but all consumers gain from a larger variety of goods. On balance, the South's welfare decreases, the North's increases, but the total welfare of the two regions rises, because of the existence of a positive inter-regional externality. The externality arises because an increase in a region's IPR protection raises the profits of firms and enlarges the product variety in another region without raising the deadweight loss in the latter. However, an agreement that requires the South to raise its IPR standard without compensation benefits the North at the expense of the South, and would not be compatible with the South's incentive.

Therefore, we extend the above IPR model to incorporate multi-sectoral bargaining between the North and South to show that multi-sectoral negotiations (or multi-issue negotiations) in GATT/WTO can be mutually beneficial to both regions. For example, it would benefit both regions for the South to harmonize its IPR standard with the North's, in exchange for the North lowering its import tariffs against South's exports of traditional products. In this case, multi-issue negotiations can achieve incentive-compatible and mutually beneficial outcomes while single-issue negotiations cannot, since it is globally welfare-improving for each side to make concessions on a different issue.

There have been many theoretical and empirical studies on the effects of IPR protection on innovation, trade, foreign direct investment and economic growth.[2] As far as we are aware, however, the present paper is among the first to assume that both the North and the South have innovative capabilities and to consider optimal degrees of IPR protection for the North, the South and the world as a whole. It is also among the first to analyze the merits of raising the South's IPR protection in the broader context of multi-sectoral (or multi-issue) negotiations, such as in the GATT or WTO. There are some other studies in the literature that are related to our study in one way or another. Both Chin and Grossman (1990) and Deardorff (1992) examine welfare effects of extending IPR protection from the North to the South. They find, as we do, that many results depend

[2]See, for example, Mansfield (1986), Maskus and Penubarti (1995), Gould and Gruben (1996), Richardson and Gaisford (1996), Horowitz and Lai (1996), Lai (1998) and Glass and Saggi (2001). For example, Lai (1998) finds that, since stronger IPR protection in the South can increase the rate of innovation, there is a tradeoff between the dynamic gains and static losses from strengthening IPR protection in the South.

on the size of the South's market.[3] However, there are two notable differences between these papers and our study. First, they assume that the South does not have innovative capability. Second, they examine only the case in which the South has either full or no IPR protection. Diwan and Rodrik (1991) also consider various degrees of IPR protection in the North and the South. Interestingly, they find that to maximize the global welfare, which is the equally weighted sum of the North's and the South's welfare, the rates of patent protection in the two regions must be identical. They emphasize the taste difference between the two regions and assume no innovative capability in the South. Helpman (1993) uses a dynamic general equilibrium North-South model to study IPR protection, growth and welfare. He assumes that the North specializes in innovation and the South specializes in imitation. He finds that tightening IPR protection in the South hurts the South and may or may not benefit the North. We believe that this result needs to be modified if we take into account the South's innovative capability. We examine this issue in our partial equilibrium model, which is able to include a more detailed microeconomic analysis of firm and government behaviors.[4] Unlike our work, none of the above-mentioned papers deals with the incentive-compatibility issue of the South's concessions in IPR. Our result that multi-issue negotiation makes both the South and North better off echoes the recent literature on linkage issue related to international trade negotiations (see Horsmann *et al.*, 2001).

More recently, McCalman (2001) makes estimates of the transfer of income from consumers to producers (mostly a transfer from South to North) resulting from the TRIPS. However, he does not estimate the welfare gains from larger product variety, which can be substantial. As we argue below, such a gain would actually outweigh

[3]In particular, Deardorff (1992) shows that global welfare will be reduced if the North's IPR standard is extended to a very large part of the South. In a related study, Yang (1998) argues that because of the free-rider problem existing among the Southern countries, the South's IPR protection is too weak.

[4]Taylor (1993) has an interesting study on how firms in the North respond to lax IPR protection in the South by creating market-made protection, i.e., technology masquing.

the deadweight loss so that a rise in the South's IPR protection is globally welfare-improving.[5]

The organization of the paper is as follows. Section 2 lays out the basic features of the model and derives the Nash equilibrium pre-TRIPS IPR standards in the two regions. Section 3 examines the effect of varying the South's IPR protection standard on global welfare. Section 4 introduces a bargaining game between the two regions in a multi-sectoral negotiation. Section 5 summarizes the findings.

2. A Multi-sectoral Model with IPR Protection

There are two regions in the world, the North and the South. The North has higher innovative capability than the South. There are two distinct regimes, the pre-TRIPS regime and the post-TRIPS regime. We assume that in the pre-TRIPS regime, the North and the South adopt their respective Nash equilibrium IPR standards. While the TRIPS Agreement covers extensive issues, it is a widely shared view that establishing a global minimum IPR standard is the key.[6] To capture the view that the TRIPS adopted the prevailing IPR standard of the North at the time of signing the agreement, we assume that in the post-TRIPS regime the North's pre-TRIPS IPR standard is set as the minimum standard for both regions. We shall derive the Nash equilibrium IPR standards in the pre-TRIPS regime in this section; in the next section, we evaluate welfare consequence of the TRIPS Agreement.

2.1. *Preliminaries*

There are two traded sectors in each region: a differentiated goods sector and a traditional good sector. First let us focus on the

[5]He finds that the net transfers the US receives from the TRIPS to be up to 40% of the gains associated with trade liberalization in the WTO, while the developing countries pay net transfers of up to 64% of the gains they receive from trade liberalization. The large amount of transfers involved shows that the IPR issue can indeed be an important leverage for the South to elicit trade concessions from the North.

[6]See Hoekman and Kostecki (1995) for example.

differentiated products sector. Consider one or many industries with very high potential for product innovation. Assume that any newly developed product will become obsolete after T periods.[7] Although IPR protection refers to a broad range of legal activities, here we use patent protection as representative of IPR protection. Region k's government sets a patent length T_k for $k \in \{s, n\}$, where s denotes the South and n denotes the North. We assume 'national treatment', i.e. governments provide the same protection to all firms, regardless of where they are invented. This had been practiced by many countries even before TRIPS. All imitated products are prohibited from being produced or sold in region k for T_k periods. The time horizon is infinite. At the beginning of period 0, both governments announce and immediately enforce patent length of T_s and T_n respectively for all goods invented in or after period 0. In each period, potential innovators decide whether or not to make individual R&D investments. If they do, differentiated products will be developed. We assume that innovators (i.e. firms) and consumers face exactly the same environment in every period. (We can imagine there is a pool of resources that can perform product development and production every period.) Thus, potential innovators will take the same R&D action in every period. In particular, the same *numbers* of differentiated products will be developed in every period. Let M_k be the number of differentiated products developed in region k in each period. We assume that the sets of products developed in the North and South are non-intersecting, and so a product developed in one region is different from any product developed in the other region. Products invented in different periods are necessarily different to qualify for IPR protection. The same firm could develop many products in many periods. Nonetheless, for ease of exposition, we treat different products (whether in the same period or not) as being invented by different firms.

Before period T, the numbers of differentiated products (invented under the new IPR regime) whose patents have expired as well as not expired change from one period to the next. After period T, these numbers become steady. Therefore, a steady state is attained after period T. To simplify the analysis, we assume that there is no

[7] T can be regarded as the length of the product cycle. After T periods, the product has no economic value.

discount of the future. Since there is no discounting, we can focus our attention on the steady-state flow welfare for the purpose of welfare analysis.

This can be justified by 'overtaking criterion' in dynamic optimization theory.[8] In every steady-state period, there are TM_S South-invented products that are economically viable and TM_n North-invented products that are economically viable, of which $T_S(M_S + M_n)$ products' patents are still in force in the South and $T_n(M_s + M_n)$ products' patents are still in force in the North. Although the number of products is discrete, we treat it as continuous in our mathematical derivation for easier handling.

Following some previous work, we assume a quasi-linear utility function for the representative consumer. With free trade in differentiated products and the traditional product, the steady state flow utility of the representative consumer in region k (where $k \in \{sn\}$) in period l is:

$$u_k(t) = T_k \left[\sum_{j\in\{n,s\}} \int_0^{M_j} x_{jk}(i)^\alpha di \right] + (T - T_k) \left[\sum_{j\in\{n,s\}} \int_0^{M_j} \tilde{x_{jk}}(i)^\alpha \, di \right] + \left(az_k - \frac{1}{2} e_k z_k^2 \right) + y_k,$$

where $0 < a < 1$ and $2a/e_k \geq z_k \geq 0$.[9] Parameters a and e_k are positive constants; $x_{jk}(i)(\tilde{x_{jk}}(i)$, respectively) is the consumption of differentiated product i developed in region j and consumed in region k, whose patent has not expired (has expired, respectively); z_k is the consumption of a traditional product z (e.g., textile products) in region k. Finally, y_k is a competitively produced non-traded

[8]See, for example, Burmeister (1980), pp. 249–250. Basically, with no discounting, a path $\{\hat{c}, \hat{k}, \hat{k}\}$ overtakes the path $\{c, k, k\}$ if $\int_0^T [u(\hat{c}) - u(c)]dt \geq 0$, dta 0, where c is the control variable, k is the state variable, and $u(c)$ is the instantaneous welfare corresponding to the path $\{c, k, k\}$. A feasible path $\{c, k, k\}$ is optimal if it overtakes all other feasible paths. It can be easily seen that if the steady state value of $u(c)$ is higher than that of any other feasible values $u(c)$, then $\{\hat{c}, \hat{k}, \hat{k}\}$ overtakes all other paths, and is therefore optimal.

[9]For $2a/e_k < z_k$, the utility derived from good z is zero. We shall maintain the assumption that a is sufficiently large to avoid corner solutions.

composite good, produced and consumed only in region k. The price of y_s is normalized to one.[10] Note that if $e_s \neq e_n$, then consumers in different regions will demand the differentiated and the traditional products in different ratios, even if prices are equal across regions. In particular, if $e_s < e_n$, a consumer in the South demands a higher ratio of traditional product to differentiated products than a consumer in the North does. In each period, each consumer in region k maximizes her utility subject to a budget constraint.

$$I_k \geq T_k \left[\sum_{j \in \{n,s\}} \int_0^{M_j} p_{jk}(i) x_{jk}(i) di \right]$$
$$+ (T - T_k) \left[\sum_{j \in \{n,s\}} \int_0^{M_j} \tilde{p_{jk}}(i) \tilde{x_{jk}}(i)\, di \right] + p_k(z) z_k + y_k,$$

where $p_{jk}(i)(\tilde{p_{jk}}(i)$, respectively) is the price of product i developed in region j and sold in region k whose patent has not expired (has expired, respectively); $p_k(z)$ is the price of product z sold in region k, and expenditure I_k is exogenously given. To simplify the notation, define $\epsilon \equiv 1/(1-\alpha)$ and $A \equiv (1-\alpha)\alpha^{(1+\alpha)\epsilon}$.

The instantaneous demand for products x (the differentiated products) whose patents have not expired, that for those whose patents have already expired, and that for product z (the traditional product) by the representative consumers are, respectively,

$$x_{jk}(i) = \left[\frac{p_{jk}(i)}{\alpha} \right]^{-\epsilon}, \quad \tilde{x}_{jk}(i) = \left[\frac{\tilde{p}_{jk}(i)}{\alpha} \right]^{-\epsilon} \quad \text{and} \quad z_k = \frac{a - p_k(z)}{e_k}.$$

When $a < p_k(z), z_k = 0$. We shall maintain the assumption that a is sufficiently large to ensure interior solutions. Let N_k be a shift parameter on aggregate demand, which can be interpreted as the number of consumers in region k. (We shall assume that $N_n > N_s$. Note that this should not be literally interpreted as the North's population being higher, but rather that the size of the market for

[10] We assume that there is free trade in order to focus on IPR policy. Qiu and Lai (2001), on the other hand, compare South's and North's tariffs but treat IPR policy as given.

differentiated products is larger in the North, as will become clear next.) Thus, the corresponding aggregate demands are, respectively:

$$x_{jk}(i) = N_k \left[\frac{p_{jk}(i)}{\alpha}\right]^{-\epsilon}, \tilde{x}_{jk}(i) = N_k \left[\frac{\tilde{p_{jk}}(i)}{\alpha}\right]^{-\epsilon} \text{ and}$$

$$z_k = N_k \left[\frac{a - p_k(z)}{e_k}\right].$$

Define $e_n = e$ and $\eta_k = eN_k/e_k$. Then, we can rewrite

$$z_k = \eta_k \left[\frac{a - p_k(z)}{e}\right].$$

Therefore, N_s/N_n is the size of the market for differentiated products in the South relative to that of the North, and η_s/η_n is the size of South's market for the traditional product relative to that of the North. Note that $\eta_n = N_n$ and $\eta_s = eN_s/e_s$. Assuming that $e_s < e_n$, so that the South's propensity to consume the traditional product relative to the differentiated products is higher, we have $\eta_s/\eta_n > N_s/N_n$. It is indeed plausible that $\eta_s/\eta_n > 1$ and $N_s/N_n < 1$. We shall discuss more about this in Section 4.

For simplicity, assume that the unit cost of production for all x products is constant and equal to one unit of good y in that region regardless of the location of production.[11] Hence, the per-period operating profit (i.e., profit not including innovation costs) of firm i based in region j selling in region k is $\pi_{jk}(i) = [p_{jk}(i) - 1]X_{jk}(i)$. Under IPR protection, firm i has a monopoly on product i. As a result, for products whose patents have not expired,

$$p_{jk}(i) = \frac{1}{\alpha}, \quad X_{jk}(i) = N_k\alpha^{2\epsilon}, \quad \text{and} \quad \pi_{jk}(i) = N_k A.$$

We assume imitation costs are zero. Therefore, for products whose patents have expired, prices are driven down to the unit cost of

[11] In general, labor costs are lower in the South than in the North while innovation costs are higher in the South than in the North. But, our emphasis here is on the North-South difference in innovation costs.

production because of imitation. Thus

$$\tilde{p_{jk}}(i) = \frac{1}{\alpha}, \quad \tilde{X_{jk}}(i) = N_k\alpha^{\epsilon}, \quad \text{and} \quad \tilde{\pi_{jk}}(i) = 0.$$

To avoid unnecessary complexity, we omit the details of the production of traditional good z by using an endowment model. Moreover, we assume that the South is relatively more abundantly endowed with good z than the North in the sense that in every period, t, region k is endowed with $\eta_k\overline{z}_k$ of the traditional good and that $\overline{z}_n < \overline{z}_s$. Therefore, in autarky, the price of good z would be lower in the South than in the North, and when there is free trade the South would export this good to the North. Let $\eta_s z_{ss}$ and $\eta_s z_{sn}$ be the quantities of the South-produced traditional good sold in South's market and exported to North's market, respectively, with $z_{ss} + z_{sn} = \overline{z}_s$. Let r be the tariff imposed on each unit of good z imported to the North. Assume that the demand intercept a is sufficiently large and that $\overline{z}_s - \overline{z}_n > \tau/e$. Then, we have the following equilibrium conditions for the traditional good sector in both markets:

$$p_n(\mathrm{z}) = a - e(\overline{z}_n + \delta z_{sn}), \quad p_s(z) = a - ez_{ss} \quad \text{and} \quad p_n(z) = p_s(z) + \tau,$$

where $\delta \equiv \eta_s/\eta_n$. Solving the above equilibrium conditions gives

$$z_{sn} = \frac{e(\overline{z}_s - \overline{z}_n) - \tau}{e(1+\delta)} \quad \text{and} \quad p_n(z) = \frac{a(1+\delta) - e(\overline{z}_n - \delta\overline{z}_s) + \delta_\tau}{e(1+\delta)}. \tag{1}$$

The total revenue per period from sector z is therefore $R_{zn} = \eta_n[p_n(z)\overline{z}_n + \tau z_{sn}]$ for the North and $R_{zs} = \eta_s p_s(z)\overline{z}_s$ for the South. Consumer surplus per period derived from this sector in the North and South are respectively $\eta_s/2e[a - p_n(z)]^2$ and $\eta_s/2e[a - p_s(z)]^2$. Note that the per-period quantities in the traditional-good sector are also the steady-state quantities.

The total steady state flow welfare in region k is

$$W_k = U_k + U_{zk},$$

where U_k is region k's steady state flow welfare derived from all sectors excluding sector z, whereas U_{zk} is the steady state flow welfare in region k derived exclusively from sector z. We shall focus on the analysis of IPR protection in the rest of this section and in Section 3. Since IPR protection affects sector x only, and will not affect U_{zk}, we shall ignore sector z until Section 4.

2.2. *Analysis of the pre-TRIPS regime*

Based on the analysis in the preceding section, region k's (where $k \in \{s, n\}$) representative consumer's steady state flow utility at time l is

$$u_k(t) = T_k(M_s + M_n)(1-\alpha)\alpha^{2a\epsilon} + (T - T_k)(Ms + M_n)(1-\alpha)^{\alpha\epsilon} + \frac{[a - p_k(z)]^2}{2e_k} + I_k.$$

The first term on the right hand side refers to goods whose patents have not expired, and the second term refers to goods whose patents have expired.

We now turn to the firms' profits. Assume that in each period the innovation costs of different products are different. Some goods are easier to develop and some goods are harder to develop. We index goods in ascending order based on the innovation costs, i.e., a good with a lower index i has a lower innovation cost than a good with a higher i. It is assumed that the innovation cost of product i based in region k is $a_k \cdot i^{1/b_k}$: where $a_k > 0$ and $0 < b_k < 1$ are parameters.[12]

All firms sell their products in both the South's and North's markets. Thus, the life-time profit of firm i based in region k (over the entire life of product i) is

$$\prod_k(i) = \int_0^{T_s} \pi_{ks}(i)dt + \int_0^{T_n} \pi_{kn}(i)dt - a_k \cdot i^{\frac{1}{b_k}}$$

$$= (N_sT_s + N_nT_n)A - a_k \cdot i^{\frac{1}{b_k}}$$

In each period, the marginal firm in the North, M_n, and that in the South, M_s, are defined as firms that earn zero profit,

[12]We could instead use a more general cost function $f(i)$, where $f(0) > 0$, $f'(\cdot)(0) > 0$, $f''(\cdot) > 0$. But our results would not be altered qualitatively. Nor would our results be affected qualitatively if the future were discounted.

i.e., $\prod_n(M_n) = 0$ and $\prod_s(M_s) = 0$, respectively. This leads to

$$M_n = \left(\frac{\mu}{a_n}\right)^{b_n} \text{ and } M_s = \left(\frac{\mu}{a_s}\right)^{b_s}, \text{ where } \mu = (N_sT_s + N_nT_n)A.$$

Thus, M_s products are developed in the South and K products are developed in the North in each period. We define the steady state flow profits of a region in a period as the total life-time profits of all firms that innovate in that period. It turns out that these flow profits are equal to $\int_0^{M_k} \prod k(i)di$.

Before we proceed further, we now make two assumptions about the asymmetry between the two regions. First, we assume that $N_n > N_s$. Although we can consider the South's population to be higher than the North's, it is widely documented that the North's demands for innovative products, such as computers, pharmaceuticals and biotechnological products, are higher than those of the South. Second, we assume that the North has higher innovative capability such that in equilibrium $M_s < M_n$. There are many combinations of a_s, a_n, b_s, and b_n that can lead to this very plausible equilibrium outcome. For example, $b_s = b_n$ and $a_s > a_n$, or $b_s < b_n$ and $a_s = a_n$, are sufficient conditions for $M_s < M_n$. It would be seen later that these two assumptions would lead to the result that the North protects IPR stronger than the South does.

The steady state flow welfare of region k is given by

$$\begin{aligned} W_k(T_s, T_n, M_s, M_n) &= N_k u_k(t) + \int_0^{M_k} \Pi_k(i)di + R_{zk} \\ &= N_kT_k[(M_s{+}M_n)(1-\alpha)\alpha^{2\alpha\epsilon}] \\ &\quad + N_k(T-T_k)[(M_s{+}M_n)((1-\alpha)\alpha^{\alpha\epsilon}] + N_kI_k + M_k(N_sT_s \\ &\quad + N_nT_n)A - \frac{b_k}{1+b_k}M_k^{\frac{1+b_k}{b_k}} + U_{zk}. \end{aligned}$$

Each region chooses its IPR protection policy T_k strategically to maximize its welfare. To characterize the Nash equilibrium, we first obtain the policy reaction functions of the North and of the South. Since the reaction functions of the North and the South are symmetric up to the values of the parameters, let us focus on the South for the time being. Assuming an interior solution, the optimal response T_s for any given T_n is obtained from the following equation:

$$\frac{dW_s}{dT_s} = \frac{\partial W_s}{\partial T_s} + \frac{\partial W_s}{\partial M_s}\frac{\partial M_s}{\partial T_s} + \frac{\partial W_s}{\partial M_n}\frac{\partial M_n}{\partial T_s} = 0. \tag{2}$$

Note that

$$\frac{\partial W_s}{\partial T_s} = -N_s\{M_s[1-(1+\alpha)\alpha^{\alpha\epsilon}]\} + M_n(1-\alpha^{\alpha\epsilon})(1(1-\alpha)\alpha^{\alpha\epsilon} < 0.$$

That is, the marginal effect of lengthening IPR protection, given that the number of products remains unchanged, is negative. It is the sum of consumer losses and producer gains, which add up to a deadweight loss. We denote this social marginal cost of IPR protection in the South as $MC_S = \left|\frac{\partial W_s}{\partial T_s}\right|$, which increases with T_s.

On the other hand, lengthening IPR protection in the South encourages more innovations in both the North and the South, which enlarges product variety and so raises consumer welfare. Thus,

$$\frac{\partial W_s}{\partial M_s}\frac{\partial M_s}{\partial T_s} = N_s[T - T_s(1-\alpha^{\alpha\epsilon})](1-\alpha)\alpha^{\alpha\epsilon}\frac{\partial M_s}{\partial T_s} > 0,$$
$$\frac{\partial W_s}{\partial M_n}\frac{\partial M_n}{\partial T_s} = N_s[T - T_s(1-\alpha^{\alpha\epsilon})](1-\alpha)\alpha^{\alpha\epsilon}\frac{\partial M_n}{\partial T_s} > 0,$$

the sum of which captures the social marginal benefit (MB_S) from extending T_s. Since

$$\frac{\partial M_s}{\partial T_s} = \frac{N_s A}{\mu} b_s M_s \quad \text{and} \quad \frac{\partial M_n}{\partial T_s} = \frac{N_s A}{\mu} b_n M_n,$$

the marginal benefit MB_S decreases in T_s.

The South's reaction function is therefore obtained from equating MC_S to MB_S, which is reduced to[13]

$$M_s[1-(1+\alpha)\alpha^{\alpha\epsilon}] + M_n(1-\alpha^{\alpha\epsilon}) = \frac{N_s A}{\mu}[T - T_s(1-\alpha^{\alpha\epsilon})](b_s M_s + b_n M_n). \tag{3}$$

[13]The second-order condition for the South is automatically satisfied as it can now be easily checked that $d^2W_s/dT_s^2 < 0$.

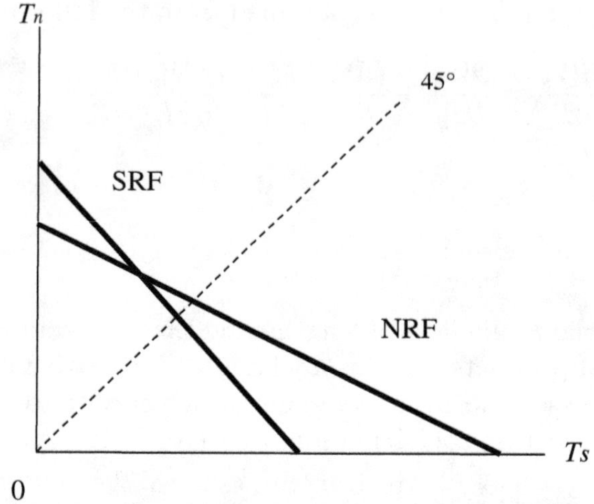

Figure 3.1. Pre-TRIPS Nash Equilibrium IPR standards. NRF indicates the North's reaction function, while SRF indicates the South's reaction function.

Invoking symmetry, we obtain the reaction function of the North

$$M_n[1-(1+\alpha)\alpha^{\alpha\epsilon}] + M_s(1-\alpha^{\alpha\epsilon}) = \frac{N_n A}{\mu}[T - T_n(1-\alpha^{\alpha\epsilon})](b_n M_n + b_s M_s). \tag{4}$$

Eqs. (3) and (4) jointly determine the Nash equilibrium, denoted by T_s^* and T_n^*. Refer to Fig. 3.1.

Note that both the South's reaction function and the North's reaction function are downward sloping in the (T_s, T_n) space. For example, the right hand side of Eq. (3) (hereinafter RHS(3)) decreases with both T_s and T_n, while the left hand side of Eq. (3) (hereinafter LHS(3)) increases with both T_s and T_n. Therefore, $(\mathrm{d}/\mathrm{d}T_n)[\mathrm{LHS}(3) - \mathrm{RHS}(3)] > 0$ and $(\mathrm{d}/\mathrm{d}T_n)[\mathrm{LHS}(3) - \mathrm{RHS}(3)] > 0$. By the Implicit Function Theorem, T_s decreases as T_n increases, as we move along the South's reaction curve in the (T_s, T_n) space. The same is true for the North's reaction function. Thus, stronger protection in the North makes it optimal for the South to protect less. The main reason for the substitution effect of the North's protection for the South's protection (as far as the South is concerned) is that as T_n increases, product variety is enlarged due to the greater incentive for firms to innovate, and so the $MC_S(T_S)$ curve, which plots MC_S on a diagram with T_s on the horizontal axis, shifts up. This calls for a reduction of IPR protection in the South. On the other hand, the $MB_S(T_S)$ curve, which plots MB_S on the same diagram, shifts down when consumers obtain increased product variety, due to the decreasing effect of variety on the marginal benefit. This also calls for a reduction of IPR protection in the South.

It can also be shown that the South's reaction curve is steeper than the North's reaction curve in the (T_s, T_n) space. Hence, the Nash equilibrium is stable (see Appendix A).

To compare the values of T_s^* and T_n^*, we first observe that because $M_n < M_s$, LHS(3) < LHS(4) for all T_s and T_n. Suppose we set $T_s = T_n = \xi$ in both (3) and (4). Then, RHS(3) < RHS(4) since $N_s < N_n$. Moreover, the RHS of both equations decreases with ξ, and the LHS of both equations increases with ξ. Hence, the value of ξ obtained from (3) is less than that obtained from (4). This, together with the fact that the South's reaction function is steeper than the North's reaction function, implies that the two curves must intersect at a point above the 45° line, which means that $T_s^* < T_n^*$ (see Fig. 3.1).

The above analysis also indicates two reasons for $T_s^* < T_n^*$. First, the North has more innovations than the South ($M_s < M_n$), because the North has sufficiently higher innovative capability. Second, the North's market size is larger than the South's ($N_s < N_n$).

Next, we check the constraints on the parameters to ensure an interior solution of *Tf*. Note that a necessary and sufficient condition for $T_s^* > 0$ is that the value of T_n (given that $T_s = 0$) on the South's reaction function is greater than the value of T_n (given that $T_s = 0$) on the North's reaction function. A necessary condition for this inequality to hold is $N_n A[T - T_n(1 - \alpha^{\alpha\epsilon})] < N_S AT$, which, together with the condition $T \geq T_n$, implies $N_s/N_n > \alpha^{\alpha\epsilon}$. Therefore, the market in the South has to be sufficiently large compared with the market in the North in order for the South to have any incentive to protect IPR.

Finally, we examine the implications of market size for equilibrium IPR standards. We find that *the equilibrium IPR protection in the South (North) is stronger when the market in the South (North) becomes larger, or the market in the North (South) becomes smaller.*

Mathematically,

$$\frac{\partial T_s^*}{\partial N_s} > 0, \quad \frac{\partial T_s^*}{\partial N_n} < 0, \quad \frac{\partial T_n^*}{\partial N_n} > 0 \quad \text{and} \quad \frac{\partial T_n^*}{\partial N_s} < 0. \tag{5}$$

The proof is given in an appendix available from the authors upon request.

It is interesting to understand why the two market sizes have opposite impacts on the optimal IPR protection. The effects of N_n on the South's reaction function is that a larger market in the North results in greater product variety, which increases the marginal cost, MC_S, of the IPR protection in the South and lowers the marginal benefit, MB_S, of the IPR protection in the South, for any given T_n. Therefore, an increase in N_n shifts the South's reaction function inward. The effects of N_s on the South's reaction function are more complicated. On the one hand, a larger market in the South also leads to greater product variety, which should lessen the IPR protection in the South. On the other hand, there are more consumers in the South who benefit from increasing the IPR protection in the South, and, as a result, the marginal benefits, MB_S, of the IPR protection in the South increase. We find that this latter effect dominates the former one and thus an increase in N_s shifts the South's reaction function outward. By the same argument, an increase in N_n shifts the North's reaction function out, while an increase in N_s shifts the North's reaction function in. Consequently, we obtain the results given in (5).

We now conclude this section. Just like Chin and Grossman (1990), we also find that it is optimal for the South to protect IPR when its market is sufficiently large. Moreover, we find that as the market in the South grows, it is individually optimal for the South to strengthen its IPR protection. However, the South's incentive to protect IPR can never be as strong as the North's incentive so long as the North has a larger market for differentiated products and has more innovations than the South does.

3. The Post-TRIPS Regime and Global Welfare

In the post-TRIPS regime, both regions are required to adopt the North's pre-TRIPS IPR protection, T_n^*, as the minimum standard. We shall evaluate the welfare consequence of such a measure. But let us first identify the equilibrium in the post-TRIPS regime, i.e. the equilibrium subject to the constraints $T_s > T_n^*$ and $T_n \geq T_n^*$. In other words, given that T_n^* is the minimum standard, what standards would the two regions adopt?

When governments adopt new IPR standards, the numbers of products invented in the regions in each period are different from those in the pre-TRIPS regime. Again, we can calculate the equilibrium policies based on the new steady-state welfare levels.[14] Thus, we can adopt a similar analysis as developed in Section 2.2. It can be easily shown that the unique post-TRIPS equilibrium is $T_s = T_n^*$ and $T_n = T_n^*$. That is, both regions simply adopt the North's pre-TRIPS IPR protection. The intuition is as follows. From the last section, we see that the North wants to lower T_n as the South increases T_s; conversely, the South wants to lower T_s as the North increases T_n. Therefore, as T_s is forced to increase from T_s^* to T_n^*, the North would want to reduce T_n below T_n^*. Given the constraint $T_n \geq T_n^*$, however, the optimal response for the North is $T_n = T_n^*$. Given that $T_n = T_n^*$, the South's unconstrained best response is $T_s = T_s^*$. However, under the constraint $T_s \geq T_n^*$, the best response of the South is $T_s = T_n^*$.

To evaluate world welfare, let us first define world (or global) welfare simply as the sum of the North's and the South's welfare, i.e., $W = W_s + W_n$. To evaluate whether the minimum IPR standard stipulated by TRIPS is welfare-improving for the world, we first find an expression for the effect of T_s on global welfare. Then, we discuss the properties of the globally optimal IPR standard of the South given that $T_n = T_n^*$. Finally, we evaluate the global welfare effect of increasing T_s from T_s^* to T_n^* given that $T_n = T_n^*$.

Based on the analysis in the last section, the North's steady state flow welfare at $T_n = T_n^*$ given by

$$\begin{aligned} W_k(T_s, T_n^*, M_s, M_n) &= N_n(M_n + M_s)(1-\alpha)\alpha^{\alpha\epsilon}[T - T_n^*(1-\alpha^{\alpha\epsilon})] \\ &\quad + N_n I_n + M_n(N_s T_s + N_n T_n^*)A - \frac{b_n}{1+b_n} M_n^{\frac{1+b_n}{b_n}} + U_{zn}. \end{aligned}$$

[14]The new steady state starts T periods after TRIPS is invoked.

Recalling that $M_n = (\mu/a_n)^{b_n}$ where $\mu = (N_S T_S + N_n T_n)A$, we can easily see

$$\frac{dW_n}{dT_s} = \frac{\partial W_n}{\partial T_s} + \frac{\partial W_n}{\partial M_n}\frac{\partial M_n}{\partial T_s} + \frac{\partial W_n}{\partial M_s}\frac{\partial M_s}{\partial T_s} > 0. \tag{6}$$

A similar inequality can be shown for the South. Therefore, *a region always benefits from stronger IPR protection in the other region, i.e.,* $dW_n/dT_s > 0$ *and* $dW_s/dT_n > 0$.[15] The benefit comes from enlarging product variety in both regions ($\partial M_k/\partial T_s > 0$ and $\partial M_k/\partial T_n > 0$, for $k = \{s, n,\}$) and increasing innovators' profits ($\partial \prod_k(i)/\partial T_s > 0$ and $\partial \prod_k(i)/\partial T_n > 0$, for $k = \{v, n,\}$). Specifically, with a stronger IPR protection in the foreign region, but with its own IPR protection unchanged, a region's consumers enjoy larger product variety with no price hikes (call it *variety spillover*), and its firms also receive more profits (call it *profit spillover*). There is, therefore, a positive inter-regional externality from strengthening IPR protection. Since a region's individually optimal IPR protection does not take into account this positive inter-regional externality, IPR is under-protected from the world's point of view if regions all adopt their individually optimal IPR standards as in the pre-TRIPS regime.

We now turn to consider the impact of increasing the South's IPR protection on global welfare given that $T_n = T_n^*$. Since $W(T_S) = W_n(T_s) + W_S(T_S)$, by (2) and (6), we have,

$$\left.\frac{dW}{dT_s}\right|_{T_s=T_s^*} = \left.\frac{dW_s}{dT_s}\right|_{T_s=T_s^*} + \left.\frac{dW_n}{dT_s}\right|_{T_s=T_s^*} > 0. \tag{7}$$

That is, provided that there is no comer solution for T_s^*, slightly increasing the South's IPR protection from its individually optimal level T^* increases global welfare. This is due to the positive externality of IPR protection indicated above. This result supports the argument for increasing the South's IPR protection. The question is how much the South's IPR protection should be increased in order to achieve global welfare optimum.

[15]If, however, consumers from the two regions have different tastes for the products, it is possible that the North (South) cannot always benefit from stronger IPR protection in the South (North), as shown by Diwan and Rodrik (1991).

Differentiating $W(T_S)$ with respect to T_s gives

$$\frac{1}{(1-\alpha)\alpha^{\alpha\epsilon}N_s}\left(\frac{dW}{dT_s}\right) = -(M_s + M_n)[1-(1+\alpha)\alpha^{\alpha\epsilon}]$$
$$+\frac{A}{\mu}(b_n M_n + b_s M_s)\}N_s[T - T_s(1-\alpha^{\alpha\epsilon})]$$
$$+N_n[T - T_n^*(1-\alpha^{\alpha\epsilon})]\}. \quad (8)$$

We can easily check that $W(T_S)$ is concave in T_s, i.e., $d^2W/dT_n^* < 0$ for all T_s. (Simply note that dW/dT_s decreases with T_s).

We next check if $dW/dT_s > 0$ at $T_s = T_n^*$. Substituting T_n^* for T_s in (8), then comparing the result with Eq. (4), we can show that it is indeed true that $dW/d\mathrm{T}_s \geq 0$ at $T_s = T_n^*$. A formal proof is given in Appendix B. Defining the South's level of IPR protection that maximizes global welfare as $T_s^w \equiv \text{argmax } W(T_n = T_n^*)$, we conclude that $T_s^w > T_n^*$. Therefore, *given that the North continues to adopt its pre-TRIPS Nash equilibrium IPR standard, global welfare is maximized when the South adopts an IPR standard which is stronger than that of the North.* Refer to Figs. 3.2a and 3.2b.

Finally, we find that *the South's IPR protection that maximizes global welfare is an increasing function of the size of the South's market. Mathematically, we have* $dT_s^w/dN_s > 0$. The proof is given in an appendix available from the authors upon request. Intuitively, as N_s increases, there is a higher demand for North-innovated goods in the South (profit spillover is stronger) as well as a greater additional variety of differentiated products developed by the South from strengthening IPR (variety spillover is also stronger), and therefore the magnitude of the positive inter-regional externality of the South's IPR protection is greater. This calls for an increase in the South's IPR protection to internalize the externality.

The above result is somewhat consistent with the conclusion of Deardorff (1992), who finds that when the fraction of the world that is weak in IPR protection is larger, it is globally optimal to extend the strong IPR protection to more of these countries. What was not addressed by Deardorff (1992), but has been addressed by us, is that the globally optimal level of IPR protection by the South would be higher than the pre-TRIPS standard of the North even when the South has lower innovative capability than that of the North.

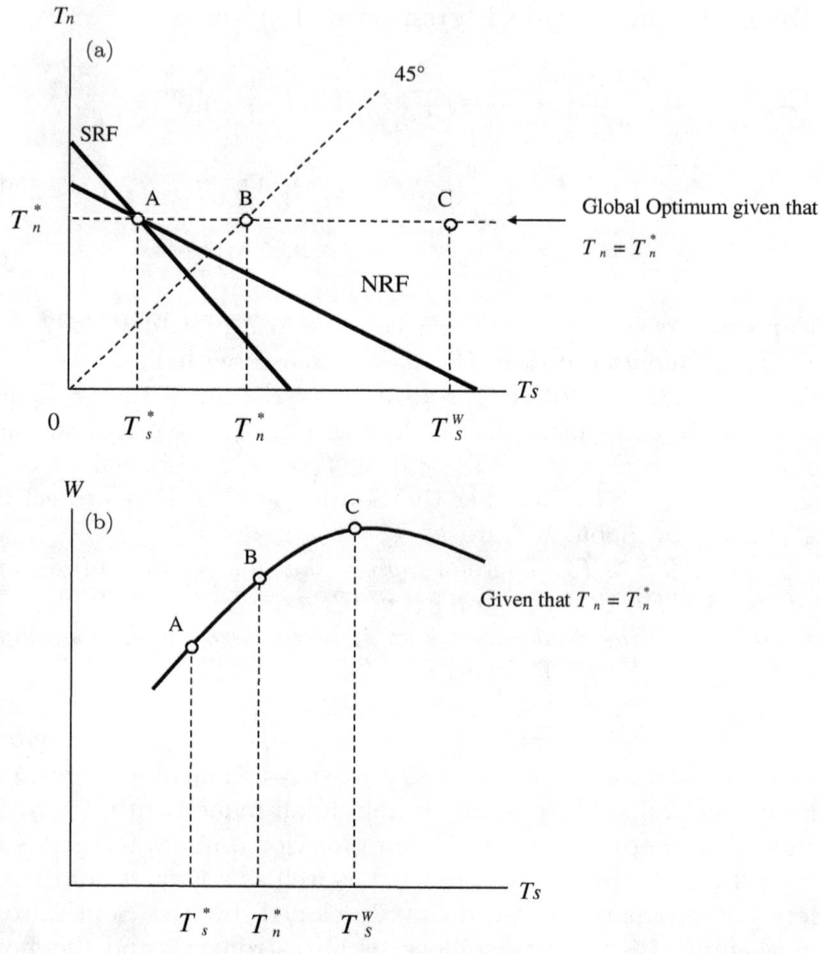

Figure 3.2. (a) The TRIPS versus global optimum. TRIPS moves the world from A to B, but the optimum is at C, given that $T_n = T_n^*$ Here, T_s^* indicates the South's pre-TRIPS patent length; T_s^w indicates the South's patent length that would maximize global welfare given that the North keeps its pre-TRIPS patent length. (b) World welfare as South's patent length changes. Points A, B and C correspond to those in Fig. 3.2a.

To conclude this section, we note that, given that the North is committed to the minimum standard, T_n^*, it would not be practical for the North to require the South to adopt any higher standard than that. This means that we can treat T_n^* as the upper bound of the minimum standard that the North can ask the South to adopt. Given this constraint, the TRIPS Agreement can be regarded as maximizing global welfare by requiring the South to adopt the North's pre-TRIPS standard, T_n^*, rather than anything lower, as the minimum IPR standard. It is in this sense that the TRIPS agreement is optimal.

4. Multi-sectoral Negotiations

In this section, we analyze the merits of the TRIPS Agreement in the context of a multi-sectoral negotiation. We consider the case in which the North wants the South to increase its IPR protection while, in return, the South wants the North to lower its trade barriers to imports of traditional goods from the South. We have seen from previous analysis that while raising the IPR standard in the South from its Nash equilibrium level T_s^* to the North's Nash equilibrium level T_n^* is globally welfare-improving, the South itself loses from such an increase. To make the TRIPS Agreement incentive-compatible for the South, the North, which is the beneficiary region, has to compensate the South. While a lump sum income transfer from the North to the South would solve the incentive-compatibility problem theoretically, it is not practical. In the Uruguay Round, the South demanded increased access to the North's markets in which it has comparative advantage, such as textile products. This sector is represented by z in this model. In the model, increasing market access amounts to lowering tariff τ on the import of z. We will show that allowing better access to the North's market in exchange for the South's strengthening of IPR standard is not only a realistic channel to solve the incentive-compatibility problem of the TRIPS, but also superior to the (impractical) lump sum income transfer mechanism.

The steady state flow welfare associated with sector z in the North and the South are, respectively.

$$U_{zn}(\tau) = \eta_n \left[p_n(z)\overline{z}_n + \frac{1}{2e}(a - p_n(z))^2 + \tau z_{sn} \right],$$

$$U_{zs}(\tau) = \eta_s \left[p_s(z)\overline{z}_s + \frac{1}{2e}(a - p_s(z))^2 \right].$$

Again, with no discounting of the future, the steady state flow welfare can be the basis of welfare analysis.

Without cooperation/negotiation with the South, the North chooses a non-cooperative optimal tariff to maximize $U_{zn}(\tau)$. Given the market equilibrium outcome obtained in Section 2, we know that this optimal tariff is

$$\tau^* = \frac{e(1+\delta-\delta^2)(\overline{z}_s - \overline{z}_n)}{2(1+\delta)-\delta^2}.$$

The corresponding welfare for the North and the South when t^* is imposed are denoted $U^*_{zn}(\tau)$ and $U^*_{zs}(\tau)$, respectively. It is easily seen that lowering τ will reduce the North's welfare in sector *2* but will increase the South's welfare in this sector:

$$\frac{\partial U_{zn}(\tau)}{\partial \tau} = \frac{\eta_n}{e(1+\delta)}[e(1+\delta-\delta_s^2)z_{sn} - \tau] > 0 \quad \text{for}\, \tau < \tau^*.$$

$$\frac{\partial U_{zs}(\tau)}{\partial \tau} = -\frac{\eta_s}{(1+\delta)}(\overline{z}_s - z_{ss}) < 0 \quad \text{for all}\, \tau.$$

Recalling that U_k is region *k's* welfare derived from all sectors excluding sector z, we denote U^*_k as the equilibrium U_k under the pre-TRIPS regime (i.e., when both regions choose their Nash equilibrium IPR levels, T^*_n and T^*_s, respectively), and define U^c_k as the equilibrium U_k under the post-TRIPS regime (i.e., when both regions choose the minimum standard equal to T^*_n).

To model the multi-sectoral negotiation, we assume that the two regions bargain simultaneously over whether the South adopts the North's pre-TRIPS IPR standard as well as over the level of r. The Nash bargaining model is adopted. Any agreement and bargaining outcome is assumed to last forever. Therefore, with no discounting, welfare consideration in the bargaining can be based on steady state flow welfare. Without having τ lowered, the South will not raise its IPR standard. So, the threat point of the bargain is such that the South maintains its pre-TRIPS IPR standard, while the North maintains tariff τ^*. To solve the bargaining problem, the tariff τ is chosen to maximize the product of two expressions that are functions of the net welfare improvements in the two regions, viz.

$$(U^c_n + U_{zn} - U^*_n - U^*_{zn})^{(1-v)}(U^c_s + U_{zs} - U^*_s - U^*_{zs})^v,$$

where $v \in [0,1]$ represents the South's bargaining power. For ease of exposition, let $N(\tau) \equiv U_n^c + U_{zn} - U_n^* - U_{zn}^*$ and $T(\tau) \equiv U_s^c + U_{zs} - U_s^* - U_{zs}^*$. It is clear that to satisfy the incentive-compatibility condition in the South, τ needs to be low enough for the South to gain sufficiently from the traditional sector to compensate for its loss in the differentiated-products sector. Since there is a natural lower bound, $\tau = 0$, for this policy, we need to assume that a, e and $\overline{z}_s - \overline{z}_n$ are sufficiently large. This will ensure that the traditional-good markets are sufficiently large, the optimal tariff τ^* is sufficiently large, and consequently, there are sufficient gains to the South from tariff-cutting by the North. This will in turn ensure that both $N(\tau)$ and $T(\tau)$ are positive.

To make sure that there indeed exists an interior solution to the bargaining game, we have to check that the welfare frontier is concave. The slope of the bargaining frontier is equal to $\frac{dN(\tau)}{dT(\tau)} = (\frac{\partial U_{zn}}{\partial \tau})/(\frac{\partial U_{zs}}{\partial \tau})$. First, the slope is equal to zero when $\tau = \tau^*$. Second, it can be easily shown that the slope is negative and increases in magnitude as r decreases, i.e. as $T(\tau)$ increases. This ensures that the frontier is strictly concave. So, if the first-order condition of the Nash bargaining yields $\tau^c \in [0, \tau^*]$, it is an optimal interior solution. Refer to Fig. 3.3.

When $\tau = 0$, the slope of the welfare frontier is equal to $(1 + \delta - \delta^2)/\delta$, which is less than one as long as $\delta > 1$. To simplify things by ensuring that tariff reduction by the North is always globally welfare-improving, we assume that $\delta > 1$, i.e. the South's market for traditional good is larger than the North's. Therefore, any decrease in τ leads to an increase in $T(\tau)$ with a magnitude greater than that of the concomitant decrease in so that global welfare is improved.[16]

The bargaining problem is equivalent to choosing τ to maximize $(1 - v)\ln(N(\tau) + vT(\tau))$, which yields the following first-order

[16]In our model, it is possible that $N_n > N_s$ while $\eta_s > \eta_n$, as long as e_s is sufficiently smaller than e_n. This simply reflects the fact that the South's consumers have, relatively speaking, a lower propensity to consume new products and a higher propensity to consume traditional products than their counterparts in the North. Casual observation confirms the presumption that the North's market for new products is larger than the South's market, while the reverse is true for the market for traditional goods.

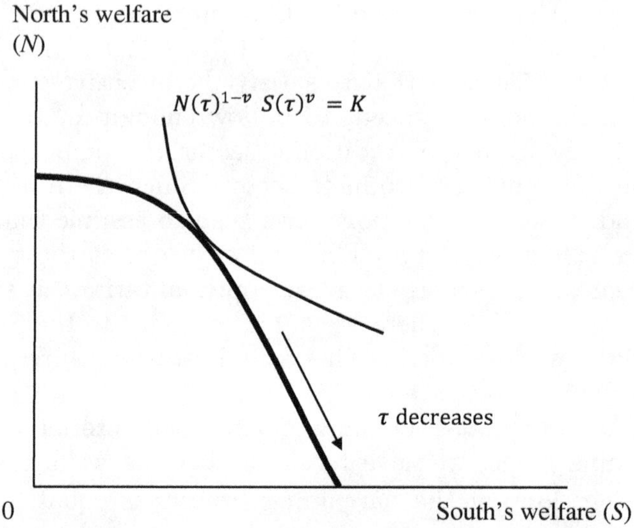

Figure 3.3. Nash bargaining over t. The two regions bargain simultaneously over whether the South adopts the North's pre-TRIPS IPR and over the value of τ. The origin is the point with no agreement.

condition.

$$\frac{(1-v)}{N(\tau)}\frac{\partial U_{zn}}{\partial \tau}+\frac{v}{T(\tau)}\frac{\partial U_{zs}}{\partial \tau}=0. \tag{9}$$

We are interested in how the bargaining outcome τ^c is affected by other factors and how global welfare is in turn affected by the bargaining outcome. First, it is straightforward to show that $\partial\tau^c/\partial v<0$, that is, trade liberalization in the traditional-good sector in the North would be deeper when the South has more bargaining power. This is the usual outcome of Nash bargaining since a lower t^c favors the South. Second, it can be easily shown that $\partial W/\partial\tau<0$. That is, global welfare increases when the South has more bargaining power. This is because higher bargaining power for the South leads to deeper trade liberalization in the North, which improves global welfare.

We have seen that both an increase in T_s and a decrease in τ yield net gains to the world, which can then be split between the two regions through Nash bargaining. So, we can say that *since bargaining leads to* $N(\tau^c)>0$ *and* $T(\tau^c)>0$, *both regions benefit* *from the multi-sectoral negotiation, of which the TRIPS Agreement is an outcome.* Although we interpret the TRIPS Agreement as one that requires all regions to adopt a minimum IPR protection standard as defined by the North's pre-TRIPS protection level, the above result can be generalized as follows: Both regions benefit from a bargain that involves the South raising its IPR protection standard to a pre-specified level $T_s \in [T_s^*, T_n^*]$ (while the North does not lower its pre-TRIPS IPR protection standard) on the one hand, and the North liberalizing trade in its traditional good sector on the other hand. The proof of this general result can be obtained by simply repeating the above analysis. This result means that even if the regions find it impossible (e.g., for political reasons) to enforce a drastic set of concessions (with T_s set to T_n^*), they can agree on a less drastic set of concessions (with $T_s \in [T_s^*, T_n^*]$ and still end up with mutual gains in a multi-sectoral negotiation.

Finally, we examine each region's marginal gain from *increases* in T_s, for all $T_s \in [T_s^*, T_n^*]$, We have found in Section 3 that as long as $T_s \in [T_s^*, T_n^*]$, any increase in T_s would lead to an increase in U_n^c but a decrease in U_s^c (now we need to reinterpret U_k^c as the value of U_k when the South and the North adopt T_s and T_n^*, respectively), and the gain in the former outweighs the loss in the latter so that $U_n^c + U_s^c$ increases. We have also proved above that as long as $\tau \in [0, \tau^*]$, any decrease in τ would lead to an increase in U_{zs} but to a decrease in U_{zn}, and the gain in the former outweighs the loss in the latter so that $U_{zs} + U_{zn}$ increases. We have assumed that the traditional goods markets are sufficiently large and the differences between the regions in endowments of traditional good are sufficiently great that tariff-cutting in the North is sufficient to compensate the South for its increase in IPR protection. Consequently, we prove in Appendix C that *whenever the South is willing to increase T_s, the North is willing to reduce τ. On balance, as T_s increases, the marginal gain to the North is always positive (i.e. $N(\tau)$ would increase), but the marginal gain to the South is positive (i.e., $T(\tau)$ increases) only if v is sufficiently large or $T(\tau)$ is sufficiently small.* This indicates that although raising the South's IPR protection T_s all the way to T_n^* is globally optimal and is in the best interest of the North, such a big move may not be in the South's best interest unless the South's bargaining power in the negotiation is sufficiently strong to elicit a large tariff reduction from the North. Otherwise, the South would prefer an agreement that requires $T_s = T_s^c < T_n^*$, since all the extra surplus from raising the IPR protection beyond Yf would accrue to the North. In other words, while both regions gain from the multi-sectoral negotiation, the South may be able to gain more if it has more freedom to choose the degree of IPR protection.

5. Summary and Conclusion

We find that it is globally welfare-improving for the South to increase its IPR protection above its (pre-TRIPS) Nash equilibrium level. Although this would hurt the South and benefit the North, the latter's gains are larger than the former's losses. Consequently, it can benefit both regions for the South to adopt the North's pre-TRIPS IPR standard, in exchange for the North lowering its import tariffs. We conclude, therefore, that the inclusion of IPR negotiations in GATT/WTO agendas is constructive.

We find that in the multi-sectoral negotiation it is globally optimal for the South to increase its IPR protection standard all the way to the North's level. However, it is not necessarily optimal for the South to do so. It is optimal for the South only if its bargaining power in the negotiation is sufficiently large to elicit a large enough tariff reduction by the North. Otherwise, the extra surplus generated from strengthened IPR protection will mostly benefit the North. In that case, if the South has the choice, it would prefer an agreement that binds it to a higher standard than before, but below that of the North. In other words, giving the South an 'all-or-nothing' choice in either adopting the North's IPR standard or maintaining the old standard might diminish the South's gain from such a negotiation. It seems evident that the South was indeed presented with an 'all-or-nothing' choice regarding IPR protection in the Uruguay Round of the GATT negotiations. If this is the case, we can say that the TRIPS Agreement requires the South to give up too much. It is therefore no wonder that many developing countries are not enforcing as high an IPR standard as the developed countries want while the developed countries seem to be retracting from their market access commitments. In spite of these seeming retractions, however, our result has demonstrated that both regions would still gain as long as they can eventually *willingly* enforce *some* bilateral concessions in both sectors. This again demonstrates the merits of multi-sectoral negotiations.

In future research, we hope to modify the existing model to a truly dynamic, and possibly general equilibrium one, and to consider interactions among trade policies, EDI policies and IPR policies in a unified model.

Acknowledgements

We thank an anonymous referee and the Editor for their very helpful suggestions. We are also grateful for the helpful comments from participants in our presentations at City University of Hong Kong, Perm State University, Oregon State University, Rutgers University, Far Eastern Meeting of Econometric Society in Kobe, and the Midwest International Economics Conferences held at Purdue U and U of Wisconsin-Madison. The work in this paper has been supported by the Research Grants Council of Hong Kong, China (Project no. CityU 1145/99H).

Appendix A. Proof of the Stability of the Nash Equilibrium

To see this, totally differentiate (3) and (4) with respect to T_s and T_n. Note that by writing M_s and M_n as functions of μ, (3) can be expressed as a function of μ and T_s only, and thus,

$$d[\text{LHS}(3) - \text{RHS}(3)] = \frac{\partial}{\partial \mu}[\text{LHS}(3) - \text{RHS}(3)](N_s dT_s + N_n dT_n) - \frac{\partial}{\partial T_s}\text{RHS}(3) dT_s = 0.$$

Since $\frac{\partial}{\partial \mu}[\text{LHS}(3) - \text{RHS}(3)] > 0$, and $\frac{\partial}{\partial T_s}\text{RHS}(3) < 0$, the following inequality holds for the South's react ion function:

$$\left|\frac{dT_n}{dT_s}\right| > \frac{N_s}{N_n}.$$

Similarly, for the North, we have

$$d[\text{LHS}(4) - \text{RHS}(4)] = \frac{\partial}{\partial \mu}[\text{LHS}(4) - \text{RHS}(4)](N_s dT_s + N_n dT_n) - \frac{\partial}{\partial T_n}\text{RHS}(4) dT_n = 0,$$

from which we conclude that the following inequality holds for the North's reaction function:

$$\left|\frac{dT_n}{dT_s}\right| < \frac{N_s}{N_n}.$$

Therefore, the South's reaction curve is steeper than the North's in the (T_s, T_n) space.

Appendix B. Proof of $dW/dT_s|_{T_s=T_n^*} > 0$

Suppose $\hat{T}_n$ solves

$$M_n[1 - (1+\alpha)\alpha^{\alpha\epsilon}] + M_s(1 - \alpha^{\alpha\epsilon}) = \frac{N_n A}{\mu}[T - T_n(1 - \alpha^{\alpha\epsilon})](b_n M_n + b_s M_s), \tag{A.1}$$

where $M_n = (\mu/a_n)^{b_n}$ and $M_s = (\mu/a_s)^{b_s}$, where $\mu = N_n T_n A$.

Comparing with Eq. (4), it is clear that $\hat{T}_\mathbf{n} > T_n^*$, since the North's reaction function is downward sloping, so that T_n increases as T_s decreases to 0. Now suppose $\hat{T'}_\mathbf{n}$ solves

$$M_n[1 - (1+\alpha)\alpha^{\alpha\epsilon}] + M_s(1 - (1+\alpha)\alpha^{\alpha\epsilon}) = \frac{N_n A}{\mu}[T - T_n(1 - \alpha^{\alpha\epsilon})](b_n M_n + b_s M_s), \tag{A.2}$$

where $M_n = (\mu/a_n)^{b_n}$, and $M_s = (\mu/a_s)^{b_s}$, where $\mu = N_n T_n A$.

We know that $\hat{T}_n > T_n$. This is because LHS $(A2) <$ LHS$(A1)$, while RHS$(A2)$ = RHS$(A1)$. Now, suppose $\tilde{T}_n$ solves

$$M_n[1 - (1+\alpha)\alpha^{\alpha\epsilon}] + M_s(1 - (1+\alpha)\alpha^{\alpha\epsilon}) = \frac{(N_s + N_n)A}{\mu}[T - T_n(1 - \alpha^{\alpha\epsilon})](b_n M_n + b_s M_s), \tag{A.3}$$

where $M_n = (\mu/a_n)^{b_n}$, and $M_s = (\mu/a_s)^{b_s}$, where $\mu = (N_s + N_n) T_n A$.

We can prove that $\tilde{T}_n > \hat{T}'_{\mathbf{n}}$. The proof is given below. Define $P \equiv A[T - T_s(1 - \alpha^{\alpha\epsilon})]b_s$; $Q \equiv [1 - (1+\alpha)\alpha^{\alpha\epsilon}]$; $R \equiv A[T - T_s(1 - \alpha^{\alpha\epsilon})]b_n$ and S $\equiv (1 - \alpha^{\alpha\epsilon})$. Eq. (A.2) can be written as

$$M_s\left(\frac{P}{AT_n} - Q\right) + M_n\left(\frac{R}{AT_n} - Q\right) = 0, \tag{A.4}$$

where $M_n = (\mu/a_n)^{b_n}$, and $M_s = (\mu/a_s)^{b_s}$, where $\mu = N_n T_n A$.

Now, we have

$$\begin{aligned}\frac{\partial LHS(A4)}{\partial N_s} &= \frac{\partial M_s}{\partial N_n}\left(\frac{P}{AT_n} - Q\right) + \frac{\partial M_n}{\partial N_n}\left(\frac{R}{AT_n} - Q\right)\\ &= \frac{M_s}{\mu}b_sT_nA\left(\frac{P}{AT_n} - Q\right) + \frac{M_n}{\mu}b_nT_nA\left(\frac{R}{AT_n} - Q\right)\\ &= \frac{M_s}{\mu}b_sT_nA\left(\frac{P}{AT_n} - Q\right) - \frac{M_s}{\mu}b_nT_nA\left(\frac{P}{AT_n} - Q\right)\\ &= \frac{M_s}{\mu}T_nA\left(b_s - b_n\right)\left(\frac{P}{AT_n} - Q\right).\end{aligned}$$

The third line of the above equation comes from using Eq. (A.4). We are now ready to prove that the last line is greater than zero. If $b_n > b_s$, then Eq. (A.4) indicates that $R/AT_n - Q > 0 > P/AT_n - Q$ since the two expressions must be of opposite signs; on the other hand, if $K < K$ then Eq. (A.4) indicates that $R/AT_n - Q < 0 < P/AT_n - Q$. Both cases imply that the last line is greater than zero. Therefore, $\partial LHS(A.4)/\partial N_n > 0$.

Now, it is quite clear that $\partial \text{LHS}(A4)/\partial T_n < 0$. Therefore, by the Implicit Function Theorem, we conclude that $dT_n/dN_n > 0$ for Eq. (A.4) to hold. Now, (A.3) is obtained from (A.2) by changing N_n to $N_s + N_n$. Therefore, we can conclude that $\tilde{T}_n > \hat{T}'_n > \hat{T}_n > T_n^*$. Since $\frac{\partial}{\partial T_n}[\text{LHS}(A3) - \text{RHS}(A3)] < 0$, and $\text{RHS}(A3) - \text{LHS}(A3) = 0$ at $T_n = \tilde{T}$, it follows that $\text{RHS}(A3) - \text{LHS}(A3) > 0$ at $T_n = T_n^*$. Since RHS(8) (at $T_s = T_n^*$) $= \text{RHS}(A3) - \text{LHS}(A3)$ (at $T_n = T_n^*$), we conclude that $dW/dT_s|_{T_s = T_n^*} > 0$.

Appendix C. $dN(\tau)/dT_n$ and $dT(\tau)/dT_S$

Note that

$$dT(\tau) = dU_s^c + dU_{zs} \quad \text{and} \quad dN(\tau) = dU_s^c + dU_{zn}.$$

From the analysis in Section 3, we have

$$\frac{dU_s^c}{dT_s} < 0, \frac{dU_n^c}{dT_s} > 0, \left|\frac{dU_s^c}{dT_s}\right| < \left|\frac{dU_n^c}{dT_s}\right|.$$

From the analysis in Section 4, we have

$$\frac{dU_{zs}}{d\tau} < 0, \quad \frac{dU_{zn}}{d\tau} > 0, \quad \left|\frac{dU_{zs}}{d\tau}\right| > \left|\frac{dU_{zn}}{d\tau}\right|.$$

From Eq. (9), we have

$$T(\tau)(1-v)\frac{dU_{zn}}{dU_{zs}} + N(\tau)v = 0.$$

Since we want to find the effect of changes in U_n^c (due to changes in T_s) on $T(\tau)$ and N, we totally differentiate the above equation with respect to r and any other variables that are affected by T_s and τ.

$$(1-v)\frac{dU_{zn}}{dU_{zs}}dT(\tau) + T(\tau)(1-v)\frac{d}{d\tau}\left(\frac{dU_{zn}}{dU_{zs}}\right)d\tau + vdN = 0,$$

which implies

$$(1-v)\frac{dU_{zn}}{dU_{zs}}(dU_s^c + dU_{zs}) + T(\tau)(1-v)\frac{d}{d\tau}\left(\frac{dU_{zn}}{dU_{zs}}\right)d\tau + v(dU_s^c + dU_{zn}) = 0.$$

Note that changes in U_n^c and U_s^c are due to T_s while changes in U_{zn} and U_{zs} are due to τAn increase in T_s leads to an increase in U_n^c and a decrease in U_s^c, thus prompting the North to decrease r in the tariff negotiation, which in turn leads to an increase in U_{zs} and a decrease in U_{zn}, as will be shown below. Differentiating the equation with respect to T_s, we have

$$(1-v)\frac{dU_{zn}}{dU_{zs}}\left(\frac{dU_s^c}{dT_s}+\frac{dU_{zn}}{d\tau}\frac{d\tau}{dT_s}\right)+T(\tau)(1-v)\frac{d}{d\tau}\left(\frac{dU_{zn}}{dU_{zs}}\right)\frac{d\tau}{dT_s}$$
$$+v\left(\frac{dU_n^c}{dT_s}+\frac{dU_{zn}}{d\tau}\frac{d\tau}{dT_s}\right)=0.$$

Let $Y = |dU_{zn}/dU_{zs}| > 1$. Recall that $dU_{zn}/dU_{zs} < 0$. From the above equation, we can solve for

$$\frac{d\tau}{dT_s}=\frac{(1-v)\dfrac{dU_s^c}{dT_s}Y-v\dfrac{dU_n^c}{dT_s}}{(1-v)\left[-Y\dfrac{dU_{zs}}{d\tau}-T(\tau)\dfrac{dY}{d\tau}\right]+v\dfrac{dU_{zn}}{d\tau}}<0.$$

Therefore,

$$\frac{dT(\tau)}{dT_s}=\frac{dU_s^c}{dT_s}+\frac{dU_{zs}}{d\tau}\cdot\frac{d\tau}{dT_s}$$
$$=\frac{-(1-v)T(\tau)\dfrac{dU_s^c}{dT_s}\dfrac{dY}{d\tau}+\dfrac{dU_s^c}{dT_s}\dfrac{dU_{zn}}{d\tau}-v\dfrac{dU_n^c}{dT_s}\dfrac{dU_{zs}}{d\tau}}{(1-v)\left[-Y\dfrac{dU_{zs}}{d\tau}-S\dfrac{dY}{d\tau}\right]+v\dfrac{dU_{zn}}{d\tau}}.$$

On the RHS of the above equation, the denominator is always positive. However, the numerator is greater than zero only if v is sufficiently large or when $T(\tau)$ is sufficiently small, based on the inequalities obtained at the beginning of the proof and $\frac{dY}{d\tau} < 0$. Hence, the expression is positive if v is sufficiently large or $T(\tau)$ is small. When $T_s = T_s^*, \tau = \tau^*$, and $T(\tau) = 0$. Therefore, $\frac{dS}{dT_s} > 0$ at $T_s = T_s^*$. Given that, as T_s increases, $|\frac{dU_s^c}{dT_s}|$ and $|\frac{dY}{d\tau}|$ both increase, while $|\frac{dU_n^c}{dT_s}| - |\frac{dU_s^c}{dT_s}|$ decreases, and $|\frac{dU_{zs}}{d\tau}| - |\frac{dU_{zn}}{d\tau}|$ decreases, we conclude that $\frac{dS}{dT_s}$ gets smaller as T_s increases. Therefore, $T(\tau)$ is maximized as T_s increases to a certain level. This level may not be much higher than T_s^* if v is small. Thus, if v is small, it is optimal for the South to increase its IPR protection only slightly. From the South's point of view, it is optimal to increase IPR protection all the way to T_n^* only when v is sufficiently large so that $\frac{dT(\tau)}{dT_s} > 0$ for any

$T_s \in [T_s^*, T_n^*]$. On the other hand.

$$\frac{dN(\tau)}{dT_s} = \frac{dU_n^c}{dT_s} + \frac{dU_{zn}}{d\tau} \cdot \frac{d\tau}{dT_s}$$

$$= \frac{(1-v)[-Y\frac{dU_n^c}{dT_s}\frac{dU_{zs}}{d\tau} + Y\frac{dU_n^c}{dT_s}\frac{dU_{zn}}{d\tau} - T(\tau)\frac{dY}{d\tau}\frac{dU_n^c}{dT_s}]}{(1-v)\left[-Y\frac{dU_{zs}}{d\tau} - T(\tau)\frac{dY}{d\tau}\right] + v\frac{dU_{zn}}{d\tau}} > 0,$$

because both the denominator and numerator are positive, based on the inequalities obtained at the beginning of the proof and $\frac{dY}{d\tau} < 0$.

References

Burmeister, E., 1980. *Capital Theory and Dynamics.* Cambridge University Press.

Chin, J. and Grossman, G.M., 1990. Intellectual property rights and North-South trade. In: Jones, R. and Krueger, A.O. (Eds.), *The Political Economy of International Trade.* Basil Blackwell, Oxford, pp. 90–107.

Deardorff, A.V., 1992. Welfare effects of global patent protection. *Economica* 59, 35–51.

Diwan, I. and Rodrik, D., 1991. Patents, appropriate technology, and North-South trade. *Journal of International Economics* 30, 27–47.

Glass, A.J. and K. Saggi, forthcoming. Intellectual property rights, foreign direct investment, and innovation. *Journal of International Economics.*

Gould, D.M. and Gruben, W.C., 1996. The role of intellectual property rights in economic growth. *Journal of Development Economics* 48, 323–350.

Helpman, E., 1993. Innovation, imitation, and intellectual property rights. *Econometrica* 61 (6), 1247–1280.

Hoekman, B.M. and Kostecki, M.M., 1995. *The Political Economy of the World Trading System.* Oxford University Press, Oxford.

Horowitz, A.W. and Lai, E.L.-C., 1996. Patent length and rate of innovation. *International Economic Review* 37 (4), 785–801.

Horsmann, I., Markusen, J. and Robles, J., 2001. Multi-issue bargaining and linked agendas: Ricardo revisited or no pain no gain. NBER Working Paper #8347.

Lai, E.L.-C., 1998. International intellectual property rights protection and rate of product innovation. *Journal of Development Economics* 55, 133–153.

Mansfield, E., 1986. Patents and innovation: an empirical study. *Management Science* 32 (2), 272–280.

Maskus, K.E. and Penubarti, M., 1995. How trade-related are intellectual property rights? *Journal of International Economics* 39, 227–248.

Maskus, K.E., 1998. The international regulation of intellectual property. *Weltwirtschaftliches Archiv* 134 (2), 186–208.

Maskus, K.E., 2000. *Intellectual Property Rights in the Global Economy.* Institute for International Economics, Washington, DC.

McCalman, P, 2001. Reaping what you sow: an empirical analysis of international patent harmonization. *Journal of International Economics* 55 (1), 161–186.

Nordhaus, W, 1969. *Invention, Growth, and Welfare.* MIT Press, Cambridge, Mass.

Qiu, L.D. and Lai, E.L.-C., 2001. *Trade and intellectual property rights protection: The roles of Northern and Southern tariffs.* Mimeo, Hong Kong University of Science and Technology.

Reichman, J.H., 1995. Universal minimum standards of intellectual property protection under the TRIPS component of the WTO agreement. *The International Lawyer* 29 (2), 345–388.

Richardson, R.S. and Gaisford, J.D., 1996. North-South disputes over the protection of intellectual property. *Canadian Journal of Economics* 29 (0), S376–S381, Special issue.

Taylor, M.S., 1993. TRIPS, trade, and technology transfer. *Canadian Journal of Economics* 26 (3), 625–637.

United Nations Conference on Trade and Development, 1997. *The TRIPS Agreement and Developing Countries.* UNCTAD, Geneva.

Yang, Y., 1998. Why do southern countries have little incentive to protect northern IPRs? *Canadian Journal of Economics* 31 (4), 800–816.

Maskus, K.E. (2000). Intellectual Property Rights in the Global Economy. Institute for International Economics: Washington, DC.
[illegible]lman, R. [illegible] 201. Doing what you can: an [illegible] analysis of [illegible] patent [illegible] Journal of [illegible]
Needham, J. (19[illegible]). [illegible] Cambridge [illegible] Press.
[illegible]
OECD [illegible] (2009). Trade and [illegible] effects of [illegible]
[illegible] Science and Technology [illegible]
[illegible] (2008). [illegible] minimum standards [illegible] intellectual property [illegible]
[illegible]
Richardson, [illegible] (199[illegible]). [illegible] intellectual property [illegible]
[illegible]
[illegible] (199[illegible]). TRIPS [illegible] Journal of [illegible] 26 (3), [illegible]
United Nations Conference on Trade and Development (199[illegible]). The TRIPS Agreement and Developing Countries [illegible] Geneva.
[illegible] (2005). [illegible] intellectual property [illegible] Journal of [illegible] 300–31[illegible]

Chapter 4

Entry, Reputation and Intellectual Property Rights Enforcement*

Abstract

We examine how reputation concerns induce a multinational to partly withhold its entry into a developing country under weak intellectual property rights (IPR) enforcement. Equilibrium IPR violations are shown to arise only in the presence of such concerns. Holding constant a multinational's incentive to innovate, better IPR enforcement encourages entry but reduces social welfare. The multinational's incentive to innovate may be inversely U-shaped in the strength of IPR enforcement. If timed properly, however, stronger IPR enforcement can foster innovation without compromising social welfare. Testable implications concerning observable IPR violations are derived.

1. Introduction

We analyze how the strengthening of intellectual property rights (IPR) enforcement in developing countries affects multinationals' entry into these countries. Existing studies typically assume weak IPR to be the only imperfection obstructing such entry. In reality, however, developing countries suffer from many other imperfections. We show that taking these imperfections into account generates new insights into our understanding of IPR enforcement in developing countries.

---

*This chapter is reproduced from *Canadian Journal of Economics*, 47(4), 1256–1281, 2014, with permission from Wiley.

The particular imperfection that we consider here is information asymmetry between consumers and multinationals with regard to the latter's product quality. Although consumers in developing countries expect multinationals to offer better quality products on average, evidence shows that they are not always aware of top-notch brand names, let alone the quality of all foreign products. A recent study of the Chinese luxury market by McKinsey and Company (2011), for example, reports that in 2008 only 23% of the country's wealthy consumers could name more than three ready-to-wear international brands and that only 44% were aware that the prices of luxury products sold in China were at least 20% higher than those in overseas markets.[1]

In the face of such asymmetric information, a multinational's entry choice will affect its reputation. We first analyze a multinational's entry under the assumption of symmetric information as a benchmark. Without any reputation concerns, a multinational will fully enter a developing country, outpricing copy-cats no matter how weak IPR enforcement is. Although no imitation takes place in equilibrium, potential competition from imitators trims the multinational's profits and hence diminishes its *ex ante* incentive to innovate. Thus, we obtain the typical insight that strengthening IPR enforcement encourages innovation and technology transfer.

Under information asymmetry, we show that a high-quality multinational can signal its quality by limiting the scale of its entry, whereas its low-quality counterpart always engages in full-scale entry. This signalling mechanism resonates with the celebrated work of Spence (1973), who showed that more capable individuals would find it less costly to signal their ability through education than their less capable peers. A similar logic underlies our result. Weak

[1]Taking advantage of this ignorance, some foreign companies export products made in China and then re-import and sell them as foreign brands that do not actually exist. In addition, multinationals sometimes fail or are unable to maintain product quality in developing countries as rigorously as they do in their home countries. McDonald's, Carrefour and Walmart have all been exposed as selling substandard products in China in recent years (http://usatoday30.usatoday.com/money/industries/food/story/2012-03-16/chinamcdonalds-carrefour-chickenes/53565980/1).

IPR enforcement forces a multinational to incur a cost to mask its technology upon entry, and that cost is higher for a high-quality multinational. Because the foregone profit will be lower, a high-quality multinational finds it less costly to signal by withholding entry than a low-quality multinational. Such withholding of entry in turn leaves room for imitation, which takes place in equilibrium if and only if IPR enforcement is sufficiently weak. This last observation highlights an important feature that is largely ignored in the existing literature: IPR violation is observable under weak enforcement only in the presence of other forms of imperfection. A number of testable implications emerge from this observation. In particular, we show that the scale of observed IPR violations increases with the growth rate of the host country's economy and the quality premium of the products and decreases with the interest rate.

Our model also allows us to examine the effects of strengthening IPR enforcement. First, a multinational will enter more aggressively when IPR enforcement is strengthened, which roughly matches empirical observations (see for example Maskus and Penubarti 1995; Smith 2001; Branstetter, Fisman and Foley 2006, BFF; Ivus 2010; Branstetter, Fisman, Foley and Saggi 2011, *BFFS*).

Second, holding constant the incentive to innovate, strengthened IPR enforcement can reduce social welfare. We obtain this result by assuming perfectly inelastic demand, such that the inefficiency does not stem from the multinational's monopoly power. Rather, imitation in unserved markets represents a social gain, and stronger IPR enforcement reduces that gain without sufficiently expanding the multinational's entry. Under symmetric information, in contrast, better IPR enforcement merely redistributes the social surplus between consumers and the multinational without changing its total amount.

Third, a multinational may not always benefit from better IPR enforcement. Imitation presents a high-quality multinational with the following tradeoffs. In the places the multinational enters, competition from potential imitators trims its profits. In the places that the multinational chooses not to enter, however, imitation brings an efficiency gain that may be shared by the multinational through litigation. The multinational's payoff may then be inversely U-shaped in IPR strength, which leads to a similar relationship between the innovation incentive and IPR strength. This relationship echoes the empirical findings of Scherer (1967) and Aghion, Bloom, Blundell, Griffith and Howitt (2005; ABBGH).

Fourth, the timing of IPR improvement is important. In an environment characterized by information asymmetry, the deferred improvement of IPR enforcement can foster innovation in multinationals without compromising social welfare.

Earlier research on IPR protection in developing countries probed the relationship between imitation in these countries and innovation in developed countries without explicitly considering the entry choices of multinationals. Segerstrom, Anant and Dinopoulos (1990) and Helpman (1993) assumed imitation to be the only means of technology transfer and suggested that imitation in developing countries allows their labour force to make use of existing innovations, thus leaving the labour force in developed countries free to specialize in future innovations.[2] This insight promoted a number of researchers to consider other channels of technology transfer. Lai (1998), and subsequently Branstetter and Saggi (2011), Dinopoulos and Segerstrom (2010) and Gustafsson and Segerstrom (2011), argued that if technologies can be transferred through direct investment, then weak IPR protection allows imitators to compete labour away from foreign investment, thus forcing multinationals to keep production in developed countries, which in turn competes labour away from innovation.

This line of research shares two assumptions. First, labour in a developing country can engage only in imitation unless employed by multinationals. Accordingly, increased imitation always takes labour away from foreign investments rather than from other indigenous

[2]Grossman and Helpman (1991) offered another explanation for why imitation in developing countries may facilitate innovation in developed countries. If continual innovation in developed countries is motivated only by the competition threat from imitation in developing countries, then any measure that reduces imitation in those countries will also reduce innovation in the former (see also Glass and Saggi 2002; Glass and Wu 2007). A similar argument lies behind the results reported by Aghion, Harris, Howitt and Vickers (2001) and ABBGH (2005) in a more general setting. Bessen and Maskin (2009) suggested that existing innovation may complement future innovation, and as a result, weak IPR protection facilitates future innovation by allowing a cheaper access to existing innovation.

economic activities. Second, there is no possibility of contracting (such as licensing) between multinationals and domestic firms. Yang and Maskus (2001, 2009) departed from these two assumptions. Both papers adopt a partial equilibrium framework in which, as the only channel of technology transfer, a multinational can licence a copycat, and the production cost is unaffected by IPR strength. Reaching the same conclusion that weak IPR protection hurts multinationals by expanding licensees' options to imitate, Yang and Maskus (2001) nevertheless observed that imitation will not take place in equilibrium when licensing is an option. This observation was confirmed by Yang and Maskus (2009), who showed that imitation will take place only in the limiting situation that IPR protection is entirely absent. Finally, Ethier and Markusen (1996) considered both licensing and direct investment in addition to exporting to a developing country in which IPR protection is completely absent. They did not examine how IPR protection affects entry mode or innovation, but they nevertheless also found imitation not to occur in equilibrium.

Our contributions can be summarized as follows. We adopt a partial equilibrium framework that considers both direct investment and licensing as entry options. The licensing option allows multinationals to contract with potential imitators. In addition to weak IPR enforcement, information asymmetry is introduced as an additional imperfection. We develop three key insights. First, when weak IPR enforcement is the only imperfection, imitators can be priced out of competition whenever licensing is feasible. Imitation takes place in equilibrium only in the presence of additional imperfections such as information asymmetry. Second, equilibrium imitation becomes a channel of technology transfer that brings efficiency gains, which can be shared by multinationals through moderately strong IPR enforcement. Third, although it transfers technology and benefits multinationals, imitation is less efficient than legitimate channels of technology transfer. It emerges as a supplement only when some other imperfections prevent multinationals from taking full advantage of legitimate transfers.

We would like to emphasize, however, that we are not arguing the case for whether multinationals benefit from weak IPR enforcement in real life, which is an empirical issue. Nor do we wish to advocate any particular nation disregarding IPR protection. Nevertheless, as a theoretical possibility, our insight that imitation can result in efficiency gains and that multinationals can share in that gain through moderately strong IPR enforcement remains an intriguing one. It also does not seem too far-fetched, as our prediction of inverted U-shaped relationships between IPR strength and multinational profits is consistent with empirical studies.

The remainder of the paper is organized as follows. After setting up the model in Section 2, we establish in Section 3 the equilibrium under both symmetric and asymmetric information conditions and show that imitation takes place in equilibrium only under asymmetric information. Section 4 discusses the effects of stronger IPR enforcement on entry scale, social welfare and a multinational's profits and innovation incentive. Section 5 concludes the paper.

2. Model Set-up

We consider a two-period model in which a multinational (M) from a developed country has to decide whether and how to bring its product to a developing country. The quality of its product is either high or low, such that $M \in \{M^h, M^l\}$. The developing country comprises a continuum of regions, each forming a separate market which is referred to as a segment. Each segment is inhabited by a unit mass of consumers who demand y_t units of the product in period $t (t = 1, 2)$. We normalize $y_1 \equiv 1$ and $y_2 \equiv y$ to reduce notation and assume a growing economy, where $y > 1$, for reasons that will become clear later in the paper. We denote by $u^j(i)$ the willingness to pay of the consumers in segment i for a unit of a product of quality $j \in \{h, l\}$ with $u^h(i) > u^l(i)$. Segments differ in consumers' willingness to pay and are indexed such that $u^j(i)$ decreases in i. Let δ be the time discount factor.

In each period, M can enter a segment through either direct investment (k) or licensing (s). The two entry modes differ in both the quality provided and cost structure. Direct investment delivers M's true quality, whereas licensing always delivers low quality because of local licensees' limited technological capacity. Direct investment requires, in each period, a country-wide setup cost f and a marginal cost c_k, which is assumed to be type-independent.[3] Licensing requires a smaller setup cost, which is normalized to zero, but a larger marginal cost because M has to use extra resources to manage its licensee, an independent entity. Let c^j be $M^{j'}s$ marginal cost of licensing for $j \in \{h, l\}$. We assume the high type's licensing cost to be greater than the low type's ($c^h > c^l > c_k$) for the following reason. To prevent its licensee from stealing its technology, M has to mask it during licensing. With better technology, M^h stands to lose more from leaking its know-how than M^l does and, hence, is willing to incur a greater cost in masking.[4]

There are numerous identical domestic firms in each segment. A domestic firm can imitate M's technology at cost c and deliver a low quality product. We assume that such imitation is possible even in segments the multinational has chosen not to enter. To ensure that we do not trivialize the welfare implications of our analysis, we assume that although both modes offer a low-quality product, imitation is (weakly) less efficient than licensing: $c \geq c^h$. The strength of IPR enforcement is represented by 7, the probability that an imitator will be prosecuted at the end of each period. Once caught out, the imitator must compensate M with its sales revenue.[5] In our main analysis we assume that the strength of IPR enforcement remains the same over the two periods, an assumption that will be relaxed later.

The timing of the game and the information structure are as follows. In the first period, the multinational chooses whether to enter each segment and, if it does so, whether to enter through licensing or investment. If it chooses licensing, it makes a take-it-or-leave-it offer to a randomly chosen domestic firm (M has all of the bargaining power because of the large number of identical domestic firms). If

---

[3]As explained later (footnote 9), our analysis remains qualitatively the same even when c_k is type-dependent.

[4]This idea is formalized in our working paper (Che, Qiu and Zhou 2012, CQZ).

[5]We assume that IPR are enforced even in the segments the multinational has not entered. Note that a convicted offender may not always make the required compensation payment in a country with weak IPR enforcement. In this regard, y should be interpreted as the probability that a local copycat is caught *and* actually pays the compensation.

the offer is accepted, the licensee is entitled to use M's technology at a fee to supply the product in that particular segment. If the offer is rejected, M does not enter that segment. In each segment, including those that the multinational has chosen not to enter, domestic firms can always engage in imitation. All imitators and the multinational's legal operation, if any, compete *àla* Bertrand in each segment. In the second period, M must make a new decision regarding investment or licensing. The two periods differ in market size, as captured by y, and in consumers' belief concerning the multinational's type.[6] We assume that consumers can distinguish between imitators and the multinational. However, they cannot directly observe product quality or M's type.[6] At the beginning of the first period, consumers' *a priori* belief is that $M = M^h$ with probability ρ_1. By the end of that period, consumers observe both M's entry mode (licensing or investment) in their own segment and its entry scale (i.e., the number of segments entered by M) through each mode in the entire country.[7] This information allows consumers to update their beliefs at the beginning of the second period, ρ_2. Finally, we assume that imitators have the same information structure as consumers.

3. The Signalling Equilibrium

3.1. *Multinational's payoff*

In period t and segment i, if an imitator is able to sell its product at price p, its expected payoff is $(1 - 1')p - c$. Competition among imitators drives the price to:

$$p \equiv \frac{c}{1-\gamma}.$$

Knowing that imitators can produce only a low-quality product, consumers in segment i will buy from an imitator only if $u^l(i) \geq p$. Therefore, imitation is feasible only in segments $i \leq x$, where x is

[6]This assumption can be relaxed to allow consumers to have a chance to observe product quality at the end of the first period, but the results remain qualitatively unchanged (CQZ 2012).

[7]Consumers can observe the entry mode and scale because the legal operations of a multinational constitute public information.

determined by:

$$u^l(x) \equiv p.$$

x is the index of the marginal segment in which domestic firms are indifferent between imitating and not imitating. Slightly abusing the notation, we also use x to denote the scale of potential imitation. Note that x decreases in strengthening IPR enforcement reduces the potential scale of imitation.

If M enters segment $i \leq x$ with an investment (after having sunk setup cost f), it faces competition from imitators. Consumers in segment i are willing to pay up to:

$$u^{\rho_t}(i) = \rho_t u^h(i) + (1 - \rho_t)u^l(i)$$

for M's product supplied through investment when their belief is ρ_t. As M enjoys both a cost advantage ($c_k < c$) and quality premium ($u^{\rho_t}(i) \geq u^l(i)$), it can charge a price that is sufficiently low to fend off imitators in the Bertrand competition. This means that M will set its price p such that $u^{\beta t}(i) - p_k = u^l(i) - p$, or $p_k = u^{\rho_t}(i) - u^l(i) + p$, and its investment profit in segment $i \leq x$ will thus be:

$$y_t[u^{\rho_t}(i) - u^l(i) + p - c_k].$$

If M enters segment $i \leq x$ through licensing, its licensee will have to charge p to fight off competition from imitators. The licensee thus will earn $y_t p$ from licensing. If the licensee does not accept the licence offer, it has the option to become an imitator and earn zero payoff Thus, M will set the licensing fee at $y_t p$ and offer the licence to a random domestic firm, which will accept the offer.

Accordingly, M's licensing profit in segment $i \leq x$ will be:

$$y_t(p - c^j).$$

Should M decide to withhold from entering a segment $i \leq x$, imitation will take place, and M's expected payoff will be $y_t \gamma p$.

In segment $i > x$, there is no competition from imitators. Thus, the price in segment i is $u^{\rho_t}(i)$ for investment and $u^l(i)$ for licensing,

Table 4.1. M^j's payoff per unit of market size in segment i and period t.

	Segment	
	$i \leq x$	$i > x$
Investment (k)	$u^{\rho t}(i) - u^l(i) + \dfrac{c}{1-\gamma} - c_k$	$u^{\rho t}(i) - c_k$
Licensing (s)	$\dfrac{c}{1-\gamma} - c^j$	$u^{\rho t} - c^j$
Withholding/imitation (x)	$\dfrac{\lambda c}{1-\gamma}$	0

and M's profit under direct investment is:

$$y_t(u^{\rho_t}(i) - c_k)$$

and under licensing is:

$$y_t(u^l(i) - c^j).$$

If M withholds in segment i, it receives nothing from this segment. Table 4.1 summarizes $M^{j'}s$ payoff per unit of market size in segment i and period t. The multinational's total profit (excluding fixed cost f in the case of investment) is this per-unit payoff multiplied by market size y_t. As previously noted, the two periods differ in y_t and possibly ρ_t.

3.2. *Entry decision*

Denote the entry choice made by M^j in period t by κ_t^j, σ_t^j, where κ_t^j is the measure of segments entered through direct investment and σ_t^j is the measure entered through licensing. Denote $M^{j'}s$ total profit in period t by Π_t^j. The entry problem faced by the multinational differs between the two periods as the first-period entry serves the additional function of signalling.

The second period

In the second period, the trade-off between direct investment and licensing is the following. Direct investment requires a setup cost, f. However, in every segment, investment dominates licensing, as $c_k < c^l < c^h$ and $u^{\rho_2}(i) \geq u^l(i)$ for all i. Therefore, investment and licensing cannot coexist.

Suppose that M^j chooses licensing. Because the licensing payoff decreases in i, licensing yields a non-negative profit in segment $i \leq s^j$, where s^j is defined by:

$$u^l(s^j) \equiv c^j. \tag{1}$$

As $c^j < \frac{c}{1-\gamma}$, we have $s^j > x$. Note that s^j depends on M's type owing to the difference in licensing cost, and s^j is the same for both periods. Define:

$$\pi_s^j \equiv \int_0^x \left(\frac{c}{1-\gamma} - c^j\right) di + \int_x^{s^j} (u^l(i) - c^j)di \tag{2}$$

as $M^{j'}s$ payoff per unit of market size under licensing. Then $M^{j'}s$ second-period profit is $\Pi_{2,s}^j = y\pi_s^j$. Suppose that M^j chooses investment. Similar to the foregoing analysis, direct investment generates a non-negative profit in segment $\leq k^{\rho 2}$, where $k^{\rho 2}$ is defined by:

$$u^{\rho 2}(k^{\rho 2}) \equiv c_k. \tag{3}$$

Because $c_k < \frac{c}{1-\gamma}$ and $u^{\rho 2}(i) \geq u^l(i)$, we have $k^{\rho 2} > x$. Note that $k^{\rho 2}$ depends on ρ_2 but not on j (i.e., the true identity of M for a given ρ_2). Define:

$$\pi_k^{\rho 2} \equiv \int_0^x \left(u^{\rho 2}(i) - u^l(i) + \frac{c}{1-\gamma} - c_k\right) di + \int_x^{k^{\rho 2}} (u^{\rho 2}(i) - c_k)di \tag{4}$$

as M's payoff per unit of market size under investment. Then M's second-period profit is $\Pi_{2,k}^{\rho 2} = y\pi_k^{\rho 2} - f$.

The second-period entry problem for M^j is therefore reduced to a choice between direct investment and licensing: $\max\{\Pi_{2,k}^{\rho 2}, \Pi_{2,s}^j\}$.

The first period

The first-period entry profile κ_1, σ_1 affects consumers' beliefs in the second period. Their off-equilibrium beliefs are assumed to follow the intuitive criterion (Cho and Kreps 1987). M^j's first-period choice is therefore:

$$\max_{\{\kappa_1^j,\sigma_1^j\}} \Pi_1^j(\{\kappa_1^j,\sigma_1^j\}) + \delta \max\{\Pi_{2,k}^{\rho 2(\{\kappa\sigma\})}, \Pi_{2,s}^j\}. \tag{5}$$

For signalling purposes, M^j may choose investment and licensing simultaneously in the first period, in which case we assume for the sake of simplicity that its investments are in lower-indexed segments: investment in segments $i \in [0,\kappa_1^j]$ and licensing in segments $\in [\kappa_1^j, \kappa_1^j + \sigma_1^j]$.[8] A perfect Bayesian equilibrium is a pair of $\{\{\kappa_1^h,\sigma_1^h\},\{\kappa_1^l,\sigma_1^l\}$ that solves (5) for $j \in \{h,l\}$ simultaneously.

3.3. *Equilibrium under symmetric information*

As a benchmark, we first consider the case of symmetric information, i.e., M's type is known to consumers. As consumers' willingness to pay and entry cost do not change over time, the entry scale of any given entry mode must be the same across the two periods: $\kappa_1^j = \kappa_2^j = k^j$ and $\sigma_1^j = \sigma_2^j = s^j$, where k^j is defined by:

$$u^j(k^j) \equiv c_k. \tag{6}$$

As before, because $c_k < \frac{c}{1-\gamma}$ and $u^j(i) \geq u^l(i)$, we have $k^j > x$

Because the second-period profit is independent of $\{\kappa_1^j,\sigma_1^j\}$, M's first-period entry simply maximizes the profit in that period. As in the second period, investment and licensing do not coexist in period 1 and, hence, the entry problem in this period is again reduced to

---

[8]This assumption helps to simplify the exposition of our analysis. Otherwise, M's entry may consist of greater dimensions (moving down the segments, the entry may be investment, licensing, then investment again and licensing again, etc which would greatly expand M's strategy space and complicate our analysis without yielding any new insights. Note that the assumed behaviour would be optimal if $u^h(i)$ declines with i faster than $u^l(i)$. To see why, suppose that M invests in segment i but licences in segment $i' < i$. Let M swap the mode of entry between the two segments. As the entry scale of each mode remains the same, the swap does not affect consumers' posterior belief, ρ_2, and, hence, M's second period profit.

Nevertheless, its first-period profit changes by the amount of $[\rho_1 u^h(i') + (1-\rho_1)u^l(i') + u^l(i)] - [\rho_1 u^h(i) + (1-\rho_1)u^l(i) + u^l(i')] = \rho_1[u^h(i') - u^h(i)] - \rho_1[u^l(i') - u^l(i)]$, which is positive given the assumption that $u^h(i)$ declines with i faster than $u^l(i)$. Thus, M is better off with the swap.

a choice between direct investment and licensing. The equilibrium entry mode, however, may differ between the two periods, as the market size grows. Define π_k^j as M^j*'s* investment payoff per unit of market size under symmetric information:

$$\pi_k^j \equiv \int_0^x (u^j(i) - u^l(i) + \frac{c}{1-\gamma} - c_k)di + \int_x^{k^j} (u^j(i) - c_k)di. \quad (7)$$

In the first period, the profit is $\pi_k^j - f$ for direct investment and π_s^j for licensing. The corresponding profits in the second period are $y\pi_k^j - f$ and $y\pi_s^j$ respectively.

Lemma 1. *Suppose that:*

$$\pi_k^h < f < y(\pi_k^h - \pi_s^h). \quad (8)$$

Under symmetric information, both types of M licence in the first period. In the second period, M^h *chooses direct investment, whereas* M^l *chooses direct investment if* $f \leq y(\pi_k^l - \pi_s^l)$, *and licensing otherwise.*

Condition (8) characterizes a growing economy, the size of which is too small in the first period for investment to be profitable even for M^h but becomes much larger in the second period, such that M^h finds investment more profitable than licensing. To simplify the exposition and focus on our scenario of interest, we assume throughout the remainder of the paper that condition (8) holds. Because $\pi_k^l < \pi_k^h$, if investment is unprofitable for M^h in the first period, it must also be unprofitable for M^l. Note that because M always operates beyond the marginal segment in which imitators are indifferent between entering and not entering, imitation does not take place in equilibrium.

We now consider the effects of strengthening IPR enforcement under symmetric information. For a given entry mode, M's entry scale is determined by its zero-profit condition and is independent of γ. In every segment that M enters, the social benefit and social cost of supplying M's product are also independent of γ. The presence of imitators merely reduces the rent that M enjoys. As the reduction in M's rent (which equals $u^l(i) - \frac{c}{1-\gamma}$) is the same whether it enters through investment or licensing, $\pi_k^j - \pi_s^j$ is independent of $1'$ for either type of multinational. Therefore, IPR strength does not affect the equilibrium choice of entry mode. In sum, stronger IPR enforcement does not change social welfare.

M's profits, however, are improved by stronger IPR enforcement:

$$\frac{d\pi_k^j}{d\gamma} = \frac{d\pi_s^j}{d\gamma} = \int_0^x \frac{c}{(1-\gamma)^2}di + \Big(p(\gamma) - u^l(x)\Big)\frac{dx}{d\gamma} = \int_0^x \frac{c}{(1-\gamma)^2}di$$

which is positive when $x > 0$. Stronger IPR enforcement has two effects. First, it raises imitators' break-even price $p(\gamma)$ which allows M^j to charge consumers a higher price. Second, it reduces the scale of potential imitation (x). The second effect is muted, however, because in the marginal segment in which imitators are indifferent between entering and not entering, their break-even price equals consumers' willingness to pay, $(\gamma) = u^l(x)$, and thus M^j loses no profits because of the threat of imitation.

Proposition 1. *Under symmetric information, IPR violations never take place in equilibrium. Stronger IPR enforcement does not affect social surplus or entry choice but (weakly) improves the multinational ś profits.*

The last property, *ie.*, that the multinational's profits increase with IPR strength, justifies the conventional wisdom in an environment in which information is symmetric. It is worth emphasizing that no matter how weak the IPR enforcement is, imitation will never take place in equilibrium in such an environment. With a cost advantage and quality premium (when M^h enters through direct investment), M is able to outprice imitators through competition. The absence of equilibrium imitation arises not from the nature of Bertrand competition but rather from the numerous copycats competing with one another.

Our result holds even under Cournot competition. The consequences of weak IPR enforcement lie not in any observed IPR violations but in M's lower profits resulting from the threat of potential imitation.

3.4. *Equilibrium under asymmetric information*

We now turn to the main focus of this paper: reputation concerns arising from information asymmetry. A better reputation enables a multinational to charge a higher price when it enters through direct investment in the second period. As a result, both multinational types may try to establish a better reputation by carefully choosing their first-period entry profile. In particular, M^l may attempt to mimic $M^{h'}s$ entry choice, and, in response, M^h may adopt an entry profile that distances it from M^l.

M^l will be discouraged from mimicking $M^{h'}s$ entry profile if being itself produces a better payoff:

$$\pi_s^l + \delta \max\{y\pi_k^l - f, y\pi_s^l \geq \Pi_1^l\}(\{\kappa_1^h, \sigma_1^h\}) + \delta(y\pi_k^h - f). \quad (9)$$

Note that the second term on the right-hand side, $(y\pi_k^h - f)$, is the low type's second-period payoff when it successfully convinces consumers that it is a high type. The following condition, which we assume throughout the rest of the paper, ensures that it is feasible for M^h to distance itself from M^l:

$$\pi_s^l - \gamma xp \geq \delta y(\pi_k^h - \pi_k^l), \quad (10)$$

where $\gamma xp = \int_0^x 1' pdi$ is the multinational's payoff should it withdraw completely. The right-hand side of (10) is the upper bound of the return that M^l obtains by successfully convincing consumers that it is M^h. The left-hand side is the maximal cost that M^h can impose on M^l by choosing to withhold its entry completely in the first period. When (10) holds, it is feasible for M^h to choose an entry profile (by withholding from enough segments) in period 1 that M^l will find unprofitable to mimic.

Given such feasibility, we now turn to $M^{h'}s$ incentive to separate itself from M^l. With a particular entry profile $\{\kappa_1, \sigma_1\}$ and posterior belief $\rho_2 M^{j'}s$ two-period total profit is:

$$\Pi^j(\{\kappa_1, \sigma_1\}, \rho_2) \equiv \Pi_1^j(\{\kappa_1, \sigma_1\}) + \delta \max\{y\pi_k^{\rho 2} - f,\ y\pi_s^j\},$$

The marginal return to a better reputation is $\frac{\partial \Pi^j}{\partial \rho 2}$. When ρ_2 is sufficiently large, both types undertake direct investment in the second period, in which case they enjoy the same marginal return:

$$\frac{\partial \Pi^h}{\partial \rho_2} = \frac{\partial \Pi^l}{\partial \rho_2} = \delta y \frac{\partial \pi_k^{\beta 2}}{\partial \rho_2}$$

Because direct investment in the first period gives the two types the same payoff, the marginal cost of reputation through period-1 investment is the same for both:

$$\frac{\partial \Pi^h}{\partial k_1} = \frac{\partial \Pi^l}{\partial k_1}.$$

The marginal cost of reputation through licensing differs, however:

$$\frac{\partial \Pi^j}{\partial \sigma_1} = \begin{cases} c - c^j > 0 & \text{if } \sigma_1 \leq x; \\ u^l(\sigma_1) - c^j \geq 0 & \text{if } \sigma_1 \in (x, s]; \\ u^l(\sigma_1) - c^j < 0. & \text{if } \sigma_1 > s^j \end{cases}$$

In particular, $c^h > c^l$ implies that:

$$\frac{\partial \Pi^h}{\partial \sigma_1} < \frac{\partial \Pi^l}{\partial \sigma_1}, \quad \forall \sigma_1$$

M^h is able to command an advantage over M^l in paying for a better reputation in two situations. The first is when $\sigma_1 \in (s^h, s^l)$, in which case a marginal reduction in licensing scale benefits M^h but hurts M^l. The second is when $\sigma_1 \leq s^h$, in which case a marginal reduction in licensing scale costs M^h less than it costs M^l.

The foregoing discussion establishes the single-crossing property: there exists $\sigma_1 \leq s^l$, such that maintaining a better reputation through a reduction in licensing scale is less costly for M^h than for M^l. Given the feasibility condition (10), there exists $s^* > 0$, such that (9) holds in equality at $\kappa_1^h, \sigma_1^h = \{0, s^*\}$:

$$\pi_s^l - \Pi_1^l(\{0, s^*\}) \equiv \Delta, \tag{11}$$

where:

$$\Delta \equiv \delta(y\pi_k^h - f) - \delta \max\{y\pi_k^l - f,\, y\pi_s^l\} \tag{12}$$

is the return to M^l from mimicking M^h. In (11) and (12), π_s^l is given by (2), π_k^j is given by (7) and:

$$\Pi_1^l(\{0, s^*\}) = \begin{cases} \int_0^x (p(\gamma) - c^l)di + \int_x^{s^*} (u^l(i) - c^l)di & \text{for } s^* > x; \\ \int_0^{s^*} (p(\gamma) - c^l)di + \int_{s^*}^x \gamma p(\gamma)di & \text{for } s^* \leq x. \end{cases}$$

We are now ready to present one of the key results of this paper.

Proposition 2. *There exists a unique and separating equilibrium, where, in the first period, M^l licences in s^l segments and M^h licences in min $\{s^*, s^h\}$ segments.*

The formal proof of proposition 2 is relegated to the appendix, but its intuition can be simply explained. Because M^h and M^l differ only in their licensing costs, M^h is unable to distance itself from M^l via direct investment alone. Because investment is unprofitable in the first period, any combination of investment and licensing is dominated by a combination of withholding and licensing. No pooling equilibrium exists because by choosing a licensing scale below s^l, M^h commands an advantage over M^l in paying for a better reputation. In a separating equilibrium, knowing that its type will be fully revealed in the second period, M^l enters fully (i.e., s^l segments) in period 1, as it does in the benchmark case. To separate itself from M^l, M^h chooses s^* when $s^* < s^h$. If $s^* \geq s^h, M^h$ will simply choose $0, s^h$ to maximize its first-period profit, as M^l will make no attempt to mimic $M^{h'}s$ entry profile.[9]

From proposition 2, it is straightforward to derive the following result.

Proposition 3. *IPR violation takes place in equilibrium if and only if $M = M^h$ and $s^* < x$, and it takes place in period 1 in segments $i \in [s^*, x]$.*

Recall that imitation is never observed when information is symmetric. Proposition 3 highlights the reason for *equilibrium* imitation: the strategic withholding of entry by the multinational in an

---

[9]For simplicity, we assume that c_k does not depend on M's type, although the results remain the same even if it does. In equilibrium, M enters in the first period through licensing such that the investment cost c_k does not matter. In the second period, M's type is fully revealed through signalling and, thus, c_k affects only M's payoff without qualitatively changing any results reported in the propositions. If c_k depends on M's type, M may signal its type in the first period through investment rather than withholding licensing scale. However, as noted, withholding in a given segment (which gives M a positive payoff) always dominates investment in that segment (which gives M a negative payoff because of the limited market size in period 1). Finally, in the incentive-compatibility condition (equations (11) and (12)), the expression of Δ will change if c_k is type-dependent, but Δ will continue to be independent of enforcement strength and thus all of the comparative static results remain unchanged.

attempt to maintain its reputation, which in turn allows imitators to survive in the market. A unique feature of this paper is that IPR violations take place in equilibrium despite the possibility of licensing. The existing literature generates equilibrium imitation by assuming away the possibility of licensing, which we consider unrealistic. By introducing reputation concerns, we are able to show how IPR violations may emerge in equilibrium in an environment that allows the multinational to licence to potential imitators.

For the remainder of the paper, we refer to the case of $s^* > x$ as a *non-imitation equilibrium* and to that of $s^* \leq x$ as an *imitation equilibrium*. We first identify the factors that affect the extent of IPR violations. Suppose that $u^i(i)$ can be shifted up by parameter θ^j for $j \in \{h, l\}$ for all i and that $\delta = 1/(1+\gamma)$ is the discount factor corresponding to an interest rate r. Condition (11) reveals the following.

Proposition 4. *In an imitation equilibrium, the scale of IPR violations increases in y and θ^h and decreases in r and θ^l.*

Proposition 4 suggests that more IPR violations will be observed in an economy with a higher growth rate, lower interest rate, or larger quality premium (higher θ^h or lower θ^l). A rapidly growing economy that expands the product market substantially in the future increases the return to a good reputation, thus enhancing the incentive for M^l to mimic M^h unless M^h withdraws its entry further to increase the cost of mimicking. As M^h withdraws further, it leaves more room for IPR violations. Likewise, a lower interest rate in a growing economy increases the present discounted value of a good reputation, forcing M^h to further withdraw its entry to prevent M^l from mimicking it. A quality premium does not increase IPR violations because imitated products can be priced at a higher amount. In our model, imitators are assumed to be competitive, and, as a result, they price at their marginal cost (adjusted by the probability of IPR enforcement) without any direct effect of a higher quality premium. Instead, a larger quality premium enhances the return to a good reputation, which, as in the case of a higher growth rate or lower interest rate, induces M^h to further withdraw its entry, leaving more room for imitation.

4. The Effects of Strengthening IPR Enforcement

Having established the equilibrium under asymmetric information, we now examine the effects of strengthening IPR enforcement (*i.e.*, a larger γ) on M's entry scale and profits and social welfare. We begin with the following observations. First, because IPR enforcement does not alter consumers' valuation of the multinational's product, it exerts its influence only through the operating decisions of the two types of M and their imitators. Second, in a separating equilibrium, the types are fully revealed in the second period. Thus, as discussed in the symmetric information case, the second-period entry decisions of both types of M are independent of 7. Third, the first-period choice made by M^l is also unaffected. Only the first-period licensing scale of M^h is subject to change. Fourth, because $x < \min\{s^l, k^h, k^l\}$ and stronger enforcement in the second period exerts an influence only through x, the marginal gain of reputation, , is independent of This last observation implies that the change in $M^{h'}s$ first-period licensing scale must come from the marginal cost of reputation, *i.e.*, the left-hand side of equation (11).

Consider first a non-imitation equilibrium ($s^* > x$), in which case equation (11) becomes:

$$\int_{s^*}^{s^l} (u^l(i) - c^l)di = \Delta.$$

Neither side of the equation involves, and thus equilibrium entry scale s* does not depend on γ. Because stronger enforcement makes it more costly for domestic firms to imitate M's product, the imitators' price (p) is higher and the imitation scale (x) is smaller. These two effects affect M^h and M^l symmetrically when s^* is beyond x, and thus the incentive compatibility constraint remains intact. As x retreats, inequality $s^* > x$ continues to hold, so M^h and M^l still operate beyond x. The retreat of x will therefore have no effect on M's profit at the margin, but its profits inside the margin will increase owing to a higher p, as in the case of symmetric information. Given that the entry scale of both types of M remains the same in both periods and is larger than that of potential imitation, it is straightforward to conclude that social welfare must also remain the same.

Proposition 5. *In a non-imitation equilibrium, stronger IPR enforcement increases the profits of both M^h and M^l but has no effect on their entry decisions or social welfare.*

Now consider an imitation equilibrium ($s^* \leq x$), in which case (11) becomes:

$$\int_{s^*(\gamma)}^{x} (c - c^l)di + \int_{x}^{s^l} (u^l(i) - c^l)di = \Delta. \tag{13}$$

Because x is a function of, s^* must also depend on γ. Strengthening IPR enforcement has two asymmetric effects on M^h and M^l, as the former operates inside the margin in which imitators operate ($s^* < x$), whereas the latter operates beyond that margin ($s^l > x$). The rising imitation price allows M^l to raise its payoff dollar by dollar in segment $i \in (s^*, x]$ but allows M^h to increase its payoff only through successful litigation, *i.e.*, only with probability A smaller imitation scale does not affect $M^{l'}s$ payoff, but it reduces $M^{h,}s$, as M^h collects compensation from fewer segments in which imitation takes place. Hence stronger IPR enforcement increases $M^{l'}s$ profits more than $M^{h'}s$ (if $M^{h'}s$ profits increase at all). As a result, the incentive compatibility constraint must become slack, allowing M^h to expand s^*. Formally, we differentiate both sides of (13) with respect to γ to get:

$$(c - c^l)\frac{ds^*}{d\gamma} + (u^l(x) - c)\frac{dx}{d\gamma} = 0. \tag{14}$$

Because $u^l(x) = p > c$ and $\frac{dx}{d\gamma} < 0$, we have:

$$\frac{ds^*}{d\gamma} > 0.$$

Proposition 6. (*Entry Scale*) *In an imitation equilibrium, stronger IPR enforcement increases $M^{h,}s$ first-period entry scale but has no effect on $M^{l,}s$ first-period entry scale or either type ś second-period entry decision.*

We turn next to social welfare. An increase in s^* is accompanied by a decrease in x: some of the segments previously served by imitators are now served by legally licensed products from M^h, whereas others are no longer served at all. The first change brings an efficiency gain, as legal licensing is less costly than imitation. The second change, however, results in an efficiency loss. Imitation creates a social surplus even though it violates M's property rights. Under symmetric information, imitation does not take place in equilibrium, and a decrease in x merely reduces the competition M faces without any effect on social welfare. Under asymmetric information, in contrast, M^h chooses not to serve certain segments. In an imitation equilibrium, some of these unserved segments are served by imitators, which represents a social gain. A smaller x reduces this social gain.

To determine the net effect on social welfare, let W_1^h denote the first-period social welfare for M^h:

$$W_1^h = \int_0^{s^*(\gamma)} (u^l(i) - c^h)di + \int_{s^*(\gamma)}^{x(\gamma)} (u^l(i) - c)di$$

Making use of (14) we obtain:

$$\frac{dW_1^h}{d\gamma} = (c - c^h)\frac{ds^*}{d\gamma} + (u^l(x) - c)\frac{dx}{d\gamma} = (c^l - c^h)\frac{ds^*}{d\gamma} < 0. \qquad (15)$$

Therefore, the efficiency loss resulting from a smaller x always outweighs the efficiency gain resulting from a larger s^*, and thus first-period social welfare decreases with γ when $M = M^h$. Because IPR strength does not affect first-period welfare when $M = M^l$ or second-period welfare for both types, we conclude that the two-period total expected social welfare must decline.

Proposition 7. (*Welfare*) *In an imitation equilibrium, strengthening IPR enforcement reduces social welfare.*

It is well known that, holding constant a multinational's incentive to innovate, stronger IPR protection results in social welfare loss because it allows distortionary monopoly pricing. By assuming unit demand, this paper stays away from such an effect, and the welfare loss arises for an entirely different reason. From (14) and (15), we know that efficiency loss $u^l(i) - c$ equals the acquired incentive for M^l to mimic M^h, whereas efficiency gain $c - c^h(i)$ is smaller than the acquired disincentive, $c - c^l(i)$, for M^l not to mimic M^h, as M^h faces a larger licensing cost. When IPR enforcement becomes stronger, s^*

must respond to the reduction in x to keep the acquired incentive in balance with the acquired disincentive. Therefore, social welfare must decrease. Finally, we analyze how better IPR enforcement influences a multinational's profits and hence its incentive to innovate. When $s^* \leq x, M^{l'}s$ operating scale exceeds that of imitators in both periods, and thus stronger IPR enforcement raises $M^{l'}s$ profits, as in the benchmark case. Similarly, $M^{h'}s$ second-period profits also increase:

$$\frac{d(y\pi_k^h - f)}{d\gamma} = y\int_0^x \frac{c}{(1-\gamma)^2}di > 0.$$

$M^{h'}s$ first-period profit is:

$$\Pi_1^h(\{0, s^*\}) = \int_0^{s^*(\gamma)} (p(\gamma) - c^h)di + \int_{s^*(\gamma)}^{x(\gamma)} \gamma p(\gamma)di.$$

Differentiating this profit with respect to, we obtain:

$$\frac{d\Pi_1^h(\{0, s^*\})}{d\gamma} = (c - c^h)\frac{ds^*}{d\gamma} + \int_0^x \frac{c}{(1-\gamma)^2}di + \gamma p^{\frac{dx}{d\gamma}}.$$

This expression reveals three effects that stronger IPR enforcement has on $M^{h'}s$ first-period profit. First, it expands s^*, which allows M^h to drive away imitators in some segments and collect social gain $c - c^h$ in each of these segments. Second, it raises the imitation price, and thus $M^{h'}s$ payoff, as M^h will raise its own price in licensed segments and collect more compensation in segments in which imitation takes place. Third, it reduces x, which reduces the compensation that M^h can collect through IPR litigation. Substituting (14) into the foregoing equation allows us to calculate the effect of stronger enforcement on $M^{h'}s$ total profits:

$$\frac{d(\Pi_1^h(\{0, s^*\}) + \delta(y\pi_k^h - f))}{\mathrm{d}\gamma} = xp\left(\frac{1+\delta y}{1-\gamma} + \frac{c^h - c^l}{c - c^l}\frac{d\ln x}{d\ln \gamma}\right).$$

Proposition 8. (*Profit*) *In an imitation equilibrium, stronger IPR enforcement increases the profits of* M^l. *It increases the profits of* M^h *if and only if.*

$$(1+\delta y)\frac{c - c^l}{c^h - c^l} + (1-\gamma)\frac{d\ln x}{d\ln \gamma} > 0. \tag{16}$$

To better understand condition (16), note that:

$$(1-\gamma)\frac{d\ln x}{d\ln \gamma} = \frac{\gamma}{1-\gamma}\frac{c}{xu^l(x)},$$

where $u^{l'}(i) \equiv \frac{du^l(l)}{di}$. Therefore, we can further conclude the following.

Corollary 1. *In any imitation equilibrium, stronger IPR enforcement:*

1) *increases the profit of M^h when γ is sufficiently small but*
2) *decreases the profit of M^h for some positive γ when $u^{lf}(\cdot)$ is sufficiently small.*

To illustrate this corollary, we consider utility function $u^l(i) = bi^{-\alpha}$, where b is some positive constant and $\alpha > 0$ measures the dispersion in willingness to pay across segments. A larger α corresponds to a more dispersed distribution. Should the willingness to pay be rooted in affordability, α also reflects income dispersion. Given that $u^l(x) = p$, we have $(1-\gamma)\frac{d\ln x}{d\ln\gamma} = -\frac{V}{\alpha}$. Hence, condition (16) is reduced to:

$$(1+\delta y)\frac{c-c^l}{c^h-c^l} > \frac{\gamma}{\alpha},$$

which holds when $1'$ is small and does not hold when α is sufficiently small.

Figure 4.1 shows how, for $u^l(i) = bi^{-\alpha}$, $M^{h'}s$ first-period entry scale, two-period total profits and social welfare respond to changes in 7. Condition (14) reveals that imitation arises in equilibrium ($s^* \leq x$) if and only if γ is below some threshold, say, $\overline{\gamma}$. In such an equilibrium, x declines with γ, whereas s^* increases with it. Social welfare decreases with γ, and $M^{h'}s$ profit is inversely U-shaped. When $\gamma \geq \overline{\gamma}$, imitation does not take place in equilibrium ($s^* \geq x$). In this region, x continues to decline as γ increases, but the profits earned by M^h begin to increase with γ. At the same time, s^* becomes independent of γ and, as a result, social welfare remains constant. When enforcement becomes sufficiently strong, imitation is no longer feasible in any segment. A further strengthening of IPR enforcement has no effect whatsoever. Because M faces no threats from local competition, its profit equals the social surplus.

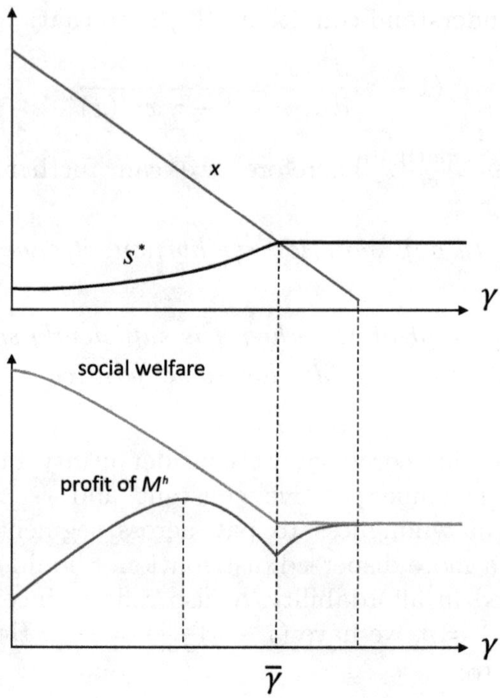

Figure 4.1. First-period entry scale, two-period profits, and social welfare when $M = M^h$ and $u^l(i) = bi^{-\alpha}$.

The comparative statics discussed thus far (propositions 5 through 8) offer a few interesting insights. First, they put into perspective the empirical observations that stronger IPR enforcement encourages multinationals' entry (Maskus and Penubarti 1995; Smith 2001; BTT 2006; Ivus 2010; BFFS 2011). Our analysis demonstrates that stronger IPR enforcement encourages the entry of multinationals only when IPR violations are observed in equilibrium.

Second, whenever such entry is expanded by stronger IPR enforcement, social welfare declines. Stronger enforcement exerts two effects on social welfare. By inducing more entry, it allows certain segments to be served more efficiently (through licensing rather than imitation). However, it also forces imitators to abandon certain segments. As explained earlier, the very reason that a multinational is induced to leave some segments unserved implies that the gain will be outweighed by the loss. This cautions welfare implications based on the afore-mentioned empirical observations.

Third, our analysis offers an alternative explanation for why stronger IPR enforcement may lead to efficiency loss *ex post*, that is, after a technology has been invented. It is well understood that IPR protection involves a social cost and that this cost arises because IPR protection allows the innovator to charge distortionary monopoly prices. This conventional channel of efficiency loss is removed from the present paper as we assume a perfectly inelastic demand. In this paper, the efficiency loss arises because stronger IPR enforcement reduces the total number of segments served (particularly those served by imitators). More fundamentally, the *ex post* efficiency loss stems from non-rivalry over knowledge: Once a knowledge has been invented, allowing it to be used by copycats in markets not served by its owner will create social gains, and forbidding such imitation constitutes a social loss. In the presence of reputation concerns, weak enforcement allows imitators to exploit such non-rivalry over knowledge; strong enforcement denies such a possibility.

Fourth, strengthened IPR enforcement does not always improve multinationals' *ex ante* incentives to innovate. As a multinational derives *ex ante* incentives from the profits it can earn *ex post*, propositions 5 and 8 imply that better enforcement can have divergent effects on innovation for different types of multinational. Stronger enforcement always encourages the innovation of low-quality products, but it may discourage the innovation of high-quality products when the enforcement has reached a certain level. In this regard, the average quality of the technology transferred to a developing country may be lower, thus representing an *ex ante* efficiency loss from IPR improvement.

Although the foregoing discussion appears to portray rather grim prospects for IPR improvement in the presence of information asymmetry, there is a situation in which stronger IPR enforcement unambiguously enhances M's profits regardless of its type. We have thus far assumed the strength of IPR enforcement to be identical across the two periods. Suppose that we relax this assumption to allow different IPR enforcement strengths in the two periods. More specifically, let γ_t be the strength of IPR enforcement in period $= 1, 2$, with $\gamma_2 \geq \gamma_1$, meaning that any improvement in the first period is also effective in the second. Per condition (11), it is easy to verify that γ_2 has no effect on the first-period behaviour of M or its copycats, and hence is inconsequential to social welfare or M's profit in period 1. Therefore, regardless of the value of γ_2, the effects of γ_1 on first-period social welfare and $M^{h'}s$ profit remain the same as described in propositions 7 and 8. Furthermore, because M's type is fully revealed in the second period in a separating equilibrium, we can apply the same logic as in proposition 1 to conclude that the only effect of an increased γ_2 is an increase in M's second-period profit.

Proposition 9. *In an imitation equilibrium, deferred improvement in IPR enforcement (i.e., increasing γ_2 without changing γ_1) strictly improves the profits of both types of multinationals without affecting the two-period total social surplus.*

As in proposition 7, the social surplus result in proposition 9 ignores the influences of improved profitability on innovation incentives. Should this effect be taken into account, deferred improvement in IPR enforcement can strictly improve social welfare. Together with propositions 7 and 8, proposition 9 offers a possible rationale for deferred IPR improvement in developing countries in which reputation concerns inhibit multinational entry. Because stronger IPR enforcement is most effective in the absence of friction, delaying IPR improvement until after multinationals' strategic entry has helped to overcome information asymmetry can bring unequivocal social gains.

5. Concluding Remarks

In this paper, we demonstrate that because developing countries suffer from many forms of imperfection, multinationals may withhold entry for reasons other than weak IPR enforcement. Such withholding allows copycats to operate, giving rise to IPR violations in equilibrium, a point that is largely ignored in the literature. We show that imitation in the shadow of IPR enforcement can be an alternative channel for technology transfer and that strengthening such enforcement may not be in the best interests of either the host country or multinationals.

In addition to imperfect IPR protection, the particular form of imperfection that we focus on herein is the information asymmetry between foreign multinationals and local consumers concerning the quality of the former's product. In the introduction, we stress the pertinence of this form of imperfection in developing countries. It also allows us to explain why the Pareto gains achieved under moderately weak enforcement cannot be attained under perfect enforcement through a contractual arrangement. It would be useful to investigate the other forms of imperfection that may prevent foreign multinationals from entering a developing country even under perfect enforcement.

Acknowledgement

We are grateful for the helpful comments of Chong-en Bai, Hongbin Cai, Jacques Cremer, Tanjim Houssain, David Levine, Zhigang Tao, Cheng Wang, Yong Wang, Li-An Zhou and the seminar participants at Katholieke Universiteit Leuven, City University of Hong Kong and the Third Asia-Pacific Trade Seminars (Shanghai). The comments and suggestions made by the editor and two anonymous referees have also greatly helped to improve this paper.

Appendix

Proof of proposition 2. We first consider the isoprofit curves. We plot the isoprofit curves of $\Pi^j(\{\kappa_1, \sigma_1\}, \rho_2)$ while fixing $\kappa_1 = 0$ in Figure A.1, where the solid curve corresponds to M^l and the dotted curve corresponds to M^h. When $\rho_2 < \rho^l$, the isoprofit curve of M^l is flat because M^l chooses licensing in the second period, and consumers' belief thus becomes immaterial. The case is similar for M^h when $\rho_2 < p^h$. When $\rho_2 < \rho'$, the isoprofit curve is highest when $\sigma^j = s^j$ because, with ρ_2 fixed, the entry profile that maximizes Π^j is $(0, s^j)$ for $j \in \{h, l\}$. Note that $\rho^h > \rho^l$ and $s^h < s^l$.

When $\rho_2 > \rho'$, M^j adopts direct investment in the second period. Fixing ρ_2 the entry profile that maximizes Π^j is $(0, s^j)$ for $j \in \{h, l\}$, and thus all isoprofit curves of M^j are tangent to ρ_2 at s^j. As the small arrows indicate, with σ_1 fixed, an isoprofit curve to the right corresponds to a larger $\Pi^j(\{0, \sigma_1\}, \rho_2)$, as a higher ρ_2 increases Π^j.

The isoprofit curves in Figure A.1 satisfy the single-crossing property in the shaded area: M^h has an advantage over M^l in paying for a better reputation provided that $\sigma_1 < s^l$. The entry profile $0, s^*$

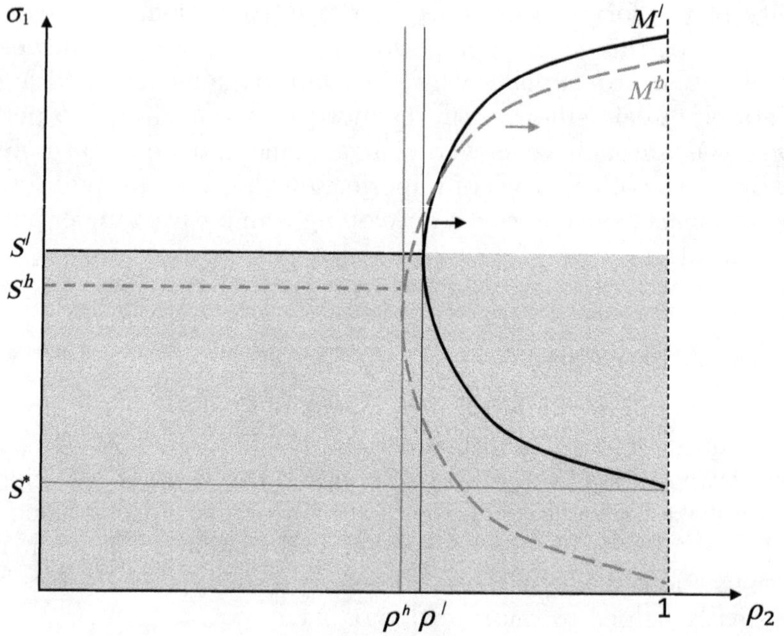

Figure A.1. Isoprofit curves when $\kappa 1 = 0$.

falls within the shaded area when $\rho_2 = 1$, indicating that it is also feasible for M^h to credibly distance itself from M^l. We now prove the proposition formally in three steps.

Step 1. There exists no pooling equilibrium. Suppose that a pooling equilibrium does exist, where both types choose κ_1, σ_1 in the first period. Then, $\rho_2 = \rho_1 \cdot M^l$ is willing to choose the equilibrium entry profile only if doing so dominates being itself, that is:

$$\Pi_1^l(\{\kappa_1, \sigma_1) + \delta \max\{y\pi_k^{\rho 1} - f, y\pi_s^l\} \geq \pi_s^l + \delta \max\{y\pi_k^l - f, y\pi_s^l\}.$$

Given the definition of s^*, the foregoing becomes:

$$\Pi_1^l(\{\kappa_1, \sigma_1\}) + \delta \max\{y\pi_k^{\rho_1} - f, y\pi_s^l\} \geq \Pi_1^l(\{0, s^*\}) + \delta \max\{y\pi_k^h - f, y\pi_s^l\}.$$

Then, there exists an $s' > 0$ such that:

$$\Pi_1^l(\{0, s + \delta \max\{y\pi_k^h - f, y\pi_s^l\} = \Pi_1^l(\{\kappa_1, \sigma_1\}) + \delta \max\{y\pi_k^{\rho 1} - f, y\pi_s^l\}.$$

The last two observations combined yield:

$$\Pi_1^l(\{0, s'\}) \geq \Pi_1^l(\{0, s^*\})$$

Because $\Pi_1^l(\{0, \sigma_1\})$ is concave (and hence quasi-concave) in σ_1 and maximized at $\sigma_1 = s^l$, s' takes two values, one of which falls between s^* and s^l. This s' lies in the region in which the isoprofit curves of M^h and M^l satisfy the single-crossing property, meaning that M^h has an advantage over M^l in paying for a better reputation. In other words, there exists an $\varepsilon > 0$ such that M^l is not interested in choosing $\{0, s' - \varepsilon\}$ regardless of how consumers respond in shaping their subsequent belief:

$$\begin{aligned}\Pi_1^l(\{0, s' - \varepsilon\}) + \delta \max\{y\pi_k^h - f, y\pi_s^l\} < \Pi_1^l(\{\kappa_1, \sigma_1\})\\ +\delta \max\{y\pi_k^{\rho 1} - f, y\pi_s^l\}.\end{aligned}$$

M^h, in contrast, will find such deviation profitable if consumers assign a sufficiently high ρ_2 after observing it. Hence, the pooling equilibrium fails the intuitive criterion test.

Step 2. In a separating equilibrium, M^h chooses no direct investment in the first period (i.e., $\kappa_1^h = 0$). Suppose that M^h does choose some $\{\kappa_1^h, \sigma_1^h\}$ in such an equilibrium. Without loss of generality, consider $s' \in (0, s^l)$ such that:[10]

$$\Pi_1^l(\{0, s'\}) = \Pi_1^l(\{\kappa_1^h, \sigma_1^h\}) \tag{A1}$$

Because direct investment in any segment in the first period is unprofitable, it must be true that:

$$s' < \sigma_1^h. \tag{A2}$$

Now consider a deviation by M^h from $\{\kappa_1^h, \sigma_1^h\}$ to $\{0, s'\}$ in the first period. As s' satisfies (A1), M^l has no incentive to deviate whatever belief consumers would assign following the deviation. However, M^h

[10]If there does not exist an $s' > 0$ such that equation (A1) holds, then it is evident that M^h can profitably deviate from $\{\kappa_1^h, \lambda_1^h\}$ to $\{0, s^*\}$ while keeping its distance from M^l. Given that $s' > 0$ solves equation (A1), as argued in step 1, s' can take two solutions, with one falling below s^l.

can profit from such deviation provided that consumers respond with a large subsequent belief, ρ_2. To see this, note that:

$$\Pi_1^l(\{0,s\}) - \Pi_1^h(\{0,s'\}) = s'(c^h - c^l),$$

whereas:

$$\Pi_1^l(\{\kappa_1^h, \sigma_1^h\}) - \Pi_1^h(\{\kappa_1^h, \sigma_1^h\}) = \sigma_1^h(c^h - c^l).$$

Following (A2) and holding $c^h > c^l$, we have:

$$\Pi_1^l(\{0,s'\}) - \Pi_1^h(\{0,s'\}) < \Pi_1^l(\{\kappa_1^h, \sigma_1^h\}) - \Pi_1^h(\{\kappa_1^h, \sigma_1^h\})$$

which in turn implies (given (A1)):

$$\Pi_1^h(\{0,s'\}) > \Pi_1^h(\{\kappa_1^h, \sigma_1^h\})$$

meaning that M^h can profit from a deviation to $\{0, s'\}$

Step 3. In a separating equilibrium, M^l licences in s^l segments in the first period, and M^h licences in $\min\{s^*, s^h\}$ segments. In such an equilibrium, as its type will be fully revealed in the second period, M^l chooses s^l as in the benchmark case. Given $M^{l'}s$ choice, M^h maximizes its own payoff without inducing any mimicking from M^l by choosing $a_1^h = s^*$ if $s^* < s^h$, and $\sigma_1^h = s^h$ if $s^h \geq s^*$.

References

Aghion, P., N. Bloom, R. Blundell, R. Griffith and P. Howitt (2005) "Competition and innovation: An inverted-U relationship." *Quarterly Journal of Economics* 120, 701–28.

Aghion, P., C. Harris, P Howitt and J. Vickers (2001) "Competition, imitation and growth with step-by-step innovation." *Review of Economic Studies* 68, 467–92.

Bessen, J. and E. Maskin (2009) "Sequential innovation, patents, and imitation." *Rand Journal of Economics* 40, 611–35.

Branstetter, L., R. Fisman and C. Γ. Foley (2006) "Do stronger intellectual property rights increase international technology transfer? Empirical evidence from U.S. firm-level panel data." *Quarterly Journal of Economics* 484, 321–49.

Branstetter, L., R. Fisman, C. Γ. Foley and K. Saggi (2011) "Does intellectual property rights reform spur industrial development?" *Journal of International Economics* 83, 27–36.

Branstetter, L. and K. Saggi (2011) "Intellectual property rights, foreign direct investment, and industrial development." *The Economic Journal* 121, 1161–91.

Che, J., L. Qiu and W. Zhou (2012) "Entry, reputation, and intellectual property rights enforcement." Working paper.
Cho, I. and D. M. Kreps (1987) "Signaling games and stable equilibria." *The Quarterly Journal of Economics* 102, 179–221.
Dinopoulos, E. and P. Segerstrom (2010) "Intellectual property rights, multinational firms and economic growth." *Journal of Development Economics* 92, 13–27.
The Economist (2004) (Still) made in Japan April 7, 2004, print edition, Ethier, W.J., and J. R. Markusen (1996) "Multinational firms, technology diffusion and trade." *Journal of International Economics* 41, 1–28.
Glass, A.J. and K. Saggi (2002) "Intellectual property rights and foreign direct investment." *Journal of International Economics* 56, 387–410.
Glass, A.J. and X. Wu (2007) "Intellectual property rights and quality improvement." *Journal of Development Economics* 82, 393–415.
Grossman, G.M. and E. Helpman (1991) "Quality ladders and product cycles." *The Quarterly Journal of Economics* 106, 557–86.
Gustafsson, P. and P. S. Segerstrom (2011) "North-South trade with multinational firms and increasing product variety." *International Economic Review* 52, 1123–55.
Helpman, E. (1993) "Innovation, imitation and intellectual property rights." *Econometrica* 61, 1247–80.
Ivus, O. (2010) "Do stronger patent rights raise high-tech exports to the developing world." *Journal of International Economics* 81, 38–47.
Lai, E.L.C. (1998) "International intellectual property rights protection and the rate of product innovation." *Journal of Development Economics* 55, 133–53.
Maskus, K.E. and M. Penubarti (1995) "How trade-related are intellectual property rights." *Journal of International Economics* 39, 227A8.
McKinsey and Company (2011) "Understanding China's growing love for luxury." *McKinsey Consumer and Shopper Insights.*
Scherer, Γ. (1967) "Market structure and the employment of scientists and engineers." *American Economic Review* 57, 524–31.
Segerstrom, P.S., T. C. A. Anant and E. Dinopoulos (1990) "A Schumpeterian model of the product life cycle." *American Economic Review* 80, 1077–91.
Smith, P.J. (2001) "How do foreign patent rights affect U.S. exports, affiliate sales, and licenses?" *Journal of International Economics* 55, 411–39.
Spence, M. (1973) "Job market signaling." *The Quarterly Journal of Economics* 87, 355–74.
Yang, G. and K. E. Maskus (2001) "Intellectual property rights, licensing, and innovation in an endogenous product-cycle model." *Journal of International Economics* 53, 169–87.
Yang, *L.* and K. E. Maskus (2009) "Intellectual property rights, technology transfer and exports in developing countries." *Journal of Development Economics* 90, 231–36.

Chapter 5

Does the Protection of Foreign Intellectual Property Rights Stimulate Innovation in the US?*

Abstract

Although standard theories suggest that patent protection helps stimulate innovative activities, some new theories argue the opposite. Empirical studies do not generate conclusive results either. This paper investigates empirically the impacts of foreign patent reforms on innovation in the US, using data on successful patent applications in the US over 33 years and major IPR reforms in 21 countries, in addition to the patent reforms in the US and the TRIPS Agreement of the WTO. We find that the TRIPS Agreement has had significant impacts on innovation in the US, which highlights the importance of international cooperation in patent protection. However, the effects of strengthening patent protection by individual countries are not statistically significant. This result seems to imply that the US market is already sufficiently large/profitable to provide innovation incentives in the US and therefore further strengthening foreign patent protection simply increases the US innovators' rent, but not their innovation.

1. Introduction

There is no disagreement on the importance of innovation for economic growth. Since the 1980s, many countries have strengthened

*This chapter is reproduced from *Review of International Economics*, 18(5), 882–895, 2010, with permission from Wiley.

their intellectual property rights (IPR) protection in order to stimulate innovation.[1] Standard theories predict that IPR protection stimulates innovation because protection raises incentives to create innovations by enabling innovators to reap the benefits of innovation (through monopoly profits) and recoup the costs of research and development (R&D) investments. However, some recent studies argue the opposite.[2] Naturally, the heated IPR-innovation debate has largely shifted its focus to empirical investigations. Unfortunately, the actual (empirical) effects of IPR protection on innovation have been found to be also inconclusive. After surveying the empirical literature, Jaffe (1999) makes a disquieting conclusion that there is little empirical evidence to support the widely accepted theory that strengthening IPR protection has a significant impact on innovation.[3] Granstrand (2005) echoes Jaffe's concern in a more recent survey of the literature. Researchers continue to search for evidence and answers with regard to the efficacy of IPR protection on innovation.

In this study, we analyze the effect of strengthening foreign countries' IPR protection on innovation in the United States. In theory,[4] increased IPR protection in other countries should spur

[1]IPR includes patent rights, copyrights, trade secrets, and others. However, in this paper the most relevant part of IPR is patent rights and hence we use the two terms, IPR protection and patent protection, interchangeably.

[2]See Jaffe and Lerner (2004) and Bessen and Maskin (2009) for examples. These studies argue that patents may be counterproductive because they incur additional application costs, discourage attempts to invent around patents, and delay spillover to sequential innovations.

[3]Hall and Ziedonis (2001) also draw the same conclusion with regard to R&D investment when innovation is cumulative; as they put it, "there remains little systematic evidence on how a shift toward stronger patent rights affects the innovative activities of firms in the context of rapidly changing, cumulative technologies Sakakibara and Branstetter (2001) find that the Japanese response (in innovation) to the 1988 patent reform in Japan was very small. However, Evenson and Kanwar (2001) and Chen and Puttitanum (2005) find some positive effects of strengthening IPR protection on innovation.

[4]In a closed economy, a country's optimal patent protection should balance the tradeoff between the *ex ante* incentives to pursue research that patent protection offers and the monopolies created by patent protection. In an open economy, the incentive-monopoly tradeoff extends to international markets. Lai and Oiu (2003) and Grossman and Lai (2004) provide a theoretical analysis of the optimal length of patent protection in an open economy.

innovation in the US because it enables US innovators to reap more profits from foreign markets, via export or foreign direct investment (FDI). However, there is no systematic empirical analysis to confirm such a link. To make a contribution to this literature, we examine US patents over 33 years (from 1967 to 1999) and find that strengthening IPR protections in individual or a small group of countries has no significant impact on US innovations, but the Trade-Related Aspects of Intellectual Property Rights (TRIPS) Agreement, which is a collective action by a large group of countries, does have a positive and significant effect on innovation in the US.

Although the above issue, to be analyzed in this study, has not been examined in the literature, there exist some studies on foreign IPR protection. Mansfield's (1994) survey evidence reveals that US multinational firms are more likely to locate research facilities in a country that has strong IPR protection. Similar effects on technology transfer and FDI are also found in some recent studies.[5] Based on a small sample and interviews in India, Lanjouw (1998) and Lanjouw and Cockburn (2000) argue that less-developed countries' (LDC) patent protections on drugs may induce more research throughout the world on treatments for diseases that are prevalent in the developing world. However, it is unlikely that a particular country's (like India's) patent reforms can substantially increase innovators' profits. This latter view is consistent with the main findings in the present study that uses cross-country and cross-industry data.

Many earlier studies in the industrial organization literature focus on understanding the impacts of a single patent policy reform on innovation.[6] Some studies in the international trade literature consider comprehensive IPR reforms in a number of countries, but focus on the IPR effects on trade and FDI, not innovation.[7] In contrast, Lerner (2002) examines the impacts on innovation by

---

[5]It is found that a host country's stronger IPR protection encourages technology transfer from the US to that country (Branstetter et al., 2005) and attracts US FDI in that country (Branstetter et al., 2007).

[6]Examples include Sakakibara and Branstetter (2001) on the broadening of the Japanese patent scope, Kortum and Lerner (1998) and Hall and Ziedonis (2001) on the establishment of the Court of Appeals for the Federal Circuit in the US, and Lanjouw (1998) on the strengthening of patent protection of pharmaceuticals in India.

177 IPR policy changes across 60 countries and over a 150-year period. He finds that strengthening patent protection has few positive effects on patent applications by entities in the country undertaking the policy change. However, foreign patent applications in countries undertaking policy changes increase. As a complement to Lerner's (2002) study, this paper uses cross-country time-series data to examine the effects of foreign IPR reforms on innovation in the US. Since the 1980s, IPR protection has been in the forefront of international trade negotiations. Developed countries, led by the US, exert great pressure on developing countries to adopt more stringent standards in protecting IPR.[8] The signing of the World Trade Organization's (WTO's) TRIPS Agreement in 1994 was a result of such pressure. One of the most important features of the TRIPS Agreement was a substantial increase in IPR protection in developing countries, although developed countries were also required to make adjustments in their IPR laws. For example, all countries were required to protect their patents for at least 20 years. Our finding, mentioned earlier, does not lend support to the US complaints that inadequate IPR protection in developing countries reduces innovation incentives in the US. It probably implies that the patent-protected US market is sufficiently large for innovators to recoup the costs of R&D investments and further strengthening IPR protection by individual foreign countries merely adds pure rent to the proceeds that US innovators earn. This hypothesis has an indirect support from McCalman's (2001) estimation that the TRIPS Agreement adds billions of dollars to the US patent holders.[9]

[7]See the literature review by Maskus (2000) and the recent study by Branstetter *et al.* (2007) on FDI.

[8]As early as in the 1980*s*, the US pushed to move IPR issues from the framework of WIPO, which was seen by the US as too weak and narrowly focused, into the Uruguay Round of multilateral trade negotiations of the General Agreement on Tariffs and Trade during 1986 and 1994.

[9]McCalman (2001) estimates that enforcement of the TRIPS Agreement will benefit the US with a net increase in the present value of patent rights of $4.5 billion (1988 dollars) on the patents applied for in 1988 and developing countries make contribution to this by transferring the rent to the US patent holders. The benefits of any increase in innovation in response to the TRIPS Agreement have not been included.

In searching for the sources of innovation in the US, we focus on economic factors (GDP), innovative capabilities (education expenditure), and IPR policies (domestic and foreign). In addition to the TRIPS Agreement, we find that the US GDP and the country's spending on higher education have significant and positive effects on the number of patent applications that are awarded by the United States Patent and Trademark Office (USPTO). According to Jaffe (1999), among the major changes in patent policy and practices that occurred in the 1980*s* and 1990*s* in the US, the most important policy change is the creation of the Court of Appeals for the Federal Circuit (CAFC) in 1982.[10] However, we do not find a significant effect of this policy shift on US innovations. This observation is consistent with that of Kortum and Lerner (1998, 2003), but in contrast to some others (e.g. Hall and Ziedonis, 2001, who find that the policy change causes an otherwise perplexing surge in US patenting rates, at least in the semiconductor industry).

The rest of the paper is organized as follows. The regression model and data are discussed in section 2. The empirical findings are presented and discussed in Section 3. In Section 4, we conduct robustness checks of our results. Concluding remarks are given in Section 5.

2. Empirical Design and Data

The objective of this study is to explore the effects of strengthening foreign IPR protection on innovation in the US. We should first determine how to measure innovation and what factors may affect innovation.

There are two ways to measure technological innovation: the output and the input. Although there is no perfect measurement of innovation input and output, it is common to use the number of patent applications within a certain period of time to capture innovation output, and to use the R&D expenditures within a certain

[10]The establishment of the CAFC is widely believed to have had a profound impact on the substantive outcomes of patent litigation. According to Granstrand (2005), the new court changes the validity of litigated patents from 30% to 89%.

period of time to indicate innovation input. Since we have industry-level patent data, but only economy-wide R&D data, in this study we will use patents to capture innovation in the US. Specifically, we use the successful number of patent applications in the US in each year to measure the innovation output in the US. Every year, thousands of patent applications are submitted to the USPTO and, on average, about 60% of them are eventually awarded for patent protection. We call these successful patent applications. Patent application in the US started to surge in the mid-1980s. US inventors filed 149,825 applications in 1999, while in 1984 there were only 61,841 applications filed. The USPTO awarded US inventors 85,072 patents in 2000, while only 38,367 patents were awarded in 1984 (Kim and Marschke, 2004). Detailed patent data can be downloaded from Bronwyn H. Hall's website http://emlab.berkeley.edu/*users*/bhhall. This dataset consists of information about almost 3.4 million US patents granted by the USPTO between 1963 and 2002. However, in this study we use the data between 1967 and 1999 because data for some explanatory variables beyond this period are not available.

Following Hall *et al.* (2002), we decompose the patented inventions into six technological categories: Chemical; Computers and Communications; Drugs and Medical; Electrical and Electronics; Mechanical; and Others.[11]

[11]The classification of these industries is (1) *Chemical*, which includes Agriculture, Food, Textiles; Coating; Gas; Organic Compounds; Resins; Miscellaneous-Chemical; (2) *Computers and Communications*, which includes Communications; Computer Hardware & Software; Computer Peripherals; Information Storage; (3) *Drugs and Medical*, which includes Drugs; Surgery & Medical Instruments; Biotechnology; Miscellaneous-Drug & Med.; (4) *Electrical and Electronics*, which includes Electrical Devices; Electrical Lighting; Measuring & Testing; Nuclear & X-rays; Power Systems; Semiconductor Devices; Miscellaneous-Elec.; (5) *Mechanical*, which includes Materials Processing & Handling; Metal Working; Motors, Engines & Parts; Optics; Transportation; Miscellaneous-Mechanical; and (6) *Others*, which includes Agriculture, Husbandry, Food; Amusement Devices; Apparel & Textile; Earth Working & Wells; Furniture, House Fixtures; Heating; Pipes & Joints; Receptacles; Miscellaneous-Others. Note that "Agriculture" appears in both industry 1 and industry 6, but it refers to different items (e.g. fertilizers (patent code 071 and plant protecting and regulating compositions (054) belong to industry 1's agriculture group while harvesters (056), planting (111) and crop threshing or separating (460) belong to industry 6's agriculture group.

Table 5.1. Patent distribution in the US, 1967–99.

Industry	Mean	Std. dev.	Min.	Max.
1. Chemical	8816	1164	7122	12,149
2. Computers and Communications	5510	5184	1928	20,062
3. Drugs and Medical	3675	3201	762	11,776
4. Electrical and Electronics	7240	2567	5023	13,563
5. Mechanical	7413	1388	5095	9929
6. Others	6964	1303	5193	10,092

Existing studies in the literature choose different sets of control variables to explain innovation activities. They include GDP, per capita GDP, domestic savings, human capital openness to trade and FDI, the political environment, and the extent of patent protection. Given the specific focus of our study and the data limitations, we choose some of those variables and introduce some new variables in our regression model given below:

$$\ln Y_{it} = \alpha_0 + \alpha_1 \ln GDP_{t-1} + \alpha_2 EDU_{t-1} + \sum_{i=1}^{5} \beta_i IND_i + \sum_{j=1}^{10} \theta_j IPR_j + \theta_0 TRIP + \theta_{US} IPR_{US} + \varepsilon_{it}.$$

where t indicates time, i represents the industry, a, β, and θ are parameters to be estimated, and ε is the disturbance term. The left-hand-side variable, Y_{it}, is the number of patent applications filed by US non-government organizations in industry i and eventually awarded by the US patent office in year t. Table 5.1 shows the minimum number, maximum number, and average number of successful patent applications per year in each of the six industries from 1967 to 1999. There are large variations over time, within the same industry and across industries.

On the right-hand side of the regression, GDP_{t-1} is the real US GDP in year $t-1$ measured in 1996 dollars.[12] A country's total

[12]The GDP data are obtained from the website of the United States Bureau of Economic Analysis (http://www.bea.gov/bea/dn/home/gdp.htm).

innovation is influenced by the size of the economy (total GDP) and the quality of the economy (GDP per capita), as suggested by Stern *et al.* (2000) who use the latter to represent the national knowledge stock. We use total GDP as one of the explanatory variables in our main regression model and let the education variable (discussed below) partially reflect the quality of the economy. Note that we replace total GDP with GDP per capita in the next section for robustness checks, and we find that the main results of this study do not change. Also note that we use the previous year's GDP rather than concurrent GDP data, because innovation and patent awards take time.[13]

Education level, especially tertiary education, is one of the most relevant measures of human capital to affect technological innovation. Following Stern *et al.* (2000), we capture education investment, denoted as EDU_{t-1}, using the share of total expenditures for all colleges and universities in GDP in year $t-1$ in the US.[14] Over the entire period (1967–99), the mean value of this variable is 2.6567 (percent) and the standard deviation is 0.1490. The variable takes the value 2.4712 for 1967, which is close to the lowest level (2.4097), and 2.8969 for 1999, which is the highest level.

As Table 5.1 indicates, innovation varies across industries. Innovators' responses to GDP and other control variables may also be different across industries. To allow for such differences, we include industry dummies $INDj$. Since there are totally six industry groups, we need only five dummies.

Recall that the main objective of our study is to investigate the impacts of strengthening IPR protection in other countries on innovation in the US. Therefore, we need to identify major IPR reforms in foreign countries. According to Branstetter et al. (2007), from 1982 to 1999, there were 16 country-level major IPR reforms in the world (excluding the US).[15] Based on Ginarte and Park's (1997)

[13]Generally speaking, it takes a long time for an application to be approved: the percentage of granted patents issued two years after application is about 85%, and the percentage for three years is about 95%. However, we have tested the model using GDP of year $t-2$ and year $t-3$, respectively, and found no qualitative changes in the results.

[14]The information is obtained from the website of the United States National Center for Education Statistics (http://nces.ed.gov/).

Table 5.2. Major IPR reforms in foreign countries.

Reforming years	Countries/Regions	IPR dummies
1977	France, Germany, the Netherlands, Switzerland	$IPR77$
1978	Sweden	$IPR78$
1986	Taiwan, Spain	$IPR86$
1987	Japan, South Korea	$IPR87$
1991	Mexico, Chile, Indonesia	$IPR91$
1992	Thailand, Portugal	$IPR92$
1993	China	$IPR93$
1994	Venezuela, Colombia	$IPR94$
1995	Turkey	$IPR95$
1996	Argentina	$IPR96$
1997	Brazil, the Philippines	$IPR97$

patent rights index, we also identify the major IPR reforms between 1967 and 1981. Table 5.2 is a list of those reforms. Our IPR dummy variables are constructed based on Table 5.2, where IPR_j is a dummy variable that takes the value of before a particular year, j, and equals unity from that year onward. For example, we set $IPR_{77} = 0$ for all the years before 1977 and $IPR_{77} = 1$ from 1977 onward, which corresponds to the year when four European countries enacted IPR reforms.

We first explain how we identify the major IPR reforms during the 1967–81 period, based on Ginarte and Park's (1997) patent rights index. The index is used to represent the degree of patent protection quinquennially (i.e. the time distance between two consecutive indices is five years). It is constructed for 110 countries from 1960 to 1990, based on five categories of each country's patent law: (1) extent of coverage, (2) membership in international patent agreements, (3) provisions for loss of protection, (4) enforcement mechanisms, and (5) duration of protection. Each category is scored a value in the range of [0, 1] and the index is the sum of these five values. A higher index represents a stronger protection level. To identify

[15]This information comes from Ginarte and Park (1997), Maskus (2000), and Oian (2007).

major IPR reforms, we choose the following criterion: a country has a major IPR reform if its Ginarte-Park patent rights index increases by no less than 0.5 between two consecutive (five-year) periods. When an IPR reform is identified, we treat the middle year of the five-year reforming period as the year of the corresponding reform. Based on this criterion, seven countries stand out: Denmark, Finland, France, Germany, the Netherlands, Sweden, and Switzerland. They are all European countries and their indices jump in the 1975–1980 period, with 1977 being the middle year. This observation is consistent with these countries' (except for Denmark and Finland's) participation in the European Patent Convention.[16] The Convention was signed by many countries in Munich in 1973. Germany, France, the Netherlands, and Switzerland all began to enforce the Convention in 1977 while Sweden did so in 1978. Therefore, we choose these years as their IPR reforming years. Some other countries, such as Belgium, Luxembourg, and the United Kingdom, also participated in the Convention in 1977, but since their indices did not jump over the 0.5 bar, they are not included in our IPR Dummies.[17]

The TRIPS Agreement was signed in 1994 and came into force on 1 January 1995. We use the dummy *TRIPS* to capture the effects of the Agreement on US innovations. Specifically, let $TRIPS = 0$ for all the years before 1995 and $TRIPS = 1$ from 1995 onward. Since Turkey's own IPR reform also took place in 1995, we drop IPR_{95}

The US set up the CAFC in 1982, which broadens the rights of patent holders and has been considered as the cornerstone of IPR policy shift in the past 20-plus years. Accordingly, we introduce the dummy variable IPR_{US}, which is equal to for all the year before 1982, and 1 for all the years from 1982 onward.[18]

[16]Branstetter *et al.* (2005) also include this dummy in their study.

[17]Denmark joined the Convention in 1990 and Finland joined in 1996. The year of their indices jumping and that of their participation in the Convention do not match. In any case, their markets for the US exports and FDI were much smaller than the above-mentioned countries. For that reason, we do not include these two countries in the IPR dummies. For the same reason, Branstetter *et al.* (2005) do not include these two countries in their study either.

[18]Branstetter *et al.* (2005) also include this dummy in their study.

3. Analysis and Results

With 31 years and six industry groups, the number of observations of the left-hand-side variable in our regression model is 186. Table 5.3 reports the preliminary OLS results derived based on our main model introduced in the preceding section. Note that except for a few industry dummies, none of the explanatory variables is significant. The two IPR dummies that have lower *p*-values are *TRIPS* (0.300) and IPR_{87} (0.312). Other *IPRj*, including IPR_{US}, have very high *p*-values. While IPR reforms in one or a few countries may not have significant impacts on US innovations, their joint impacts might be significant. To test this, we conduct the *F*-test on the 10 IPR dummies (excluding *TRIPS* and IPR_{US}). We obtain $F(10, 166) = 0.60$ and $\text{Prob} > F = 0.8103$. Thus, the 10 IPR dummies are not jointly significant.

Table 5.3. Preliminary regression results.

Independent variable	Coefficient	Standard error	*t*-Statistics	*p*-Value
GDP	0.262	0.541	0.48	0.629
EDU	0.197	0.594	0.33	0.741
*IND*1	0.248	0.081	3.07	0.002
*IND*2	−0.474	0.081	−5.88	0.000
*IND*3	−0.873	0.081	10.82	0.000
*IND*4	0.018	0.081	0.22	0.826
*IND*5	0.055	0.081	0.69	0.493
IPR_{77}	−0.050	0.155	−0.33	0.745
IPR_{78}	−0.013	0.180	−0.07	0.942
IPR_{86}	0.046	0.155	0.29	0.768
IPR_{87}	0.163	0.161	1.01	0.312
IPR_{91}	0.093	0.165	0.56	0.574
IPR_{92}	0.073	0.185	0.39	0.694
IPR_{93}	0.057	0.184	0.31	0.758
IPR_{94}	0.126	0.184	0.68	0.497
IPR_{96}	−0.067	0.184	−0.37	0.715
IPR_{97}	0.079	0.158	0.50	0.618
TRIPS	0.192	0.184	1.04	0.300
IPR_{US}	−0.004	0.100	−0.04	0.966
Constant	5.906	4.096	1.44	0.151
R-squared	0.750			

Table 5.4. Revised regression results.

	Independent variable	Coefficient	Standard error	*t*-Statistics	*p*-Value
Model 1	GDP	0.367	0.256	1.44	0.153
	EDU	0.788	0.315	2.50	0.013
	*IPR*87	0.138	0.123	1.12	0.262
	TRIPS	0.365	0.092	3.97	0.000
	*IPR*US	−0.043	0.092	−0.47	0.641
	Constant	3.496	2.341	1.49	0.137
	R-squared	0.743			
Model 2	GDP	0.286	0.188	1.52	0.129
	EDU	0.795	0.314	2.53	0.012
	TRIPS	0.380	0.086	4.41	0.000
	*IPR*US	0.138	0.122	1.13	0.261
	Constant	4.146	1.878	2.21	0.029
	R-squared	0.742			
Model 3	GDP	0.517	0.218	2.37	0.019
	EDU	1.021	0.238	4.30	0.000
	TRIPS	0.338	0.089	3.80	0.000
	*IPR*US	−0.043	0.093	−0.47	0.642
	Constant	1.657	1.676	0.99	0.324
	R-squared	0.741			
Model 4	GDP	0.436	0.133	3.29	0.001
	EDU	1.028	0.237	4.34	0.000
	TRIPS	0.353	0.083	4.26	0.000
	Constant	2.306	0.930	2.48	0.014
	R-squared	0.740			

Since the IPR dummies are not jointly significant, following the approach taken by Evenson and Kanwar (2001), we delete the high *p*-value IPR dummies from the main model and re-run the regression. In fact, we do this through a few steps. We run various regression models and report their results in Table 5.4. Note that cross-industry patenting is not our focus and there is no change to the sign and significance of each industry dummy in all the regressions in this study. Hence, to save space, we do not report the estimates of the industry dummies any more.

In Model 1, we keep IPR_{US} because of its particular interest. The new regression does not improve the significance of IPR_{87} by very much. Although the *p*-value of IPR_{US} is reduced, the 1982 US IPR reform is still not significant. However, three other variables, P_{t-1} EDU_{t-1}, and *TRIPS*, are statistically significant.

In Model 2, we further delete IPR_{US}, but there is no change to the significance of the 1987 IPR reforms in Japan and Korea. In Model 3, we delete IPR_{87} but add IPR_{US} back to the regression. The 1982 US IPR reform remains an insignificant factor for US innovations. In both Models 2 and 3, the three common factors, namely GDP education, and the TRIPS Agreement, are significant. Based on the results from these two models, we drop both IPR_{US} and IPR_{87} to get Model 4. In Model 4, all remaining variables have significant impacts on innovation in the US.

3.1. *Summary*

Both the US GDP and investment in education have positive effects on innovation in the US. A 10% increase in GDP leads to a 4.36% increase in successful patent applications, while a 10% increase in the share of higher education expenditure in GDP increases successful patent applications by 10%. Strengthening an individual country's IPR protection does not help to stimulate innovation in the US. A series of individual countries' IPR reforms, which spread over a long period of time, do not affect the successful patent applications in the US either. However, the TRIPS Agreement does have a significant positive effect on innovation in the US. In contrast to a series of IPR reforms, the TRIPS Agreement involves all countries and occurs in the same year (although it took a few years for developing countries to completely enforce the Agreement). This finding underscores the importance of international agreements. We also find that the US IPR reform in 1982 did not significantly affect successful patent applications in the US. This finding is consistent with some of the studies in the literature (see Jaffe, 1999).

4. Robustness Examination

In this section, we analyze several possibilities that might undermine or overturn the results obtained in the preceding section. Nonetheless, these robustness checks confirm our conclusions stated above.

4.1. *Elimination*

Recall that before deleting some IPR dummies from the main model, none of the IPR variables, the GDP variable, or the education variable shows statistically significant influences on the successful patent applications in the US. Instead of removing those high p-valued IPR dummies from the main model, should we drop the GDP and/or education variables? To answer this question, we conduct the following experiments. First, by deleting EDU only, the p-value of the GDP variable reduces from 0.629 (see Table 5.3) to 0.464, that of IPR_{87} reduces from 0.312 to 0.245, that of $TRIPS$ increases from 0.300 to 0.329, while all other IPR dummies retain high p-values. That is, none of remaining factors becomes statistically significant. Second, by deleting both the GDP and education variables from the main model, the p-values of IPR_{87} and $TRIPS$ change to 0.165 and 0.292, respectively, while all other IPR dummies have quite high p-values. That is, none of the remaining variables becomes statistically significant explanatory variables for innovation in the US. Third, if we delete GDP from the main model, the p-values of EDU, IPR_{87}, and $TRIPS$ are 0.59, 0.282, and 0.271, respectively. Further deleting other high p-value IPR variables does not help us to find any significant explanatory variables. Therefore, the approach adopted in the preceding section for Model 4 seems to be the only option to identify the factors that have statistically significant effects on innovation in the US.

4.2. *GDP per capita*

As shown earlier, a country's total innovation is affected by the size of the economy (total GDP), but it could also be influenced by the richness of the country (GDP per capita). To examine the latter effect, we replace the total GDP in the main model with per capita GDP denoted as $PGDP$.[19] The regression results do not change: when we include all variables on the right-hand side of the main model, none of them (except a few industry dummies as before) is statistically significant; when we drop some IPR dummies with high

[19]For a given country, GDP and GDP per capita are highly correlated. Thus, we should not include both variables in the same regression.

Table 5.5. GDP per capita.

Independent variable	Coefficient	Standard error	t-Statistics	p-Value
PGDP	0.543	0.380	1.43	0.154
EDU	0.819	0.318	2.58	0.011
IPR_{87}	0.126	0.128	0.98	0.327
TRIPS	0.372	0.090	4.14	0.000
IPR_{US}	−0.036	0.089	−0.40	0.687
R-squared	0.743			
PGDP	0.757	0.312	2.43	0.016
EDU	1.030	0.235	4.38	0.000
TRIPS	0.348	0.086	4.03	0.000
IPR_{US}	−0.038	0.089	−0.42	0.674
R-squared	0.741			

p-values, we obtain the upper part of Table 5.5, which indicates that IPR_{87} and IPR_{US} are not significant either; when we further delete IPR_{87} from the model, we obtain the lower part of Table 5.5. Thus, *PGDP*, *EDU*, and *TRIPS* are statistically significant, but other IPR dummies are not.

4.3. *Time lag*

In the main regression model, we set the dummy variables of various countries' IPR reforms according to the years when their IPR regimes were changed. However, it could take a few years for US innovations to respond to changes in those IPR systems.[20] To see whether our results are sensitive to the choice of timing the IPR dummies, we modify the main regression model by taking a lag of two years for the IPR dummy variables. For example, we let $IPR_{86} = 0$ for all the years before 1988 and $IPR_{86} = 1$ from 1988 onward, which corresponds to the IPR reforms of Taiwan and Spain in 1986. The dummies IPR_{US} and *TRIPS* are also amended accordingly.[21] We delete high p-value

[20] In fact, it also takes some time for the policy-changing countries to fully implement their IPR reforms.

[21] This is particularly true for TRIPS as the Agreement allows some developing countries to fully amend their IPR laws a few years after 1995.

Table 5.6. Two-year lags.

Independent variable	Coefficient	Standard error	*t*-Statistics	*p*-Value
GDP	0.251	0.175	1.43	0.155
EDU	0.673	0.333	2.02	0.045
*IPR*86	0.197	0.126	1.56	0.120
*IPR*93	0.342	0.108	3.17	0.002
TRIPS	0.058	0.118	0.49	0.624
R-squared	0.744			
GDP	0.262	0.174	1.51	0.133
EDU	0.666	0.332	2.00	0.047
*IPR*86	0.194	0.125	1.55	0.124
*IPR*93	0.375	0.084	4.48	0.000
R-squared	0.744			

IPR dummies (but still keep TRIPS for its particular importance) and report the regression results in the upper part of Table 5.6. Note that the *p*-value of IPR_{86} is quite small, which closely corresponds to IPR_{87} in the main model for IPR reforms in Japan and Korea. We further delete the high *p*-value *TRIPS* and report the new regression results in the lower part of Table 5.6.

Why does IPR_{93} become statistically significant, when the *TRIPS* does not? Note that when using the two-year lag, IPR_{93} represents China's IPR reform. The year 1995 corresponds to the TRIPS Agreement if the US innovations are affected immediately by foreign IPR reforms, but it corresponds to China's IPR reform if IPR reforms have a two-year lag. Therefore, the above analyses, as summarized in Tables 5.4 and 5.6, suggest two possible explanations: (1) if foreign IPR reforms have immediate impacts on the successful patent applications in the US, then the TRIPS Agreement has significant impacts on innovation in the US (Table 5.4); (2) if there is a two-year lag before foreign IPR reforms affect innovation in the US, then it is China's IPR reform, not the TRIPS Agreement, that has significant impacts on innovation in the US (Table 5.6). How do we know which explanation is more plausible? It is reasonable to assume that although China had its IPR reforms stipulated in its law, the implementation of these reforms was still very weak even up to today. As pointed out by Branstetter *et al.* (2007), foreign managers still regard China as an insecure place as far as IPR is concerned. This casts doubt on the China-effect explanation. But then, if the TRIPS-effect explanation holds, why does innovation not take time to respond to policy changes? It does, perhaps. Although the TRIPS Agreement was signed in 1995, it had been negotiated for several years before 1995. Hence, people might have well anticipated the establishment of the WTO and introduction of the TRIPS Agreement.[22]

4.4. *Time trend*

There may exist some time-related factors that affect innovation in the US. For example, past cumulative innovation helps future innovation. We can include a time trend to capture the unobservable time-related explanatory variables (other than *GDP* or). In particular, we add a time variable $T (T = 1, 2, ..., 33$, for 33 years) to the right-hand side of the main regression model. We conduct the same analysis as before by first running the regression including all IPR dummies and then deleting some high p-value IPR dummies and re-running the regression. The final results are reported in Table 5.7. The p-value for T is high (0.310). Thus, there is no other unobservable time trend that significantly affects US innovations. Moreover, including the time trend does not affect the results obtained in Section 3.

4.5. *Export and FDI*

A country's IPR protection may be important for innovation in the US because it leads to higher incentives for innovation creation by US inventors by allowing them to reap more profits from that country's

[22]In order to further "test" the TRIPS-effect story, let us perform another analysis: assume that there is a one-year lag for the IPR reforms to impact innovations in the US. For example, let $IPR_{86} = 0$ for all the years before 1987, and $IPR_{86} = 1$ from 1987 onward. Other IPR variables are defined similarly. As a result, the only IPR dummy that has significant explanatory power is IPR_{94}. The year 1994 corresponds to IPR reforms in Venezuela and Colombia. However, we can hardly argue that these two countries' IPR reforms have more significant effects on innovations in the US than other countries, such as Japan, Korea, and Mexico. Therefore, it is more plausible that it is the TRIPS Agreement that spurs innovation in the US.

Table 5.7. Time trend.

Independent variable	Coefficient	Standard error	t-Statistics	p-Value
T	−0.035	0.035	−1.02	0.310
GDP	1.576	1.127	1.40	0.164
EDU	1.088	0.244	4.46	0.000
$TRIPS$	0.353	0.083	4.27	0.000
R-*squared*	0.742			

market. There are two channels through which US inventors can earn profits from foreign markets: exporting and FDI. Therefore, the total value of US exports to and FDI in a foreign country at least partially capture the extent of the importance of that country's IPR protection to innovation in the US. To capture this idea, we replace the IPR dummies in the main model with $IPR_j * \ln EX_{jt}$, where EX_{jt} is the total value of US exports to and FDI in country j in year t (or a group of countries j when there is more than one country undertaking IPR reforms in the same year, referring to Table 5.2), measured in millions of 1996 dollars. For example, in IPR_{87}, 87 represents Japan and Korea together and so EX_{87t} is the sum of the US exports to and FDI in Japan and Korea in year t. However, in $TRIPS * \ln EX_{TRIPSt}$, we use one-half of total US exports and outward FDI in the calculation. This is because not all countries in the world participate in the TRIPS Agreement. Also note that there is no change to the US IPR dummy, i.e. IPR_{US}. The data on goods exports of the US to the IPR reforming countries in each year can be obtained from the Foreign Trade Division of the US Census Bureau. We obtained the US outward direct investment data from the websites of the Bureau of Economic Analysis and the World Bank. We first run the regression with all explanatory variables. Similar to the results reported in the previous section, most variables do not exhibit having significant effects on innovations in the US. Again, $IPR_{87} * \ln EX_{87t}$ and $TRIPS * \ln EX_{TRIPSt}$ have the lowest p-values at, respectively, 0.315 and 0.320, among all IPR variables. We delete the other high p-value IPR variables and re-run the regression. The results are reported in the upper part of Table 5.8. $IPR_{87} * \ln EX_{87t}$ is still not statistically insignificant. We delete it and re-run the new regression. The results are reported in the lower part of Table 5.8.

Table 5.8. Linkage term.

Independent variable	Coefficient	Standard error	t-Statistics	p-Value
GDP	0.278	0.189	1.47	0.142
EDU	0.781	0.318	2.46	0.015
$IPR * \ln EX87t$	0.013	0.011	1.17	0.244
$TRIPS * \ln EXTRIPSt$	0.029	0.007	4.42	0.000
R-squared	0.742			
GDP	0.435	0.133	3.28	0.001
EDU	1.029	0.237	4.35	0.000
$TRIPS * \ln EXTRIPSt$	0.027	0.006	4.26	0.000
R-squared	0.740			

Again, the TRIPS Agreement has a statistically significant impact on innovations in the US.

5. Conclusion

Conventional wisdom suggests that IPR protection will stimulate innovation activities, but some recent theories argue the opposite. Empirical studies do not generate conclusive results on this supposition. This paper empirically investigates the impacts of foreign IPR reforms on innovation in the US, using data on successful patent applications in the US over 33 years and major IPR reforms in 21 countries, in addition to the reforms in the US and the TRIPS Agreement of the WTO. We find that the TRIPS Agreement, which represents worldwide IPR reforms, has significant impacts on innovations in the US, but the effect of strengthening patent protection by individual countries is not statistically significant. This finding generates many implications. It perhaps suggests that the US market is large/profitable enough to provide innovation incentives in the US, and so further strengthening foreign patent protection simply increases the US innovators' rent, but not innovation. It also indicates the importance of international cooperation in IPR protection.

Data limitations constrain our research. There are a number of directions that we would like to take in order to improve the paper once we are able to collect more detailed data. First, in this paper, we use numbers of patent to measure innovation activities. We would like to check the result using other measures of innovation activities; for example, R&D investments. These two measures (innovation output and input) may not lead to the same conclusion, especially in cross-industry analysis (Scherer, 1983). However, we do not have industry-level R&D expenditures data.

Second, although the time coverage is quite long in our dataset, the industry breakdown is too broad (only six groups), and, as a result, our dataset is not sufficiently large. A more detailed industry-level dataset would allow us to test the IPR-innovation linkage more precisely by separating cross-industry effects.

References

Bessen, James and Eric Maskin, "Sequential Innovation, Patents, and Imitation" *Rand Journal of Economics* 40 (2009): 611–35.

Branstetter, Lee, Raymond Fisman, and Fritz Foley, "Does Stronger Intellectual Property Rights Increase International Technology Transfer? Empirical Evidence from U.S. Firm-Level Data" *Quarterly Journal of Economics* 121 (2005): 321–49.

Branstetter, Lee, Ray Fisman, Fritz Foley, and Kamal Saggi, (2007). "Intellectual Property Rights, Imitation, and Foreign Direct Investment: Theory and Evidence NBER" working paper 13033.

Chen, Y. and T. Puttitanum, "Intellectual Property Rights and Innovation in Developing Countries" *Journal of Development Economics* 78 (2005): 474–93.

Evenson, R. and S. Kanwar, (2001). "Does Intellectual Property Protection Spur Technological Change?" Yale Economic Growth Center discussion paper 831.

Ginarte, J. and W Park, "Determinants of Patent Rights: A Cross-National Study" *Research Policy* 26 (1997): 283–301.

Granstrand, Ove, (2005). "Innovation and Intellectual Property Rights ch. 10" in J. Fagerberg, D. Mowery, and R. Nelson (eds), *Oxford Handbook of Innovation*, Oxford: Oxford University Press.

Grossman, Gene M. and Edwin L.-C. Lai, "International Protection of Intellectual Property" *American Economic Review* 94 (2004): 1635–53.

Hall, Bronwyn and Rosemarie Ziedonis, "The Determinants of Patenting in the U.S. Semiconductor Industry, 1980–94," *Rand Journal of Economics* 32 (2001): 101–28.

Hall, Bronwyn H., Adam Jaffe, and Manuel Trajtenberg, (2002). "The NBER Patent Citations Data File: Lessons, Insights and Methodological Tools" in A. Jaffe and M. Trajtenberg (eds), *Patents, Citations and Innovations*, Cambridge, MA: MIT Press 403–60.

Jaffe, Adam B., (1999). "The U.S. Patent System in Transition: Policy Innovation and the Innovation Process NBER" working paper 7280.

Jaffe, Adam B. and Josh Lerner, (2004). *Innovation and Its Discontents: How Our Broken Patent System is Endangering Innovation and Progress, and What To Do About It*, Princeton, NJ: Princeton University Press.

Kim, Jinyoung and Gerald Marschke, "Accounting for the Recent Surge in U.S. Patenting: Changes in R&D Expenditures, Patent Yields, and the High Tech Sector" *Economics of Innovation and New Technology* 13 (2004): 543–58.

Kortum, Samuel and Josh Lerner, "Stronger Protection or Technological Revolution: What Is Behind the Recent Surge in Patenting?" *Carnegie-Rochester Conference Series on Public Policy* 48 (1998): 247–304.

———, (2003). "Unraveling the Patent Paradox working paper", Harvard University.

Lai, Edwin L.-C. and Larry D. Oiu, "The North's Intellectual Property Rights Standard for the South?" *Journal of International Economics* 59 (2003): 183–209.

Lanjouw, J., (1998). "The Introduction of Pharmaceutical Product Patents in India: 'Heartless Exploitation of the Poor and Suffering'?" NBER working paper 6366.

Lanjouw, J. and I. Cockburn, (2000). "Do Patents Matter? Empirical Evidence after GATT NBER" working paper 7495.

Lerner, Josh, "150 Years of Patent Protection *American Economic Review, Papers and Proceedings* 92 (2002): 221–25.

Mansfield, Edwin, (1994). "Intellectual Property Protection," Foreign Direct Investment, and Technology Transfer Γ*C* discussion paper 19, World Bank.

Maskus, Keith E., (2000). *Intellectual Property Rights in the Global Economy*, Washington, DC: Institute for International Economics.

McCalman, Phillip, "Reaping What You Sow: An Empirical Analysis of International Patent Harmonization" *Journal of International Economics* 55 (2001): 161–86.

Oian, Yi, "Do Additional National Patent Laws Stimulate Domestic Innovation in a Global Patenting Environment? A Cross-Country Analysis of Pharmaceutical Patent Protection, 1978-2002," *Review of Economics and Statistics* 89 (2007): 436–53.

Sakakibara, Mariko and Lee Branstetter, "Do Stronger Patents Induce More Innovation? Evidence from the 1988 Japanese Patent Reforms" *Rand Journal of Economic* 32 (2001): 771–800.

Scherer, F. M., "The Propensity to Patent" *International Journal of Industrial Organization* 1 (1983): 107–28.

Stern, Scott, Michael Porter, and Jeffrey Furman, (2000). "The Determinants of National Innovation Capacity NBER" working paper 7876.

Chapter 6

Intermediate Input Imports and Innovations: Evidence from Chinese Firms' Patent Filings*

Abstract

Innovation plays a key role in economic growth. In this paper, we investigate the effects of intermediate input tariff reduction on the innovation activities of domestic firms. Input tariff reduction has two opposite effects on the innovation decision of a firm: it may promote innovation because the cost of innovation activities decreases, but it may also result in a decrease in innovation because foreign technologies become cheaper. We use Chinese firm-level data from 1998 to 2007, which features a drastic input tariff cut in 2002 because of China's WTO accession, and find that input tariff cut results in *less* innovation undertaken by Chinese firms. The findings are obtained using the difference-in-differences technique and are robust to various specifications checks of the model. We also provide a theoretical framework to generate insights to the empirical findings.

1. Introduction

Innovation and technological progress are key determinants of economic growth. In his 2014 State of the Union Address, US President Barack Obama claimed that "the nation that goes all-in on innovation today will own the global economy tomorrow". The past

*This chapter is reproduced from *Journal of International Economics*, 103, 166–183, 2016, with permission from Elsevier.

few decades have witnessed the race for innovation and deepening globalization worldwide. How does trade liberalization influence the incentive of firms to engage in innovation activities? This important question has been addressed by a large body of literature. Most existing studies are based on final goods trade and confirm that trade is one of the most important factors that drive innovation (Kiriyama, 2012). In contrast, this paper examines the effects of intermediate input tariff liberalization on firm innovation activities. Our study is based on Chinese firm-level data.

A growing share of international trade is in capital goods and intermediate inputs. At the global level, the share of capital goods in total trade increased from 21.0% in 1970 to 26.5% in 2006 while the share of intermediate goods in total trade increased from 7.5% to 13.0% (Onodera, 2009). From 2000 to 2006, the total value of China's capital and intermediate input imports increased by 151% and 256%, respectively. Another notable change is China's growing innovations. For example, China's share of global research and development (R&D) jumped from 2.2% in 2000 to 14.5% in 2011.[1] In 2011, China's patent office received the highest number of applications worldwide.[2] Thus, China is a good case for analyzing the effects of intermediate input imports on innovations. Drastic trade liberalization in China also makes the country a good case for valid empirical investigation of such an issue. On the one hand, the aver-age input tariff rate in China dropped from 13.74% in 1998 to 8.13% in 2007, with the greatest cuts after 2001 when the country became a member of the WTO. On the other hand, the degrees of input tariff liberalization differ tremendously across industries. By utilizing these two features, namely, large and sudden tariff cuts due to the WTO accession and cross-industry variations of the cuts, we are able to use the difference-in-differences (DID) technique to assess empirically the effects of input tariff cuts on the innovation activities of domestic firms.

Against backdrop, our analysis shows that China's input tariff liberalization *reduces* innovation activities of firms as measured by patent filings. This negative effect is both statistically significant

[1] *Foreign Policy*, "It's official: China is becoming a new innovation powerhouse", Feb. 6th, 2014.

[2] *The Economist*, "How innovative is China? Valuing patents", Jan. 5th, 2013.

and economically important: a one-percentage point cut in input tariff rate results in about 0.15% to 0.28% drop in innovations. This finding is robust to different model specifications and concerns of the model. This finding is also interesting because it is neither obvious nor expected.

A cut in intermediate input tariffs could have positive and negative incentives to innovation activities. On the one hand, input tariff reduction enables a firm to purchase a larger quantity of input with more varieties and higher quality. This capability lowers a firm's incentive to undertake innovation because the firm can raise its production productivity or output quality through a cheaper channel (i.e., importing intermediate inputs). On the other hand, a firm may undertake R&D by using intermediate inputs, and its innovation activities may benefit from the technology embedded in imported inputs. As a result, the cost of undertaking R&D decreases or the effectiveness increases, and hence, a firm's incentive to do R&D increases. Our empirical finding implies that the innovation-reducing effect dominates the innovation-raising effect in China.[3] We introduce a simple theoretical model to understand the mechanism at work, and find that under some very plausible conditions, a firm imports higher quality inputs in response to a tariff cut in intermediate input, which results in a reduction in innovation.

To the best of our knowledge, the present paper is the first to investigate the *direct* effects of intermediate input imports on innovation based on firm-level data. Two strands of related literature exist.[4] In the first strand, some papers have examined the effects on innovations by trade liberalization in general, but not by intermediate input imports in particular, and thus their conclusions and

[3]A good example which supports this general empirical finding is Changhong's response to imported technology. Changhong is a large TV maker in China. Through "imitation" the company was able to introduce many new product lines in early 1980s. Beginning in 1986, Japanese TV makers dumped the new generation of color TV production lines and key components to the Chinese market. In response, Changhong stopped its own R&D but just purchased the Japanese technology because of the low cost. The full story can be found in http://news.xinhuanet.com/fortune/2011-05/03/c_121370462.htm.

[4]Grossman and Helpman (1991) provide a very comprehensive study on the relationship between trade and innovation. See Atkeson and Burstein (2010) and Burstein and Melitz (2013) for the recent approaches.

mechanisms differ considerably from the present paper. Generally speaking, trade affects innovation through various channels, such as transferring embedded technology, increasing market size, changing competition, realizing scale economies, and generating spillovers. Examples in this strand include Baldwin and Gu (2004), de Negri and Turchi (2007), Almeida and Fernandes (2008), Lileeva and Trefler (2010), Aw *et al.* (2011), Bustos (2011), and Bloom *et al.* (2016).[5] In particular, Bloom *et al.* (2016) find that import competition from China leads to more innovations of European firms, but imports from other developed countries have no significant effect. Using firm-level data covering 43 developing countries, Almeida and Fernandes (2008) report that on average 53% of the technological innovations are embodied in new machinery or equipment and transferred from developed to developing countries through exports and multinational firms. In their analysis of 43,595 firms in Brazil and Argentina, de Negri and Turchi (2007) find that national exporters are in general more innovative than non-exporters, with the percentage of innovating firms in these two categories being 48% and 36%, respectively.

The second strand of literature includes the recently emerging empirical studies on the effects of intermediate input imports on firm's performance.[6] Several studies (Halpern *et al.*, 2011 on Hungarian firms; Kasahara and Rodrigue, 2008, on Chilean firms) find that imports of intermediates or declines in input tariffs are conducive to productivity gains. Productivity can increase through three channels via imported intermediate inputs: learning, improved input quality, and increase in input variety. Using Indonesian manufacturing plant-level data, Amiti and Konings (2007) find that a 10% fall in input tariffs leads to a 12% gain in the productivity of

[5]Earlier empirical studies are based on country-level or industry-level data. For example, Coe and Helpman (1995) find strong international R&D spillovers through trade, based on evidence that the productivity growth of a country depends not only on its domestic R&D capital stock but also on the R&D capital stock of its foreign trading partners.

[6]Theoretical studies have painted a clear picture (e.g., Ethier, 1982). Firms' performance can improve from intermediate input imports because of the increased variety of inputs and the utilization of technology embedded in imported inputs.

importing firms, which is much higher than the productivity gain from reducing output tariffs. Qualitatively similar results are also found by Topalova and Khandelwal (2011) based on Indian data. Goldberg *et al.* (2010) examine the effects of trade liberalization in India during the 1990s and find that domestic firms increase their product scope because they can access previously unavailable new input varieties. Approximately 31% of the new products are results of lower input tariffs. Using firm-level data from the French agri-food sector, Chevassus-Lozza *et al.* (2013) discover that lowering input tariffs increases the export sales of high-productivity firms at the expense of low-productivity firms. Bas (2012) shows that Argentine firms in industries experiencing larger input tariff reductions have higher probability of entering the export market. Using French data, Bas and Strauss-Kahn (2014) find that using more varieties of imported input results in higher TFP and export scope. However, not all results are positive. For example, van Biesebroeck (2003) finds that there is no productivity improvement for Columbia firms through the use of input import.[7] Muendler (2004) also finds that the use of foreign inputs plays a minor role in the productivity change of Brazilian firms.

Similar to the present research, several studies have also examined the effects of Chinese input tariff reductions, but with different focuses. Using data on Chinese firms from 2000 to 2006, Yu (2015) finds that both input tariff and output tariff reductions improve firm productivity for both processing-trade and non-processing-trade firms. In particular, the effect of input tariff reduction on productivity is stronger than that of output tariff reduction. Ge *et al.* (2011) investigate the channels of firm productivity gains from input tariff cut and find supports for the learning, variety, and quality channels. Fan *et al.* (2015) and Bas and Strauss-Kahn (2015) examine the effect of Chinese input tariff reduction on the change in quality of export goods and find significant quality upgrade. Feng *et al.* (2016) study the connection between firm imports and exports, based on

[7]Zhang (2014) decomposes productivity gains to static and dynamic gains. Dynamic gains come from the increase in knowledge and/or innovation of the importers because of imported intermediate inputs. He uses Columbia data to show that dynamic gains are more important than static gains.

Chinese firm-level data from 2002 to 2006. They find that firms that expand their intermediate input imports raise the volume of their exports and increase their export scope. All these studies suggest that the channel through which intermediate input imports affect firm performance is the increased technology or quality embedded in imported inputs.[8]

Similar to this second strand of literature, our paper also focuses on intermediate input import. However, different from all those studies, we explore *directly* the effects on *innovation*, which distinguishes the present study from this strand of literature. Of course, the performance measures studied by the above-mentioned papers are not independent of innovation. For example, new products introduced by firms may be the result of firms' product R&D, and the improved quality of their products could be the outcome of their innovation specifically targeting quality improvement. However, those measures are not equivalent to innovation. The improvements of those performance could be the results of other efforts by firms, such as improved management practice or changes in organizational form along with trade liberalization, or as Ethier (1982) shows, improved performance could be the results of intermediate input imports because of the increased variety of inputs and the utilization of technology embedded in imported inputs.[8]

Our finding is also different from all above-mentioned studies even if we consider the good performance being (partly) the result of innovations. For example, the increased product scope of Indian firms can be contributed to the larger amount of product R&D by firms, and the productivity gain by Indonesian importers is a result of more process R&D undertaken by these firms. While innovation has been "found" to *increase* in all studies discussed above (with the exception of two cases with insignificant results, i.e., van Biesebroeck, 2003, and Muendler, 2004) in response to intermediate input tariff reduction, in contrast, we directly show that patent applications of

[8]Using new product sales as a measure of innovation, Liu and Buck (2007) show that Chinese firms increase their innovations when they import more technology. Using data from 1965 to 1995 for 86 countries, Connolly (2003) finds that high technology imports from developed countries increase domestic innovations (perhaps through initial imitation), especially for developing countries. He argue that this is perhaps through reversed engineering.

Chinese firms *decrease*, which indicates that innovation is different from other performance measures and separately investigating the trade effect on innovation of firms is important.

Innovation is an important topic in many disciplines including economics and management. Two of the many issues that the innovation literatures emphasize are incentive for innovation and spillovers/diffusion of innovation. Factors affecting incentives and spillovers include intellectual property rights (IPR) protection, market competition, education levels, and institutions. We can view the issue studied in the present paper as how embodied technology from upstream (intermediate inputs) affects, via diffusion, downstream innovation incentives. In this regard, our paper is also loosely related to the MAKE-or-BUY issue discussed mostly in the industrial organization and management literatures. With the MAKE decision, firms conduct R&D in-house and develop their own technology, while with the BUY decision, they acquire technology externally. Veugelers and Cassiman (1999) provide a useful review of this literature. On the one hand, there is substitution between the MAKE and BUY decisions. This view is developed based on transaction cost economics (Williamson, 1985) and property rights theory (Grossman and Hart, 1986). There are costs and benefits of using external technology as it helps lower innovation costs and gain time, but inevitably incurs transaction or agency costs. On the other hand, there is complementarity between MAKE and BUY. It has been argued that in-house R&D may serve to absorb, modify and improve external technology purchased by the firms (Cohen and Levinthal, 1989). Evidence for both substitution and complementarity can be found in the literature (Cassiman and Veugelers, 2006; Lyons, 1995). The mechanism which works in our paper is related but not exactly the same as those underlying the MAKE-or-BUY decision. Cheaper imported intermediate inputs can make the MAKE option less attractive because the importers can use the embodied technology directly, but can also make the BUY option less attractive because the cost of doing R&D is lower.

The remainder of this paper is organized as follows. In the next section, we describe our estimation strategy and data. We conduct empirical analysis and discuss the findings in Section 3. We explore the underlying mechanisms in Section 4. Concluding remarks are provided in Section 5.

2. Background, Empirical Strategy, and Data

2.1. *China's patent applications*

Similar to its impressive economic growth, China has also experienced drastic growth in patent applications received by the State Intellectual Property Office (SIPO). The total patent applications increased from 8558 in 1985 to 928,177 in 2014, indicating an average annual growth of 17.54% according to the World Intellectual Property Office (WIPO). Although patent applications started late and from a small base, China has become the largest country receiving patent applications since 2011, overtaking Japan in 2010 and the US in 2011. Many studies have attempted to provide explanations for the explosion of China's patent applications. Hu and Jefferson (2009) suggest and test five factors that account for the patent rise including intensification of R&D, growth of foreign direct investment (FDI), amendments to the patent law, ownership reform, and industry structural shift.

In fact, since China passed its first patent law in 1984, it has amended the law several times including 1992, 2000, and 2008 in addition to those made in accordance with the Agreement on Trade-Related Aspects of Intellectual Property Rights (TRIPS). Interestingly enough, well before China's entry to the WTO, China's 1992 amendment had extended the duration of invention patent protection from 15 to 20 years, which is a major part of the TRIPS requirement. Hence, the TRIPS does not completely coincide with the 2002 tariff reduction from China's WTO accession.

According to the quantitative study of Future (2012), from 1986 to 2010, 2.106 million invention patent applications were published by SIPO, with about 53% of them are from entities within China. The growth during the period of 2000–2010 is even more spectacular, at an average annual rate of 28.4%. State-owned enterprises (SOE) were the main corporate inventors before the mid-1990s, but private companies have become the main corporate inventors in the later period. Geographically, the center of gravity of innovation focused on three cities (Beijing, Shanghai and Shenzhen) in the early years, but later spread all over the country. The Kairos Future's Report (2012) attributes the driving forces for the phenomenal growth of patent applications in China to factors such as policy incentives, increased R&D spending, rising levels of education, and liberalization of many sectors.

2.2. *China's accession to WTO*

China began its economic reform and adopted an opening-door policy in 1979. The economy was still very closed at the beginning of the reform period. Hence, to open up its economy, the Chinese government introduced a series of trade liberalization policies, including decentralizing foreign trade decisions, allowing manufacturing firms to engage directly in imports and exports, reducing import and export controls, removing import quotas, and lowering tariff rates. With the aim to integrate fully into the global market and make a strong commitment to trade liberalization, China began preparing its application for WTO entry in the late 1980s and was eventually accepted by the end of 2001. During the long negotiation period of WTO accession, China had unilaterally cut its tariffs many times, and its tariff cut in 2002, right after the accession, was very drastic. China's simple average tariff rates (including both intermediate inputs and final goods) dropped from 42.9% in 1992 to 26.6% in 1996, 17% in 2000, and 9.8% after the WTO accession.

Fig. 6.1 plots the time trend of China's simple average *input* tariffs during the period 1996–2007. The figure shows that tariff rates dropped substantially in 1997, remained more or less unchanged during 1997–2001, and started to decrease in 2002 until it reached a steady state in 2005. While Fig. 6.1 shows the general pattern of changes in input tariffs from all industries, a clear heterogeneity across industries can be observed behind the graph. Fig. 6.2 shows the relation between input tariffs in 2001 and the decrease in average input tariffs between pre-WTO (1998–2001) and post-WTO accession (2002–2007) periods across industries, which is defined based on China's Input–Output Table 2002. Clearly, a strong positive correlation between the initial tariff level and the change of the tariff exists because of the WTO accession. That is, industries with higher initial tariff levels had larger reductions. As a result, input tariff levels in the post-WTO accession period are more uniform across industries than the levels in the pre-WTO accession period.

The input tariff liberalization of China offers us a great opportunity to examine the effects of input tariff reductions on firm behavior because of its large variations of changes over time and across industries.

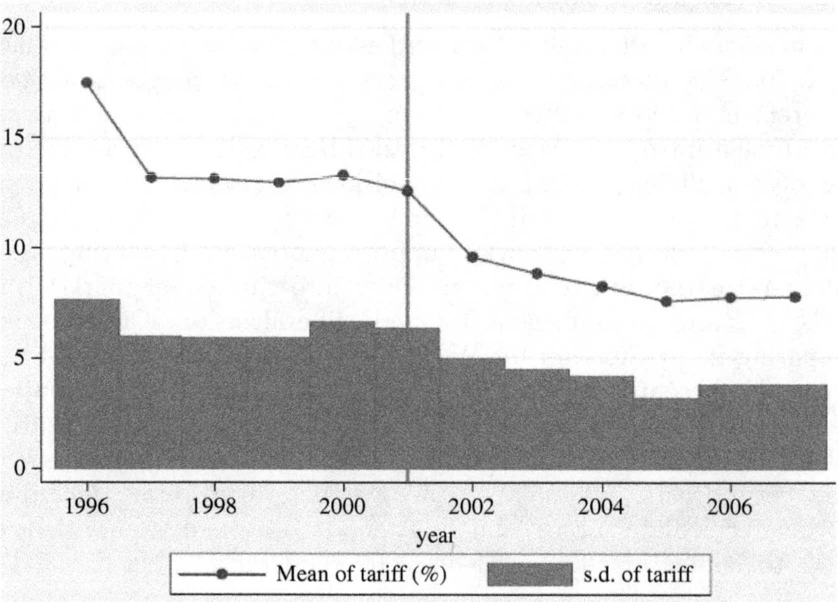

Figure 6.1. China's input tariff trend: 1996–2007.

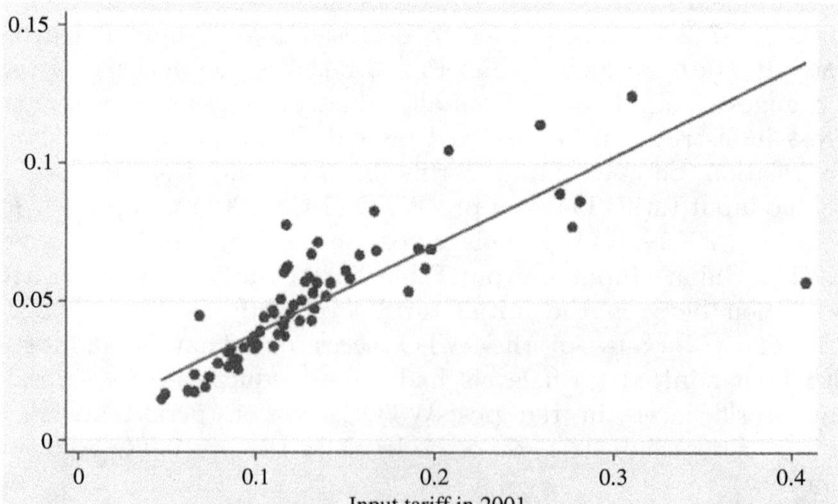

Figure 6.2. Initial input tariffs and their reductions cross industries defined based on Input-Output Table.

2.3. *Estimation specification*

Our analysis is based on the period of 1998–2007. Our objective is to estimate the effects of input tariff reduction on innovation activities of domestic firms. We overcome the identification problem by exploiting the presence of large variations in input tariff reduction across industries because of China's WTO accession, which is treated as an exogenous shock in most empirical studies using Chinese trade data (e.g., Fan *et al.*, 2015; Bloom *et al.*, 2016). We employ the DID technique to conduct the estimation. Industries with larger input tariff cuts are expected to make bigger adjustments. We thus examine the difference between the change in innovation activities by firms in industries with larger input tariff reductions because of the WTO accession (the treatment group) and the corresponding change by firms in industries with smaller input tariff reductions (the control group).

Specifically, we propose the following specification for our DID estimation:

$$y_{fit} = \beta InT01_i \cdot Post02_t + X'_{fit}\gamma + \lambda_f + \lambda_t + \gamma_{fit}, \qquad (1)$$

where y_{fit} is the innovation activity of firm f in industry i in year t; $InT01_i$ is the average tariff rate of inputs employed in the production of industry i in year 2001, which is used to measure the degree of input tariff reduction in industry i because of the WTO accession given that this initial tariff level is positively correlated with the degree of tariff cut (Fig. 6.2); $Post02_t$ is an indicator of the post-WTO accession period, which is equal to one if $t \geq 2002$, and zero other-wise; k_f is the firm fixed effect, used to control for all time-invariant characteristics of firms (as well as industries and regions); k_t is the year fixed effect, used to control for all yearly shocks common to all industries, such as business cycles; $\mathbf{X'}_{fit}$ is a set of time-varying firm characteristics; and e_{fit} is the error term. Following Bertrand *et al.* (2004) and Amiti and Konings (2007), we cluster the standard errors at the firm level to deal with the potential heteroskedasticity and serial autocorrelation. We control for time-varying firm characteristics ($\mathbf{X'}_{fit}$) that may affect innovation activities. Characteristics include firm age, size, capital–labor ratio, exporting status, and equity share owned by foreign investors. The innovation of a firm may have a life cycle, and hence, we include in particular the square term of firm age, in addition to the linear term.

Our main interest focuses on parameter b. A positive sign of b indicates that input tariff cut increases the innovation activity of a firm, while a negative sign indicates the opposite effect. After obtaining our main empirical results from the above specifications, we will conduct a series of robustness checks to confirm the findings.

2.4. *Key variables*

Our empirical model (1) has two key variables: firm-level innovation activity (dependent variable) and industry-level input tariff (the key explanatory variable).

Innovation activities can be measured by using either innovation input (e.g., R&D expenditure) or innovation output (e.g., patent filing). Different disadvantages and advantages are associated with each measure. Patent filing is generally considered as a better measure of innovation activities because it captures the effectiveness of innovation effort (including both observable and unobservable inputs), whereas R&D expenditure is only one particular (observable) input for innovation and fails to capture the quality of innovation. Following some studies in the literature (e.g., Aghion *et al.*, 2009) Hashmi, 2013, Hu and Jefferson, 2009), we use patent filing as the measure of innovation in this study.

Our dependent variable is the number of patents filed by a firm in a given year. We encounter a large number of observations of zero patent filing because many firms do not have any patent application in some of the years. We construct and use the following transformed measure as our dependent variable $y_{fit} = \ln[Y_{fit} + (Y_{fit}^2 + 1)^{\frac{1}{2}}]$, where Y_{fit} is the total number of patent filings by firm f in industry i in year t, to avoid the problem of too many zeros. This transformation allows us to keep all observations of zero patent filing and interpret our estimate b as the percentage change in patent filing. We prefer this transformation to other log-like transformations, such as $\ln(Y_{fit} + 1)$, because of its flexibility. However, our results are robust to using $\ln(Y_{fit} + 1)$ as dependent variable.[9]

[9]Our results are also robust to using alternative estimation methods particularly suitable for dealing with the problem of many zeros. It will be shown in the subsection of robustness check later (Subsection 3.3).

Our key explanatory variable is industry-level input tariffs. We construct this measure following the approach of Amiti and Konings (2007), Goldberg *et al.* (2010), and Topalova and Khandelwal (2011), who use Input–Output Tables. Specifically, input tariff for industry i (according to the classification in Input–Output Table) in year t is defined as the weighted average of the tariffs of goods that are used as inputs for industry i; that is

$$\ln T_{it} = \sum_j CostShare_{ij} \cdot OutT_{jt}$$

where InT_{it} is the input tariff of industry i in year t, $OutT_{jt}$ is the out-put tariff of industry j in year t (calculated as the simple average of tariffs of the Harmonized System (HS) six-digit products covered in industry j), and $CostShare_{ij}$ is the cost share of industry j in the production of a good in industry i. $CostShare_{ij}$ is calculated based on China's Input—Output Table of 2002. Accordingly, the industry classification in our study is also defined following the Input–Output Table of 2002. We use the year 2002 because China's Input–Output Table is only available every five years and 2002 is the middle year of our sample period. With this construction, we define input tariff of industry i in year 2001 as $InT01_i \equiv InT_{i2001}$, which is the main regressor we will employ in our empirical analyses.[10]

As pointed out by Amiti and Konings (2007), one drawback of using Input–Output Table in constructing input tariff is that the industrial classification of the table is at a highly aggregate level, consequently the resulting input tariffs would also be at the same level. Hence, to obtain input tariffs at a more disaggregate level, we also construct InT_{it} from China's Customs Data by using the share of imports of industry j in the total imports by industry i to proxy $CostShare_{ij}$. In this latter measure, industries are defined at the four-digit level of the China Industrial Classification (CIC). Although this

[10]Input subsidies prevailed in China in the period considered in this study. However, without knowing the details on the subsidies, one cannot construct precise or effective input tariffs. Probably because of this difficulty, all other papers on China (and many other developing countries) simply ignore the subsidies, and so does the present paper. However, as long as the subsidies are not closely correlated with tariff cuts, the results will not be systematically biased. The subsidy problem led us to exclude processing trade firms in our sample because they receive the largest subsidies in the form of tariff exemption.

measure has other drawbacks (for example, input imports are affected by tariffs, and the share does not take domestic intermediate inputs into account), it has the advantage of being more disaggregate, and hence was used as a robustness check.

2.5. *Data*

Our empirical analysis relies on data that includes information on firm-level operation, firm-level innovations, and industry-level input tariffs. To this end, we construct our unique dataset by merging three data sources manually.

Our first data source is the Annual Survey of Manufacturing Enterprises, which is maintained by the National Bureau of Statistics (NBS) of China. This data includes all years from 1998 to 2007, and is the most comprehensive firm-level dataset in China, covering all SOEs and large non-SOEs with annual sales above five million yuan Renminbi (around US$800,000). The number of firms in this dataset varies from over 140,000 in the late 1990s to over 336,000 in 2007. Firms are from all 31 provinces and direct-controlled municipalities in China and all manufacturing industries. The dataset provides detailed information on each firm, including official name, industry, and location as well as most items of each firm's operation and performance, based on the firms' accounting statements, such as age, employment, capital, intermediate inputs, new product sales, and ownership.

Following Cai and Liu (2009), we clean this dataset by dropping observations according to the basic rules of the Generally Accepted Accounting Principles. In particular, we drop firms from the data if any of the following is observed: (1) liquid assets are greater than total assets, (2) total fixed assets are greater than total assets, and (3) the net value of fixed assets is greater than total assets. We drop firms with fewer than eight workers because they fall under a different legal regime (Brandt *et al.*, 2012), firms with obviously wrong year of establishment (e.g., later than 2007 or earlier than 1900), and non-manufacturing firms (i.e., firms in mining, tobacco, and public utility industries according to China Industrial Classification System).

Processing trade is popular in China. However, we remove processing-trade firms from our data for two reasons. First, according to government policy, processing trade is exempted from import duties on imported inputs and materials, and the effective rate of input tariffs for processing-trade firms is zero, in both pre-WTO and post-WTO accession periods, hence, input tariff reduction does not have direct effects on them. Second, processing-trade firms may have very different production functions, import and export behaviors, and innovation motivations because they are provided with technologies, intermediate inputs, or product design by foreign parties.[11] However, firms engage in processing trade at different degrees. We drop manufacturing firms whose ratios of processing exports over their total exports are higher than 0.5.

The second data source is SIPO. The SIPO dataset contains detailed information on each patent filing since 1985, including date of filing, official name and address of the applicant, name of the patent, and type of patent classified according to China's Patent Law, i.e., whether the application is for an invention patent, a utility model patent, or a design patent.

Some remarks on the use of SIPO data are in order. In general, measuring innovation activities is difficult. The report of OECD (2009) provides a good description of the advantages and drawbacks of using patent as a measure of innovation. In addition to patent filing data, other types of data to measure innovations exist, but some are almost impossible to obtain while some are even less satisfactory than patent filing. First, R&D expenditure measures innovation input, but R&D data is available only for years 2001–2003 and 2005–2007, and thus is not good for our DID estimation because data for only one year in the pre-WTO period is available.[12] Moreover, R&D data

---

[11]Some recent papers, for example, Ge *et al.* (2011) and Yu (2015), use processing-trade firms as control group in their DID estimation when investigating the productivity effect of input tariff cut in China. In our view, processing-trade firms are not a proper control group for other manufacturing firms as far as innovation is concerned because the two types of firms are incomparable qualitatively and should not share a common innovation trend. Thus, using processing-trade firms as the control group will result in biased estimates. For example, if processing-trade firms do not do any innovation and an upward trend exists for the innovation of other manufacturing firms, then using the processing-trade firms as the control group will significantly overestimate the impact of the tariff cut and may even change the sign of the estimate from negative to positive.

[12]Despite this shortcoming of R&D data, we have also tried to replace patent filing with R&D expenditure in the same regression model used in this study

can also be severely distorted when various subsidy schemes are provided, which is the case in China. It is true that patent filing activities could be distorted by government policies, but the matter is the relative degrees. As for incentive for patent, Li (2012) provides a description of various policy initiatives at regional levels such as patent subsidy programs. The most important part of the subsidy programs is subsidizing patent filings, which varies across regions, but it is on average around just a few hundred RMB (Chinese currency unit, around RMB6.7 per USD at the present) per patent filing. In contrast, there is huge incentive for R&D. For example, companies classified as High and New Technology Enterprise can get a corporate income tax (CIT) rate cutting from the standard rate 25% down to only 15%. In addition, companies that meet the government's criteria can get 150% of eligible R&D expenses deducted before CIT. According to PWC (2015), slight change in R&D behavior might result in more eligible R&D tax benefits. Hence, we expect that distortion of R&D data is much severer than patent data.[13]

Second, China's patent filing and/or granting abroad is a good alternative because it may reflect more genius innovation, as argued by Holmes *et al.* (2015). Such data can be found in WIPO dataset. However, linking the WIPO data to the NBS data is almost impossible.[14] In fact, at the aggregate level, we find that the ratio of total patents applied abroad by Chinese residents over all patents applied by Chinese residents is very stable over time and very small (only a few hundred per year in the late-1990s), ranging from

and found that the estimate of the response of R&D to import tariff cut has the same sign (negative) as that of patent but is statistically insignificant. However, we do not want to make any conclusion based on this analysis unless we have longer-period R&D data, which is left for future research when data becomes available.

[13]There is an ongoing debate on the correlation between R&D and patents in China. Hu and Jefferson (2009) find weak linkage between patent and R&D, but Dang and Motohashi (2015) argue that patent count is correlated with R&D input and financial output and so patent statistics are meaningful indicators of innovations. Following this debate, we also check the relationship between firms' R&D expenditure and patents based on our sample. We find that firms' R&D investment increases their patent filings.

[14]The two datasets have no common identifier; WIPO contains English names only while NBS contains Chinese names only.

minimum 3.50% to 5.70% over the period 1999–2013, with an average 4.66%. Moreover, Wunsch-Vincent *et al.* (2015) show that China's foreign patents are concentrated in a few technology fields and in a few firms, mostly in the information technology sector. Hence, using these data in our study would not be of high value.

We match NBS and SIPO data using common information included in both datasets. Specifically, we merge the two datasets using the official names of firms, and then double-check the matched outcomes using location information of the firms. Our matching out-come is reasonably good, for two reasons. First, according to a report by NBS, about 8.8% of manufacturing firms in China applied for patents during 2004–2006. During the same period, the number of firms in our matched dataset constitutes about 4% of the total number of firms in the NBS dataset. This is a reasonably good match, given that the NBS dataset is very large (with more than 1.3 million observations after cleaning). Second, our matching technique is based on the names and location of firms, and we use the same technique for all industries and for the whole sample period (before and after WTO accession). Therefore, the degree of mismatch across industries does not appear to be correlated with the degree of input tariff reduction across industries. This alleviates considerably the potential estimation biases arising from the matching process.

Our third data source is the World Integrated Trade Solution (WITS) database, which is maintained by the World Bank, and contains tariff data at the HS six-digit level.[15] The data are given at different HS versions over the years, and hence, we convert them to the HS02 version using the UN Statistics Division Concordance Table. We calculate industrial-level input tariffs by using this dataset together with the 2002 Input–Output Table of China. We construct our unique dataset by merging the three databases. The matched dataset has an unbalanced panel of 337,257 firms and a total of around 1.3 million observations, with both detailed patent filing information and firm characteristics during the period of 1998–2007. Our analyses are based on this unique dataset.

In the robustness checks, we need to identify the processing trade status of firms (that is, whether or not the firm is a processing trade

[15]WITS does not provide 2002 data and we obtain 2002 data from WTO.

firm) and their importing status (that is, whether or not the firm imports inputs directly or not), which requires information from another data source, that is, China's Customs Data (2000–2006). Hence, we also merge Customs data with NBS data by using the same method as Yu (2015). The Customs data contains most detailed information of each international trade transaction conducted by Chinese firms, including product code at HS six-digit level, value and quantity. This data also allows us to do our mechanism test.

Ge *et al.* (2011) and Yu (2015) use the merged Customs and NBS data in their studies, whereas we use it only for robustness check. Specifically, they confine their analyses to manufacturing firms that also make direct imports, which we call direct importers. Their studies omit a large number of manufacturing firms that do not make direct imports, which we call non-importers. However, non-importers may buy imported inputs from intermediaries and employ these inputs in their production. As pointed out by Goldberg *et al.* (2010), using the sample of direct importers may result in a bias. In the main analysis of our study, we use the entire NBS dataset. There-fore, our analysis will provide a more complete picture of how input tariff cut affects the innovation of firms.[16]

Table 6.1 presents the summary statistics and definitions of the main variables used in this study. Overall, a Chinese manufacturing firm applied for 0.15 patents per year on average, and the patent applications increased significantly from the pre-WTO to the post-WTO accession period. Input and output tariffs decreased significantly because of WTO accession. Almost all firm-level performances and industrial characteristics were improved. The degree of industrial competition also increased after 2001.

One potential concern is whether our key explanatory variable, the 2001 input tariff levels, is exogenous to individual firms. This concern is generally legitimate, but is alleviated here by the observation on the actual liberalization process in China. As shown in Fig. 6.1, both mean tariff rate and standard deviation remained

[16]A related problem of using the whole sample is that some non-importers may not use any imported inputs. This possibility may bias the impact of intermediate input imports downwards. We do find stronger impact on importers than on non-importers, as shown in Subsection 3.4.

Table 6.1. Summary statistics.

Variables	All (1)	Pre-WTO (2)	Post-WTO (3)	Difference (3) – (2)	Definition
Patent	0.1057	0.0698	0.1787	0.1089	Total no.
	(0.0089)	(0.0037)	(0.0120)	(0.0205)	of patents
Invention	0.0465	0.0073	0.0601	0.0528	No. of invention
	(0.0080)	(0.0015)	(0.0107)	(0.0183)	patents
Utility	0.0467	0.0225	0.0551	0.0326	No. of utility
	(0.0012)	(0.0013)	(0.0015)	(0.0027)	patents
Design	0.0574	0.0400	0.0634	0.0234	No. of design
	(0.0016)	(0.0021)	(0.0020)	(0.0037)	patents
Input tariff	0.0996	0.1285	0.0821	−0.0464	Industrial input
	(0.0009)	(0.0016)	(0.0009)	(0.0017)	tariff
Age	10.1022	13.7903	8.8264	−4.9639	Firm age
	10.1022	13.7903	8.8264	−4.9639	
Age	234.0097	393.7576	178.7502	−215.0074	Firm age
squared	(0.5156)	(1.3160)	(0.5117)	(1.1645)	squared
Exporting	0.2784	0.2651	0.2830	0.0179	Firm exporting
	(0.0004)	(0.0008)	(0.0005)	(0.0009)	status indicator
Labor	4.7841	5.0096	4.7062	−0.3035	Log of firm
	(0.0010)	(0.0020)	(0.0011)	(0.0022)	employment
Capital/	3.2936	3.0529	3.3764	0.3235	Log of capital-
labor	(0.0012)	(0.0024)	(0.0014)	0.0028	labor ratio
Foreign	0.0641	0.0518	0.0683	0.0164	Foreign share
Share	(0.0002)	(0.0003)	(0.0002)	(0.0005)	holding
TFP	2.4688	2.2031	2.5610	0.3579	Firm
	(0.0011)	(0.0021)	(0.0012)	(0.0024)	productivity
Output	0.1328	0.1700	0.1102	−0.0598	Industrial output
tariff	(0.0016)	(0.0030)	(0.0016)	(0.0031)	tariff
SOE share	0.1672	0.2863	0.0949	−0.1914	Share of
	(0.0032)	(0.0055)	(0.0028)	(0.0056)	SOEs
FIE no.	3.7195	3.3805	3.9209	0.5405	Logarithm of
	(0.0270)	(0.0439)	(0.0334)	(0.0550)	no. of FIEs
HHI	0.0520	0.0547	0.0504	−0.0043	Herfindahl-
	(0.0015)	(0.0025)	(0.0019)	(0.0031)	Hirschman index

Standard errors in parentheses.

constant in the 1998–2001 period. This feature implies that the stability of tariffs holds not only for industry average, but also for individual industries. Thus, the input tariffs in 2001 were largely determined by the previous round of liberalization in 1997. That is, tariff rates in 2001 are *pre-determined* before our sample period and do not appear to be affected by innovation activities during the pre-WTO accession period. This finding can be confirmed by the data. Following Goldberg *et al.* (2010), we regress industrial innovation activities in the pre-WTO accession period on tariff rates in 2001 and find that tariff rates in 2001 are uncorrelated with innovation activities (see column 1 of Table 6.2). As shown in Table 6.2 (columns 2–5), other industrial performances are also not correlated with the 2001 input tariff rates. This independence result also holds for actual input tariff cuts from the WTO accession (instead of initial tariff rates in 2001), as shown by columns 6–10 of Table 6.2. This observation implies that either the users of imported inputs did not engage in serious lobbying activities during 1998–2001, or lobbying by users of imported inputs was not effective.

Timing of China's accession to WTO is regarded commonly as an exogenous shock at least to individual firms. Hence, a number of studies such as Fan *et al.* (2015) and Bloom *et al.* (2016) use it as an exogenous variable to proxy China's trade liberalization. We also take this approach.

3. Empirical Analysis and Findings

3.1. *Main results*

Table 6.3 presents the regression results based on our DID specification (1), with control variables introduced step by step. All estimations show that input tariff reduction leads to a *decline* in innovation of firms. In column 1, with only firm fixed effect and year fixed effect being controlled for, we find a statistically significant and negative estimate for $InT01_i \cdot Post02_t$. The negative sign indicates that after China's WTO accession, firms in industries which face a larger cut in input tariffs (higher $InT01_i$) undertake less innovation. In column 2, we include several time-varying firm characteristics that may influence innovation activities, such as age, size, capital–labor ratio, export status, and equity share owned by foreign investors.

Table 6.2. Correlation between input tariff and pre-WTO industrial.

	(1)	(2)	(3)	(4)	(5)
Variables	In(patent)	Output	Output share of domestic firms	Value-add per capita	Capital-labor ratio
Input tariff in 2001	−1.6748	−0.0636	−0.0072	0.0357	−0.1041
	(1.2713)	(0.1118)	(0.0353)	(0.0776)	(0.0897)
Observations	280	280	280	280	280
R-squared	0.0058	0.0010	0.0002	0.0007	0.0031
	(6)	(7)	(8)	(9)	(10)
Decrease in input tariff	0.2204	0.3833	−0.0130	0.0211	−0.1451
	(3.3125)	(0.3449)	(0.0841)	(0.1807)	(0.2786)
Observations	280	280	280	280	280
R-squared	0.0000	0.0047	0.0001	0.0000	0.0008

The dependent variable in each column is the growth rate of the corresponding industrial performance during 1998–2001. Robust standard errors in parentheses.

Table 6.3. Basic results.

Variables	(1) In(patent)	(2) In(patent)	(3) In(patent)	(4) In(patent)	(5) In(patent)	(6) In(patent)	(7) In(patent)	(8) In(patent)
$InT01 * Post02$	−0.1555****	−0.1561****	−0.1561****	−0.1886****				
	(0.0189)	(0.0190)	(0.0194)	(0.0203)				
$DInT * Post02$					−0.2847****			
					(0.0549)			
Input tariff						0.1853****		
						(0.0405)		
$InTA01 * Post02$							−0.0286**	
							(0.0116)	
$FITA01 * Post02$								−0.0231**
								(0.0109)
Firm Controls								
Age		−0.0014***	−0.0014***	−0.0011***	−0.0011***	−0.0011***	−0.0011***	−0.0011***
		(0.0003)	(0.0003)	(0.0002)	(0.0002)	(0.0002)	(0.0003)	(0.0002)
Age Squared		0.000***	0.000***	0.000***	0.000***	0.000***	0.000***	0.000***
		(0.0000)	(0.0000)	(0.0000)	(0.0000)	(0.0000)	(0.0000)	(0.0000)
Exporting		0.0110***	0.0110***	0.0109***	0.0109***	0.0109***	0.0109***	0.0107***
		(0.0016)	(0.0016)	(0.0016)	(0.0016)	(0.0016)	(0.0017)	(0.0018)
In(Labor)		0.0225***	0.0225***	0.0228***	0.0228***	0.0228***	0.0214***	0.0196***
		(0.0011)	(0.0011)	(0.0011)	(0.0011)	(0.0011)	(0.0011)	(0.0011)

Variables								
In(Capital/labor)		0.0047***	0.0047***	0.0047***	0.0047***	0.0047***	0.0044***	0.0039***
		(0.0005)	(0.0005)	(0.0005)	(0.0005)	(0.0005)	(0.0005)	(0.0005)
Foreign Share		−0.0010	−0.0010	−0.0012	−0.0012	−0.0013	−0.0022	−0.0002
		(0.0035)	(0.0035)	(0.0035)	(0.0035)	(0.0035)	(0.0037)	(0.0046)
Industrial controls								
Output tariff			0.0151	−0.0024	0.0039	−0.0090	0.0172	0.0148
			(0.0132)	(0.0133)	(0.0133)	(0.0147)	(0.0135)	(0.0132)
SOE no.				−0.0889***	−0.0785***	−0.0781***	−0.0712***	−0.0653***
				(0.0114)	(0.0111)	(0.0111)	(0.0117)	(0.0114)
FIE no.				0.0006	0.0010	0.0004	0.0007	0.0007
				(0.0010)	(0.0010)	(0.0010)	(0.0011)	(0.0011)
Firm FE	Y	Y	Y	Y	Y	Y	Y	Y
Year FE	Y	Y	Y	Y	Y	Y	Y	Y
Observations	1,280,731	1,270,473	1,270,473	1,268,326	1,268,326	1,268,326	1,162,812	1,084,519
R-squared	0.5117	0.5132	0.5132	0.5141	0.5140	0.5140	0.5149	−0.5078

Robust standard errors clustered at firms in parentheses.
*** $p < 0.01$.
** $p < 0.05$.

Evidently, the negative effect of input tariff reduction on innovation is very robust to these additional controls. As for the effects of the control variables, we find that firms having a shorter history, larger employment, or higher capital-labor ratio have more innovations. Exporters also have more innovations than non-exporters, which is consistent with the findings in the literature (e.g., Baldwin and Gu, 2004). However, the effect of foreign ownership is not statistically significant. As shown below (in columns 3–8), these findings are also robust after we introduce other control variables and use alternative measures of the key explanatory variable.

China's WTO accession brings changes in both input and output tariffs. Output tariff change may affect market competition in China, and consequently influence innovation incentives of firms. In column 3, we add a control for industrial output tariff $OutT_{it}$. We find that the estimate of $InT01_i \cdot Post02_t$ is still negative and statistically significant with a very similar magnitude as in columns 1–2. The effect of output tariff on innovation is statistically insignificant, which holds even when we introduce additional control variables and use alter-native measures of the key explanatory variable (in columns 5–8).[17] That is, input tariff liberalization has a stronger effect on firm innovation than output tariff liberalization. This comparison is similar to the findings in the literature that focus on firm productivity. For example, Amiti and Konings (2007) disentangle the effect of input tariff reduction from that of output tariff reduction and find that input tariff effect is at least twice as high as the output tariff effect in Indonesia.

If there exist any policy reforms introduced in China around the time of the WTO accession which may affect our treatment and control groups differently, then the effects of those policy reforms may also be captured in the DID estimates. In that case, the regression result from Eq. (1) will not be the pure effect of input tariff cuts.

[17]How import competition in final goods affects innovation is a different topics. Bloom *et al.* (2016) provide a good review of this line of study and their own empirical study finds that trade liberalization that leads to more Chinese imports in Europe increases innovations of European firms. As the effect depends on the sources of competition, i.e., origin of the exporting countries, our finding (insignificant result) merely represents the average effect of output tariff reduction.

Indeed, two important reforms took place in the early 2000s: the SOE reform and the relaxation of FDI entry regulations. These reforms were on-going reforms that had started in the 1980s and 1990s, respectively, and accelerated after the WTO accession. The SOE reform resulted in a large-scale privatization, close-down of small SOEs, and an improvement in the efficiency of surviving (large) SOEs. The new FDI regulations relaxed the entry requirements for foreign investors and reduced the range of industries restricted to foreign investment. These reforms may not have differentiated effects on the treatment and control groups. However, to control for any possible confounding effects from these two policy reforms, we include two additional control variables in our DID estimation: $SoeShare_{it}$ (the ratio of the number of SOEs over the total number of domestic firms) and FDI_{it} (the logarithm of the number of foreign invested firms). The regression result (column 4) indicates that the negative effect of input tariff reduction on innovation is still present. Firms in industries with higher SOE shares tend to undertake less innovation, possibly because SOEs undertake less innovation on average, or the presence of SOEs in the market crowds out innovation activities of private firms. However, the presence of foreign firms has no significant effect on innovation activities of the domestic firms.

Thus far, we have used input tariff rates of 2001, $InT01_i$, to represent the degrees of tariff liberalization from China's WTO accession.[18] We have strong reasons for using this measure as the key explanatory variable instead of yearly input tariff rates or actual input tariff reduction to interact with $Post02_t$. First, the schedule of tariff reductions upon WTO accession was released in 2002, and the schedule may be endogenous; hence, the phase-out process could be exploited by firms (Guadalupe and Wulf, 2010). Second, initial input tariffs are pre-determined in China. For this reason, in their analysis, Amiti and Konings (2007) also employ initial tariffs as the instrument for actual tariff changes. However, even though our choice of $InT01_i$ is well justified, we still want to check whether the results will be qualitatively different if these alternative measures are used. We first replace $InT01_i$ with actual input tariff changes, denoted

[18]Using the average tariffs over 1998–2001 or tariffs in 1998 generates similar results. The results are available upon request.

as $DInT_i$. We define $DInTi = InT_{i1998-2001} - InT_{i2002-2007}$, where $InT_{i1998-2001}$ is the average input tariff over the period 1998-2001, and $InT_{i2002-2007}$ is the average input tariff over the period 2002–2007. In column 5, we run the regression by replacing $InT01_i \cdot Post02_t$ in model (1) with $DInT_i \cdot Post02_t$. The effect of input tariff reduction is still statistically significant, negative, and even stronger than that using $InT01_i$. We then run simple OLS regression with yearly input tariff levels, denoted as InT_{it}, as key regressor, i.e., replacing $InT01_i \cdot Post02_t$ in model (1) with InT_{it}. Column 6 shows the regression results. The coefficient of InT_{it} is positive and statistically significant, indicating that lower input tariffs lead to significantly less innovation. Both results are qualitatively consistent with our main DID estimations.

We followed a common practice in literature (e.g., Goldberg, *et al.*, 2010) to calculate industry-level input tariff using China's Input–Output Table. However, as pointed out earlier, such an approach is restrictive as the obtained input tariffs are available only at a highly aggregate level. We need to find a way that does not rely on Input-Output Table to obtain input tariffs at a finer level of industry disaggregation. The approach we take is to calculate the weighted average industry-level input tariffs at the CIC 4-digit level, denoted as $InTA01_i$, by using the import share constructed from Customs data as weights instead of using the cost share constructed from the Input-Output Table. We replace $InT01_i$ by $InTA01_i$ to run the regression with this new $InTA01_i$. The results are reported in column 7. The effect of input tariff reduction on innovation remains negative and statistically significant.

While industry-level input tariff is commonly used to proxy trade liberalization, a firm's production and corresponding decisions will not be affected by a change in tariffs of some intermediate inputs that the firm does not use in its production. For this reason, using firm specific (or firm-level) input tariff is desirable, i.e., only considering tariffs relevant to the firm. We follow Yu (2015) in calculating the weighted input tariff for each firm ($FIT01_i$), where the firm's import of each input in the initial year is used to construct the weight.[19] However, this approach applies to direct importers

---

[19]See Yu (2015) for details of the construction.

only. For non-importers, we use the average of firm-specific input tariffs (of direct importers) in each CIC four-digit industry for all of these firms in the same industry. In contrast, we drop all processing firms. We use the average pre-WTO firm-specific tariffs (i.e., firm-specific tariffs in 2000 and 2001) as the initial tariffs to keep as many observations with firm-specific tariffs as possible. With firm-specific tariffs, we run the regression using $FIT01_i \cdot Post02_t$ to replace $InT01_i \cdot Post02_t$ as regressor of interest. The results are reported in column 8 of Table 6.3. The main results are robust.[20]

In summary, we find that input tariff cut reduces innovation of the firms. This finding is statistically significant and robust to various model specifications and input tariff measures. The effect is also economically significant. For example, with the estimated coefficient (−0.2847) in the specification with actual tariff cut as key regressor (column 5), the average 4.64% input tariff cut because of China's WTO accession reduces the patent filings of firms by 0.0132. This decrease is quite significant because the average patent filings of the entire sample are 0.1507. That is, patent filings of firms drop by 8.76% as a result of input tariff liberalization.

3.2. *Validity of the DID specifications*

The reliability of our estimates, which are reported in Table 6.3, depends on the validity of our DID specifications. In this subsection, we conduct a series of validity checks. The new regression results presented in Table 6.4 confirm the validity of our specifications.

[20]However, in this approach the direct importers account for only about 1% of the firms in our whole sample. This sample of direct importers is so small because these firms must exist and directly imports in year 2000 or 2001 (while there are many new entries after 2001), and many Chinese firms use imported intermediate inputs through intermediaries or trade companies. For example, our sample shows that during 2000–2006 22.73% of Chinese ordinary imports are conducted by intermediaries. Thus, we believe that it is not representative to use the tariff of these 1% firms in the main analysis.

Table 6.4. Validity of the specifications.

	(1)	(2)	(3)	(4)	(5)
	In(patent)	In(patent)	In(patent)	In(patent)	In(patent)
Variable	Flexible	Linear trend	Pre-WTD	Processing firms	Processing firms
$lnT01 * Post02$		−0.1981***		−0.3636	−0.2775
		(0.0215)		(0.6725)	(0.2099)
Input tariff			−0.0485		
			(0.0535)		
$lnT01$ * Year 1999	0.0263				
	(0.0224)				
$lnT01$ * Year 2000	0.0101				
	(0.0230)				
$lnT01$ * Year 2001	−0.0739***				
	(0.0255)				
$lnT01$ * Year 2002	−0.1275***				
	(0.0272)				
$lnT01$ * Year 2003	−0.1645***				
	(0.0280)				
$lnT01$ * Year 2004	−0.2133***				
	(0.0313)				
$lnT01$ * Year 2005	−0.2704***				
	(0.0326)				
$lnT01$ * Year 2006	−0.3414***				
	(0.0335)				
$lnT01$ * Year 2007	−0.3938***				
	(0.0349)				
Firm Controls	Y	Y	Y	Y	Y
Industrial Controls	Y	Y	Y	Y	Y
Firm FE	Y	Y	Y	Y	Y
Year FE	Y	Y	Y	Y	Y
Observations	1,268,326	1,268,326	323,879	89,316	131,293
R-squared	0.5142	0.5141	0.6127	0.8145	0.6500

Robust standard errors clustered at firm in parentheses.
*** $p < 0.01$.

3.2.1. *Flexible estimation*

In our main DID regression model, we use a time dummy variable, $Post02_t$, to separate the pre-WTO and post-WTO accession periods. The estimate from the interaction term, $InT01_i \times Post02_t$, yields the average treatment effect, which compares the difference between the treatment and control groups in their *average* differences between the pre-WTO and post-WTO accession periods. One drawback of such an approach is that it does not consider year to year changes. Hence, we now compare the difference between the treatment and control groups for *every* year in the entire period to remedy this weakness. Specifically, we use a flexible estimation specification to replace the interaction term $InT01_i \times Post02_t$ in model (1) with a series of interaction terms between $InT01_i$ and the year dummies, that is, $InT01_i \times t$ with t indicating 1999 through 2007. We run this regression and report the results in column 1 of Table 6.4. The estimated coefficients are statistically insignificant for all years before 2001, but become negative and statistically significant for every year from 2001 onwards. The magnitudes also become larger. These results clearly indicate the similarity between the two groups before the WTO accession, the innovation-reducing effect of input tariff cuts, and the increasing trend of the effect.

3.2.2. *Industry-specific time trend*

In the DID estimation, we assume that, conditional on $\mathbf{X}_{fit}$, k_f, k_t, innovation activities of the treatment and control groups follow the same time trend. This assumption allows us to use innovation activities of the control group as the counterfactual of the treatment group in the post-WTO accession period. However, innovation trends in different industries (or different groups) could be different because they may be affected by industry-specific confounding factors. Normally, this issue can be dealt with by con-trolling for sector-year fixed effect, but cannot be done here because the key regressor (i.e., $InT01_i{\cdot}Post02_t$) of our empirical model is defined merely at industry-year level, which rules out the possibility of including industry-year fixed effect in the regressions. Alternatively, to check whether unobserved industry-specific factors would bias our estimates, we add an industry-specific linear time trend, $k_i \cdot t$, to model (1). This addition enables us to control for all unobserved industry characteristics if they affect firm innovation in the form of a linear time trend. The regression result for the key explanatory variable is presented in column 2 of Table 6.4. The estimate is −0.1981, which is negative and statistically significant. Thus, our estimate is not driven by any unobserved industry trends.

3.2.3. *Placebo test I: pre-WTO accession period*

Following Topalova (2010), we conduct our first placebo test to examine the effect of input tariffs on firm innovation in the pre-WTO accession period (1998–2001). The premise is that because tariffs did not change much during that period, we should not expect any significant effect of input tariffs on innovation; if the result is the contrary, then it indicates the existence of some underlying confounding industrial factors (other than the WTO accession) that drive innovation. Accordingly, we replace $InT01_i \cdot Post02_t$ by InT_{it} in Eq. (1) and run the regression for the sample in the pre-WTO accession period. The estimates are given in column 3 of Table 6.4. The effect of InT_{it} is not statistically significant. Hence, we can rule out the possibility that some underlying confounding factors drive innovation.

3.2.4. *Placebo test II: subsample of processing-trade firms*

In our second placebo test, we run the regression model (1) using the subsample of processing-trade firms. As processing-trade firms enjoy zero input tariff rate during the entire period, their innovation decisions should not be affected much by the input tariff liberalization from China's WTO accession, and the estimation using the sample of processing-trade firms should produce an insignificant liberalization effect. We use two criteria to define processing-trade firms. One includes all firms with average ratios of processing exports over total exports larger than 90%, and the other consists of firms with average ratios larger than 50%. The processing export ratios are calculated based on the Chinese Customs Data.

The regression results are presented in columns 4 and 5 for the 90% and 50% criteria, respectively. Clearly, the coefficient of $InT01_i \times Post02_t$ in both cases is highly insignificant, confirming the conjecture. This test suggests that manufacturing firms adjust their innovation activities in response to input tariff reduction after the WTO accession if, and only if, their imported inputs are actually affected by tariff reduction.

3.3. *Robustness checks*

In this subsection, we further check the robustness of our results to address other concerns. Most of the results are presented in Table 6.5.

3.3.1. *Industrial competition*

The fact that market competition affects innovation activities is well known in innovation literature. In the main model, we have taken into account changes in import competition resulting from China's output tariff reduction. We further control for overall industrial competition by including the Herfindahl–Hirschman Index (HHI) in the model. The new variable, HHI_{it}, is the HHI for industry i in year t. Column 1 of Table 6.5 shows that our result is robust to including this competition variable.

3.3.2. *Export opportunity*

While China undertook considerable trade liberalization during the period of 1998–2007, trade liberalization also occurred in other countries. When foreign countries lower their tariffs on Chinese products, the market opportunity for Chinese exporters is increased, which may also induce them to adjust their innovation decisions. We handle this issue in two ways. First, we control for the export expansion opportunity by adding a term of industry-level total exports, $IndExp_{it}$. The regression results are reported in column 2 of Table 6.5.

We find a positive and significant effect of industry export on a firm's innovation activity (estimated coefficient 0.0042). More importantly, the estimate of our key variable, $InT01_i \times Post02_t$, remains negative and statistically significant. Second, to isolate the export expansion effect, we run the regression using the subsample of non-exporting firms. The results are reported in column 3 of the table. The main result also holds for this sub-group of firms.

Table 6.5. Robustness checks.

	(1)	(2)	(3)	(4)	(5)	(6)	(7)	(8)	(9)
	ln(patent)	ln(patent)	ln(patent)	ln(patent)	ln(patent)	ln(patent)	ln(patent)	ln(patent)	ln(patent)
Sample	All	All	Non-exporters	Life-cycle	Single-product	Surviving firms	Two-period	TFP	Initial size
$lnT01 * Post02$	−0.1887***	−0.1851***	−0.1151***	−0.1971***	−0.1737***	−0.2000***	−0.1627***	−0.1919***	−0.1776***
	(0.0203)	(0.0205)	(0.0185)	(0.0227)	(0.0210)	(0.0203)	(0.0273)	(0.0212)	(0.0202)
HHI	−0.0037								
	(0.0402)								
Total exports		0.0042***							
		(0.0013)							
Length $* Post02$				−0.0087***					
				(0.0031)					
$Post02$							0.0210***		
							(0.0039)		
ln(output/labor)								0.0131***	
								(0.0007)	
Firm controls	Y	Y	Y	Y	Y	Y	Y	Y	Y
Industrial controls	Y	Y	Y	Y	Y	Y	Y	Y	Y
Firm FE	Y	Y	Y	Y	Y	Y	Y	Y	Y
Year FE	Y	Y	Y	Y	Y	Y		Y	Y
Observations	1,268,326	1,267,582	913,640	973,993	1,174,680	572,405	475,172	1,195,919	1,268,326
R-squared	0.5141	0.5141	0.5110	0.5195	0.5100	0.4497	0.7913	0.5136	0.5156

Robust standard errors clustered at firm in parentheses. In column 9 we include a series of interaction terms between the initial labor size and year dummies.
$^{***}p < 0.01$

3.3.3. *Intellectual property rights (IPR) protection*

In the main analysis, we already controlled for SOE privatization and FDI entry deregulation, which occurred during China's WTO accession and could potentially affect the estimation. Another important policy change during the same period with even more obvious effect on innovation was the strengthening of IPR protection as required by TRIPS. One can argue that the average effect of TRIPS on innovation has already been controlled for by year dummies, but we can still explore the policy's differential effects across industries. As shown by Bilir (2014), the extent that an industry is affected by IPR changes is correlated with the length of the industry life cycle. Inspired by this observation, we control for the industry-differentiated effect of TRIPS by including the interaction term between the length of product life cycle and post-WTO dummy, i.e., $T_i \cdot Post02_t$. The data of product life-cycle length can be obtained from Bilir (2014), but we need to match the SIC industry code in Bilir (2014) with the CIC. As Bilir's (2014) measure of product life-cycle length is only available for a limited number of industries, a significant loss of observations will take place when we include this control variable.

Following Bilir (2014), in our test, we also use different measures of product life-cycle length, i.e., the average life-cycle length, the life-cycle length based on the seventy-fifth and eighty-fifth percentiles of each citation lag distribution, in our test. We report the result of the use of the average life-cycle length in column 4 of Table 6.5. Our result is robust, and so are the results obtained from the use of other length measures which are omitted in the table.

3.3.4. *Multi-product firms*

Many firms produce multiple products that may span over different industries.[21] Thus, our dependent variable (i.e., a firm's total number of patent filings) may cover many industries that experience different degrees of input tariff cut. Thus, the analysis will lead to an imprecise estimation of the impact of input tariff cut on firm innovation. Hence, to check whether our result is contaminated by this problem, we

[21]Note that each firm reports one industry which it belongs to in the NBS survey even if it is a multi-product firm spanning many industries.

restrict our analysis to a subsample of firms that produce products all belonging to the same 3-digit industry.[22] We run regression (1) based on this subsample of "single-industry" firms and find that the effect of input tariff reductions on innovation remains negative and statistically significant, as shown in column 5 of Table 6.5.[23]

3.3.5. *Surviving firms*

We notice from the summary statistics in Table 6.1 the presence of a decrease in average age of firms. This observation implies that a significant number of firms entered after 2001. From the data, we also observe a significant number of firms exiting. If the new entrants and/or exiting firms have different patenting behaviors, our earlier estimation results may also capture the selection effect, instead of the true effect of input tariff reductions. Hence, to check whether our estimates are driven by entry and exit, we focus on a subsample of surviving firms (i.e., firms in both the pre- and post-WTO accession periods). Results are reported in column 6 of Table 6.5. We still find negative effect of input tariff reductions and the magnitude becomes even larger, implying that the selection from entry and exit does not drive our findings and if it does, it causes a bias on our estimate downwards at the most.

3.3.6. *Two-period estimation*

The DID estimation and resulting statistical inference crucially depend on the accuracy of standard errors. In the main analysis, we followed Bertrand *et al.* (2004) to cluster standard errors at the firm level. As a robustness check, we use another approach, which is also suggested by Bertrand *et al.* (2004), to calculate the standard errors.

---

[22] We obtain product-level data from NBS of China for the period 2000–2006, which contains information of each product (defined at the five-digit product level) produced by every firm. As product-level data and NBS data use the same firm identity, we can easily match these two datasets and identify firms producing all goods within only one three-digit industry.

[23] Some firms may change location or industry affiliation over the sample period. Though these firms are very few and we have controlled for firm fixed effects, we conduct regressions with the sample of firms without such a change, and find similar results.

In particular, we first collapse the panel structure into two periods (pre-WTO and post-WTO accession) and then use the White-robust standard errors. The regression results are presented in column 7 of Table 6.5. The results are qualitatively similar to the ones obtained before.

3.3.7. *Firm-level productivity*

Firms with different productivity levels may have different abilities or incentives to conduct innovation. Recall that in the main analysis, we included firm fixed effects in all regressions, which control for all firm-level time-invariant characteristics, including the *initial* productivity and other factors (e.g., corporate culture) that may affect innovation. However, productivity changes over time. Hence, to further control for the effects of productivity on innovation, we also introduce *contemporary* productivity levels of the firms to the model. In this robustness check, we use labor productivity (output/labor) to represent firm productivity. The new results are reported in column 8 of Table 6.5. Our key finding remains robust. The results also show that more productive firms are more innovative, which is consistent with the findings in literature.

3.3.8. *Firm size*

Firms of different sizes may have different incentives to undertake innovation because of different investment returns. Firms of different sizes may also have different innovation trends. Thus, to check whether introducing a control for the differential trends across sizes will affect our estimation, we add a series of interaction terms between the initial labor size (to capture firm size) and year dummies in our regression. The new results are reported in column 9 of Table 6.5. We find that our key estimation is robust to this size consideration.[24]

[24]Note that in column 9 of the table, we do not report the estimates of the newly introduced interaction terms; for otherwise, the table will be too long. Our regression result shows that all these interaction terms are positive and statistically significant, implying that larger firms are always more innovative.

3.3.9. *Alternative estimation methods*

In the main model, we use the OLS method to estimate the effect of input tariff cut on firm innovation. Now, we check our results using alternative estimation methods. First, we use the Fixed-effect Poisson model. Column 1 of Table 6.6 reports the result (the coefficients are incidence-rate ratios). We still obtain significantly negative effect of input tariff cut on firm patent filings. However, only 98,868 observations (about 7.8% of the whole sample) remain in the regression because all firms with just one observation or firms with all zero outcomes are dropped automatically in such nonlinear regressions for panel data. Second, to remedy the severe data loss problem associated with the Fixed-effect Poisson model, we also use the Random-effect Poisson model, which keeps all observations. We obtain very similar results, as shown in column 2 of Table 6.6.

Third, firms may make innovation decisions in a sequential manner, that is, they first decide whether to innovate and then how much to innovate. In this case, a two-step selection model is more appropriate. We check whether our results are robust to this two-step selection model estimation, and to do so requires an excluded variable that affects firms' decision on whether to innovate but not affect firms' decision on how much to innovate. Following Sanyal and Ghosh (2013), we use each firm's patent stock since 1995 (denoted by lnpatentr95) as exclusion restriction in the first step Fixed-effect Logit regression, with patenting indicator as dependent variable. Then, in the second step, we include the inverse Mill's ratio from the first step to correct the potential selection bias in the regression. The results of the two-step selection model are reported in columns 3 and 4 of Table 6.6. The results show that past innovation behavior affects current innovation decision and the existence of a selection effect in innovation. Most importantly, input tariff cut clearly decreases both the likelihood and the intensity of innovation. However, a similar problem as in the Fixed-effect Poisson model occurs, that is, we experience a significant loss of observations in the first-step regression.

In sum, our findings are robust to alternative nonlinear regression models despite the significant cost of using such regressions (i.e., a substantial loss in observations).

Table 6.6. Alternative estimation methods.

	(1)	(2)	(3)	(4)	(5)	(6)
	Patent	Patent	Patent indicator	ln(patent)	ImpStart	ln(patent)
Variables	FE Poisson	RE Poisson	1st step	2nd step	1st stage	2nd stage
$lnT01 * Post02$	−3.3218***	−3.5040***	−2.0515***	−0.8275**	0.0384***	
	(1.1609)	(0.7862)	(0.5660)	(0.3282)	(0.0146)	
ImpStart						−2.9826***
						(0.7515)
Age	−0.016	−0.0116	−0.0311***	−0.0131***	0.0017***	0.0046***
	(0.0119)	(0.0097)	(0.0057)	(0.0032)	(0.0002)	(0.0014)
Age squared	0.0002	0.0002	0.0004***	0.0002***	−0.000***	−0.0001***
	(0.0002)	(0.0002)	(0.0001)	(0.0001)	0.0000	0.0000
Exporting	−0.0217	0.0402	−0.0056	0.001	0.0231***	0.0759***
	(0.0614)	(0.0563)	(0.0432)	(0.0231)	(0.0015)	(0.0176)
ln(Labor)	0.6446***	0.7795***	0.1758***	0.1544***	0.0220***	0.0808***
	(0.0837)	(0.0532)	(0.0337)	(0.0194)	(0.0010)	(0.0166)
ln(Capital/labor)	0.1050***	0.2361***	−0.0137	0.403***	0.0035***	0.0136***
	(0.0406)	(0.0306)	(0.0198)	(0.0118)	(0.0004)	(0.0028)
Foreign share	−0.3359*	−0.2004	−0.1489	0.0346	0.0176***	0.0523***
	(0.1974)	(0.1627)	(0.0952)	(0.0493)	(0.0050)	(0.0149)

(*Continued*)

Table 6.6. (*Continued*)

	(1)	(2)	(3)	(4)	(5)	(6)
	Patent	Patent	Patent indicator	ln(patent)	ImpStart	ln(patent)
Variables	FE Poisson	RE Poisson	1st step	2nd step	1st stage	2nd stage
Output tariff	0.0821	0.0071	0.8485**	−0.2534	−0.0117	−0.0238
	(1.1219)	(0.7686)	(0.4135)	(0.2413)	(0.0106)	(0.0242)
SOE no.	−1.1608*	−1.0104**	−0.1161	−0.4275***	0.1452***	0.3759***
	(0.6122)	(0.5011)	(0.2538)	(0.1460)	(0.0100)	(0.1076)
FIE no.	−0.0908	−0.1291***	0.0424	0.0284*	0.0038***	0.0107***
	(0.0720)	(0.0458)	(0.0277)	(0.0158)	(0.0009)	(0.0032)
lnpatentr95			4.5846***			
			(0.0432)			
Lambda				−0.6782***		
				(0.0339)		
Observations	98,868	1,268,326	96,201	31,127	870,661	870,661
R-squared				0.7638		
Number of firm	17,241	335,998	16,446			309,713

Robust standard errors clustered at firm in parentheses.
*** $p < 0.001$.
** $p < 0.05$.
* $p < 0.1$.

3.3.10. *Importing behavior*

After focusing on the effect of input trade liberalization on innovation, we now turn to the direct relation between intermediate input imports and innovation. Specifically, we check whether the reduction in patenting occurs after firms begin to import, or in other words, whether input tariff cut affects firm innovation through the change in importing behavior of firms. We therefore use a two-stage IV regression method to investigate (i) whether input tariff cut affects firms' importing behavior (first-stage regression), and (ii) whether the changed importing behavior in turn affects firms' innovation behavior (second-stage regression), using input tariff cut to instrument the importing behavior. Because we need firms' importing behavior information to perform this method, we combine NBS data with Customs data for the period 2000–2006. We identify each firm's importing status in each year from Customs data, and define a dummy variable $ImpStart_{ft}$ that indicates whether firm f starts to import intermediate inputs in year t. The dummy variable equals zero for the years before the firm starts to import and unity after-wards. We restrict our sample to initial non-importers, that is, firms that did not export in the first year they entered the sample. The IV regression results are reported in columns 5 and 6 of Table 6.6. The first-stage result shows that input tariff cut increases the likelihood of importing intermediate inputs, which in turn reduces innovation as shown by the second-stage result.

3.4. *Heterogeneous effects*

Firms are heterogeneous in many dimensions, and so are innovations. We explore the possible heterogeneous effects of input tariff reductions on innovations. Results are reported in Table 6.7.

3.4.1. *Types of innovation*

Our data have detailed information with regard to the types of innovation. Chinese Patent Law classifies patents into three categories, namely, invention, utility model, and design. Invention patents refer to technical innovations on products, methods, or both; utility model patents refer to technical proposals on the shape and/or structure of a product; and design patents refer to changes in the shape and/or

Table 6.7. Heterogeneous effects.

	(1)	(2)	(3)	(4)	(5)	(6)
Variables	Invention	Utility	Design	ln(patent)	ln(patent)	ln(patent)
Sample	All	All	All	Low K/L	High K/L	Low TFP
$lnT01 * Post02$	−0.0821***	−0.1027***	−0.0464***	−0.0961	−0.3564***	-0.0267
	(0.0082)	(0.0109)	(0.0160)	(0.0643)	(0.0533)	(0.0228)
Firm controls	Y	Y	Y	Y	Y	Y
Industrial controls	Y	Y	Y	Y	Y	Y
Firm FE	Y	Y	Y	Y	Y	Y
Year FE	Y	Y	Y	Y	Y	Y
Observations	1,268,326	1,268,326	1,268,326	357,154	334,867	112,972
R-squared	0.4871	0.4928	0.4690	0.4837	0.5630	0.3670
	(7)	(8)	(9)	(10)	(11)	(12)
Variables	ln(patent)	ln(patent)	ln(patent)	ln(patent)	ln(patent)	ln(patent)
Sample	High TFP	SOEs	Private	Foreign	Importer	Non-importer
$lnT01 * Post02$	−0.2963***	−0.1272***	−0.1476***	−0.2678***	−0.3246***	0.0928***
	(0.0516)	(0.0466)	(0.0230)	(0.0605)	(0.1192)	(0.0180)
Firm controls	Y	Y	Y	Y	Y	Y
Industrial controls	Y	Y	Y	Y	Y	Y
Firm FE	Y	Y	Y	Y	Y	Y
Year FE	Y	Y	Y	Y	Y	Y
Observations	771,325	116,023	902,130	250,173	112,983	843,283
R-squared	0.5535	0.4996	0.5259	0.5472	0.6872	0.5642

Robust standard errors clustered at firm in parentheses.
*** $p < 0.01$.

color of a product. The requirements for obtaining each of the three patents are very different, with the invention application having the most difficult requirements and the design application having the easiest requirements. Thus, asking whether the effects of input tariff cuts on these innovations differ significantly is also reasonable. Columns 1–3 present the empirical results obtained from regressions based on each of the three types of innovation. We find that input tariff cuts reduce all types of innovation significantly.

3.4.2. *Capital intensity*

Industries differ in many dimensions, which could potentially affect firms' responses to input tariff reductions. Capital-labor ratio, or simply capital intensity, is a determinant of innovation, and differs significantly across industries. We ascertain if the main result of our analysis is sensitive to capital intensity of the industries by rerunning the regression using a subsample of industries with high capital intensity and a subsample of industries with low capital intensity, respectively. We calculate the capital–labor ratio of each four-digit CIC industry in the pre-WTO accession period (the simple average of the ratios in those years) to construct the two subsamples. The low capital-intensity industry group includes all industries with a capital intensity lower than the 25th percentile of the entire sample, whereas the high capital-intensity industry group includes all industries with a capital intensity higher than the 75th percentile of the entire sample. Column 4 of Table 6.7 reports the regression results from the low capital-intensity group while column 5 reports those from the high capital-intensity group. We find negative effects of input tariff reduction on innovation in both groups. The effect is stronger for firms from high capital-intensity industries than from low capital-intensity industries. This comparison is consistent with the fact that firms with high capital-intensity undertake more innovations and thus are more affected by the reduction.

3.4.3. *Distance from technology frontier*

Aghion *et al.* (2009) argue that the distance from the world's technology frontier is an important factor in determining firm responses in innovation to market competition. We explore whether the input tariff reductions also lead to different responses by firms with different distance from the world's technology frontier.

We divide the sample into five quantiles based on the average total factor productivity (TFP) of firms in the pre-WTO accession period.[25] Quantiles are constructed within each CIC four-digit industry. We run regressions for the subsample of the first quantile firms (i.e., firms far from the frontier) and the subsample of the fifth quantile firms (i.e., firms close to the frontier), respectively. Columns 6 and 7 report the results. We find that for low-productivity firms, the effect of input tariff reductions on innovation is insignificant, whereas for high-productivity firms, the effect is significantly negative. One possible reason for such a difference is that low-productivity firms do not use much imported intermediate input in their production nor do they engage actively in innovation, and thus, their innovation activities are not sensitive to changes in input tariffs.

3.4.4. *Ownership*

In terms of ownership structure, three types of firms primarily exist in China: SOEs, domestic private firms, and foreign invested enterprises (FIEs). FIEs are all business entities established in China with part or all of foreign capital. They include both Sino-foreign joint ventures and wholly foreign-owned enterprises. Determining whether firms with different ownership structures have different responses to input tariff reduction would be an interesting exercise. Columns 8–10 show the results for SOEs, domestic private firms, and FIEs, respectively. All types of firms reduce their innovations significantly in response to input tariff liberalization. The negative effect on SOEs is the weakest. Perhaps, the innovation incentives of SOEs are less responsive to market and cost conditions. The effect on FIEs is the strongest, which may suggest that they depend more on imported intermediate inputs for production and innovations.

---

[25]TFP is estimated using the Levinsohn and Petrin (2003) method at the level of two-digit CIC industry and with information of value added, employment, fixed assets, and intermediate inputs. All nominal variables are deflated using the deflators from Brandt *et al.* (2012).

3.4.5. *Direct importers and non-importers*

We classified firms into direct importers, which are firms that import intermediate inputs directly by themselves, and non-importers. While direct importers are affected directly by input tariff cuts, non-importers may also be affected indirectly because they may purchase imported inputs from intermediaries. Amiti and Konings (2007) show that direct importers in Indonesia are affected more by tariff reductions than non-importers. We examine whether the difference obtained for Indonesian firms also exists for Chinese firms by running regressions using the sample of direct importers and non-importers, respectively. Columns 11 and 12 show the effect on direct importers and non-importers, respectively. We find that both types of firms reduce their innovations, with direct importers reducing more than non-importers.

4. Mechanism: A Simple Model and Evidence

Why does a tariff cut in intermediate input imports reduce firm innovations? To understand this interesting observation, we provide one explanation derived from a highly simplified and stylized model in Subsection 4.1. We put the equilibrium analysis (the proof of the results) in the Appendix. In Subsection 4.2, we conduct further empirical analysis which generates results consistent with the main predictions from the model, thereby providing support for the model.[26]

4.1. *Model and results*

Consider a firm facing demand for its product as $P(y)$, where y is the quantity and P is the price with $P(y) < 0$. Production requires both domestic intermediate input, denoted as d, and imported intermediate input, denoted as x. Assume that production function takes the following form: $y = f(x, d)h(b, r)$, where $f(\cdot)$ is a usual production function and $h(\cdot)$, which represents the level of productivity, is

[26]The model of endogenous input and output quality choices proposed by Kugler and Verhoogen (2012) can also be modified to provide insights on how firms respond to intermediate input tariff cut by adjusting their decisions.

an increasing function of the quality of the imported intermediate input b and the firm's innovation r. Let p^d be the price of domestic intermediate input, $p^x(b)$ the price of imported intermediate input, which is an increasing function of quality (i.e., $p^x > 0$), p^r the price of imported input for innovation activity, and t the import tariff.

Given p^x, p^r, p^d and t, the firm's optimization problem is

$$\max\left[\mathrm{P}(y)y - \tau p(\beta)\chi - \tau p^r r - p^d d\right].$$

Suppose that the second order conditions for optimization hold. Let us use subscript to denote partial derivative. In the Appendix, we prove the following proposition.

Proposition 1. *Suppose that θ_r or $\frac{p^{x'}}{p^x}$ is sufficiently small and $\theta_{\beta\beta} > 0$. Then, a decrease in the tariff (τ) on intermediate input will result in a rise in intermediate input quality (β), but a reduction in innovation activity (r). The firm's productivity (θ) will increase.*

When τ decreases, many possible combinations of optimal responses from the three decision variables, namely, x, β and r, exist and the possibility of all three increasing is very possible because of the price effect (cheaper now). However, our analysis identifies an interesting (and somewhat surprising) outcome: r decreases. This decrease is accompanied with an increase in β. The intuition is in fact very clear. Note from the analysis leading to the corollary that the condition on θ_r and that on $\frac{p^{x'}}{p^x}$ are in relative terms. Thus, understanding the result based on the condition that both θ_r and $\frac{p^{x'}}{p^x}$ are small is a better option. In this case, although everything (x and r) is cheaper, spending the money most efficiently to improve output and profit remains a concern. Because the marginal improvement in productivity by increasing innovation is small (θ_r), and the percentage increase in the price of intermediate input with higher quality ($\frac{p^{x'}}{p^x}$) is also small but the effect of further raising productivity from using higher quality intermediate input increases ($\theta_{\beta\beta} > 0$), increasing the quality of the intermediate input by reducing innovation raises profits, because these inputs serve as substitutes in raising productivity.

The implications of increasing intermediate input quality and reducing innovation on the quantity of import (x) are less clear.

With the increase in productivity ($\theta_\tau < 0$), the marginal revenue of increasing input rises, and so x should go up. However, if the cost of import, τp^x, has also increased because of higher quality input, then x will have a tendency to decrease. Our analysis shows that under the condition stated in Proposition 1, in response to a tariff cut, x may increase or decrease.

4.2. *Empirical evidence: Input quality or quantity?*

We now turn to further empirical analysis to determine the relevance of the above proposed mechanism on how the intermediate input imports of firms respond to tariff cuts. Specifically, we investigate how input tariff cuts affect the value (exclusive of tariffs), quantity, and quality (or price, exclusive of tariffs) of intermediate input imports.

From Customs data, we can obtain detailed information on imports at the HS six-digit level; thus, our regressions are conducted at a more disaggregate level. We first drop all processing imports to process the data before running the regressions. We then identify imports of intermediate inputs using the Classification by Broad Economic Categories (BEC) published by the United Nations Statistics Division. This classification requires us to convert product affiliations in all the years before 2002 to the HS2002 version with the concordance table from the United Nations Statistics Division.

Following Goldberg *et al.* (2010), we conduct the regression analyses (for import price, quantity and value) based on the following model:

$$y_{ijt} = aTariff01_i \cdot Post02_t + \lambda_i + \lambda_t + \lambda_j \cdot t + \varepsilon_{ijt},$$

where y_{ijt} is the logarithm of quantity, value, and unit value of imported intermediate input i (at HS six-digit level) of industry j (at HS two-digit level) in year t; $Tariff01_i$ is the tariff of input i in year 2001; $Post02_t$ is the WTO accession dummy as defined previously; and ε_{ijt} is the robust error term. We control for product fixed effect (λ_i) and year fixed effect (λ_t) in all regressions. Because industries may have different time trends, we further control for HS two-digit industry-specific linear time trend ($\lambda_j \cdot t$).

The regression results are reported in Table 6.8. For each dependent variable, we run the regressions for China's total intermediate

Table 6.8. Effects on import value, quantity and price.

	Import price			Import quantity				Import value			
Sample	(1) All sources	(2) From OECD	(3) From non OECD	(4) All sources	(5) From OECD	(6) From non OECD	(7) Share from OECD	(8) All sources	(9) From OECD	(10) From non OECD	(11) Share from OECD
$Tariff01$	0.0046***	0.0063***	0.0063***	−0.0123***	−0.0129***	−0.0218***	0.004	−0.0072***	−0.0063***	−0.0135***	0.0007**
$Post02$	(0.0014)	(0.0015)	(0.0014)	(0.0030)	(0.0034)	(0.0038)	(0.0004)	(0.0028)	(0.0031)	(0.0037)	(0.0003)
Year FE	Y	Y	Y	Y	Y	Y	Y	Y	Y	Y	Y
HS6 FE	Y	Y	Y	Y	Y	Y	Y	Y	Y	Y	Y
HS2 trend	Y	Y	Y	Y	Y	Y	Y	Y	Y	Y	Y
Observations	25,212	24,845	25,533	25,212	24,845	23,533	24,855	25,233	24,876	23,576	24,876
R-squared	0.9676	0.9642	0.9459	0.9240	0.9176	0.8914	0.6666	0.9058	0.9058	0.8499	0.6870

In all regressions we control for year and HS 6-digit industry fixed, and HS 2-digit industry linear time trend. Robust standard errors in parentheses.
*** $p < 0.01$.
** $p < 0.05$.

input imports from all countries, from OECD countries, and from non-OECD countries, respectively.

As predicted by Proposition 1, if θ_r or $\frac{p^{x'}}{p^x}$ is sufficiently small, which we think is quite plausible for China. Then, in response to input tariff cuts, firms may switch from importing low-quality to high-quality inputs. In this case, import price will be higher because higher quality means higher price. This view is confirmed by columns 1–3.[27] However, the prediction on the import quantity is less clear, depending on other conditions. Our results show that import quantity drops, as reported in columns 4-6. Because price increases while quantity decreases, the change in value is generally ambiguous. Nevertheless, we find that imported value also decreases, as shown by columns 8–10.

An alternative way to proxy input quality is to look at the origin of the exporting country, with OECD countries' exports representing higher quality. Although both total quantity and value decrease, the share of input imports from OECD increases in both quantity (column 7) and value (column 11), lending further support to the quality upgrade.

As intermediate inputs are classified into intermediate and capital goods in the BEC classification, we also check the two types of intermediate inputs separately and the results are similar.

5. Conclusion

The effects of trade on innovation have long been a hot topic in both academic and policy circles. Trade in intermediate inputs has become increasingly important in the world economy. This paper investigates the effects of intermediate input trade liberalization on firm innovation, which complements the emerging literature that investigates the effects of intermediate input trade liberalization on

[27] This finding complements Bas and Strauss-Kahn (2015). There is an important difference though. Bas and Strauss-Kahn (2015) find that, relative to processing-trade firms, ordinary-trade firms increase their import quality after the trade liberalization. Here we show that among ordinary-trade firms, those facing higher trade liberalization intensity increase their import quality more.

firm performance from different perspectives such as productivity, product scope, and product quality.

We exploit the quasi-natural experiment of China's WTO accession in 2001 and the rich data on Chinese firms and find that input tariff reductions in China reduce innovations of the Chinese firms. This result is robust to a series of model specifications, and significant both statistically and economically.

The driving force underlying the negative effect of intermediate input imports on firm innovation is that high-quality input imports substitute for internal innovation of firms. Theoretically, intermediate input imports can be complements to internal innovation in the sense that high-quality inputs help lower innovation cost. On the contrary, cheaper intermediate inputs from abroad can be substitutes for firm innovation because firms can buy instead of making them. Our empirical evidence show that the input tariff cut leads firms to opt for lesser imports but choose higher-quality intermediate inputs, whereby reducing innovations.

Although the results are somewhat surprising, they are not incompatible with results obtained by other studies on the effects of intermediate input tariff reductions on the other aspects of the performances of the Chinese firms, such as productivity (Yu, 2015) and export quality (Bas and Strauss-Kahn, 2015; Fan *et al.*, 2015). Introducing a general theoretical framework that can produce all these results and provide a clear mechanism is an attractive prospect. Such a model will also be helpful in predicting whether our negative effect can also be found in other countries. Further empirical studies on the experiences of other countries on the effects of intermediate input trade liberalization on innovation are also encouraged, such as Goldberg *et al.*, 2010 on India.

Acknowledgments

We benefitted from discussions with Elhanan Helpman, Hong Ma, Marc Melitz, Tommy Wu, Xi Weng, Li-an Zhou and the presentation at The UIBE International Trade Workshop (October 2014) and The Hong Kong Economic Association Conference (December 2014), seminar at Guanghua School of Management, Peking University (March

2015) and Bologna University (April 2015), Summer Work-shop of HKIMR (August 2015), The HKU International Trade Work-shop (December 2015), Kobe University (2015), The Hitotsubashi-Peking University Workshop on Trade & Development (March 2016). We thank Chaoqun Zhan for his assistance in our research and the referees for their excellent comments and suggestions. Qiu appreciates financial support from HKIMR for visiting scholarship and Chung Hon-Dak Endowed Professorship in Economic Development.

Appendix

Proof of Proposition 1. In this proof, we reduce the number of decision variables to make our points as simple as possible. To this end, we make two simplifying assumptions. First, we assume that all inputs for R&D are imported. Second, to focus on import decisions, assume that $f(\cdot)$ takes the Leontief form and the price of domestic input is sufficiently low that the firm always chooses the level of domestic input equal to that of the imported input. This step allows us to omit the domestic input from the production function, and ignoring the cost of domestic input from the profit will not affect the qualitative results. With further simplification, we can write the production function as $y = x\theta(\beta, r)$. We will return to discussing the implications of relaxing these two assumptions later. Relaxing these assumptions will not alter the qualitative aspect of the result and may even reinforce it. Consequently, the firm's optimization problem becomes

$$\max_{(\beta,r,x)} [\mathrm{P}(y)y - \tau p^{\chi}(\beta)\chi - \tau p^{r} r]$$

Using subscript to denote partial differentiation, we obtain first-order conditions:

$$\begin{aligned} P' x^2 \theta\theta_{\beta b} + P x \theta_{\beta} - \tau p^{x'} x &= 0, \\ P' x^2 \theta\theta_{r} + P x \theta_{r} - \tau p^{r} &= 0, \\ P' x \theta^2 + P\theta - \tau p^{x} &= 0, \end{aligned}$$

which can be rewritten as

$$P'X\theta + P = \tau P^{X'}\frac{1}{\theta_\beta} \tag{2}$$

$$P'X\theta + P = \tau p^{r}\frac{1}{\theta_r}\frac{1}{x} \tag{3}$$

$$P'X\theta + P = \tau p^{x}\frac{1}{\theta}. \tag{4}$$

Combining Eq. (2) with Eqs. (3) and (4), respectively, we obtain

$$x = \frac{p^r}{p^{x'}}\frac{\theta_\beta}{\theta_r} \tag{5}$$

$$\theta = \frac{1}{p^{x'}}p^{x}\theta_\beta. \tag{6}$$

Let us focus on a simple case in which $P'' = 0$ and $p^{x''} = 0$. Differentiating Eq. (6) with respect to τ and using $\theta_\tau = \theta_\beta\beta_\tau + \theta_r r_\tau$ yields.

$$\beta_\tau = \mathrm{A}r_\tau, \quad \text{where A} \equiv \frac{\theta_r}{\theta_{\beta\beta}}\left(\frac{p^{x'}}{p^{x}} - \frac{\theta_{\beta r}}{\theta_r}\right) \tag{7}$$

Similarly, differentiating Eq. (5) with respect to t and using

$$x_\tau = \mathrm{B}r_\tau, \quad \text{where B} \equiv \frac{p_r}{p^{x}} - \frac{x}{\theta_r}(A\theta_{\beta r} + \theta_{rr}). \tag{8}$$

Differentiating Eq. (1) with respect to τ, we have

$$2P'[\chi(\theta_\beta\beta_\tau + \theta_r r_\tau) + \theta\chi_\tau] = p^{x'}\left[\frac{1}{\theta_\beta} - \frac{\tau}{\theta_\beta^2}\left(\theta_{\beta\beta}\beta_\tau + \theta_{\beta r}r_\tau\right)\right].$$

Substituting Eqs. (7) and (8) into the above equation and rearranging the terms yields

$$\left[2P'(Ax\theta_\beta + \chi\theta_r + B\theta) + \tau\left(\frac{P^{x'}}{\theta_\beta}\right)^2\frac{\theta_r}{p^{x}}\right]r_\tau = \frac{p^{x'}}{\theta_\beta}. \tag{9}$$

Hence, if $C < 0$, we will have $r_\tau > 0$ because $D > 0$. Using Eqs. (5)–(8), we can rearrange the terms to get

$$C = \frac{p^X p^r}{\theta_{\beta\beta}} \left(\frac{\theta_\beta}{p^{x'}}\right)^2 \left[\left(\frac{\theta_{\beta r}}{\theta_r} - \frac{p^{x'}}{p^x}\right)^2 - \frac{\theta_{\beta\beta}\theta_{rr}}{\theta_r^2}\right] + x\theta_r + \frac{p^r}{p^{x'}}\theta_\beta.$$

Then, with some manipulation, we have $C < 0$ if and only if

$$(\theta_{\beta\beta}\theta_{rr} - \theta_{\beta r}^2)\frac{1}{\theta_r^2} > \frac{p^{x'}}{p^x}\left[\frac{p^{x'}}{p^x} - 2\left(\frac{\theta_{\beta r}}{\theta_r} - \frac{\theta_{\beta\beta}}{\theta_\beta}\right)\right]. \tag{10}$$

Note from Eq. (7) that if $A < 0$, then β_τ and r_τ will have the opposite signs, and if $\theta_{\beta\beta} > 0$, then $A < 0$ if and only if

$$\frac{p^{x'}}{p^x} < \frac{\theta_{\beta r}}{\theta_r}. \tag{11}$$

The above analysis leads to the following lemma:

Lemma 1. *Suppose $\theta_{\beta\beta} > 0$. Conditions (10)–(11) are sufficient conditions for $\beta_\tau < 0$ and $r_\tau > 0$.*

Let us further suppose that $\theta_{\beta\beta}\theta_{rr} - \theta_{\beta r}^2 > 0$ to obtain more meaningful conditions. Then, LHS of Eq. (10) is decreasing in θ_r while RHS is increasing in θ_r. Moreover, LHS can be very large when hr is very small. Thus, Eq. (10) holds when θ_r is sufficiently small. Even if θ_r is not very small (so that LHS is not very large), Eq. (10) still holds if $\frac{p^{x'}}{p^x}$ is sufficiently small. An interesting observation is that Eq. (11) also requires to be sufficiently small or $\frac{p^{x'}}{p^x}$ be sufficiently small. Hence, the effects of tariff on intermediate input quality and innovation activity are established.

Let us turn to the effect on productivity. Note that $\theta t = \theta_\beta\beta_\tau + \theta_r r_\tau$. Thus, when θr is sufficiently small, we also have $\theta_r < 0$ because according to Corollary 1, $\beta_\tau < 0$ although $r_\tau > 0$. Alternatively, using the fact that $\beta_\tau = Ar_\tau$ and $\theta_r > 0$ and with the result $r_\tau > 0$, we can easily show that the necessary and sufficient condition for $\theta t < 0$ is

$$\frac{p^{x'}}{p^x} < \frac{\theta_{\beta r}}{\theta_r} - \frac{\theta_{\beta\beta}}{\theta_\beta}. \tag{12}$$

Thus, we have a result on productivity similar to Corollary 1; that is, when θ_r or $p^{x'}/p^x$ is sufficiently small, a decrease in tariff (t) on intermediate input will result in higher productivity (θ).

Note that condition (12) is stronger than Eq. (11). Thus, the condition stated in Proposition 1 should be the condition that satisfies Eq. (12). Recall that we imposed two simplifying assumptions to carry out the above analysis. If the firm uses both domestic input and imported input for R&D, as the imported input becomes cheaper, the firm will substitute domestic input with imported input. However, compared to the case without domestic input, the decrease in R&D cost as a result of a decrease in t is smaller. Hence, given the condition in Corollary 1, the firm will have a stronger incentive to reduce R&D. That is, the result stated in Corollary 1 is reinforced.

If substitution between domestic input and imported intermediate input for production is performed, then the level of domestic input (d) will be chosen optimally. As a direct effect, tariff drop will clearly reduce the use of domestic input. The firm will face a similar situation in choosing the other three variables, x, b and r. We do not expect to see the qualitative aspect of Corollary 1 to change. The increase in productivity as a result of higher b may push the use of domestic input, which is the indirect effect. Whether the use of domestic input will go up or down remains ambiguous.

References

Aghion, P., Blundell, R., Griffith, R., Howitt, P., Prantl, S., 2009. The effects of entry on incumbent innovation and productivity. Rev. Econ. Stat. 91 (1), 20–32.

Almeida, R., Fernandes, A.M., 2008. Openness and technological innovations in developing countries: evidence from firm level surveys. J. Dev. Stud. 44 (5), 701–727.

Amiti, M., Konings, J., 2007. Trade liberalization, intermediate inputs, and productivity: evidence from Indonesia. Am. Econ. Rev. 97, 1611–1638.

Atkeson, A., Burstein, A., 2010. Innovation, firm dynamics, and international trade. J. Polit. Econ. 118, 433–484.

Aw, B.Y., Roberts, M.J., Daniel, Y.U., 2011. R&D investment, exporting, and productivity dynamics. Am. Econ. Rev. 101, 1312–1344.

Baldwin, J., Gu, W., 2004. Trade liberalization: exporting-market participation, productivity growth and innovation. Economic Analysis Research Paper Series No. 027, Statistics Canada.

Bas, M., 2012. Input-trade liberalization and firm export decisions: evidence from Argentina. J. Dev. Econ. 97, 481–493.

Bas, M., Strauss-Kahn, V., 2014. Does importing more inputs raise exports? Firm-level evidence from France. Rev. World Econ. 150(2), 241–475.

Bas, M., Strauss-Kahn, V., 2015. Input-trade liberalization, export prices and quality upgrading. J. Int. Econ. 95(2), 250–262.

Bertrand, M., Duflo, E., Mullainathan, S., 2004. How much should we trust Differences-in-Differences estimates? Q. J. Econ. 119, 249–275.

Bilir, L.K., 2014. Patent laws, product lifecycle lengths, and multinational activity. Am. Econ. Rev. 104 (3), 1979–2013.

Bloom, N., Draca, M., Reenen, J.V., 2016. Trade induced technical change: the impact of Chinese imports on innovation, diffusion and productivity. Rev. Econ. Stud. 83 (1), 87–117.

Brandt, L., Biesebroeck, J.V., Zhang, Y., 2012. Creative accounting or creative destruction? Firm-level productivity growth in Chinese manufacturing. J. Dev. Econ. 97 (2), 339–351.

Burstein, A., Melitz, M., 2013. Trade liberalization and firm dynamics. Advances in Economics and Econometrics Tenth World Congress. Applied Economics. Econometric Society Monographs. vol. 2. Cambridge University Press, UK.

Bustos, P., 2011. Trade liberalization, exports, and technology upgrading: evidence on the impact of MERCOSUR on Argentinian firms. Am. Econ. Rev. 101, 304–340.

Cai, H., Liu, Q, 2009. Competition and corporate tax avoidance: evidence from Chinese industrial firms. Econ. J. 119 (537), 764–795.

Cassiman, B., Veugelers, R., 2006. In search of complementarity in innovation strategy: internal R&D and external knowledge acquisition. Manag. Sci. 52 (1), 68–82.

Chevassus-Lozza, E., Gaigne, C., Mener, L.L., 2013. Does input trade liberalization boost downstream firms' exports? Theory and firm-level evidence. J. Int. Econ. 90, 391–402.

Coe, D., Helpman, E., 1995. International R&D spillovers. Eur. Econ. Rev. 39, 859–887.

Cohen, W., Levinthal, D., 1989. Innovation and learning: the two faces of R&D. Econ. J. 99, 569–596.

Connolly, M., 2003. The dual nature of trade: measuring its impact on imitation and growth. J. Dev. Econ. 72, 31–55.

Dang, J., Motohashi, K., 2015. Patent statistics: a good indicator for innovation in China? Patent subsidy program impacts on patent quality. China Econ. Rev. 35, 137–155.

de Negri, J.A., Turchi, L.M., 2007. Technological Innovation in Brazilian and Argentine Firms. IPEA, Brasilia.

Ethier, W.J., 1982. National and international returns to scale in the modern theory of international trade. Am. Econ. Rev. 72 (1), 389–405.

Fan, H., Li, A., Yeaple, S., 2015. Trade liberalization, quality, and export price. Rev. Econ. Stat. 97 (5), 1033–1051.

Feng, L., Li, Z., Swenson, D.L., 2016. The connection between imported intermediate inputs and exports: evidence from Chinese firms. *J. Int. Econ.* 101, 86–101.

Future, K., 2012. China's Three Waves of Innovation: A Quantitative Study of China's New Invention Landscape, Sweden.

Ge, Y., Lai, H., Zh, S., 2011. Intermediates import and gains from trade liberalization. Working Paper.

Goldberg, P.K., Khandelwal, A.K., Pavcnik, N., Topalova, P., 2010. Imported intermediate inputs and domestic product growth: evidence from India. Q. J. Econ. 125 (2), 1727–1767.

Grossman, G., Helpman, E., 1991. Innovation and Growth in the Global Economy. The MIT Press, MIT Press, MA.

Grossman, S., Hart, O., 1986. The costs and benefits of ownership: a theory of vertical and lateral integration. J. Polit. Econ. 94, 691–719.

Guadalupe, M., Wulf, J., 2010. The flattening firm and product market competition: the effect of trade liberalization on corporate hierarchies. Am. Econ. J. Appl. Econ. 2, 105–127.

Halpern, L., Koren, M., Szeidl, A., 2011. Imported inputs and productivity. CeFiG Working Papers 8.

Hashmi, A.R., 2013. Competition and innovation: the inverted-U relationship revisited. Rev. Econ. Stat. 95 (5), 1653–1668.

Holmes, T., McGratten, E.R., Prescott, E.C., 2015. Quid pro quo: technology capital transfers for market access in China. Rev. Econ. Stud. forthcoming.

Hu, A.G., Jefferson, G.H., 2009. A great wall of patents: what is behind China's recent patent explosion? J. Dev. Econ. 90 (1), 57–68.

Kasahara, H., Rodrigue, J., 2008. Does the use of imported intermediates increase productivity? J. Dev. Econ. 87, 106–118.

Kiriyama, N., 2012. Trade and innovation: synthesis report. OECD Trade Policy Papers, No. 135. OECD Publishing.

Kugler, M., Verhoogen, E., 2012. Prices, plant size, and product quality. Rev. Econ. Stud. 79 (1), 307–339.

Levinsohn, J., Petrin, A., 2003. Estimating production functions using inputs to control for unobservables. Rev. Econ. Stud. 70 (2), 317–341.

Li, X., 2012. Behind the recent surge of Chinese patenting: an institutional view. Res. Policy 41, 236–249

Lileeva, A., Trefler, D., 2010. Improved access to foreign markets raises plant-level productivity. . . for some plants. Q. J. Econ. 125 (1), 1051–1099.

Liu, X., Buck, T., 2007. Innovation performance and channels for international technology spillovers: evidence from Chinese high-tech industries. Res. Policy 36, 355–366.

Lyons, B., 1995. Specific investment, economies of scale, and the make-or-buy decision: a test of transaction cost theory. J. Econ. Behav. Organ. 26 (1), 431–443.
Muendler, M.-A., 2004. Trade, technology, and productivity: a study of Brazilian manufacturers, 1986-1998. Working Paper.
OECD, 2009. Patent Statistics Manual. OECD Publications, Paris.
Onodera, O., 2009. Trade and innovation: a synthesis. OECD J. Gen. Pap. 2008/4,
PWC, 2015. China Research & Development Tax Services: an opportunity for tax savings. Available from the company's website: www.pwccn.com.
Sanyal, P., Ghosh, S., 2013. Product market competition and upstream innovation: evidence from the US electricity market deregulation. Rev. Econ. Stat. 95 (1), 237–254.
Topalova, P., 2010. Factor immobility and regional impacts of trade liberalization: evidence on poverty from India. Am. Econ. J. Appl. Econ. 2 (2), 1–41.
Topalova, P., Khandelwal, A., 2011. Trade liberalization and firm productivity: the case of India. Rev. Econ. Stat. 93 (1), 995–1009.
van Biesebroeck, J., 2003. Revisiting some productivity debates. NBER Working Paper No. 10065.
Veugelers, R., Cassiman, B., 1999. Make and buy in innovation strategies: evidence from Belgian manufacturing firms. Res. Policy 28 (1), 63–80.
Williamson, O., 1985. The Economic Institutions of Capitalism, Firms, Markets, Relational Contracting. The Free Press, New York.
Wunsch-Vincent, S., Kashcheeva, M., Zhou, H., 2015. International patenting by Chinese residents: constructing a database of Chinese foreign-oriented patent families. China Econ. Rev. 36, 198–219.
Yu, M., 2015. Processing trade, tariff reductions, and firm productivity: evidence from Chinese firms. Econ. J. 125, 943–988.
Zhang, H., 2014. Static and dynamic gains from importing intermediate inputs: theory and evidence. Working Paper, The University of Hong Kong.

Part II

International Trade and Trade Policy

Chapter 7

Optimal Strategic Trade Policy under Asymmetric Information*

Abstract

When cost is private information in the Brander-Spencer model, the home government is confronted by a decision of choosing between two policy options: a menu of policies and a uniform policy. The former induces separation and so reveals the cost information to the foreign competitors. The latter helps the weak firm by concealing the cost information. The main result from this study is that policy menu is preferred to uniform policy under Cournot competition while the opposite occurs under Bertrand competition.

1. Introduction

As Stegemann (1989, p. 89) has put in a survey article, 'the evidence around us — increasing international economic interdependence, rekindled protectionism, and the increase in policy actions with real or perceived strategic intent — will continually force the economics profession to address the issues that authors of models of strategic trade policy have tried to address. One of the most influential models of strategic export policy is the well-known Brander-Spencer model (1985), in which it is shown that the home government has a unilateral interest in adopting an export subsidy policy if the home

*This chapter is reproduced from *Journal of International Economics*, 36, 333–354, 1994, with permission from Elsevier.

firm competes with a foreign firm in quantities. The central motive for these types of strategic policies is to 'shift profits' from foreign firms to the home country. Subsequently, Eaton and Grossman (1986) demonstrated that the optimal policy is an export tax when the home firm competes with a foreign firm in prices. One important implication of these two studies is that the type of optimal strategic export policy is sensitive to many industrial-specific factors such as market conduct. It then becomes clear that lacking the relevant information, the government could very likely adopt the wrong type of policy. Moreover, it is reasonable to expect that policymakers have less information than firms concerning production and markets.

Information is also crucial in determining the appropriate policy. Wong (1990) has shown that if policymakers do not have complete information about the home firm's costs, some export policies could be welfare worsening. In particular, Wong (1990) demonstrated that in the Brander-Spencer model with asymmetric information (about cost), the optimal export subsidy scheme derived from the full information case is no longer incentive compatible in general and may even be detrimental to the home country. The reason is simple. The home firm has an incentive to misreport its cost in order to maximize its subsidy-cum-profit. The production decision is thus distorted (compared with the equilibrium outcome without government intervention) and the distortion could be sufficiently large such that national welfare is reduced to a level lower than that under free trade. However, Wong (1990) did not go any farther to explore incentive-compatible policies.

This paper develops strategic trade policies taking into account the constraints arising from incentive compatibility. We assume that the home firm's marginal cost is private information. Being uninformed, the home government faces two policy options. It can offer a menu of policies or simply a uniform policy. In the case of a policy menu, the home firm makes a selection from the menu, after which another uninformed party, the foreign firm, observes the policy selection. The two firms then compete in a third market for their exports.

The distinguishing feature of this model is that it is a mix of screening and signalling problems. We can divide the game into two stages: the policy stage and the market stage. The former is a screening sub-model in which the uninformed party (government) offers a menu to the informed party (home firm). The latter is a signalling sub-model in which the informed party (home firm) takes an action (policy selection) before it meets another uninformed party (foreign firm).[1] Moreover, the two tasks, screening and signalling, are accomplished in one action — when the home firm makes a selection from the given menu. The home government faces a dilemma because of this. On the one hand, it wants to discern the home firm's type in order to provide export subsidies or taxes for the purpose of profit-shifting. On the other hand, it wishes to have the high-cost firm sending out a low-cost signal under Cournot competition in order to reduce the foreign firm's production, or the low-cost firm signalling a high cost under Bertrand competition to raise the foreign firm's price. In this study we find that under Cournot competition it is optimal for the home government to offer a menu of policies which leads to a separating equilibrium, but under Bertrand competition it is optimal to adopt a uniform policy which results in a pooling equilibrium.

As is well known in the strategic trade literature, the role played by the government is to make the home firm's output expansion credible. In the model with private cost information, we find that there is a second role that the government can play. By offering a separation inducing menu, the government enables the home firm to credibly reveal its true type to its rival.

Recently Brainard and Martimort (1992) and Maggi (1992) also examine the impacts of asymmetric information in the Brander-Spencer model.[2] However, the focus of their papers is somewhat different. Brainard and Martimort (1992) incorporate a cost of raising government funds and Maggi (1992) considers non-linear policies. Neither paper is concerned with the signalling aspect of the design of government policy.

The remainder of the paper is organized as follows. In Section 2 we present a model with screening and signalling characteristics when firms compete in a Cournot fashion. A complete analysis of the model is contained in Section 3. Section 4 discusses Bertrand

---

[1] See Kreps (1990, p. 651) for the conceptual difference between screening and signalling models.

[2] These papers came to my attention after the initial submission of my paper to this journal.

competition and gives results contrary to those obtained under Cournot competition. Section 5 concludes the paper.

2. The Model

Consider the following situation. Two firms, 1 and 2, who respectively are located in countries 1 and 2, produce homogeneous goods for a third market. Both firms are assumed to produce strictly positive outputs and, unless stated otherwise, compete in a Cournot fashion. The inverse demand function takes the form: $p = a - b(q_1 + q_2)$, where $a > 0, b > 0, p$ is the price of the product, and q_i the output of firm i, $i = 1, 2$. Only the government in country 1 is involved in policy intervention.[3]

The information structure is as follows. Firm 1's marginal cost, c, is constant and private information but it is common knowledge that firm 1 is of either high cost, c_H, or low cost, c_L, with Prob $(c = c_L) = \mu$.[4] Firm 2's marginal cost is assumed known to all parties and equal to zero for simplicity. The reason for this assumption is that in the present setting, even if there were some uncertainties associated with firm 2's marginal cost, there is no way for firm 2 to signal it. Both government 1 and firm 1 would base their decisions on the expected value. Randomness in firm 2's marginal cost complicates the model without changing the qualitative aspect of the results. In contrast, firm 1 is able to signal its cost through its policy selection.

In the environment described above, we consider the following two-stage, one-shot game. At the beginning of the first stage, called the policy stage, government 1 designs (and commits to) its policy.[5] The government has two options: it can use a uniform policy or a

[3]This supposition is common in the literature on trade policies and is made for simplicity. It can be justified, for instance, if government 2 unilaterally adopts a free trade policy.

[4]Allowing government 1 and firm 2 to have different priors will not change our results as long as these priors are common knowledge.

[5]The government's ability to commit is commonly assumed in the literature. If this is not assumed, precommitment effects should be carefully investigated, as in Caillaud *et al.* (1990).

menu of policies.[6] Under the uniform policy regime, the government sets a specific (per unit) export subsidy rate for firm 1 regardless of its type. The alternative possibility, a menu of policies, gives firm t a choice as to the policies that will be applied. After the government has announced its menu of policies, firm 1 makes its policy choice. When information-revealing is desirable, a policy menu plays a role in inducing this revelation. Without such policy menus, a simple announcement by firm 1 about its cost is not credible.

The menu approach allows the policy to be conditional on the firm's type. In our setting, each choice on the menu consists of two policies: a specific export subsidy rate and a level of lump-sum tax.[7] If the subsidy rate were the only instrument available to the government, firm 1 would have chosen the highest subsidy rate independently of its type and no information would be revealed.

We confine policy options to linear subsidies, i.e. the subsidy rate does not vary with other informative variables such as output and price. This has the advantage of simplicity. Some possible implications of non-linear policies are discussed in the concluding remarks.

In the second stage, referred to as the market stage, the two firms compete in quantities on the basis of their respective information sets. Between the two stages there is a transition period in which firm 2 observes the policy choice made in the first stage and then updates its belief concerning firms 1's true marginal cost. This belief is correctly inferred by firm 1 and government 1. In particular, if government 1 designs a menu of policies inducing firm 1 to reveal its true type, then firm 2 observes this and the outputs of both firms are determined as if there were full in government 1 believe the marginal cost of firm 1 is given by its prior distribution.

---

[6]Policy menus have been explored extensively in the regulation literature. The studies of incentive-compatible policies can also be found in the literature on trade policy. See, for example, Feenstra (1987) and Prusa (1990).

[7]In a real-world context, one could perhaps view the lump-sum tax as a tax on profit. However, it is hard to find a case in which an industry-specific profit tax is tied to an export subsidy. As suggested by a referee, another possibility is that the fixed cost represents a cost of lobbying. To be viewed as a low-cost firm, the firm must incur a lobbying cost that exceeds some threshold set by the government.

3. Analysis

We analyze the model by solving the game backwards. Since we consider pure strategies only, the policy selection is either pooling or separating. The analysis proceeds as follows. We first determine the optimal policy among the class of policies that lead to separating equilibria (in Subsections 3.1 and 3.2). We then consider pooling equilibria (in Subsection 3.3). Finally, we derive the optimal policy (in Subsection 3.4) by comparing the maximum social welfare achieved under these two types of policies. In considering pooling equilibria, we assume, without loss of generality, that the government sets a uniform policy. A uniform policy causes pooling (involuntarily).

For the purpose of comparison, we briefly illustrate the optimal policy in the case of full information. Obviously, neither a policy menu nor a *lump-sum* tax is necessary. We denote variables in the full information case with a superscript f. Then, given any export subsidy rate, s, the second stage game yields

$$q_1^f = \frac{a - 2c + 2s}{3b} \quad \text{and} \quad q_2^f = \frac{a + c - s}{3b}.$$

Government 1 chooses s^f to maximize its objective function, denoted $W^f(s)$, which is simply the profit the home firm earns from exports less any subsidy payments. With linear demand, this can be expressed as

$$W^f(s) = \left[a - b\left(q_1^f(s) + q_2^f(s)\right) - c\right] q_1^f(s)$$

Thus to obtain

$$s^f = \frac{a - 2c}{4}. \tag{1}$$

3.1. *Separation-inducing menus*

We now consider separating equilibria. Let $t = (t_L; t_H)$ denote a policy menu, where t_L is a policy intended for the low-cost firm and t_H is a policy intended for the high-cost firm. Each policy $t_i = (s_i; \tau_i)$ for $i - L$, H consists of two elements, a specific export subsidy rate, s_i, and a lump-sum tax, τ_i.

Let $\pi^i(t_j)$ denote firm 1's profit when it is of type i and chooses policy t_j for $i, j = L, H$. A menu t is called a *separation-inducing menu* if for $i \neq j$

(i) $\pi^i(t_i) \geqq \pi^i(t_j)$, and
(ii) $\pi^i(t_i) \geqq 0$, $i, j = L, H$.

Condition (i) is the self-selection constraint while condition (ii) is the participation constraint. As mentioned above, if a separation-inducing menu is used by government 1, firm 2 will be able to discern firm 1's type and it then follows that all parties act as if they have complete information in the second-stage Cournot game.

Given a separation-inducing menu t, the market-stage game can be described by the following maximization problems, $i = L, H$:

$$\max_{q_{si}}\{[a - b(q_{si} + q_{2i}) - c_i + s_i]q_{si} - \tau_i\} \tag{2}$$

$$\max_{q_{2i}}[a - b(q_{si} + q_{2i})]q_{2i} \tag{3}$$

where q_{si} is firm 1's output and q_{2i} firm 2's output under the policy menu regime and when firm 1 is type i. If t_L (t_H) is adopted, then $i = L$ (H) in both (2) and (3), which constitute a Cournot game between firm 2 and a low (high) cost firm 1 with firm 2 knowing firm 1's true type. Thus, the respective reaction functions are

$$\begin{aligned} q_{si} &= \frac{a - c_i + s_i - bq_{2i}}{2b}, \quad i = L, H, \\ q_{2i} &= \frac{a - bq_{si}}{2b}, \quad i = L, H. \end{aligned} \tag{4}$$

Given s, the market-stage equilibrium outputs are

$$q_{si} = \frac{a - 2c_i + s_i}{3b} \quad \text{and} \quad q_{2i} = \frac{a + c_i - s_i}{3b}, \qquad i = LH \tag{5}$$

As mentioned in the introduction, the model incorporates both screening and signalling. Use of a menu of policies allows the government to screen for the type of firm so as to better design its export policy, but at the same time, firm 1's policy selection signals the same information to firm 2. To understand the implications of this, it is helpful to first consider a pure screening version of the model in which firm 2 knows firm 1's marginal cost. In this case, firm 2's output level will be affected by the policy imposed by the government, but the means by which the policy is chosen conveys no information. In particular, if firm 1 chooses a policy t_j that is not consistent with its type i, then firm 2 will produce $q_{2i} = (a + c_i - s_j)/3b$, the Cournot output based on firm 1's true marginal cost, c_i, and subsidy, s_j. Therefore, we have

$$\pi^i(t_j) = \frac{1}{9b}(a - 2c + 2s_j)^2 - \tau_j,\ ij = L, H. \tag{6}$$

If the firm selects policy t_i corresponding to its type i, its profit, $\pi^i(t_i)$, is given by setting $j = i$ in (6).

If menu t is separation-inducing, condition (i) must be satisfied. Comparing $\pi^i(t_i)$ with $\pi^i(t_j)(j \neq i)$, we obtain Lemma 1.

Lemma 1. *In the pure screening model, if t is a separation-inducing mem, then $s_L \geqq s_H$ and $\tau_L \geqq \tau_H$. Conversely, if $s_L \geqq s_H$, there exists $\tau_L \geqq \tau_H$ such that (t_L, t_H) is a separation-inducing menu, where $t_i = (s_i, \tau_i)$ for $i = L, H$.*

Proof: See the appendix. □

Next, we provide some intuitions for Lemma 1. First and foremost, the two instruments in a separation-inducing menu have to go hand in hand, with a high subsidy associated with a high tax and vice versa. Otherwise both types would pick the policy with higher subsidy and lower tax. Second, a separation-inducing menu must have $s_L \geqq s_H$. To see this, note that $\partial\pi^i/\partial s_j$ is the marginal rate of substitution of taxes for subsidies, by (6). Moreover, the isoprofit curves of the types satisfy the single crossing property, since $\frac{\partial^2\pi^i}{\partial s_j \partial c_i} = -8/9b$, also by (6). The single crossing property implies monotonicity of the subsidies, by a standard argument from the incentive literature. By both (5) and Lemma 1, it is necessary that $q_{SL} > q_{SH}$. Thus, an alternative intuition is that the low-cost firm benefits more than the high-cost firm from an increase in the subsidy rate. For the converse, moving along the high type's isoprofit curve, in the direction of increasing subsidy and tax, raises the profit of the low type. Thus, pairs of policies that are equally profitable for the higher type satisfy self-selection for the low type.

We now return to our original model incorporating both signalling and screening. Since firm 2 does not know firm 1's marginal cost, its output level will depend on its updated belief which is influenced by firm 1's policy selection. Suppose that the government offers a separation-inducing menu and firm 2 believes firm 1's type is signalled by the adopted policy. More precisely, if firm 1 chooses t_j, then firm 2 believes that firm 1 is of type j and correspondingly sets $q_{2j} = (a + c_j - s_j)/3b$. Taking this into account, firm 1 with type i will optimally set $q_{si} = (2a - 3c_i - c_j + 4s_j)/6b$. Consequently,

$$\begin{aligned} \pi^i(t_j) &= \frac{1}{36b}(2a - 3c_i - c_j + 4s_j)^2 - \tau_j \\ \pi^i(t_i) &= \frac{1}{9b}(a - 2c_i + 2s_i)^2 - \tau_i \end{aligned} \tag{7}$$

Lemma 2 gives a necessary condition for the separation of types (the proof is similar to that of Lemma 1).

Lemma 2. *In the model with screening and signalling, if t is a separation- inducing menu, then* $s_L - s_H - (c_H - c_L)/4$. *Conversely, if* $s_L - s_H - (c_H - c_L)/4$ *there exists* $\tau_L \tau_H$ *such that* (t_L, t_H) *is a separation-inducing mem.*

The inclusion of signalling weakens the constraint required for the separation of types. When signalling is taken into account, the separation does not rule out the possibility that $s_L < s_H$. This follows because it is still necessary that $q_{SL} \geqq q_{SH}$ by (5) and Lemma 2. Thus, as in the case of the pure screening model, the low-cost firm benefits more than the high-cost firm from an increase in the export subsidy rate, holding the beliefs of firm 2 fixed. In addition, the low-cost firm loses more than the high-cost firm when firm 2's belief about firm Ps type changes from low to high, because firm 2 will increase its output in response to this change in its beliefs. This second effect is absent in the case of the pure screening model. With the second effect, the subsidy need not do as much work to induce separation.

3.2. *Optimal separation-inducing menu*

In designing its optimal profit-shifting policy in stage 1, the objective of the government is to maximize the expected social welfare in country 1. This is simply the profit of each type of firm 1 less any net subsidy, since the subsidy is already counted in the profit, weighted by the probability of that type. When menus induce separation, the expected social welfare is given by

$$W(t) = \mu(\pi^L(t_L) - s_L q_{SL} + \tau_L) + (1-\mu)(\pi^H(t_H) - s_H q_{SH} + \tau_H),$$

where outputs q_{SL} and q_{SH} are given by (5) and $\pi^L(t_L)$ and $\pi^H(t_H)$ are given by (7).

To derive the optimal menu, we first maximize $W(t)$ by ignoring the separation constraints. The first-order condition yields the optimal subsidy rates, s_L^* and s_H^*:

$$s_L^* = \frac{1}{4}(a - 2c_L) \quad \text{and} \quad s_H^* = \frac{1}{4}(a - 2c_H), \tag{8}$$

from which, and (5), we obtain the equilibrium outputs of each type of firm 1 and firm 2:

$$q_{si} = \frac{a - 2c_i}{2b} \quad \text{and} \quad q_{2i} = \frac{a + 2c_i}{4b}, \quad i = L, H. \tag{9}$$

As expected, the optimal subsidy rates (8) are just the full information subsidy rates corresponding to the firm's particular type. Since the optimal menu imposes no restrictions on the lump-sum tax instrument, we are free to use lump-sum taxes to ensure separation. For convenience, we first normalize the lump-sum tax by setting $\tau_H^* = 0$. When s_L^* and s_H^* are set at their optimal levels as in (8), we demonstrate in the appendix that the menu $t*$ induces separation [i.e. $\pi^L(t_L^*) \geqq \pi^L(t_H^*)$; and $\pi^H(t_H^*) \geqq \pi^H(t_L^*)$] if

$$\tau_L^* = \frac{1}{2b}(c_H - c_L)(a - c_H - c_L). \tag{10}$$

These results are summarized in Proposition 1.

Proposition 1. *t^*, as defined in* (8) *and* (10), *is an optimal separation-inducing menu.*

The intuition behind Proposition 1 is clear. It is well known in the literature of strategic trade policy that when demand is linear, the optimal profit-shifting policy requires that a higher export subsidy rate s_L^* (relative to s_H^*) be granted to the low-cost firm.[8] Thus, these

[8]This can be seen from the formula for the optimal subsidy in Brander and Spencer (1985) or eq. (1).

subsidies satisfy Lemma 2. A lump-sum tax, τ_L^*, is levied on the low-cost firm in order to prevent the high-cost firm from pooling so as to obtain the higher subsidy rate. The tax τ_L^* is chosen so that the low-cost firm still selects t_L^* but the high-cost firm chooses t_H^*.

3.3. *Optimal uniform policy*

We now consider uniform policies. Whenever a uniform policy is adopted by the government, firm 2 receives no information from the policy stage, so it remains uninformed. It follows that the market-stage game is a quantity competition with asymmetric information (firm 2 has incomplete information about firm 1's cost). Let s denote the common subsidy rates, q_{pi} denote firm 1's output under the uniform policy regime when it is type $i (i = L, H)$, and $\overline{q}_2$ denote firm 2's output. Then the market-stage game is characterized by the following maximization problems:

$$\max_{q_{pi}} \left[a - b(q_{pi} + \overline{q}_2) - c_i + s\right] q_{pi}, \quad i = L, H,$$

where $\overline{q_1} = \mu q_{PL} + (l - \mu) q_{PH}$. Let $\tilde{\pi}^i(s)$ denote firm 1's equilibrium profit when it is of type i and under subsidy rate s. Firm 1's reaction function is the same as (4) except $q_{2i} = \overline{q}_2$, but firm 2 now reacts to firm 1's expected output q_u giving rise to the reaction function

$$\tilde{q}_2 = \frac{a - b\overline{q}_1}{2b}. \tag{11}$$

Hence, given s, the market-stage equilibrium outputs are

$$q_{pi} = \frac{1}{6b}(2a - 3c_i - \overline{c} + 4s) \quad \text{and} \quad \overline{q}_2 = \frac{1}{3b}(a + \tilde{c} - s), \ i = L, H, \tag{12}$$

where $\tilde{c}$ stands for the expected value of firm 1's marginal cost, i.e. $\tilde{c} = \mu c_L + (1 - \mu) c_H$. Thus, the resulting firm 1's profit given s is [using (12)]

$$\tilde{\pi}^i(s) = \frac{1}{36b}(2a - 3c_i + 4s - \overline{c})^2, \quad i = L, H.$$

Under the uniform policy regime, the expected social welfare in country 1 is the weighted sum of each type's profit net of subsidy, which is given by

$$\tilde{W}(s) = \mu(\tilde{\pi}^L(s) - Sq_{PL}) + (1-\mu)(\tilde{\pi}^H(s) - sq_{PH}).$$

From the first-order condition for the maximization of IF(s), we can easily derive the optimal subsidy rate, s*, and the equilibrium outputs:

$$S_P^* = \frac{a - 2\bar{c}}{4},\ q_{pi} = \frac{a - c_i - \tilde{c}}{2b} \quad \text{and} \quad \tilde{q}_2 = \frac{a + 2\bar{c}}{4b},\ i = L, H. \quad (13)$$

Relative to the complete information case, asymmetric information creates some distortions when the optimal uniform policy, s_P^*, is adopted and the prior is non-degenerate. Then, by comparing s_P^* in (13) with s^f in (1), we realize that s* does not shift profit from firm 2 optimally since $c_L < \bar{c} < c_H$. It oversubsidizes (undersubsidizes) firm 1 and causes overproduction (underproduction) when firm 1 is a high (low) cost firm.

3.4. *Optimal policy and equilibrium*

In this subsection we derive the overall optimal policy by comparing the social welfare under the optimal separation-inducing menu with the welfare under the optima! uniform policy.

We first illustrate the equilibria under the two different optimal policies using Fig. 7.1. Note that the level of per unit subsidy rate affects the position of firm 1's reaction curve. Since $S_L^* > S_P^*$, the low-cost firm's reaction curve in the separating case, R_{SL}, is to the right of R_{PL}, its reaction curve in the pooling case. Similarly, the high-cost firm's reaction curve in the separating case, R_{SH}, is to the left of R_{PH}, its reaction curve in the pooling case because $s_H^* < s_P^*$. However, firm 2's reaction curve in the separating case, as shown by R_2, is unaffected by the subsidy level in country 1. Thus, in Fig. 7.1, S^{SL} and S^{SH} are the equilibria in the separating case.

In the pooling case, firm 2's output, $\overline{q}_2$, is a function of firm 1's expected output, $\overline{q}_1$ [see (11)]. If firm 1 is actually a low-cost firm, then the equilibrium is at S^{PL}, where the horizontal line at q_2 intersects firm 1's reaction function, R_{PL}. Similarly, the equilibrium

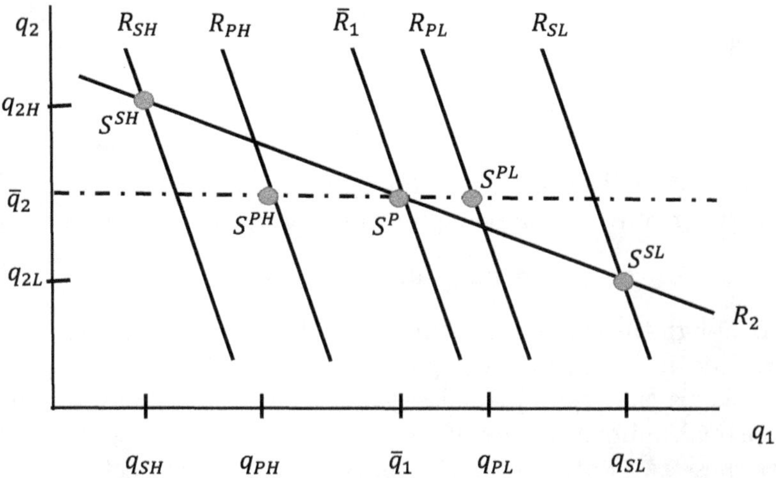

Figure 7.1. Cournot equilibria under the two policies.

is at S^{PH} if firm 1 is a high-cost firm. The expected value of these two equilibria is shown by S^p, the intersection of $\overline{q}_2$ and firm 1's expected reaction curve, $\overline{R}_1$ (which is derived as if firm 1 had marginal cost c).

It is well known in the strategic trade literature that the optimal subsidies place the home firm (firm 1) in a Stackelberg leader position vis-a-vis the foreign firm (firm 2). Thus, S^{SL} and S^{SH} are the respective Stackelberg quantity equilibria in the separating case when firm 1 is respectively the low-cost firm and the high-cost firm. In the pooling case, S^p could be viewed as a modified Stackelberg equilibrium in which a Stackelberg leader reveals only its average output $\overline{q_1}$ (and firm 2 responds by committing to $\overline{q_2}$) but the leader's actual output subsequently varies with its type. Due to the linear reaction function (R_2), it is not difficult to see that firm Ts average outputs are the same under both cases and that firm 2's output in the pooling case is equal to its average output in the separating case. Our previous results in subsections 3.2 and 3.3 also prove this. By (9) and (13),

$$\begin{aligned} \overline{q}_1 &\equiv \mu q_{PL} + (1-\mu)q_{PH} = \frac{a-2\overline{c}}{2b} = \mu q_{SL} + (1-\mu)q_{SH}, \\ \overline{q}_2 &= \frac{a-2\overline{c}}{4b} = \mu q_{2L} + (1-\mu)q_{2H}. \end{aligned} \tag{14}$$

Moreover, the total outputs in the market are unchanged in the two cases since using (9) and (13):

$$q_{si} + q_{2i} = \frac{3b - 2c_i}{4b} = q_{pi} + \overline{q}_2, \quad i = L, H.$$

Thus, the optimal separation-inducing menu and the optimal uniform policy give rise to the same equilibrium price for the product, i.e.

$$p_{SL} = p_{PL} \quad \text{and} \quad p_{SH} = p_{PH}. \tag{15}$$

Although the expected outputs and the equilibrium price of firms 1 and 2 do not vary in the separating and pooling cases, Lemma 3 below shows that the optimal separation-inducing menu dominates the optimal uniform policy. If we denote the expected social welfare under these two optimal policies as W^* and W^*, respectively, where

$$W* = \mu(p_{SL} - c_L)q_{SL} + (1 - \mu)(p_{SH} - c_H)q_{SH}, \tag{16}$$

$$\tilde{W}^* = \mu(p_{PL} - c_L)q_{PL} + (1 - \mu)(p_{PH} - c_H)q_{PH}, \tag{17}$$

then we have Lemma 3.

Lemma 3. *The optimal separation-inducing menu gives country l higher welfare than the optimal uniform policy:* $W^* > \tilde{W}^*$.

Proof: Using (14) and (15) in (16) and (17), the welfare difference can be expressed by

$$W^* - \tilde{W}^* = \mu(p_S L - c_L)q_{SL} + (1 - \mu)(p_{SH} - c_H)q_{SH} \tag{18}$$

$$= \mu(q_{sL} - q_{PL})[(p_{SL} - c_L) - (p_{SH} - c_H)]. \tag{19}$$

Because the low-cost firm produces more in the separating case than in the pooling case, i.e. $q_{sL} > q_{PL}$ the low-cost firm's price-cost margin is higher than the high-cost firm's since

$$p_{SH} - c_L = \frac{a - 2c_L}{4} > \frac{a - 2c_H}{4} = p_{SH} - c_H, \tag{20}$$

(18) shows $W^* - \tilde{W}^* > 0$. □

Note that the first term in (18) is positive (since $q_{SL} > q_{PL}$) but the second term is negative (since $p_{SH} < p_{PH}$). This implies that use of the optimal separation-inducing menu instead of the optimal uniform policy results in a welfare gain if firm 1 turns out to be a low-cost firm but a welfare loss if it is in fact a high-cost firm. Thus, there is an ex ante tradeoff using the optimal separation-inducing menu.

To understand how the tradeoff is resolved, let us make use of Fig. 7.1. Since points S^{SH} and S^{PH} entail the same total output and the same price, all points on the segment (which is not depicted in the figure) between these two points also entail the same total output and the same price. Similarly, all points on the segment between points S^{SL} and S^{PL} (including these two points) entail the same total output and the same price. It follows that firm 1 has equal price-cost margin $(p_{SH} - c_H)^{at}$ all points on the segment between S^{SH} and S^{PH} and equal price-cost margin $(p_{SL} - c_l)^{at}$ all points on the segment between S^{SL} and S^{PL}. Note that at both the pooling equilibrium [shown by (S^{PH}, S^{PL})] and the separating equilibrium [shown by (S^{SH}, S^{SL})], firm 1 has the same expected output (q_t) but a higher variance in its output at the separating equilibrium. Thus, the issue is whether country 1's welfare is increasing or decreasing in the variance of firm 1's output. To answer this, let us consider a continuum of 'outcomes' between the pooling and separating equilibria. An 'outcome' here is represented by a pair of points with one on the segment between S^{PL} and S^{SL}, the other on the segment between S^{PH} and S^{SH}, and the expectation at S^p. Then an increase in the variance in firm 1's output is achieved by an increase in the low-cost firm's output (a point on the segment between S^{PL} and S^{SL}) and a decrease in the high-cost firm's output (a point on the segment between S^{PH} and S^{SH}) keeping expected output unchanged at q_v Since the low-cost firm's price-cost margin is higher than the high-cost firm's [see (20)], welfare in country 1 must rise as the variance in firm 1's output increases. Hence, the optimal separation-inducing menu is preferred to the optimal uniform policy.

With Lemma 3 we are now ready to analyze the entire game described in Section 2. To do this, we must consider all policy options, both menu and uniform, at the same time.

Since government 1 is a Stackelberg leader vis-a-vis the firms, it will choose a policy that results in the highest social welfare in country 1. This, together with Lemma 3, rules out the uniform policies. Moreover, Lemma 3 and Proposition 1 indicate that t^* is the optimal one among all policies. Once the government adopts t^*, we have all results obtained in Subsection 3.2. We now conclude the above analysis in Proposition 2.

Proposition 2. *In the two-stage sequential game with asymmetric information and Cournot competition, there exists a separating equilibrium with t^* as the separation-inducing menu. The full information equilibrium allocation is achieved. Pooling is never an equilibrium.*

The result that the full information allocation is attained is not surprising. On the one hand, the export subsidy rate that firm 1 receives in an optimal separation-inducing menu is identical to that in the full information case corresponding to the firm's type.[9] On the other hand, the additional policy instrument used in our model has no impact on the export market, i.e. the introduction of a lump-sum tax per se does not cause the firms' outputs and price to differ from those in the full information model.[10]

Lemma 3 and Proposition 2 seem to suggest that it is always preferable for the government to set a policy so as to induce firm 1 to reveal its information. This result, however, is sensitive to the nature of market competition. We will see this in the next section.

4. Bertrand Competition

The government always wants to learn firm 1's true cost in order to design a precise policy. However, if firm 1 tries to inform the government or if the government uses some rules to induce firm 1 to reveal its cost, in our setting, the information is also released to firm 1's rival (firm 2), which may not be desirable. Earlier results indicate that information revelation is desirable in a Cournot game.

---

[9]Because of this, the government's commitment is not a problem in the Cournot model. Although the government knows the firm's type after the firm has chosen a policy from this optimal menu, there is no need to revise the level of that policy because it is already equal to the optimal level in the full information case.

[10]This result of course depends upon a common assumption that monetary transfer either from the government to firm 1 (i.e. subsidy) or from firm 1 to the government (i.e, tax) is costless. The government is never reluctant to introduce an additional instrument when it is necessary, for example a lump-sum tax in this model, as it can be implemented at no expense. For the possible effects of relaxing this assumption, see Caillaud *et al.* (1988) and Brainard and Martimort (1992).

The question is whether revelation is always optimal. To answer this, we now consider another model which differs from the earlier one in two respects: the firms produce imperfect substitutes and compete in prices.

Suppose the demand system is given by

$$q_i = \alpha - \beta p_i + \gamma p_j \quad \text{where } i,\ j = 1, 2, \quad i \neq j,\ \alpha > 0, \quad \text{and} \quad \beta > \gamma > 0. \tag{21}$$

We adopt the same notations defined before but interpret them in the context of a Bertrand game. For brevity, we only present results related to Lemma 3 and Proposition 2. In doing so, we first derive the optimal uniform policy. We then characterize the optimal separation-inducing menu. Finally, we compare the social welfare under these two optimal policies. Results are summarized in Proposition 3.

Given s under the uniform policy regime, the market-stage game is characterized by the following two maximization problems:

$$\max_{p_{pi}} (p_{pi} - c_i + s)(\alpha - \beta p_{pi} + \gamma \overline{p}_2),\ i = L, H,$$
$$\max_{\tilde{p}_{pi}} \tilde{p}_2(\alpha - \beta \tilde{p}_2 + \gamma \tilde{p}_1), \tag{22}$$

where p_{pi} is firm 1's price when it is type i in the pooling case, $\tilde{p}_1 = \mu p_{PL} + (1-\mu)p_{PH}$ is the expected price charged by firm 1, and p_2 is firm 2's price in the pooling case. By solving these problems simultaneously, we obtain the market-stage equilibrium prices ($i = L, H$):

$$\tilde{p}_2 = \frac{1}{4\beta^2 - \gamma^2}[\alpha(2\beta + \gamma) + \beta\gamma(\overline{c} - s)],$$
$$p_{pi} = \frac{1}{2(4\beta^2 - \gamma^2)}[2\alpha(2\beta + \gamma) + \gamma^2(\overline{c} - c_i) + 4\beta^2(c_i - s)]$$

Maximizing the expected social welfare, which is

$$\tilde{W}(s) \equiv \mu(p_{PL} - c_H)(\alpha - \beta p_{PL} + \gamma \overline{p}_2) + (1-\mu)(p_{PH} - c_H)(\alpha - \beta p_{PH} + \gamma \overline{p}_2),$$

gives the optimal uniform policy s_p^*:

$$s_p^* = -\frac{\gamma^2}{4\beta^2 - \gamma^2}[\alpha(2\beta + \gamma) - (2\beta^2 - \gamma^2)\bar{c}]$$

Therefore, the equilibrium prices are

$$p_{pi} = \frac{1}{2}\left[c_i + \frac{\alpha(2\beta + \gamma)}{2\beta^2 - \gamma^2}\right], \quad i = L, H \quad \text{and}$$
$$\bar{p}_2 = \frac{1}{4\beta}\left[\alpha + \gamma\bar{c} + \frac{2\alpha\beta(\beta + \gamma)}{2\beta^2 - \gamma^2}\right], \tag{23}$$

and analogously to (17), country 1's expected welfare at the pooling equilibrium is

$$\tilde{W}^* = \mu(p_{PL} - c_L)p_{PL} + (1 - \mu)(p_{PH} - c_H)q_{PH}, \tag{24}$$

where

$$q_{PL} = \alpha - \beta p_{PL} + \gamma\bar{p}_2 \quad \text{and} \quad q_{PH} = \alpha - \beta p_{PH} + \gamma\bar{p}_2$$

To avoid repetition, we omit the derivation of the optimal separation-inducing menu and the resulting market equilibrium. The optimal separation-inducing menu has the per unit subsidy rates[11]

$$s_i^* = -\frac{\gamma^2}{4\beta^2(2\beta^2 - \gamma^2)}[\alpha(2\beta + \gamma) - (2\beta^2 - \gamma^2)c_i], i = L, H,$$

and the market equilibrium prices are

$$p_{si} = \frac{1}{2}\left[c_i + \frac{\alpha(2\beta + \gamma)}{2\beta^2 - \gamma^2}\right] \quad \text{and} \quad p_{2i} = \frac{1}{4b}\left[\alpha + \gamma c_i + \frac{2\alpha\beta(\beta + \gamma)}{2\beta^2 - \gamma^2}\right],$$
$$i = LH, \tag{25}$$

Moreover, analogously to (16), the separating equilibrium welfare of country 1 is

$$W^* = \mu(p_{SL} - c_L)q_{SL} + (1 - \mu)(p_{SH} - c_H)q_{SH}, \tag{26}$$

---

[11]The levels of lump-sum tax are chosen to make the policy satisfy the separation constraints.

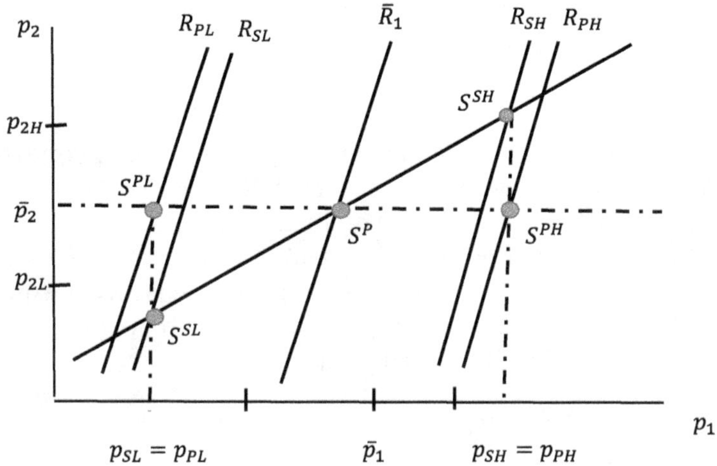

Figure 7.2. Bertrand equilibria under the two policies.

where

$$q_{SL} = \alpha - \beta p_{SL} + \gamma p_{2L} \quad \text{and} \quad q_{SH} = \alpha - \beta p_{SH} + \gamma p_{2H}.$$

We illustrate the above equilibria in Fig. 7.2. Note that the position of firm 1's reaction curve (shown as R_{SL}, R_{SH}, R_{PL}, and R_{PH} in Fig. 7.2) depends on its type and the tax rate. When changing from the optimal uniform policy to the menu, the low-cost firm's reaction curve is shifted downward (because $s_L^* < s_P^*$, i.e. the firm faces a higher tax); and the high-cost firm's reaction curve is shifted upward (since $s_H^* > s_P^*$, i.e. the firm faces a lower tax). Also in Fig. 7.2, S^{SL} and S^{SH} represent the Stackelberg price equilibria in the separating case. S^p would be the Stackelberg price equilibrium if the firm had marginal cost $\bar{c}$. S^{PL} and S^{PH} are the actual equilibria in the pooling case.

Similar to the Cournot case, linearity of the reaction function implies that the price $\overline{p}_2$ charged by firm 2 in the pooling case is equal to the average price in the separating case: i.e. by (23) and (25)

$$\mu p_{2L} + (1 - \mu) p_{2H} = \frac{1}{4b}\left[\alpha + \gamma\bar{c} + \frac{2\alpha\beta(\beta + \gamma)}{2\beta^2 - \gamma^2}\right] = \overline{p}_2. \tag{27}$$

Also by (23) and (25), we have

$$p_{SL} = p_{PL} \quad \text{and} \quad p_{SH} = p_{PH}, \tag{28}$$

Meaning that each type of firm 1 sets the same price under these two cases, but

$$p_{2L} < \overline{p}_2 \quad \text{and} \quad p_{2H} > \overline{p}_2. \tag{29}$$

Due to the strategic complementarity of Bertrand competition, firm 2 sets a lower price if it knows that its rival is a low-cost firm than if it does not know. Similarly, firm 2 sets a higher price when it knows that it is competing with a high-cost firm. We now make welfare comparison between the pooling and separating equilibria. From (24) and (26), the welfare difference can be expressed in the same form as (18) for the Cournot case:

$$\begin{aligned} W^* - \widetilde{W}^* = \mu(p_{SL} - c_L)(q_{SL} - q_{PL}) \\ + (1-\mu)(p_{SH} - c_H)(q_{SH} - q_{SH}). \end{aligned} \tag{30}$$

Note from the demand system (22) and (29),

$$\begin{aligned} q_{SH} - q_{PL} = \gamma(p_{2L} - \overline{p}_2) < 0 \quad \text{and} \\ q_{SH} - q_{PH} = \gamma(p_{2H} - \overline{p}_2) > 0. \end{aligned} \tag{31}$$

Thus, the first term of (30) is negative, implying a loss from using the separation-inducing menu when firm 1 is a low-cost firm. However, the second term is positive, which captures the gain from adopting the menu when firm 1 is a high-cost firm. Moreover, the gain and loss are proportional to firm 1's price-cost margin. To show that welfare is lower at the separating equilibrium than at the pooling equilibrium, we need only to show that firm 1 earns a higher price-cost margin when it is low cost than it is high cost. To do this, we use (27) and (31) to rewrite the welfare difference (30) as

$$W^* - \widetilde{W}^* = \frac{1}{\gamma}\mu(q_{SL} - q_{PL})[(p_{SL} - c_L) - (p_{SH} - c_H)]. \tag{32}$$

By (25),

$$\begin{aligned} p_{SL} - c_L &= \frac{1}{2}\left[\frac{\alpha(2\beta+\gamma)}{2\beta^2 - \gamma^2} - c_L\right] > \frac{1}{2}\left[\frac{\alpha(2\beta+\gamma)}{2\beta^2 - \gamma^2} - c_H\right] \\ &= p_{SH} - c_H. \end{aligned} \tag{33}$$

Using (31) and (33) in (32), we immediately obtain $W^* < \widetilde{W}^*$. This establishes Proposition 3.

Proposition 3. *In the two-stage sequential game with asymmetric information and Bertrand competition,* $\widetilde{W}^* > W^*$, *i.e. the optimal uniform policy achieves higher social welfare than a separation-inducing mem. The equilibrium is pooling.*

The welfare difference (30) for the Bertrand case is identical in form to (18) for the Cournot case. Moreover, since firm 1 has the same expected output ($\bar{q}_1$) at the separating and pooling equilibria,[12] it is again true that the difference between the separating and pooling equilibria could be explained on the basis of the difference in the variance of output. However, in the Bertrand case it is more convenient to use Fig. 7.2 to express the explanation in terms of the difference in the variance of firm 2's price. As can be seen from (31), when firm 2's price is high, then firm 1's output is high (and vice versa) and an increase in the variance of firm 2's price causes a proportional increase in the variance of firm 1's output.

In Fig. 7.2 and from (28), firm 1 has the same price and price-cost margin at all points on the segment between S^{PL} and S^{SL} and likewise on the segment between S^{PH} and S^{SH}. However, firm 2's price varies as an 'outcome' moves from the separating equilibrium [shown by (S^{sl}, S^{SH})] to the pooling equilibrium [shown by (S^{PL}, S^{PH})]. The variance in firm 2's price is higher at the separating equilibrium than at the pooling equilibrium. In fact, a reduction in firm 2's price variance is achieved by a rise in firm 2's price when firm 1 is a low-cost firm (a point moving upwards from S^{SL} towards S^{PL}) and a drop in firm 2's price when firm 1 is a high-cost firm (a point moving downwards from S^{SH} towards S^{PH}) keeping the expected price unchanged at p_2. Thus, to select between these two equilibria, we must know whether country 1's welfare is increasing or decreasing in firm 2's price variance.

Since the welfare difference (30) for the Bertrand case is identical in form to (18) for the Cournot case and that the low-cost firm has a higher price- cost margin than the high-cost firm in both cases [see (20) and (30)], as discussed before (for Lemma 3), we prefer a higher output from the low-cost firm. Note that a higher output for the low-cost firm is achieved by a lower variance in firm 2's price (and thus a

[12]Following (27) and (28), one can easily check this by calculating the two expected outputs.

low variance in firm 1's output). Consequently, the optimal uniform policy that results in a smaller variance in firm 2's price is preferred to the menu in Bertrand competition.

The sharp difference between Lemma 3 and Proposition 3 arises because the pooling and separating equilibria have significantly different consequences for outputs in the Bertrand case than in the Cournot case. It is known from (31) that, in the Bertrand case, the low-cost firm produces less while the high-cost firm produces more in the separating equilibrium than in the pooling equilibrium. However, in the Cournot case, the low-cost firm produces more but the high-cost firm produces less in the separating equilibrium than in the pooling equilibrium, i.e. the expressions in (31) have opposite signs in the Cournot case.[13]

When government 1 adopts an optimal uniform policy, the equilibrium necessarily differs from the full information equilibrium. Interestingly enough, Proposition 3 indicates that country 1 achieves higher social welfare in a world with incomplete information than in a world with full information. This is because firm 1's cost information has positive net effects on the social welfare if it is kept private. One important implication of this finding is that in a 'rivalrous agency' model,[14] it is better not to induce the agent to reveal its information, in some cases, because the revelation has a signalling effect.

5. Conclusion

When information asymmetry problems are present in the Brander-Spencer model, the home government can design a menu of policies, by introducing an additional policy instrument, to induce information revelation and achieve the full information social welfare. But the rival firm is also uninformed. Hence, the model is characterized by a mix of screening and signalling. In models of this kind it is not always optimal for the uninformed government to design a mechanism that

[13]It can be easily verified that this is also true if we had differentiated products instead of homogeneous products in the Cournot case.

[14]Our model differs from Fershtman and Judd's (1987) owner-manager model. In a 'rivalrous agency' environment we consider a hidden information problem while they deal with issues of hidden action.

induces the informed home firm to reveal its information, because this also informs the foreign firm. The nature of the optimal policy is sensitive to the type of competition between home and foreign firms. Under Cournot competition, the government offers a menu of policies that induces the home firm to reveal its type. Under Bertrand competition, however, the government chooses a uniform policy, allowing the home firm to conceal its information.

As suggested by a referee, it would be of interest to investigate non-linear policies that do not reveal the home firm's cost information to the foreign firm and compare them with linear polices.[15] Under the non-linear policy regime, the government first offers a subsidy scheme in which subsidy rates are contingent on output level, then firms produce, and finally the home firm receives subsidy payments at the rate corresponding to its output. This has the advantage that different types of the home firm receive different marginal subsidy rates. Also the types are separated only *after* the foreign firm has produced and so the home firm's cost information does not influence the foreign firm's output decision. Such non-linear policies might dominate linear policies, especially when information-concealing is desirable, for the reason that the non-linear policies share the advantages that are respectively attained by separation-inducing menus and uniform policies.

Appendix

Proof of Lemma 1

By (6), $\pi^L(t_H) - \pi^H(t_H) = \frac{4(c_H - c_L)(a - c_L - c_H + 2s_H)}{9b}$. Since $\pi^L(t_H) \geqq \pi^H(t_H)$ from the separation constraint, we obtain

$$\pi^L(t_L) - \pi^H(t_H) \geqq \frac{4}{9b}(c_H - c_L)(a - c_L - c_H + 2s_H). \qquad \text{(A.1)}$$

Similarly,

$$\pi^H(t_H) - \pi^L(t_L) \geqq -\frac{4}{9b}(c_H - c_L)(a - c_L - c_H + 2s_L). \qquad \text{(A.2)}$$

[15] In a model in which the foreign firm knows the home firm's marginal cost (no signalling), Maggi (1992) shows that non-linear policies enhance the government's degree of freedom to implement the Stackelberg outcome.

Combining (A.1) and (A.2) yields

$$\frac{4}{9b}(c_H - c_L)(a - c_L - c_H + 2s_H) \leqq \frac{4}{9b}(c_H - c_L)(a - c_L - c_H + 2s_L)$$

So $s_L \geqq s_H$. Using $\pi^H(t_H) \geqq \pi^L(t_L)$ once again, we have

$$\frac{(a - 2c_H + 2s_H)^2}{9b} - \tau_H \geqq \frac{(a - 2c_H + 2s_L)^2}{9b} - \tau_L,$$

which confirms $\tau_H \leqq \tau_L$.

For the converse, set

$$\tau_L = \frac{(a - 2c_H + 2s_L)^2}{9b} \quad \text{and} \quad \tau_H = \frac{(a - 2c_H + 2s_H)^2}{9b}$$

Proof of Proposition 1. We shall show that t^* induces separation. By using optimal subsidy levels (8) and the normalization $\tau_H^* = 0$, we obtain

$$\pi^L(t_L^*) = \frac{(a - 2c_L)^2}{4b} - \tau_L^*, \quad \pi^H(t_H^*) = \frac{(a - 2c_H)^2}{4b},$$

$$\pi^L(t_H^*) = \frac{(a - c_L - c_H)^2}{4b}, \quad \pi^H(t_L^*) = \frac{(a - c_L - c_H)^2}{4b} - \tau_L^*.$$

Therefore, $\pi^L(s_L^*) \geqq \pi^L(s_H^*)$ iff

$$\begin{aligned} \tau_L^* &\leqq \frac{1}{4b}[(a - 2c_L)^2 - (a - c_L - c_H)^2] \\ &= \frac{1}{4b}(c_H - c_L)^2 + \frac{1}{2b}(c_H - c_L)(a - c_L - c_H) \end{aligned}$$

and $\pi^H(t_H^*) \geqq \pi^H(t_L^*)$ iff

$$\begin{aligned} \tau_L^* &\leqq \frac{1}{4b}[(a - c_L - c_H)^2 - (a - 2c_H)^2] \\ &= \frac{1}{2b}(c_H - c_L)(a - c_L - c_H) - \frac{1}{4b}(c_H - c_L)^2 \end{aligned}$$

Hence the separation constraints are satisfied iff

$$-\frac{1}{4b}(c_H - c_L)^2 \leqq \tau_L^* - \frac{1}{2b}(c_H - c_L)(a - c_L - c_H) \leqq \frac{1}{4b}(c_H - c_L)^2$$

Obviously, τ_L^* defined as in (10) satisfies the above condition. Thus t^* induces separation.

References

Brainard, S.L. and D. Martimort, (1992). Strategic trade policy with incomplete informed policymakers, NBER Working Paper 4069.

Brander, J.A. and B.J. Spencer, (1985). Export subsidies and international market share rivalry, *Journal of International Economics* 18, 83–100.

Caillaud, B., R. Guesnerie, P. Rey and J. Tirole, (1988). Government intervention in production and incentives theory. A review of recent contributions, *Rand Journal of Economics* 19, no. 1, 1–26.

Caillaud, B., B. Jullien and P. Picard, (1990). On precommitment effects between competing agencies, CEPREMAP Working Paper 9033.

Eaton, J. and G. Grossman, (1986). Optimal trade and industrial policy under oligopoly. *Quarterly Journal of Economics* 101, 383–406.

Feenstra, R.C., (1987). Incentive compatible trade policies, *Scandinavian Journal of Economics* 89, no. 3, 373–388.

Fershtman, C. and K.L. Judd, (1987). Strategic incentive manipulation in rivalrous agency, Hoover Institute (Standard University) Discussion Paper 8711.

Kreps, D.M., (1990). *A course in microeconomic theory* (Princeton University Press, Princeton, NJ).

Maggi, G., (1992). Strategic trade policy under asymmetric information, Stanford University, Mimeo.

Prusa, T.J., (1990). An incentive compatible approach to the transfer pricing problem, *Journal of International Economics* 28, 155–172.

Stegemann, K., (1989). Policy rivalry among industrial states: What can we learn from models of strategic trade policy? *International Organization* 43, 73–100.

Wong, K., (1990). Incentive incompatible, immiserizing export subsidies, University of Washington Discussion Paper 9020.

Chapter 8

Keiretsu and Relationship-Specific Investment: A Barrier to Trade?*

Abstract

This article develops a model of informal procurement within Japanese keiretsu so as to consider effects on intermediate-good imports, such as auto parts. Parts-suppliers make relationship-specific investments that benefit the automaker and prices are determined by bargaining after investment has been sunk. Although this investment raises efficiency, it limits the range of imports to less important parts, such as tailpipes, and it is possible that no parts are imported, despite lower foreign costs. Lack of information concerning investment rents combined with counterintuitive responses of imports to changes in output and costs could create unwarranted perceptions of a trade barrier.

1. Introduction

Persistent and large deficits in U.S. trade with Japan, reaching US \$55.7 billion in 1997, have led to significant economic tension between the two countries. Since US \$32.2 billion of this 1997 deficit, or 58 percent, involved automobile trade, with US \$10 billion attributable to trade in auto parts,[1] it is not surprising that a main focus of tension has been auto and auto-parts trade. Indeed, a trade dispute over autos almost resulted in a trade war between

*This chapter is reproduced from *International Economic Review*, 42(4), 871–901, 2001, with permission from Wiley.

[1]Source: U.S. Bureau of Census, unadjusted data, report FT900 (CB-98-104).

the U.S. and Japan in 1995. Since it is evident that visible and formal trade barriers, such as tariffs and import quotas, applied to manufactures are low in Japan, the central U.S. complaint is that invisible and informal barriers arising from typical Japanese business practices and regulations have substantially blocked legitimate access of American products to the Japanese market. Particularly with respect to auto parts, the concern is that vertical relationships within Japanese corporate groups, known as *keiretsu*, could act as a structural impediment to trade.[2] The special nature of these relationships is perhaps one of the most distinguishing features of the Japanese auto industry. Auto producers, such as Nissan and Toyota, are involved in long-term arrangements with their keiretsu suppliers or subcontractors. As explained by Aoki (1988: pp. 216–18), in return for long-term commitment by the automaker, subcontractors make relationship-specific investments that are specifically directed toward the needs of the automaker and are of no value to firms outside the keiretsu group.[3] Such investments would include the design costs of modifications that improve the fit or ease of assembly with other parts produced by the keiretsu, but which are not relevant to the particular production processes of other auto manufacturers. Another example might involve investment by the supplier in "just in time" delivery, such as building a plant close to the automaker's

[2]See, for example, Levinsohn (1997). According to Church (1995), the keiretsu "do business mainly with each other, freezing out competing buyers and sellers, both foreign and domestic. This system forms the very fabric of the way the Japanese do business, and it does more than outright trade barriers or even government 'administrative guidance' to keep out foreign products. Especially, it seems, U.S. auto parts, such as shock absorbers, mufflers, tailpipes and disk-brake pads . . . sell for less than half to only a third the price of made-in-Japan parts of comparable quality. What then limits American parts to around 1.5 percent of the Japanese market? The keiretsu system, American conclude."

[3]As Aoki (1988: p. 216) states, "the prime manufacturer must maintain its reputation of commitment to the subcontractor in order to elicit the subcontractor's commitment regarding relationship-specific investments in expertise, equipment, and research and development Conversely, "the subcontractor must maintain its reputation for quality, timely delivery of supplies, continual innovative effort, and so on, if it is to secure a stable and profitable position in the subcontracting group"

plant or cooperating with other suppliers to coordinate delivery.[4] "Just in time" production methods are a prominent feature of Japanese supply arrangements. A main aim of this article is then to determine the effects of these relationship-specific investments within keiretsu on the ability of foreign suppliers to export auto parts or other intermediate inputs to Japan. To explore this issue, we develop a model of procurement with the feature that, within the keiretsu, relationship-specific investments by suppliers create rent[5] for the automaker. In keeping with the informal nature of supply arrangements, auto-parts prices are determined through bargaining between individual suppliers and the automaker after investment has been sunk. A key aspect of the model is its consideration of a large variety or range of parts so as to define the margin at which a part is imported or produced within the keiretsu. As we show, relationship-specific investment limits access to the Japanese market by making it profitable for the keiretsu to produce a range of parts that otherwise would be imported. The rents from these investments create a net benefit to the keiretsu automaker, more than offsetting the lower U.S. production costs for parts. Generally, higher levels of investment reduce the range of imported parts, causing a fall in the U.S. share of the Japanese auto-parts' market. Since Japanese auto production also rises, the total value of U.S. parts imports need not fall. However, for a sufficiently high level of investment, the reduction in the range of imported parts dominates and eventually imports would be reduced to zero.

Even supposing this last worst case scenario for U.S. exports, it is not obvious that these keiretsu supply relationships create an "unfair" trade barrier, potentially justifying the use of countervailing trade remedies. A central issue is one of exclusive dealing: are U.S. and other non-Japanese suppliers unfairly excluded from long-term or other supply arrangements with keiretsu? We would argue that the simple exclusion of imports does not prove the case because the informational requirements for the effective design of relationship-specific investments could require a local presence in Japan and close communication with other keiretsu suppliers. For example, detailed

---

[4]See Dyer and Ouchi (1993: p. 55) for other examples.

[5]This is a form of *relational quasi rent* as termed by Aoki (1988).

information about the production processes of other suppliers may be required to improve the compatibility or fit of a particular part and close coordination with these suppliers may be required for just in time delivery.[6] Also, if U.S. and other non-Japanese firms do locate in Japan, language and other cultural barriers may make it difficult for these firms to be effective in creating rents for the keiretsu automaker. In addition, since in our model relationship-specific investment enhances efficiency, even if exclusionary, the long-term keiretsu arrangements could be defended as a method to improve incentives for investment.[7]

Apart from these general comments, the article does not provide further insight as to whether keiretsu long-term supply arrangements are in fact exclusionary practices. Rather, having developed the basic effects of relationship-specific investment within keiretsu on the range and value of imported intermediate goods, a central theme of the article is then to argue that these relationships could create a strong impression of the existence of an "unfair" barrier to trade, even if the practices are not truly exclusionary. First, if the rents created by relationship-specific investment are not observable outside the keiretsu, then the inability to export parts that are cheaper in the U.S. could appear to be due to a trade barrier. Also, relationship-specific investment can lead to counterintuitive effects. For example, a move from a prohibitive Japanese tariff to free trade or, alternatively, a reduction in the price of U.S. parts could raise Japanese marginal cost, reducing Japanese auto output and total demand for parts. Also, to the extent Japanese auto output increases, this tends to reduce the range of parts that would be imported at free trade. We argue that these counterintuitive effects could easily be misunderstood, leading to significant perceptions of a trade barrier.

[6]Branstetter (2000) finds strong empirical support for the importance of the flow of technological information within vertical keiretsu groups in enhancing efficiency. Also, the need to transport parts from the U.S. would complicate "just in time" delivery. Further, exchange rate fluctuations could raise the risk to U.S. firms in making investments that are specific to the Japanese buyer.

[7]See Marvel (1982) for the general point. McMillan (1996) provides an excellent description of the sources of keiretsu efficiency and makes this argument in the context of the trade dispute over auto parts. Lawrence (1991) finds some support for the idea that vertical, as opposed to horizontal, keiretsu enhance efficiency.

To develop these results, we take the existence of long-term supply arrangements involving relationship-specific investments within keiretsu as given.[8] We also make the simplifying, but generally realistic, assumption that suppliers exporting from the United States are unable to make relationship-specific investments of value to the keiretsu automaker. As discussed above, we do not need to specify whether this is due to the need to overcome cultural barriers and produce locally in Japan or to some exclusionary practice. Indeed, our results concerning the implications for U.S. exports to Japan do not depend on whether keiretsu firms are domestically or foreign owned. Although not necessary for the results, an additional assumption is that U.S. parts suppliers do not make relationship-specific investments of value to the U.S. automaker.[9] Since contracts made by U.S. automakers with outside suppliers are relatively short term (reducing the profitability of relationship-specific investments), whereas in Japan they are open ended, this simplifying assumption partially reflects this institutional difference.[10] In the absence of relationship-specific investment, parts, whether from Japan or the

[8]Keiretsu are very stable. For instance, "member firms of Kyohokai, an association formed by Toyota parts suppliers, numbered 171 in 1984. Of these firms, 153 had been continual members of Kyohokai during the 11 years since 1973" (Asanuma, 1989: p. 5). Also subcontractors differ as to whether they are top ranked firms with technological expertise and long-term supply relationships or more marginal firms that may be used as a short-term capacity buffer so as to help maintain permanent employment in the core manufacturer (see Asanuma, 1989: pp. 16–18; Aoki, 1988; pp. 208–209). Our analysis applies to the top ranked suppliers.

[9]The model could be developed with symmetric institutions, in which U.S. and Japanese suppliers make relationship-specific investments of value to the U.S. and Japanese automakers respectively. The nature of results concerning the range and value of U.S. parts imported into Japan would not change. However, instead of simply importing those parts that can be produced more cheaply in Japan, the results developed for imports into Japan would now also apply to imports into the U.S.

[10]The average length of contract in the U.S. auto industry was only 2.5 years in 1989, up from 1.3 years in 1984 (Dyer and Ouchi, 1993). Some theoretical justification for asymmetry is provided by McLaren (2000), who argues that the "thickness of the market" for specialized inputs produced by unintegrated firms can lead to multiple equilibria in which countries differ as to the degree of vertical integration. Vertical integration "thins" the market, reducing the incentive for up-front production by unintegrated firms.

U.S., are priced competitively at marginal cost.[11] While there is a large literature concerning vertical integration, contract design, and the institutional differences between Japanese and U.S. contracting arrangements,[12] specific modelling of the informal procurement arrangements within keiretsu is relatively recent. Of particular relevance here is McLaren (1999), who argues that less formal bargaining arrangements can dominate formal contracts in encouraging cooperative investment.[13] More generally, well known managerial costs arising from incentive problems within organizations can favor informal supply arrangements of the sort exemplified by the keiretsu (see Aoki, 1988). Empirical work examining the effects of keiretsu on the pattern of Japanese trade include Lawrence (1991, 1993) and Fung (1991), who argue that industries with a high keiretsu presence tend to have low imports.[14] Also, Weinstein and Yafeh (1995) present evidence that strong relationships with their main bank can cause keiretsu expansion at the expense of imports and Cheng and Kreinin (1996) consider the preferential use of keiretsu suppliers.[15]

[11]Although U.S. auto producers tend to be more vertically integrated than their Japanese counterparts, treating U.S. suppliers as purely competitive is not unreasonable given the large number of establishments (4856 in 1992 according to the Office of Automotive Affairs) with relatively short-term contracts. However, one might want to relax this assumption to allow for a rent-shifting motive if the aim were to model the political economy aspects of lobbying by the U.S. auto industry for greater access to Japan.

[12]See for example, Perry (1989), Aoki (1988), Asanuma (1985, 1989), and Holmstrom and Roberts (1998).

[13]In McLaren (1999), the incentive for cooperative investments is increased by unintegrated buyers who raise the "threat point" of suppliers in the event that bargaining breaks down. Also see Taylor and Wiggins (1997) for the implications of U.S. and Japanese subcontracting systems for quality control.

[14]Saxonhouse (1991) presents an opposing view, arguing that there is little evidence that Japan's trade regime is different from other countries. Data to be explained include Japan's low share of manufactured goods imports, low share of intraindustry trade, etc. (see Lawrence, 1993: pp. 6–7).

[15]Also see Feenstra *et al.* (1999) for estimates as to the proportion of within group purchases by Asian business groups (e.g., 31 percent for autos in Japan). Related theoretical work includes Krishna and Morgan (1998), who consider trade policy in the U.S.-Japan auto-parts dispute, and Greaney (1999), who is concerned with distortions in firm behavior due to claims of an implicit trade barrier. For vertical

This article provides a natural basis for further work concerning the effects of trade policy in the context of the U.S./Japan trade dispute.[16] However, the model's consideration of a large number of parts, with differing importance for downstream costs, could also have applications in other procurement settings. Since a higher share of downstream costs tends to make relationship-specific investment more valuable for the downstream purchasing firm, this suggests that, even with different contracting arrangements, parts with high-cost shares are more likely to be associated with long-term supply arrangements or, at the extreme, full vertical integration. In the current context, the model predicts that such parts will be produced within the keiretsu and only lower value parts will be imported. This has some real world counterpart, as shown by U.S. complaints that Japanese firms preferentially reserve high value auto parts for their own suppliers.[17]

In Section 2, the model is developed in an initial closed market setting, with the effects of moving to free trade presented in Section 3. Section 4 then develops the effects of relationship-specific investments within keiretsu for the ability of foreign suppliers of intermediate goods to access the Japanese market. Next, in Section 5, we explain why the use of imports could raise Japanese marginal costs and also discuss the implications of this and other counterintuitive results for perceptions of a trade barrier. Finally Section 6 contains concluding remarks.

2. The Model of Relationship-specific Investment

2.1. *Costs and relationship-specific rents with general numbers of parts*

We suppose that a final good, such as an auto, is produced in both Japan and the United States based on Cournot competition between

relations between markets and trade see Spencer and Jones (1992) and Spencer and Raubitschek (1996) among others.

[16]Qiu and Spencer (2001) use this model to examine the effects of VIEs (voluntary import expansions) and VERs (voluntary export restraints) aimed at opening the Japanese market.

[17]See, for example, Lachica (1995).

a Japanese firm, referred to as a J-maker, and a U.S. firm, referred to as an A-maker. Our results also apply to the case in which the J-maker has a world monopoly, but the extension to oligopoly seems appropriate given the institutional reality of oligopolistic competition between U.S. and Japanese auto producers. Autos are assumed homogeneous (for convenience) and are sold in a unified world market at a price $F = F(Y)$ where $Y \equiv y^J + y^A$ and y^J and y^A are the respective outputs of the J- and A-makers.

A large number N of parts is required to produce an auto, with parts and labor combined in fixed proportion. Without loss of generality, we set the units of output of each part i so that each auto is produced using just *one* part of each type. In modelling the keiretsu, a central role is played by the fact that parts differ with respect to their costs of production and hence their importance for downstream costs. The cost of production of parts also differs across the two countries. Letting c^j and c^{*i} represent the constant average (and marginal) cost of production of part i in Japan and the U.S., respectively, we arrange parts i in order of increasing average cost. This ordering is assumed to be the same in both countries. Exploiting the fact that the number N of parts is large, it is convenient to express costs c^i and c^{*i} as differentiable and increasing functions $c^i = c^*(i)$ and $c^{*i} = c(i)$ on the continuum $[0, N]$. For the keiretsu parts producers, the importance of part i for downstream costs is then captured by the cost-share[18]

$$\sigma^i = \sigma(i) = c(i)/C(N) \text{ for } C(N) \equiv \int_0^N c^j di$$

(σ is Greek s for share) where the ordering of parts implies $\sigma'(i) > 0$.

As previously discussed, the U.S. parts producers act as purely competitive firms with no commitment to the J- or A-makers. Within the keiretsu, we assume for simplicity that there is just one

[18]To see the correspondence between the discrete and continuous versions of the model, suppose that $c(j) = a+\rho j$ for $= 1, 2, \ldots, N$, which implies $\sigma^j \equiv c(j)/C(N)$ for $C(N) \equiv \int_{j=1}^{n} c^j = N[a + (\rho/2)(N + 1)$ If $c(i) = c^0 + \rho i$ for $i \in [0, N]$, then $(N) = \int_0^N c(i)di = N[c^0 + (\rho/2)N]$. For $c^0 \equiv a + \rho/2$ and $j = i + 1$, we obtain $c(i + 1/2) = \int_1^{i+1} (c^0 + \rho i)di = c^0 - \rho/2 + \rho(i + 1) = c^j$ and $\sigma^{i+1/2} = \sigma^j$. If $c(j)$ is nonlinear then $\sigma^{i+1/2} \approx \sigma^j$.

J-supplier[19] of each part i. Each J-supplier i (or more simply supplier i) potentially makes a relationship-specific investment, denoted k^j, which creates rent for the J-maker (but not for the A-maker) in the form of a reduction in assembly costs.[20] Since the J-maker gains rent only through the use of the part, the level of rent, denoted r^i, is assumed to be constant for each unit of part j purchased from supplier i. Recalling that each auto is produced with just one unit of each part, r^j also represents the J-maker's rent per auto from investment k^j. The magnitude of r^j is assumed to be proportional to the initial value, denoted w^o, of the J-maker's assembly cost per auto in the absence of relationship-specific investments and also to the relative contribution of part i to cost, as measured by the cost-share $\sigma(i)$. This last condition reflects the idea that the greater the proportion of costs associated with the part, the greater the potential for cost reduction. For example, *a* given amount of investment is likely to be more effective in reducing costs when it applies to engines rather than to seat covers. Also, we obtain the reasonable feature that the level of rent created per auto is invariant to an inflation in the costs of all parts. Finally, letting θ denote the productivity of investment in creating rent, the rent created per auto by investment k^i is given by

$$r^i = w^o\sigma(i)\theta h(k^i) \quad \text{for} \quad 0 < \theta \le \theta^{\max}, \tag{2.1}$$

where $\theta^{\max} \equiv \min\{1, C(N)/w^o\}$ and $h(k^j)$ satisfies

$$h(0) = 0h'(k^j) > 0h''(k^j) < 0 \quad \text{and} \quad h(k^j) < 1. \tag{2.2}$$

[19]If there is more than one long-term supplier for part i, this may weaken the bargaining power of these suppliers. However, it is in the interest of the J-maker to allow suppliers some bargaining power in order to gain the benefit from relationship-specific investments (see Proposition A.1 (ii) of the Appendix). Assuming investment takes place, most of our results are not sensitive to the level of bargaining power.

[20]From Dyer and Ouchi (1993: Figure 8.2), in 1984, assembly costs were 23.1 percent of total costs for a U.S. car and only 15. 7 percent for a comparable Japanese car. Relationship-specific investments can reduce assembly costs by improving the "fit" with other parts or by facilitating "just in time" delivery so as to reduce inventory costs.

Two examples of functions satisfying (2.2)[21] are $h(k^i) = 1-\exp\{-k^i\}$ and $h(k^i) = 1 - 1/(1 + k^i)$.

From (2.1) and (2.2), it follows that rent, r^j, is increasing in k^j, but at a decreasing rate:

$$dr^i/dk^i = w^o\sigma(i)\theta h'(k^i) > 0 \quad \text{and}$$
$$d^2r^i/(dk^i)^2 = w^o\sigma(i)\theta h''(k^i) < 0. \tag{2.3}$$

Also, the conditions $\theta \leq \theta^{\max}$ and $h(k^i) < 1$ sufficiently restrict the magnitude of the rent, r^j, that there is no "free lunch" from assembly or from the production and use of keiretsu parts. Since $r^j < w^o\sigma(i)$ from $\theta^{\max} \leq 1, h(k^j) < 1$, and (2.1), the J-maker's assembly cost per auto, denoted w, is strictly positive; i.e.,

$$w = w^o - \int_0^N r^i di = \int_0^N (w^o\sigma(i) - r^i)di > 0.$$

Correspondingly, since $r^j < \sigma^j C(N) = c^j$ from $\theta^{\max} \leq C(N)/w^o, h(k^j) < 1$, and (2.1), the marginal resource cost, $c^j - r^j$, from the production and use of keiretsu parts once investment k^i has been sunk, is also strictly positive.

Adjusting for relationship-specific investment and letting p^i represent the price paid to supplier i, the J-maker's marginal cost for part i is given by $\gamma^i \equiv p^i - r^i$ if the part is purchased from within the keiretsu and by c^{*i} if the part is imported. The J-maker's overall marginal cost, denoted γ^J, then equals the sum of these costs for parts plus w^0. To focus on the question of access to the Japanese market, we assume that parts can be freely imported into the U.S. from Japan and hence that the A-maker buys part i at a price equal to the $\min\{c^{*i}, c^i\}$. Thus, given a constant assembly cost, the A-maker's marginal cost, denoted γ^A, is a constant. The J-maker, supplier i, and the A-maker respectively earn profits:

$$\pi^J = y^J(P(Y) - \gamma^J)\phi^i = y^J(p^i - c^i) - k^i \quad \text{and}$$
$$\pi^A = y^A(P(Y) - \gamma^A). \tag{2.4}$$

[21]If $h(k^i) = 1-\exp\{-k^i\}$ then $h(0) = 0, h'(k^i) = \exp\{-k^j\}h''(k^j) = -h'(k^i)$, and $h(k^j) < 1$. If $h(k^j) = 1 - 1/(1 + k^j)$, then $h(0) = 0, h'(k^j) = 1/(1 + k^j)^2, h''(k^i) = -2/(1 + k^j)^3$, and $h(k^i) < 1$.

2.2. *Order of moves and bargaining over price within Keiretsu*

Relationship-specific investments within keiretsu take place at arm's length. Consequently, even if such investment would be beneficial to the J-maker, payment is typically determined only after investment is sunk and there is no guarantee that the cost will be covered.[22] The model captures this idea by assuming that J-suppliers commit to their investments prior to bargaining with the J-maker as to the price they will receive for their product. Although the bargained price, p^j, can depend on the rent, r^j, created by investment, k^j, it is assumed that third party verification problems[23] prevent payments based on k^i directly. As outlined in Section A.1 of the Appendix, it is possible to formulate a model of incomplete contracts with the same results, but a bargaining framework would seem to best reflect the institutional arrangements within keiretsu.[24] We assume the following order of moves. In stage 1, each supplier i commits to its investment k^i, which becomes sunk at this stage, and simultaneously, the J-maker and A-maker both specify their respective outputs y^J and y^A. Since each firm sets its choice variable to maximize own profit taking the other choice variables as given, this gives rise to a Nash equilibrium in k^j, y^J, and y^A. If the J-maker has a monopoly, then $y^A \equiv 0$. Profits π^J and π^A (in the duopoly case) are strictly positive, but it is possible that a J-supplier would make a loss by producing in stage 2 (i.e., $\phi^j < 0$ for all $k^i \geq 0$) or that bargaining would break down and the supplier would not produce the part. In both these cases, anticipating the outcome of stage 2, supplier j sets $k^i = 0$ and exits the market at stage 1. In stage 2, the J-maker

[22]As stated by Dyer and Ouchi (1993: p. 52), "Japanese suppliers frequently give automakers a head start in development by starting work on projects even before they are assured of winning the project."

[23]It is possible that a judge would not be able to verify the value of k^j, even if all parties can estimate the value of k^j from knowledge of $r^j\sigma^j$, and θ. Adding uncertainty to the model would disguise the value of k^i, but although a suitably designed model would give similar results, the model becomes rather more complex.

[24]The role of bargaining is supported by Asanuma (1985), who observes that parts prices are revised at regular intervals, by bilateral negotiation, incorporating both risk and incentives for innovation and effort.

engages in simultaneous Nash bargaining[25] over price p^j with each supplier i remaining in the market. If an agreement is reached, the J-maker orders its desired number of parts. Otherwise the J-maker purchases part i at the lowest price available, either at a price c^i from a competitive spot market in Japan or at a price c^{*i} from U.S. suppliers if imports are not prohibited. Parts and final-good output are then produced and sold.

An alternative possibility[26] would be to assume that investments k^j are determined in stage 1 and y^J, y^A, and p^j in stage 2. Suppliers would then strategically choose k^j considering the effect on the Cournot equilibrium outputs in stage 2 as well as the bargained price p^j. However, since with a continuum of parts it is reasonable to assume that the effect of an individual variation in k^j on y^J is negligible, the outcome is then the same as with the assumed order of moves.

We initially develop the model in a closed market setting in which the import of parts into Japan is prevented through government regulations or a prohibitive tariff.

Considering stage 2 first, the J-maker's objective in bargaining with supplier i is to minimize the total cost, $y^J\gamma^j = y^J(p^j - r^j)$, of part i for the given output y^J committed in stage 1. Since the J-maker's disagreement or "threat point" is to buy the part at a price c^i from the spot market, this implies a payoff from reaching agreement of $y^J(c^i - \gamma^i)$. Correspondingly, since k^i is sunk, supplier i maximizes variable profit $\phi^i + k^i = y^J(p^i - c^i)$ with a threat point of no production and zero variable profit.

Hence, setting p^j to maximize $G^j \equiv y^J(c^j - \gamma^j)^\alpha(p^j - c^j)^{1-\alpha}$ for $\alpha \in [0, 1]$, where α represents the bargaining power of the J-maker and $1 - \alpha$ the bargaining power of each J-supplier, it

[25]See Binmore *et al.* (1986) for a justification of the Nash bargaining concept as a subgame perfect equilibrium in a game where participants alternate offers until one side accepts.

[26]This may be the more natural order of moves for the example in which relationship-specific investment involves building a plant near the J-maker. However, if the investment involves small design changes to make the part a better fit with other keiretsu parts, then the importance of knowing exact production requirements may make the simultaneous choice of y^J with k^j a more natural assumption.

follow,[27] using $c^i - r^i > 0$, that at the Nash bargaining equilibrium

$$p^i - c^i = (1-\alpha)r^i \geq 0 \quad \text{and} \quad \gamma^i \equiv p^i - r^i = c^i - \alpha r^i > 0. \quad (2.5)$$

As can be seen from (2.5), supplier i gains a share, $1-\alpha$, of the rent it creates, resulting in a reduction of αr^j in the marginal cost of part i for the J-maker. Since the respective payoffs to the J-maker and supplier i are non-negative for all $k^i \geq 0$, i.e.,

$$y^J(c^i - \gamma^i) = y^J \alpha r^i \geq 0 \quad \text{and} \quad \phi^i + k^i = y^J(1-\alpha)r^i \geq 0, \quad (2.6)$$

agreement is always reached for supplier i to produce the part. However, if $k^i = 0$, then, since $\gamma^i = c^i$ from (2.5), the J-maker's cost is the same as if the part had been purchased on the spot market.

2.3. *Stage 1: Relationship-specific investments and output decisions*

In stage 1, there is a Nash equilibrium in which the J- and A-makers set their outputs and J-suppliers simultaneously set their investment levels. Examining the investment decisions first, if supplier i remains to produce in stage 2, it sets $k^i \geq 0$ to maximize ϕ^i as in (2.6), taking y^J, y^A, and k^j for $j \neq i$ as given.[28] Since ϕ^i is concave[29] in k^i, the Kuhn-Tucker first order conditions, given by

$$d\phi^i/0k^i = y^J(1-\alpha)(dr^i/dk^i) - 1 \leq 0 \quad \text{and} \quad (d\phi^i/dk^i)k^i = 0, \quad (2.7)$$

define k^i as a function, $k^i = k(\sigma^i, y^J)$, where k^i satisfies $d\phi^i/dk^i = 0$ if $k^i > 0$ and $k^i = 0$ if $d\phi^i/0k^i < 0$. Taking into account stage 2, from (2.6) evaluated at $k^i = k(\sigma^i, y^J)$, supplier i earns a stage 1

---

[27] From $d\ln G^j/dp^i = (1-\alpha)/(p^j - c^j) - \alpha/(c^j - \gamma^i) = 0$, we obtain $\alpha(p^j - c^j) = (1-\alpha)(c^i - \gamma^j)$ for $\gamma^j = p^j - r^i$.

[28] From (2.6), y^A and investments k^j for $j = i$ influence k^i only through their effects on y^J.

[29] We have from (2.6) that $\partial^2\phi^i/(dk^i)^2 = y^J(1-\alpha)w^\circ\sigma(i)\theta h(k^j) < 0$.

profit given by

$$\phi^i = \phi(\sigma^i, y^J) = y^J(1-\alpha)r^i - k(\sigma^i, y^J) \text{ for } r^i = w^o\sigma^i\theta h(k(\sigma^i, y^J)), \tag{2.8}$$

where the parameters θ and α are omitted for convenience. Since, from (2.8), J-suppliers have the option of earning zero profit by setting $k^j = 0$, all J-suppliers produce in stage 2 and from (2.7), supplier i engages in relationship-specific investment, setting $k^i > 0$, if and only if $d\phi^i/dk^i > 0$ at $k^i = 0$.

Since a requirement for relationship-specific investment is that J-suppliers receive a positive share of the rent they create (see (2.7)), we assume $\alpha < 1$. Evaluating (2.7) at $k^j = 0$, using dr^j/dk^j from (2.3), the ordering of parts from lowest to highest cost-share then ensures that $d(0\phi^j/0k^j)/di = y^J(1-\alpha)w^o\sigma'(i)\theta h'(0) > 0$ and hence that $k^i > 0$ implies $k^j > 0$ for all $j > i$. Thus, letting part $i = Z(Z$ for zero investment) satisfy

$$k^Z = 0 \text{ and } d\phi^Z/0k^Z = y^J(1-\alpha)w^o\sigma(Z)\theta h'(0) - 1 = 0, \tag{2.9}$$

(2.9) defines the cutoff point, $Z = Z(y^J; \theta, \alpha)$ at which $k^i = k(\sigma^i, y^J) > 0$ if $i > Z$ and $k^i = 0$ for $i \leq Z$. We assume that some suppliers set $k^i > 0$, which implies $< N$. An important case is $k^i > 0$ for all $i \in [0, N]$, which, for convenience, we refer to as satisfying $i > Z$. This case applies at $\theta = \theta^{\max}$, since we assume

$$d\phi^0/dk^0 = y^J(1-\alpha)w^o\sigma^0\theta^{\max}h'(0) - 1 > 0, \tag{2.10}$$

which implies that $k^0 = k(\sigma^0, y^J; \theta^{\max}) > 0$ and hence $k(\sigma^i, y^J; \theta^{\max}) > 0$ for all $i \in [0, N]$.

The conditions under which J-suppliers make relationship-specific investments are summarized in Proposition 1 (i). Also, as shown in Proposition l (ii), the ordering of parts in terms of increasing cost shares σ^i has the useful feature that for $i > Z$, parts are also ordered in terms of increasing levels of k^i, r^i and ϕ^i. Supposing that suppliers i and j for $i > j$ make the same level of investment, then since part i involves a higher cost-share, this generates a higher level of rent for the J-maker.

Since the outcome of bargaining is that each supplier receives a share $1-\alpha$ of the rent created, this translates into a higher return to supplier i from investment, with the result that supplier i sets $k^i > k^j$.

Proposition 1. *Assume parts cannot be imported into Japan.*

(i) *For $i > Z$, supplier i invests $k^j = k(\sigma^j, y^J) > 0$, earns profit $\phi^i = \phi(\sigma^i, y^J) > 0$, and creates rent $r^i > 0$ per unit of the J-maker's output. For $i \leq Z, k^i = k(\sigma^i, y^J) = 0$ and $\phi^i = \phi(\sigma^i, y^J) = 0$.*

(ii) *For $i > Z$, higher cost-shares σ^i are associated with greater levels of k^i, r^i, and ϕ^j.*

Proof:

(i) Since $k^i > 0$ for $i > Z$ (proved in the text), it follows that $h(k^i) > 0$ from (2.2) and hence that $r^i = w^o\sigma^i\theta h(k^i) > 0$ for $> Z$. If $k^i = 0$, then $h(0) = 0$ implies $r^i = 0$ and $\phi^i = 0$. Using $y^J(1-\alpha)w^o\sigma^i\theta = 1/h^f(k^i)$ (from (2.7) for $k^i > 0$ and (2.3)) in (2.8) and $h(k^j)/k^j > h'(k^j)$ (from $h(0) = 0$ and $h''(k^j) < 0$), we obtain

$$\phi^i = \phi(\sigma^i, y^J) = [h(k^i) - k^i h'(k^i)]/h'(k^i) > 0 \text{ for } i > Z. \quad (2.11)$$

(ii) For the comparative statics, a useful expression is

$$\lambda^i \equiv -(h^f(k^i))^2/h(k^i)h^{ff}(k^i) > 0 \text{ for } k^i > 0, \quad (2.12)$$

where the sign follows from (2.2). Since from (2.7) and (2.3), $d^2\phi^i/(dk^i)(d\sigma^i) = y^J(1-\alpha)w^o\theta h'(k^i)$ and $\partial^2\phi^i/(\partial k^i)^2 = y^J(1-\alpha)w^o\sigma(i)\theta h''(k^i)$, we obtain $dk^i/d\sigma^i = -h'(k^j)/\sigma^j h''(k^j) > 0$ for $\geq Z$. Also, from $dr^i/d\sigma^i = w^o\theta h(k^i)[1 + \sigma^i h'(k^i)(dk^i/d\sigma^i)/h(k^i)]$ using (2.12) and from (2.8) using $d\phi^i/0k^i = 0$ we have that for $i > Z$,

$$dr^j/d\sigma^j = r^j(1+\lambda^j)/\sigma^j > 0 \quad \text{and} \quad d\phi^i/d\sigma^i = y^J(1-\alpha)r^i/\sigma^i > 0. \quad (2.13)$$

□

From Proposition 1 and (2.5), we can express the J-maker's marginal cost as

$$\gamma^J = \int_0^Z c^j di + \int_Z^N (c^j - \alpha r^j)di + w^0. \quad (2.14)$$

Since from (2.14), $\gamma^J = C(N) + w^O - \int_Z^N \alpha r^i di$, it follows that for $0 < \alpha < 1$, the rent created by $k^i > 0$ reduces the J-maker's marginal cost below the level $\gamma^J = C(N) + w^o$ achieved either at $\alpha = 0$, where J-suppliers capture all the rent created by $k^i > 0$, or at $\alpha = 1$, where J-suppliers have no incentive to invest ($r^j = 0$).

Now considering the stage 1 determination of output, at the Nash equilibrium in y^J, y^A, and k^i, the J-maker treats k^i and hence γ^J as fixed. Thus, there is no strategic role for output in influencing the prices paid for parts at the second stage bargaining game. From (2.4), using subscripts J and A to represent partial derivatives with respect to y^J and y^A, respectively, it follows that y^J and y^A satisfy the standard Cournot first order conditions

$$\pi_J^J = F + y^J P' - \gamma^J = 0 \pi_A^A = F + y^A P' - \gamma^A = 0. \tag{2.15}$$

Assuming that the following second order and stability conditions,

$$\begin{aligned} &\pi_{JJ}^J = 2P' + y^J p'' < 0 \quad \pi_{AA}^A = 2P' + y^A P'' < 0 \quad \text{and} \\ &H^o \equiv \pi_{JJ}^J \pi_{AA}^A - \pi_{JA}^J \pi_{AJ}^A = p'(3p' + Yp'') > 0, \end{aligned} \tag{2.16}$$

hold globally, conditions (2.15) define the equilibrium output levels $y^J = y^J(\gamma^J)$ and $y^A = y^A(\gamma^J)$ as functions of the J-maker's marginal cost, where the constant γ^A is omitted for convenience.

However, the dependence of $k^i = k(\sigma^i, y^J)$ on y^J means that $\gamma^J = \gamma^J(y^J)$ is also dependent on y^J and hence, for the comparative statics, we require the additional stability conditions:

$$\pi_{JJ}^J - dy^J/dy^J < 0 \quad \text{and} \quad H \equiv H^o - \pi_{AA}^A \left(\frac{d\gamma^J}{dy^J}\right) > 0. \tag{2.17}$$

From (2.15), holding γ^J fixed with respect to variations in y^J, we first obtain the standard result that an increase in γ^J reduces y^J and we then use (2.17) to take account of the effect of y^J on γ^J; i.e., we obtain

$$\begin{aligned} dy^J/dy^J = \pi_{AA}^A/H^o < 0 \quad \text{and} \quad & 1 - (dy^J/d\gamma^J)(d\gamma^J/dy^J) \\ &= H/H^o > 0. \end{aligned} \tag{2.18}$$

If the J-maker has a monopoly, (2.18) reduces to

$$\begin{aligned} dy^J/dy^J = 1/\pi^J_{JJ} < 0 \quad \text{and} \quad & 1 - (dy^J/d\gamma^J)(d\gamma^J/dy^J) \\ &= (\pi^J_{JJ} - d\gamma^J/dy^J)/\pi^J_{JJ} > 0. \end{aligned} \tag{2.19}$$

3. Opening the Japanese Market

With the removal of the government imposed trade restriction, there is free trade in the sense that there are no laws restricting trade, but the extent to which parts are imported is affected by the long-term supply arrangements within the keiretsu. This section develops the implications of free trade for the bargaining model, relationship-specific investment, and imports.

The potential for Japanese imports arises from the assumption that at least some range of parts can be produced more cheaply in the U.S. Letting $\delta^i = \delta(i) \equiv c(i) - c^*(i)$ represent the efficiency gap between U.S. and Japanese production costs for part i, the simplest assumption is that $c(i)$ and $c^*(i)$ are linear in i with equal slopes leading to a constant efficiency gap across all parts; i.e., for all $i \in [0, N]$,

$$\delta^j = \delta = c(0) - c^*(0) \geq 0 \; c'(i) = c^{*'}(i) \text{ and } c''(i) = c^{*''}(i) = 0. \tag{3.1}$$

The case $\delta = 0$ is retained as a benchmark. However, for greater generality and to better specify the range of parts for which relationship-specific investment causes keiretsu production to displace imports, we focus on the possibility that δ^j differs across parts, with part $i = 0$ potentially imported due to $\delta^0 > 0$ and part $i = E$, satisfying $\delta^E = 0$ (E for equal costs), produced within the keiretsu. To help ensure that there is only one region of imports (namely, parts with low cost-shares), we make the simplifying assumption[30] that the efficiency gap

[30]For a unique region of imports, it is sufficient that J-supplier profits be strictly increasing in i for $i \in [Z, N]$. This tends to be an endogenous outcome of the model since profits increase due to rising levels of σ^i and k^j. This ordering is reinforced by $\delta'(i) \leq 0$, but our results also apply if $\delta'(i) > 0$ and not too large.

is decreasing or constant as the cost-share rises, and hence that

$$\delta(0) > 0, \delta(E) = 0 \quad \text{and} \quad \delta'(i) \leq 0 \text{ for all } i \in [0, N]. \tag{3.2}$$

If $\delta(N) < 0$, then $E < N$ and Japan has an actual cost advantage for parts with the highest cost-shares.[31] Finally, we focus on the case in which keiretsu investment is potentially relevant for imports by assuming that $Z \leq E$. If $Z \geq E$, then all parts for which the U.S. has a cost advantage are imported.

With respect to bargaining at stage 2, free trade gives the J-maker the additional option of importing parts at prices c^{*i} from U.S. producers. Using a superscript F to distinguish values at free trade, for parts $i \geq E$ where Japan has a cost advantage, the payoffs from agreement at the Nash bargaining equilibrium are unchanged from (2.6). Hence, as in Proposition 1, supplier i sets $k^{iF} = k(\sigma^j, y^J) > 0$ and earns profits

$$\phi^{iF} = \phi(\sigma^j, y^J) = y^J(1-\alpha)r^j - k(\sigma^j, y^J) > 0 \text{ for } i \geq E > Z, \tag{3.3}$$

with $k^{EF} = k(\sigma^E, y^J) = 0$ and $\phi^{EF} = 0$ for $Z = E$. By contrast, in bargaining with supplier i for $i < E$, the availability of lower cost imports changes the J-maker's "threat point with the consequence that[32]

$$\begin{aligned} p^{iF} - c^j &= (1-\alpha)(r^j - \delta^j) \quad \text{and} \\ \gamma^{iF} &= c^{*i} - \alpha(r^j - \delta^j) \text{ for } i \leq E. \end{aligned} \tag{3.4}$$

Comparing (3.4) with (2.5), since $\delta^j = c^j - c^{*i} > 0$ for $i < E$, competition from imports reduces the price paid to the J-supplier by $(1-\alpha)\delta^j$, while the J-maker absorbs the amount, $\alpha\delta^i$, of the

[31] For example, if there are three parts, with $c(1) = \$230$, $c(2) = \$310$, and $c(3) = \$390$ in Japan, but $c^*(1) = \$200, c^*(2) = \$300$, and $c^*(3) = \$400$ in the U.S., then $\delta(1) = \$30$, $\delta(2) = \$10$, and $\delta(3) = -\$10$. Since c^j is the total cost of part i required per auto, parts at the high end of the scale $i \in [0, N]$ could involve both high cost parts produced in average volume or average cost parts produced in high volume.

[32] Maximizing $G^{iF} \equiv y^J(c^{*i} - \gamma^{iF})^{\alpha}(p^{iF} - c^j)^{1-\alpha}$, this follows from $(1-\alpha)(c^{*i} - \gamma^{iF}) - \alpha(p^{iF} - c^i) = 0$ for $\gamma^{iF} = p^{iF} - r^i$.

efficiency gap.[33] Analogously to (2.6), the respective payoffs of the J-maker and supplier i (relative to the disagreement point) become

$$\begin{aligned} y^J(c^{*i} - \gamma^{iF}) &= y^J\alpha(r^i - \delta^i) \quad \text{and} \\ \phi^{iF} + k^{iF} &= y^J(1-\alpha)(r^j - \delta^j) \text{ for } i \leq E. \end{aligned} \tag{3.5}$$

Agreement is then reached for supplier i to produce the part if and only the rent created is sufficiently large to make $r^j - \delta^j \geq 0$. If $r^j - \delta^j < 0$, then part i is imported. Hence, supplier i's profit at stage 2 is

$$\begin{aligned} \phi^{iF} &= y^J(1-\alpha)(r^j - \delta^j) - k^j \text{ if } r^j - \delta^j \geq 0 \quad \text{and} \\ \phi^{iF} &= -k^j \text{ if } r^j - \delta^j < 0. \end{aligned} \tag{3.6}$$

Turning to stage 1, profit maximization by supplier i involves, first, the optimal choice of k^i conditional on remaining to bargain with the J-maker and, second, the decision whether to remain in the market. With respect to the first choice, supplier i sets $k^i \geq 0$ to maximize ϕ^{iF} as in (3.6), taking y^J and y^A as given. Since the potential for imports reduces the revenue to supplier i by an amount $(1-\alpha)y^J\delta^i$, which is independent of the level of investment, this gives rise to the same first order conditions for the choice of k^j as before (see (2.7)). This is convenient, since the opening of trade then has no effect on the investment function, $k^i = k(\sigma^i, y^J)$, for firms that remain as producers. As for the decision whether to remain in the market, if supplier i produces the part, from (3.6) and (2.8), it earns a stage 1 equilibrium profit given by

$$\phi^{iF} = \phi^F(i, y^J) \equiv \phi(\sigma^i, y^J) - y^J(1-\alpha)\delta(i) \text{ for } i \leq E. \tag{3.7}$$

Alternatively, if bargaining would break down (i.e., if $r^j - \delta^j < 0$) or if revenues from production are positive (due to $r^i - \delta^i \geq 0$) but are not sufficient to cover the sunk cost of investment, then supplier i chooses not to invest, exiting the market at stage 1. Thus, noting that $\phi^{iF} \geq 0$ implies $r^i - \delta^i \geq 0$, supplier i remains to produce part i if and only if $\phi^{iF} = \phi^F(i, y^J) \geq 0$. Also, since $r^i - \delta^i \geq 0$ for $\delta^i > 0$

[33] Although γ^{iF} is reduced by $(1-\alpha)\delta^j, c^i - r^j > 0$ implies $\gamma^{iF} = (1-\alpha)c^{*i} + \alpha(c^j - r^j) > 0$.

implies $k^i > 0$, it follows that all J-suppliers remaining to produce parts $i < E$ must engage in relationship-specific investment.

To specify the range of imported parts, letting $i = T$ (T for trade) denote the marginal part just produced by the keiretsu, then $T \leq E$ satisfies

$$\phi^F(T, y^J; \theta, \alpha) = y^J(1-\alpha)(r^T - \delta(T)) - k(\sigma^T, y^J; \theta) = 0, \quad (3.8)$$

which defines[34] $T = T(y^J; \theta, \alpha)$ for $y^J = y^J(\gamma^{J\Gamma})$. Proposition 2 describes the pattern of trade and investment.

Proposition 2. *Assume $\delta(i)$ satisfies (3.2). If $Z = E$ ⅂ then $T = E$. If $Z < E$, then T satisfies $Z < T < E$ and supplier i produces part i, investing $k^j = k(\sigma^j, y^J) > 0$ for $i \geq T$, including parts i for $T \leq i < E$ with $\delta(i) > 0$. Parts i for $i < T$ are imported, but no parts are imported if $\phi^F(0, y^J) \geq 0$.*

Proof: Since $\phi(\sigma^i, y^J) = 0$ at $k^i = 0$, we obtain $\phi^{iF} = -y^J$ $(1-\alpha)\delta(i) < 0$ for $j \leq Z$ and $i < E$ from (3.7). This implies that if $Z = E$, part i is imported for $i < E$ and hence $Z = T = E$. If $Z < E$, then part i is imported for $i \leq Z$ and hence $T > Z$ Also, since $d\phi^{iF}/di = y^J(1-\alpha)[r^i\sigma'(i)/\sigma(i) - \delta'(i)]$ from (3.7) and (2.13), we obtain

$$d\phi^F(i, y^J)/di = y^J(1-\alpha)\sigma'(i)r^i(1+x^i)/\sigma(i) > 0 \text{ for } Z < i \leq E, \quad (3.9)$$

where $X^i \equiv -\sigma(i)\delta'(i)/\sigma'(i)r^i > 0$ if $\delta'(i) < 0$ and $X^i = 0$ if $\delta'(i) = 0$. Since $T > Z$ for $Z < E$, it follows, using (3.9), that $k^{iF} = k(\sigma^i, y^J) > 0$ for $i \geq T$ and parts are imported for $i < T$. Since $\phi^F(E, y^J) > 0$ for $k^{EF} > 0$, we also obtain $< E$. If $\phi^F(0, y^J) \geq 0$, then no parts are imported, since $\phi^{iF} > 0$ for all i from (3.9). □

As illustrated in Figure 8.1, parts i with equal or higher cost-shares (i.e., for $i \geq T$) are produced within the keiretsu and parts i with lower cost-shares (i.e., for $i < T$) are imported. Consequently, imported parts represent the lowest value parts in the sense that they make the least contribution to the cost of an auto. Since from

[34]This follows since ϕ^F is increasing in i (see (3.9) below). Although y^J is determined endogenously, expressing $T = T(y^J)$ helps separate out the important relationship between imports and keiretsu output.

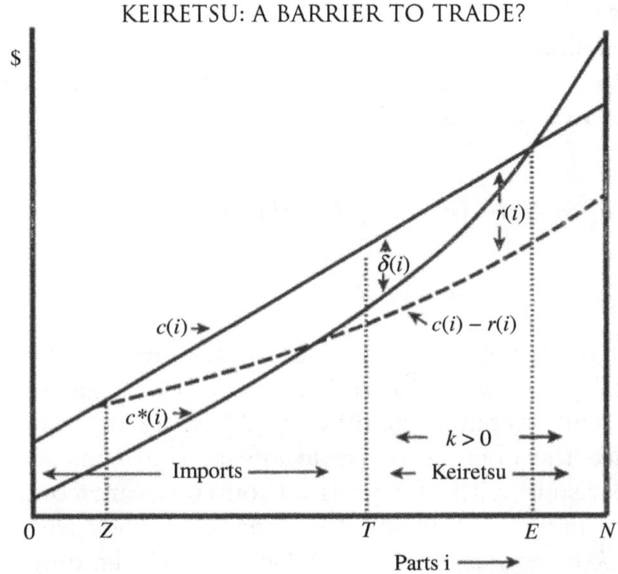

Figure 8.1. Costs and the range of imported parts.

Proposition 2, T satisfies $< T < E$, all keiretsu suppliers remaining at free trade invest, setting $k^i > 0$, including the producer of the marginal part T. Also, production by keiretsu suppliers covers a range of parts $i \in [T, E)$ for which the U.S. has lower production costs.[35] However, this production takes place only if the investment by each supplier raises efficiency relative to importing.[36] Thus, for $i \geq T$, the rent from investment, k^i shown as the difference between $c(i)$ and the dashed line, $c(i) - r(i)$, more than offsets the efficiency gap, δ^j. For $i < T$, the difference between these lines is the rent that would have been created if the part had been produced in the keiretsu. Nevertheless, as we will subsequently argue, this failure to import

[35]The assumption that $\delta(i)$ satisfies (3.2) ensures that part $i = E$ exists and that $i \in [T, E)$ is not empty.

[36]For $T \leq i < E$, it follows from $\phi^{iF} \geq 0$ and $k^j > 0$ (see Proposition 2) that $r^j - \delta^j = c^{*i} - (c^j - r^i) > 0$. Thus the import cost, c^{*i}, exceeds the marginal resource cost, $c^i - r^j$, of keiretsu production. The cost, k^i, is also covered since supplier i produces only if $\phi^i \geq 0$.

the cheaper U.S. parts can be significant if the rents are unobservable outside the keiretsu.

From Proposition 2, using (2.5) and (3.4), the J-maker's marginal cost at free trade becomes

$$\gamma^{J\Gamma} = \int_0^T c^{*i} di + \int_T^E (c^{*i} - \alpha(r^j - \delta^j))di + \int_E^N (c^j - \alpha r^j)di + w^0. \tag{3.10}$$

Consequently, at the stage 1 Nash equilibrium in y^J, y^A, and k^i, the outputs $y^J = y^J(\gamma^{J\Gamma})$ and $y^A = y^A(\gamma^{J\Gamma})$ satisfy the same first order and stability conditions (2.15), (2.16), and (2.17) as before. Since the opening of trade affects the J-maker's marginal cost, comparisons with the pretrade outcome are complicated by endogenous changes in output. However, since the investment function $k^i = k(\sigma^i, y^J)$ is unchanged (see above), holding output y^J fixed, the opening of trade has no effect on the level of k^i for parts that continue to be produced in the keiretsu. Nevertheless the range of parts produced with $k^i > 0$ is reduced by the import of parts $i \in (Z, T)$.

Although both output and relationship-specific investment are endogenously determined in the full model, it is useful to first explore the partial effects of an exogenous increase in the J-maker's output. As shown in Proposition 3, since an increase in y^J increases the incentives for relationship-specific investment, leading more J-suppliers to stay in business, it also tends to reduce the range of imported parts. This requires that some parts be imported (i.e., that $T(y^J) \geq 0$ is defined[37] from (3.8)) and that J-suppliers produce some parts for which the U.S. has a cost advantage (i.e., that $Z < E$ and hence $T < E$ from Proposition 2). For the case (3.1) in which the U.S. cost advantage is constant, we assume that $T \leq N$. The endogenous choice of relationship-specific investment also creates economies of scale for the J-maker. This last result requires that $0 < \alpha < 1$, since

[37]If $\phi^F(0, y^J) > 0$ then all J-suppliers make strictly positive profits from (3.9) and T is not defined.

if $\alpha = 0$ or if $\alpha = 1$, then $\gamma^i = \min\{c^{*i}, c^i\}$ and marginal cost remains constant.[38]

Proposition 3. *An exogenous increase in the J-maker's output: (i) narrows the range of imported parts for < E, (ii) increases rents from relationship-specific investment, and (iii) reduces the J-maker's marginal cost γ^{JF} for $0 < \alpha < 1$.*

Proof:

(i) From (3.8), using $\partial\phi^{TF}/\partial k^T = 0$, and $r^T - \delta^T > 0$ for $Z < E$ (since $k^T > 0$ from Proposition 2), we obtain $\partial\phi^{TF}/dy^J = (1-\alpha)(r^T - \delta^T) > 0$. Using (3.9), we then obtain

$$dT/\partial y^J = -\sigma(T)(r^T - \delta^T)/y^J\sigma'(T)r^T(1+X^T) < 0. \quad (3.11)$$

(ii) From $\partial\phi^i/\partial k^i = 0$ as in (2.7), we obtain $dk^i/dy^J = -h'(k^i)/y^J h''(k^i) > 0$ (see (2.2)) and hence

$$dr^j/dy^J = (dr^i/dk^i)(dk^i/dy^J) = r^i\lambda^i/y^J > \text{ for } i \geq T, \quad (3.12)$$

where $\lambda^i > 0$ from (2.12). From part (i) and $k^i > 0$ for $i \geq T$, the range of parts with $k^j > 0$ is increased for $Z < E$. For $Z = E$, then $T = Z = E$ is unchanged.

(iii) From (3.10), (3.12), and (3.11) we obtain

$$d\gamma^{JF}/dy^J = -\alpha\left[\int_T^N (dr^i/dy^J)di - (r^T - \delta^T)(dT/dy^J)\right] \leq 0, \quad (3.13)$$

where $b\gamma^{JF}/dy^J < 0$ for $\alpha > 0$ and $d\gamma^{JF}/dy^J = 0$ for $\alpha = 0$. □

[38]Although it is not obvious what mechanism would ensure the credibility of a commitment to a particular value of α, there is no presumption that it is best to set $\alpha = 0$ so as to fully internalize the returns from investment to the J-suppliers. As shown in Proposition A.1 of the Appendix, holding output fixed, total keiretsu profit is maximized at $\alpha = 0$. However, if output is allowed to vary, both the J-maker's profit and aggregate keiretsu profit are maximized at strictly positive values of α.

4. Access to the Japanese Market

This section concerns the implications of keiretsu relationship-specific investment for the ability of foreign suppliers of intermediate goods to access the Japanese market.

Recalling that θ represents the productivity of relationship-specific investment, an initial step is to show in Proposition 4 that an increase in θ expands both keiretsu output (i.e., $dy^J/d\theta > 0$) and the range of parts for which keiretsu firms potentially make investments (i.e., $dZ/d\theta < 0$). Thus for θ sufficiently large, we move into the region $Z < E$ in which some J-suppliers produce parts for which the U.S. has a cost advantage. In this region, further increases in θ restrict access to the Japanese market by reducing the range of imported parts (i.e., $dT/d\theta < 0$). More J-suppliers stay in business because the increased rent from investment raises both the price and volume of each part sold to the J-maker. At the extreme, no parts are imported. Letting $\theta = \theta^{Z=E}$ denote[39] the value of θ at which $Z = E$, the range of imported parts falls as θ is increased above $\theta^{Z=E}$. If θ increases to $\theta^{T=0}$, defined by $\phi^F(0, y^J; \theta^{T=0}) = 0$, the keiretsu supplier of part just breaks even and imports are reduced to zero.[40] Assuming that supplier would earn strictly positive profits[41] at $\theta = \theta^{\max}$, then $\theta^{T=0} < \theta^{\max}$ and no parts are imported for $\theta \in [\theta^{T=0}, \theta^{\max}]$.

Proposition 4. *(i) $dy^J/d\theta > 0$ for $\alpha > 0 (= 0$ for $\alpha = 0)$, (ii) $dZ/d\theta < 0$ for $Z \geq 0$, and (iii) $dT/d\theta < 0$ for $\theta \in (\theta^{Z=E}, \theta^{T=0}]$. No parts are imported for $\theta \in [\theta^{T=0}, \theta^{\max}]$.*

Proof: See the Appendix. □

The effect of relationship-specific investment in reducing the range of imported parts has significant consequences for a number of measures of access to the Japanese market. As shown in Proposition 5, with fewer parts imported, the level of U.S. content

[39] From (2.9), we obtain $\theta^{Z=E} \equiv 1/y^J(1-\alpha)w^o\sigma(E)h'(0) > 0$.

[40] Since $d\phi^F/di > 0$, all J-suppliers produce at $\theta^{T=0}$. From (3.7), using $\theta = 1/y^J(1-\alpha)w^0 \times \sigma(i)h'(k^j)$ (from (2.7) and (2.3)) and $\phi(\sigma^0, y^J) > 0$ for $k^0 > 0$ (see (2.11)), we obtain $\theta^{T=0} = \delta(0)/w^o\sigma^0\phi(\sigma^0, y^J)h'(k^0) > 0$.

[41] We assume $\phi^F(0, y^J; \theta^{mu}) > 0$, which, since $d\phi^F(0, y^J, \theta)/d\theta > 0$, holds for θ^{mu} sufficiently large.

per Japanese auto, denoted $v^{AJ} = \int_0^T c^{*i}di$, is reduced. Since the prices, p^{iF}, paid to keiretsu firms also increase, this implies a reduction in the U.S. share, $S^{AJ} \equiv v^{AJ}/v^J$ for $v^J \equiv v^{AJ} + \int_T^N p^{iF}di$, of the Japanese parts market. A further and perhaps more direct indicator of the possible presence of a trade restriction is $S^c = \int_T^E c^{*i}di / \int_0^E c^{*i}di$, which represents the proportion of parts that are not imported, despite an efficiency gap favoring the U.S. Since S^c is increased, this measure also suggests that relationship-specific investment limits access to the Japanese market.

Proposition 5. *For $\theta \in (\theta^{Z=E}, \theta^{T=0}]$, an increase in θ:*

(i) *reduces U.S. content, v^{AJ}, per Japanese auto,*
(ii) *reduces the U.S. share, S^{AJ}, of the Japanese market for parts, and*
(iii) *increases the proportion, S^c, of parts that are not exported to Japan, despite a U.S. cost advantage.*

Proof:

(i) Using $dT/d\theta < 0$ from Proposition 4(iii), we obtain $dv^{AJ}/d\theta = c^{*T}(dT/d\theta) < 0$.
(ii) Since $dp^{iF}/d\theta = (1-\alpha)(dr^i/d\theta) > 0$ from (3.4) and (A.11) and $dT/d\theta < 0$, we obtain

$$dS^{AJ}/d\theta = [((v^J - v^{AJ})c^{*T} + v^{AJ}p^{TF})(dT/d\theta) \\ -v^{AJ}\int_T^N (dp^{iF}/d\theta)di]/(v^J)^2 < 0.$$

(iii) Using $dT/d\theta < 0$, we obtain $dS^c/d\theta = -c^{*T}(dT/d\theta)/\int_0^E c^{*i}di > 0$. □

The results in Proposition 5 all suggest that relationship-specific investment limits access to the Japanese market. However, since this investment also increases the J-maker's output, there is an opposing effect due to an increase in the volume of imports for those parts that continue to be imported. This opens the possibility that aggregate imports might rise. Summing over the range of imported parts, since one of each part is required per auto, we can express the total volume,

O^{AJ}, and value, V^{AJ}, of parts imports as

$$Q^{AJ} \equiv T(y^J;\theta)y^J \text{ and } V^{AJ} \equiv v^{AJ}y^J \text{ where } v^{AJ} = \int_0^T c^{*i}di. \tag{4.1}$$

However, for the case (3.1) in which the efficiency gap, $\delta^i = \delta$, is constant, Proposition 6 shows that there exists a value of θ, denoted $\theta = \theta^L$ (L for large), such that if $> \theta^L$, then the reduction in the range of imported parts from an increase in y^J dominates, causing both the volume, Q^{AJ}, and value, V^{AJ}, of Japanese imports to fall. Eventually, at $\theta = \theta^{T=0}$, imports are reduced to zero. In addition, since an increase in θ preferentially reduces the imports of higher value parts, the value of U.S. exports falls more than in proportion to the fall in the volume of U.S. exports. Nevertheless, since it is possible that for low values of θ, an increase in θ would raise both Q^{AJ} and V^{AJ}, this undermines any general claim that relationship-specific investment within the keiretsu is an impediment to trade. Letting $\theta = \theta^{T=N}$ denote[42] the value of θ at which $T = N$, the condition $\theta \geq \theta^{T=N}$ ensures that at least one part is produced by a J-supplier.

Proposition 6. *Assume $\delta^i = \delta$ as in (3.1). There exists some $\theta^L \in [\theta^{T=N}, \theta^{T=0})$ such that for all $\theta \in (\theta^L, \theta^{T=0}]$, the total volume Q^{AJ} and value V^{AJ} of U.S. exports are reduced by (i) a small increase in output, y^J, OR (ii) an increase in θ. An increase in θ reduces V^{AJ} more than in proportion to Q^{AJ}.*

Proof: See the Appendix. □

Figure 8.2 illustrates the effect of θ on both the value, V^{AJ}, and share, S^{AJ}, of U.S. parts exports to the Japanese market assuming that $\delta^i > 0$ for every part. All parts are imported for $\theta < \theta^{T=N}$, but for $\theta \geq \theta^{T=N}$, the range of imported parts falls (from Proposition 5(*i*)), reducing S^{AJ} below one (as measured on the right hand axis). The figure illustrates the case in which V^{AJ} initially rises (due to the increase in the J-maker's output). However, as Proposition 6 shows, V^{AJ} eventually falls for $\theta \geq \theta^L$ and imports cease for $\theta \geq \theta^{T=0}$.

[42] Analogously to $\theta^{T=0}$ (see footnote 40), we obtain $\theta^{T=N} \equiv \delta^N/w^O\sigma(N)\phi(\sigma^N, y^J)h'(k^N) > 0$.

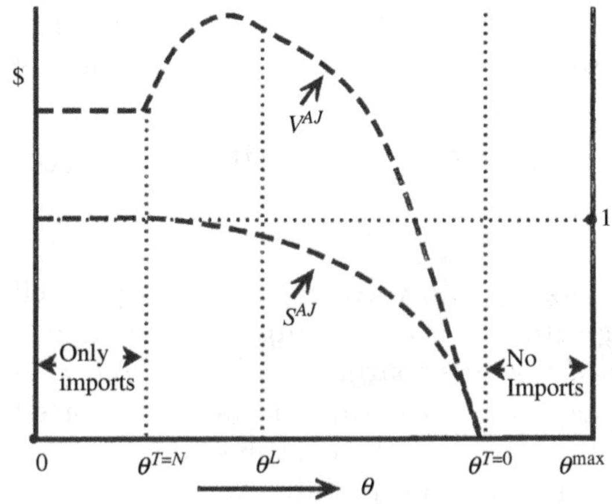

Figure 8.2. Productivity, θ, and the value of U.S. parts exports.

5. Perceptions of a Trade Barrier

As previously mentioned, our result in Proposition 2 that a range of parts is produced by the keiretsu when U.S. costs are lower can be explained by the presence of rents from relationship-specific investment. Thus one might be tempted to dismiss it as simply due to incomplete accounting. We would argue, however, that the result has considerable relevance when considering the perceptions of a trade barrier that lie behind the *U.S.*/Japan trade dispute concerning access to the Japanese market. Since it seems reasonable to suppose that the rents created by relationship-specific investments are, in fact, not observable outside the keiretsu, U.S. market participants and other interested parties could easily fall into this accounting trap. For example, by complaining that U.S. parts are not exported, despite prices that are less than half of made-in-Japan parts (see the quote, footnote 3), Church (1995) may well be suffering from this misperception. In the remainder of this section, we further develop the argument that relationship-specific investment can create perceptions of a trade barrier, by first examining the behavior of the J-maker's marginal cost and then considering effects arising from the size of the efficiency gap between the U.S. and Japan. As we will show, some of these effects of investment can mimic a government imposed trade barrier or simply create suspicion because they are counterintuitive and hard to understand.

Comparing (3.10) with (2.14), for a given output y^J, the effect of the opening of trade on the J-maker's marginal cost is given by

$$\gamma^{JF} - \gamma^J = -\left[\int_0^Z \delta^i di + \int_Z^T (\delta^i - \alpha r^i) di + \int_T^E (1-\alpha)\delta^i di\right]. \tag{5.1}$$

Since parts i for $i \leq Z$ involve no relationship-specific investment, they are all imported with the opening of trade and, as can be seen from (5.1), the J-maker's marginal cost for each part i falls by δ^i. However, it is not necessary that parts be imported for marginal cost to fall. Parts i for $i \in [T, E)$ continue to be produced by keiretsu suppliers, but marginal cost is reduced by $\gamma^{iF} - \gamma^i = -(1-\alpha)\delta^i$ due to potential competition from imports. Indeed, since there is no change in marginal cost for parts $i \geq E$ where Japan has a cost advantage, the J-maker's overall marginal cost falls if imports remain at zero with the removal of the trade restriction.

However, for parts $i \in (Z, T)$, which are produced with relationship-specific investment prior to trade and are imported subsequently, it is possible that the J-maker's marginal cost is increased. The problem is that if the J-maker's bargaining power, α, is large, it can be unprofitable for J-suppliers to invest, even though the rent created would exceed the efficiency gap by more than the cost of the investment.[43] It is even possible that the opening of trade would raise the J-maker's overall marginal cost.[44] Recalling that, prior to trade, marginal cost is $\gamma^i = c^i - \alpha r^i$, the opening of trade raises the marginal cost of part $i \in (Z, T)$ if and only[45] $c^{*i} - \gamma^i = -(\delta^i - \alpha r^i) > 0$. If all J-suppliers set $k^i > 0$ prior to

[43]If $\alpha > 0$, it is possible that $\phi^{iF} < 0$, but that $y^J(r^j - \delta^j) - k^j > 0$ (see (3.6)).

[44]This is an extreme example of the well-known inefficiencies in ex ante investment incentives associated with incomplete contracts (see for example, Laffont and Tirole, 1993).

[45]If $c^{*i} - \gamma^j > 0$, then since $\gamma^{iF} = \gamma^j - (1-\alpha)\delta^i$ due to the threat of imports, keiretsu production of part i would lower the J-maker's marginal cost with or without trade (i.e., $\gamma^{iF} < \gamma^j < c^{*i}$). However, even if $c^{*i} - \gamma^i < 0$, it is possible that $\gamma^{iF} < c^{*i} < \gamma^i$ and hence that keiretsu production of part i at free trade would lower J maker costs. From (3.5), this requires $c^{*i} - \gamma^{iF} = \alpha(r^j - \delta^i) > 0$ which holds for $i \geq T$, but which may also hold for some parts $i \in (Z, T)$, which would be imported at free trade.

the opening of trade, but subsequently all parts are imported (which requires $\delta^i > 0$ for all i), then the first and third terms of (5.1) vanish and since $\delta^j - \alpha r^j$ is decreasing[46] in i, it follows that

$$\gamma^{JF} - \gamma^J = -\int_0^N (\delta^i - \alpha r^i)di > 0 \quad \text{if} \quad \delta^0 - \alpha r^0 < 0. \tag{5.2}$$

This increase in cost requires that the J-maker's bargaining power be relatively large. Greater bargaining power has two opposing effects. It tends to reduce the J-maker's marginal cost, by lowering the bargained prices, p^{iF}, of parts for given levels of investment, but it also causes J-suppliers to reduce their relationship-specific investments, which reduces rents, making the suppliers more vulnerable to being replaced by imports. Thus as α is increased, the opening of trade causes a greater shift towards the use of imports, making it more likely that the loss of relationship-specific investment will cause the J-maker's marginal cost to rise. As Proposition A.2 of the Appendix shows, even if α is set at the J-maker's preferred level, satisfying $d\gamma^{JF}/d\alpha = 0$, we may have $\gamma^{JF} - \gamma^J > 0$ under some parameter values. Nevertheless, the possibility that $\gamma^{JF} - \gamma^J > 0$ remains a special case.

Further insight into the effects of trade on the J-maker's marginal cost is obtained by varying the size of the efficiency gap. For simplicity, we assume $\delta^i = \delta \equiv c^0 - c^{*0} \geq 0$ as in (3.1) and, to abstract from changes in γ^A, we assume that the J-maker is a monopolist. Variation in δ is achieved by varying c^{*0} holding c^0 fixed. Letting $\theta = \theta^{Z=0}$ denote the value of θ at which $Z = 0$, we assume for Proposition 7 that $\theta > \theta^{Z=0}$, and hence that all J-suppliers would set $k^j > 0$ at $\delta = 0$ or, equivalently, that all J-suppliers would invest in the presence of a prohibitive trade barrier. Letting $\delta = \delta^{T=0}$ represent the value of δ at which $T = 0$, we demonstrate that $\delta^{T=0} > 0$ and hence that no parts are imported for $\delta \in [0, \delta^{T=0}]$. Imports take place for $\delta > \delta^{T=0}$, but, as we show, this could increase the J-maker's marginal cost. All parts are imported if δ becomes sufficiently large.

Proposition 7. *Assume* $> \theta^{Z=0}$, *the* J*-maker is a monopolist, and* $\delta^i = \delta = c^0 - c^{*0}$ *as in (3.1). In response to the removal of the*

[46]This follows since $d(\delta^i - \alpha r^i)/di = \delta'(i) - \alpha(dr^i/di) < 0$ for $i > Z$.

Japanese trade barrier or alternatively a reduction in U.S. costs at free trade:

(i) *no parts are imported for* $\delta \in [0, \delta^{T=0}]$ *where* $\delta^{T=0} > 0$*, but the J-maker's output* y^J *increases, and*
(ii) *parts are imported for* $\delta > \delta^{T=0}$*, but it is possible that* $dy^{JF}/dC^{*0} < 0$ *and hence that* $y^{JF} - \gamma^J > 0$.

Proof: See the Appendix. □

From standard models, one would expect that the removal of protection or a reduction in import prices for intermediate goods would reduce domestic costs and that the associated increase in domestic final-good production would raise intermediate-good imports. By contrast, we have shown that relationship-specific investment can cause this line of reasoning to break down at two places. First, it is possible that the J-maker's cost is increased by the opening of trade (i.e., $\gamma^{JF} - \gamma^J > 0$ and $dy^{JF}/dC^{*0} < 0$). Second, an increase in the J-maker's output causes the range of intermediate-good imports to fall, reducing the total value of these imports if θ is sufficiently large. In addition, given that the rents from relationship-specific investment are unobservable to potential U.S. exporters, they might expect that parts for which the U.S. has a cost advantage would all be imported at free trade. However, from Proposition 7(i), it is possible that no parts are imported. More generally, recalling the results of Propositions 2 and 6, a proportion S^c of lower cost U.S. parts would not be imported and the parts that are not imported are the "more important" parts involving a larger share of production costs. The fact that these responses go against the conventional wisdom and are not readily understandable from standard trade models could easily give rise to negative perceptions of a continuing trade barrier.

Supposing that U.S. suppliers form expectations of the J-maker's demand for their products based on Japanese pretrade production levels and on conventional responses to the opening of trade, under the first possibility of an increase in marginal cost, Japanese auto output and volume of demand for imports would be lower than expected. However, since this first possibility occurs only if the range of imported parts is "large," driving out investment that would otherwise lower the J-maker's marginal cost, this makes significant perceptions of a trade barrier less likely.[47] By contrast, in the more likely case that the opening of trade lowers the J-maker's marginal cost, the response of imports could create a particularly negative impression. Import levels are likely to be low relative to keiretsu production, and for a small efficiency gap, i.e., for $0 < \delta < \delta^{T=0}$, imports would remain at zero. This mimics a government imposed trade barrier since a reduction in import prices for parts or a move from protection to free trade in this region would not result in any imports. Also, the fact that there are no imports despite an increase in the J-maker's output ($\gamma^{J\Gamma}$ falls in this region) could further strengthen the impression that the market is not really open. More generally, it would seem highly suspicious if in response to a fall in U.S. costs, the J-maker's output increases, but the range of imported parts falls.

Finally, some analysis of welfare effects seems worthwhile. World welfare, denoted W, is represented by the additively separable utility function, $W = u(Y) + Z$, where $u(Y)$ is the utility from final-good output, Y, and Z is the output of a tradable numeraire good produced under pure competition by labor alone. Imposing the budget constraint that all income is spent, we obtain $W \equiv u(Y) - FY + \pi^A + \pi^J + \Phi^F$ where, from (3.3) and (3.6), the total profit, Φ^F, of J-suppliers is given by

$$\Phi^F \equiv \int_T^N \phi^{iF} di = y^J(1-\alpha)\left[\int_T^E (r^i - \delta^i)di + \int_E^N r^i di\right] - \int_T^N k^i di. \tag{5.3}$$

From (5.3), using $d\phi^j/dk^j = 0$ for $\geq T, \phi^T = 0$, and $dy^J/d\theta \geq 0$, we obtain

$$d\Phi^F/d\theta = (l-\alpha)\left[y^J\left(\int_T^N (r^j/\theta)di + \int_T^E (r^j - \delta^j)di + \int_E^N r^j di\right)(dy^J/d\theta)\right] > 0.$$

[47]However, since y^J falls, if θ is not too high (see Proposition 6), U.S. suppliers might be suspicious that the volume and value of their exports is somehow restricted.

For $\alpha = 0$, since output y^J and hence y^A, Y, π^J, and π^A are unchanged (see Proposition 4), this effect of θ in raising Φ^F implies that relationship-specific investment raises Japanese and world welfare. For $\alpha > 0$, it follows using (B.4) and $dy^A/dy^J = -\pi^A_{AJ}/\pi^A_{AA}$ from (2.15) that

$$dy^J/d\theta > 0 \; dy^A/d\theta = -\pi^A_{AJ}(d\gamma^{JF}/d\theta)/H \quad \text{and}$$
$$dY/d\theta = (p'/H)(d\gamma^{JF}/d\theta) > 0. \qquad (5.4)$$

As can be seen from (5.4), both y^J and Y increase, but if $\pi^A_{AJ} < 0$ (the strategic substitutes case), then the A-maker's output, y^A, falls. This can reduce world welfare, since if the A-maker is the lower cost producer (i.e., if $\gamma^{JF} > \gamma^A$), the average cost of world production rises to the extent that J-maker's market share, y^J/Y, is increased. Nevertheless, if the J-maker is the lower cost producer (i.e., if $\gamma^{JF} \leq \gamma^A$), we show in Proposition 8 that an increase in θ increases both y^J/Y and world welfare.[48] This result applies independently of whether y^A and y^J are strategic substitutes or strategic complements.

Proposition 8. *Assume* $> \theta^{Z=E}$. *If* $\gamma^{JF} \leq \gamma^A$ *and* $\alpha > 0$, *then* $d(y^J/Y)/d\theta > 0$ *and* $dW/d\theta > 0$.

Proof: See the Appendix. □

With respect to Japanese welfare for $\alpha > 0$, there is some ambiguity as to the sign of $d\pi^J/d\theta$, but since π^J rises if y^A falls and Φ^F and Y both increase, Japan is certainly better off in the strategic substitutes case. For the U.S., since $d\pi^A/d\theta = y^A p'(dy^J/d\theta) < 0$ for $\alpha > 0$, it is a matter of weighing a consumer gain against a loss by the A-maker. Examining this trade-off, we let $W^A = u(Y^{AC}) - FY^{AC} + \pi^A$ denote U.S. welfare, where Y^{AC} is U.S. consumption. Since $dW^A/d\theta = -Y^{AC}p^f(dY/d\theta) + y^A p^f(dy^J/d\theta)$ (using (2.15)), this implies

$$dW^A/d\theta = -Y^{AC}p'(dy^A/d\theta) + (y^A - Y^{AC})p'(dy^J/d\theta).$$

[48]This result is related to Fung (1998), who argues that although U.S. exports may be hurt by the activities of main banks in Japan, this can raise efficiency and world welfare.

It follows that if U.S. production exceeds U.S. consumption (i.e., if $y^A > Y^{AC}$) and if y^A falls, then the reduction in U.S. profits dominates, causing W^A to fall. However, W^A rises for strategic complements and $y^A \leq Y^{AC}$.

6. Concluding Remarks

We have shown that the links between the J-maker and its suppliers due to relationship-specific investment within the keiretsu reduce the range of imported parts, making it harder for U.S. suppliers to access the Japanese market. Also, despite the associated increase in Japanese auto production and demand for parts, a sufficiently high level of relationship-specific investment will reduce the total value of parts imports from the U.S. and it is possible that no parts will be imported. Although we do not address the issue of whether membership in the keiretsu is "unfairly" exclusionary, since imports are driven out by the effect of relationship-specific investment in raising keiretsu efficiency, our analysis suggests that long-term supply arrangements within keiretsu could be defended on the basis that they are efficiency enhancing.

However, even if imports are not "unfairly" restricted, keiretsu supply relationships are likely to give rise to a perception of an "unfair" trade barrier. This is because the endogenous choice of investment within keiretsu can lead to counterintuitive responses in the levels of keiretsu production and imports, making it hard for outside observers to understand what is really happening. In particular, the removal of a government ban on imported parts can actually raise Japanese production costs, reducing Japanese auto output and total demand for parts. Also, if relationship-specific investment is sufficiently productive, then imports will remain at zero with the opening of trade or in response to a small reduction in U.S. costs at free trade, giving the appearance of a continuing "unfair" trade barrier. Strengthening this likely misperception is the fact that Japanese marginal costs fall in this case, raising Japanese production of both autos and parts. As a final point, we hope that recognition of these effects in the context of the policy debate concerning *U.S.*/Japan trade issues would create a better understanding by the parties involved, helping to ease trade tensions.

Appendix

A.1. *Formal contracts as an alternative to bargaining*

The payment scheme for keiretsu suppliers obtained in our bargaining framework could also be implemented through the use of contracts, signed in stage 0 before investment takes place. Assuming relationship-specific investment k^j is not verifiable by a third party and hence not contractible, but the rent r^j is contractible, the contract price can be represented as a linear sharing rule (see Laffont and Tirole, 1993),

$$p^i = c^i + (1 - \alpha^c)(r^i - \delta^i) \text{ for } i \leq E \quad \text{and} \quad p^i = c^i + (1 - \alpha^c)r^i \text{ for } i \geq E, \tag{A.1}$$

where α^c and $1 - \alpha^c$ for $\alpha^c \in [0, 1]$ respectively represent the shares of the J-maker and supplier i in the net cost reduction achieved by investment k^j. By signing the contract, supplier i agrees to supply any quantity of parts demanded at the price determined by (A.1). As previously mentioned, uncertainty could be added so as to disguise the value of k^j, but this is not necessary and the model becomes rather more complex.

Although the same outcome is achieved under the contract and bargaining models if the same sharing rule $\alpha^c = \alpha$ is used, the difference in the institutional settings could affect which sharing rule is chosen. The tradition in the procurement literature has been to choose the optimal contract from the viewpoint of the firm issuing the contracts or, alternately, based on considerations of efficiency and consumer welfare in a regulatory environment. Since the J-maker is responsible for purchasing inputs from a large number of suppliers, this suggests that the choice of α^c in a contracting framework might involve maximization of the J-maker's profit. However, in our keiretsu bargaining context, a more natural objective might be to maximize the aggregate profit of all keiretsu firms, including the J-suppliers. Despite these comments, it is not obvious what mechanism that would ensure the credibility of a commitment to a specific value of α, particularly in the bargaining framework. Fortunately, apart from the possibility that the opening of trade would raise the J-maker's marginal cost, our results are generally robust to the value of α.

A.2. *The sharing rule and profits within the Keiretsu*

Now considering the incentives for the choice of α, we simplify the presentation by assuming the J-maker is a monopolist and that all parts can be produced more cheaply in the U.S. (i.e., $\delta^j > 0$ for all i). For purposes of comparison, we first set out the conditions determining the optimal choice of output and investment if the keiretsu were fully vertically integrated and if investment k^i were observable. From (2.4) and (5.3), the aggregate profit, denoted $\Pi \equiv \pi^J + \Phi^F$, of the keiretsu can be expressed as

$$\Pi = y^J(F(y^J) - \gamma) - \int_T^N k^i di \quad \text{where}$$

$$\gamma \equiv \gamma^{J\Gamma} - \int_T^N (1-\alpha)(r^j - \delta^j)di = \int_0^T c^{*i} di + \int_T^N (c^j - r^j)di + w^0, \tag{A.2}$$

represents the marginal cost of the integrated firm. Hence, maximizing Π from (A.2), y^J and k^i satisfy

$$\begin{aligned} d\Pi/dy^J &= F + y^J F' - \gamma = 0 \quad \text{and} \quad d\Pi/dk^i = y^J(dr^i/dk^i) - 1 = 0 \\ &\text{if } i \geq T, \quad \text{where } y^J(r^i - \delta^i) - k^i \geq 0 \text{ for } i \geq T \quad \text{and} \\ &y^J(r^i - \delta^i) - k^i < 0 \text{ for } i < T. \end{aligned} \tag{A.3}$$

Returning to the setting in which J-suppliers are independent and k^j is not contractible, if y^J is chosen to maximize aggregate keiretsu profit, Π, taking k^j as given, or if the objective is to minimize total keiretsu costs of production for a given level of output, then as shown in Proposition A. 1(i), we obtain the standard result that returns to J-suppliers from investment should be fully internalized by setting $\alpha = 0$. Investments k^i and output y^J are then at the same joint profit maximizing levels as in (A.3). However, the inability to pay suppliers in the form of fixed costs, based on actual levels of investment, means that the markups paid to J-suppliers raise the J-maker' marginal cost. Thus, from (A.2) and (3.4), γ^{JF} exceeds γ by $\int_T^N (p^i - c^i)di$, creating a distortion from double marginalization. Consequently, output, y^J, is reduced below the joint profit maximizing level when the J-maker maximizes π^J as in our model. Since at $\alpha = 0$ and at $\alpha = 1, \gamma^{JF}$ is at the maximum determined by the cost of importing all parts, this distortion can be partially offset by setting $\alpha > 0$ so as to reduce the J-maker's marginal cost. The effect on J-supplier profit is ambiguous, but, from Proposition A.1 (ii), a small increase in α above zero raises both π^J and aggregate keiretsu profit, Π. More specifically, letting α^J and α^K represent the values of α that maximize π^J and Π respectively, we obtain $0 < \alpha^K < \alpha^J < 1$, where γ^{JF} is minimized at α^J.

Proposition A.1. *Assume the J-maker has a monopoly of the final-good,* $\delta^i > 0$ *for all* i *and* $T \leq N$. *If J-suppliers choose* k^j *to maximize* ϕ^j *for a given level of* y^J:

(i) *then, holding* y^J *fixed, or, if* y^J *maximizes* Π *for given* k^j, *keiretsu profit* Π *is maximized at* $\alpha = 0$, *and*
(ii) *if* y^J *maximizes* π^J *forgiven* k^i, *we obtain* $0 < \alpha^K < \alpha^J < 1$, *where* α^J *satisfies* $\partial y^{JF}/\partial a = 0$.

Proof: Assuming that $\phi^F(T, y^J; \theta, \alpha) = 0$ for some part T (as in (3.8)), then holding y^J fixed, we obtain $dT(y^J;\alpha)/d\alpha = -(d\phi^{FT}/d\alpha)/(d\phi^{FT}/dT)$ and hence, from (3.8), (3.9), and (2.7),

$$\frac{\partial T}{\partial \alpha} = \frac{\sigma(T)(r^T - \delta^T)}{1 - \alpha\sigma'(T)r^T(1 + \lambda^T)} > 0. \tag{A.4}$$

For $i \geq T$, from $d\phi^j/dk^j = 0$ as in (2.7) we obtain $dk^j/d\alpha = h'(k^j)/(1-\alpha)h''(k^j) < 0$ (see (2.2)) and hence

$$\frac{\partial r^i}{\partial \alpha} = \left(\frac{dr^j}{dk^j}\right)\left(\frac{\partial k^j}{\partial \alpha}\right) = -\frac{r^j \lambda^j}{1-\alpha} < 0, \tag{A.5}$$

where $\lambda^i \equiv -(h^f(k^i))^2/h(k^i)h^{ff}(k^i) > 0$ from (2.12). Also, we can show from (3.10) and (A.2) that

$$y^{JF}/\partial \alpha = -\int_T^N (r^i - \delta^i)di + \alpha(\partial\gamma/\partial\alpha), \tag{A.6}$$

where $dy/d\alpha = -[\int_T^N (dr^j/d\alpha)di - (r^T - \delta^T)(dT/d\alpha)] > 0$ from (A.4) and (A.5). Next, from (5.3), $d\phi^{iF}/dk^j = 0$ for $i \geq T$ and $\phi^{TF} = 0$

and, also, from (2.4), we obtain

$$d\Phi^F/d\alpha = -[y^J - (1-\alpha)(dy^J/d\alpha)]\left(\int_T^N (r^i - \delta^i)di\right)$$

$$d\pi^J/d\alpha = (P + y^J F' - \gamma^{JF})(dy^J/d\alpha) - y^J\left(\frac{d\gamma^{JF}}{d\alpha}\right) \quad \text{(A.7)}$$

It then follows from $\Pi \equiv \pi^J + \Phi^F$, using (A.7), (A.2), and (A.6), that

$$\begin{aligned} d\Pi/d\alpha = &(F + y^J P' - \gamma)(dy^J/d\alpha) \\ &- y^J[d\gamma^{JF}/d\alpha - d\gamma^{JF}/d\alpha + \alpha(\partial\gamma/\partial\alpha)] \end{aligned} \quad \text{(A.8)}$$

(i) If $d\Pi/dy^J = F + y^J F^f - \gamma = 0$, then $y^J = y^J(\gamma)$ and $dy^{JF}/d\alpha - d\gamma^{JF}/d\alpha = (d\gamma^{JF}/dy^J)(dy^J/d\gamma)(d\gamma/d\alpha)$ where $d\gamma/d\alpha = (d\gamma/d\alpha)/[1 - (dy/dy^J)(dy^J/dy)] > 0$. Since $dy^J/dy < 0$ and $dy^{JF}/dy^J \leq 0(= 0$ at $\alpha = 0)$ from (3.13), we obtain $dy^{JF}/d\alpha - \gamma^{J\Gamma}/d\alpha \geq 0(= 0$ for $\alpha = 0)$ and hence from (A.8), $d\Pi/d\alpha \leq 0(= 0$ at $\alpha = 0)$ and also $\partial\Pi/\partial\alpha = -\alpha y^J(\partial\gamma/\partial\alpha) \leq 0$ $(= 0$ at $\alpha = 0)$, proving the result.

(ii) If $\pi_J^J = P + y^J P' - \gamma^{JF} = 0$, then, using $d\gamma^{JF}/dy^J = 0$ at $\alpha = 0$ (see (3.13)), we obtain $dy^{JF}/d\alpha - \gamma^{JF}/0\alpha = (d\gamma^{JF}/dy^J)(dy^J/d\alpha) = 0$ at $\alpha = 0$. However, since $dy^{JF}/d\alpha = \partial y^{JF}/\partial\alpha < 0$ at $\alpha = 0$ (see (A.6)), it also follows that $dy^J/d\alpha = (dy^J/dy^{JF})(dy^{JF}/d\alpha) > 0$ at $\alpha = 0$ and hence from (A.8), using $\gamma^{J\Gamma} - \gamma > 0$ from (A.2), that $d\Pi/d\alpha = (\gamma^{JF} - \gamma)(dy^J/d\alpha) > 0$ at $\alpha = 0$. This proves $\alpha^K > O$. Next, from (A.7), using (A.2) and (2.19), we obtain $\pi^J/d\alpha = -y^J(d\gamma^{JF}/d\alpha) = -y^J\pi_{JJ}^J \quad (\partial\gamma^{JF}/\partial\alpha)/(\pi_{JJ}^J - d\gamma^{JF}/dy^J)$. Since $\partial y^{JF}/0\alpha < 0$ at $\alpha = 0$ and since γ^{JF} is continuous with the same value at $\alpha = 0$ as at $\alpha = 1$, it follows that $0 < \alpha^J < 1$ and that α^J satisfies $d\pi^J/d\alpha = d\gamma^{JF}/d\alpha = d\gamma^{JF}/d\alpha = 0$. Finally, using (A.7) and $dy^J/d\alpha = 0$ at $\alpha = \alpha^J$, we obtain $\alpha^K < \alpha^J$ since $d\Pi/d\alpha = d\Phi/d\alpha = -\int_T^N y^J(r^i - \delta^i)di < 0$ at $\alpha = \alpha^J$. □

Next, we show in Proposition A.2 that if $\partial\gamma^{JF}/\partial\alpha = 0$ and hence $\alpha = \alpha^J$ is at the level preferred by the J-maker, then it is possible that marginal cost is increased (i.e., $\gamma^{JF} - \gamma^J > 0$) by the opening of trade.

Proposition A.2. *Assume $\delta^i > 0$ for all i and $T \leq N$. If $\delta^0 - \alpha r^0 \leq 0$ where α satisfies $\partial\gamma^{JF}/\partial\alpha = 0$, then there exists some ä∈(O, 1) such that $\gamma^{JF} - \gamma^F > 0$ if $\alpha >$ ä.*

Proof: Since $\delta^1 - \alpha r^1 \leq 0$ implies $k^1 > 0$, it follows from (5.1) that

$$\gamma^{JF} - \gamma^J = -\int_0^T (\delta^i - \alpha r^i)di - (1-\alpha)\int_T^N \delta^i di. \qquad \text{(A.9)}$$

Since $\int_T^N (r^i - \delta^i)di = \alpha(\partial\gamma/\partial\alpha) > 0$ from $\partial\gamma^{JF}/\partial\alpha = 0$ and (A.6), rearranging (A.9), we obtain

$$\gamma^{JF} - \gamma^J = -\left(\int_T^N r^i di + \int_0^T \delta^i di\right)$$
$$+\alpha\left[\int_0^N r^i di + (1-\alpha)(\partial\gamma/\partial\alpha)\right]. \qquad \text{(A.10)}$$

Letting ä $\equiv \Omega/(\Omega + \xi)$ where $\Omega \equiv \int_T^N r^j di + \int_0^T \delta^j di$ and $\equiv \int_0^T (r^i - \delta^i)di + (1-\alpha)(d\gamma/d\alpha)$, it follows from $\Omega > 0$ and $\xi > 0$ that ä∈(O, 1) and hence, from (A.10), that $\gamma^{JF} - \gamma^J > 0$ iff $\alpha \in$ (ä, 1). □

A.3. *Proofs of Propositions 4, 6, 7, and 8*

Proposition 4. *(i) $dy^J/d\theta > 0$ for $\alpha > 0 (= 0$ for $\alpha = 0)$, (ii) $dZ/d\theta < 0$ for $Z \geq 0$, and (iii) $dT/d\theta < 0$ for $\theta \in (\theta^{Z=E}, \theta^{T=0}]$. No parts are imported for $\theta \in [\theta^{T=0}, \theta^{\max}]$.*

Proof: (i) For $i \geq Z$, from $\partial\phi^i/\partial k^i = 0$ as in (2.7), we obtain $\partial k^i/\partial\theta = -h'(k^i)/\theta h''(k^i) > 0$ for a given y^J (see (2.2)). Since $\partial r^i/\partial\theta = w^o\sigma^i h(k^i)[1 + \theta h'(k^i)(\partial k^i/\partial\theta)/h(k^i)]$ using λ^j from (2.12), we obtain

$$\partial r^i/\partial\theta = r^i(1+\lambda^i)/\theta > 0 \text{ for } k^i > 0. \qquad \text{(A.11)}$$

Also, from (3.9) and $d\phi^{TF}/0\theta = y^J(1-\alpha)r^T/\theta$ (from (3.8) using $d\phi^{TF}/0k^T = 0$ and $dr^j/0\theta = r^j/\theta$), we obtain

$$\partial T/\partial\theta = -\sigma(T)/\theta\sigma'(T)(1+\chi^T) < 0 \text{ for } Z < E, \qquad \text{(A.12)}$$

where $X^i > 0$ if $\delta'(i) < 0$ and $X^j = 0$ if $\delta'(i) = 0$. For $Z = E$, then $T = Z = E$ is constant. Next, from (3.10), using (A.11), (A.12), and

$r^T - \delta^T \geq 0(= 0 \text{ for } = Z = E)$, we obtain

$$\partial\gamma^{JF}/\partial\theta = -\alpha\left[\int_T^N (dr^i/d\theta)di - (r^T - \delta^T)(dT/d\theta)\right] < 0 \text{ for } \alpha > 0. \tag{A.13}$$

and $\partial y^{J\Gamma}/\partial\theta = 0$ at $\alpha = 0$. Finally, from $\gamma^{JF} = \gamma^J(y^{JF};\theta)$, $y^{JF} = y^J(\gamma^{JF})$ and (2.18), it follows that $dy^{JF}/d\theta = (d\gamma^{JF}/d\theta)/[1-(d\gamma^{JF}/dy^J)(dy^J/dy^{JF})] = (H^o/H)(d\gamma^{JF}/d\theta)$ and hence, from (2.18) and (A.13), that

$$dy^J/d\theta = (\pi^A_{AA}/H)(d\gamma^{JF}/d\theta) > 0 \text{ for } \alpha > 0 (= 0 \,\text{for}\, \alpha = 0). \tag{A.14}$$

(ii) Assuming $k^0 = 0$ and hence ≥ 0, it follows from (2.9) that $dZ/dy^J = -\sigma(Z)/y^J\sigma^f(Z) < 0$ and $dZ/d\theta = -\sigma(Z)/\theta\sigma^f(Z) < 0$. Hence, using part (i), we obtain $dZ/d\theta = (0Z/0y^J)(dy^J/d\theta) + 0Z/0\theta < 0$.

(iii) Since $Z = E$ at $\theta = \theta^{Z=E}$, it follows from part (ii) that $Z < E$ for $\theta > \theta^{Z=E}$. Hence, using (A.12), (A.14), and $dT/dy^J < 0$ from (3.11), we obtain $dT/d\theta = dT/d\theta + (dT/dy^J)(dy^J/d\theta) < 0$ for $\theta \in (\theta^{Z=E}, \theta^{T=0}]$. Since imports are zero at $T = 0$, no parts are imported for $\in [\theta^{T=0}, \theta^{\max}]$. □

Proposition 6. *Assume $\delta^i = \delta$ as in (3.1). There exists some $\theta^L \in [\theta^{T=N}, \theta^{T=0})$ such that for all $\in (\theta^L, \theta^{T=0}]$, the total volume, Q^{AJ}, and value, V^{AJ}, of U.S. exports are reduced by (i) a small increase in output, y^J OR (ii) an increase in θ. An increase in θ reduces V^{AJ} more than in proportion to Q^{AJ}.*

Proof: (i) For $\in [\theta^{T=N}, \theta^{T=0}]$, we obtain $dQ^{AJ}/dy^J = T + y^J(dT/dy^J)$ where $T = T(y^J, \theta)$. Thus, using $dT/dy^J < 0$ from (3.1), we have $dQ^{AJ}/dy^J < 0$ at $\theta = \theta^{T=0}$ (i.e., at $T = 0$). Since $d(dQ^{AJ}/dy^J)/d\theta < 0$ (see (A.16) below), it follows that if $dQ^{AJ}/dy^J > 0$ at $\theta = \theta^{T=N}$, then there exists some $\theta^L \in (\theta^{T=N}, \theta^{T=0})$ for which $dQ^{AJ}/dy^J = 0$ at $T = T(y^J, \theta^L)$ and hence $dQ^{AJ}/dy^J < 0$ for all $\theta \in (\theta^L, \theta^{T=0}]$. If $dQ^{AJ}/dy^J \leq 0$ at $\theta = \theta^{T=N}$, then the result follows for $\theta^L = \theta^{T=N}$. Next, since

$dV^{AJ}/dy^J = v^{AJ} + y^J c^{*T}(dT/dy^J)$ from (4.1), we obtain

$$dV^{AJ}/dy^J = c^{*T}(dQ^{AJ}/dy^J) + v^{AJ} - Tc^{*T} \tag{A.15}$$

where $v^{AJ} - Tc^{*T} \leq 0 (< 0 \text{ for } T > 0)$ from $dv^{AJ}/dT = c^{*T} > 0$ and $d^2v^{AJ}/(dT)^2 = c^{*'}(T) > 0$. Hence from (A.15), using $dQ^{AJ}/dy^J < 0$, we obtain $dV^{AJ}/dy^J < 0$ at $T = T(y^J, \theta)$ for all $\theta \in (\theta^L, \theta^{T=0}]$.

To show $d(dQ^{AJ}/dy^J)/d\theta < 0$, we first expand it into the form $d(dQ^{AJ}/dy^J)/d\theta = d(dQ^{AJ}/dy^J)/\partial\theta + (d^2Q^{AJ}/(dy^J)^2)(dy^J/d\theta)$. Since $\partial(dQ^{AJ}/dy^J)/\partial\theta = \partial T/\partial\theta + y^J(\partial^2 T/(\partial y^J)(\partial\theta))$, using $\delta^i(i) = 0$ and $\sigma''(i) = 0$ from $\delta^i = \delta$ we next obtain $\partial T/\partial\theta = -\sigma(T)/\sigma'(T)\theta$ from (A.12) and $\partial^2 T/(\partial\theta)(\partial y^J) = -(dT/dy^J)/\theta$ where $\partial T/\partial y^J = -(\sigma^T/\sigma'(T))(1 - (\delta/r^T))/y^J$ from (3.11). It then follows that $\partial(dQ^{AJ}/dy^J)/d\theta = -(\delta/r^T)(\sigma^T/\sigma'(T))/\theta < 0$. Also, from $d^2Q^{AJ}/(dy^J)^2 = 2(dT/dy^J) + y^J(d^2T/(dy^J)^2) = (\delta/r^T)[(dT/dy^J) - (\sigma^T/\sigma'(T))(dr^T/dy^J)/r^T]$ and $dr^T/dy^J = r^T\lambda^T/y^T + r^T(1 + \lambda^T)(\sigma'(T)/\sigma^T)(dT/dy^J)$ (see (3.12) and (2.13)), gathering terms in dT/dy^J, we can show $d^2Q^{AJ}/(dy^J)^2 = -(\delta/r^T)\lambda^T[\sigma^T/\sigma'(T)y^J + dT/dy^J] = -(\delta/r^T)^2(\sigma^T/\sigma'(T))\lambda^T/y^J < 0$. Hence, we obtain

$$\frac{d\left(\frac{dQ^{AJ}}{dy^J}\right)}{d\theta} = -\left(\frac{\delta}{r^T}\right)\left(\frac{\sigma^T}{\sigma'(T)}\right)\left[\left(\frac{1}{\theta}\right) + \frac{\left(\frac{\delta}{r^T}\right)\lambda^T\left(\frac{dy^J}{d\theta}\right)}{y^J}\right] < 0. \tag{A.16}$$

(ii) Since $dQ^{AJ}/d\theta = (dQ^{AJ}/dy^J)(dy^J/d\theta) + y^J(dT/d\theta)$, using $\partial T/\partial\theta < 0$ from (A.12), $dy^J/d\theta \geq$ from (A.14), and $dQ^{AJ}/dy^J \leq 0$ from part (i), we obtain $dQ^{AJ}/d\theta < 0$ for $\theta \in [\theta^L, \theta^{T=0}]$. Similarly, since $dV^{AJ}/d\theta = (dV^{AJ}/dy^J)(dy^J/d\theta) + y^J(\partial v^{AJ}/\partial\theta)$, it follows using (A.15), $v^{AJ}/d\theta = c^{*T}(\partial T/\partial\theta)$, and $v^{AJ} - Tc^{*T} \leq 0$ that $dV^{AJ}/d\theta = c^{*T}(dQ^{AJ}/d\theta) + (v^{AJ} - Tc^{*T})(dy^J/d\theta) < 0$ for $\theta \in [\theta^L, \theta^{T=0}]$. Dividing by V^{AJ}, we then obtain $(dV^{AJ}/d\theta)/V^{AJ} = T(c^{*T}/v^{AJ})(dQ^{AJ}/d\theta)/Q^{AJ} + (v^{AJ} - Tc^{*T})(dy^J/d\theta)/V^{AJ}$ Since $Tc^{*T}/v^{AJ} > 1$ for $T > 0$, this implies $(dV^{AJ}/d\theta)/V^{AJ} < (dQ^{AJ}/d\theta)/Q^{AJ} < 0$ for all $\theta \in [\theta^L, \theta^{T=0})$. □

Proposition 7. *Assume* $> \theta^{Z=0}$, *the* J*-maker is a monopolist, and* $\delta^j = \delta = c^0 - c^{*0}$ *as in* (3.1). *In response to the removal of the Japanese trade barrier or alternatively a reduction in U.S. costs at free trade:*

(i) *no parts are imported for* $\delta \in [0, \delta^{T=0}]$ *where* $\delta^{T=0} > 0$*, but the J-maker's output* y^J *increases, and*
(ii) *parts are imported for* $\delta > \delta^{T=0}$*, but it is possible* $dy^{JF}/dc^{*0} < 0$ *and hence that* $\gamma^{JF} - \gamma^J > 0$.

Proof: (i) Since $dy^J/dc^{*0} = (dy^J/d\gamma^{JF})(dy^{JF}/dc^{*0})$ where $dy^J/d\gamma^{JF} = 1/\pi^J_{JJ} < 0$ from (2.19) and $d\gamma^{JF}/dc^{*0} = (\partial\gamma^{JF}/\partial c^{*0})\pi^J_{JJ}/(\pi^J_{JJ} - (d\gamma^J/dy^J))$ from $\gamma^{JF} = \gamma^F(y^J; c^{*0})$ and (2.19), it follows that

$$dy^J/dc^{*0} = (\partial\gamma^{JF}/dc^{*0})/(\pi^J_{JJ} - (dy^J/dy^J)) < 0 \,\text{iff}\, \frac{\partial\gamma^{JF}}{\partial c^{*0}} > 0. \tag{A.17}$$

Since $> \theta^{Z=0}$, we have $k(\sigma^0, y^J) > 0$ as defined by (2.7) and hence $\phi^0 = \phi(\sigma^0, y^J) > 0$ from (2.11). For $\equiv \delta^{T=0}$, since $\phi^{0F} = \phi^0 - y^J(1-\alpha)\delta^{T=0} = 0$ (from (3.7) and (3.8)), $\phi^0 > 0$ implies $\delta^{T=0} = \phi^0/y^J(1-\alpha) > 0$. If $\delta^{T=0}$ is unique,[49] or alternatively, letting $\delta^{T=0}$ represent the smallest value of δ at which $T = 0$, it follows that $\phi^{0F} \geq 0$ and hence that no parts are imported for $\delta \leq \delta^{T=0}$. Setting $T = 0$ in (3.10), we obtain $d\gamma^{JF}/dc^{*0} = (1-\alpha)N > 0$ for $\delta \leq \delta^{T=0}$ and hence $dy^J/dc^{*0} < 0$ from (A.17). Also, since from (5.1), $\gamma^{JF} - \gamma^J = -(1-\alpha)N\delta < 0$ for $\delta \leq \delta^{T=0}, y^J$ increases with the opening of trade.

(ii) Expressing $T = T(y^J, c^{*0})$ from (3.8), it follows from (3.10), holding y^J fixed, that

$$\partial y^{JF}/\partial c^{*0} = T + (1-\alpha)(N-T) + \alpha(r^T - \delta)(\partial T/\partial c^{*0}), \tag{A.18}$$

where $\partial T/\partial c^{*0} = -\sigma(T)/\sigma'(T)r^T < 0$ for $\delta \geq \delta^{T=0}$ (from (3.8), (3.9), and $X^j = 0$) . Noting that $d\gamma^{J\Gamma}/dc^{*0}$ is discontinuous at $\delta = \delta^{T=0}$, it then follows from (5.1), using the mean value theorem, that $\gamma^{JF} - \gamma^J = -(1-\alpha)N\delta^{T=0} - (d\gamma^{JF}/dc^*)(\delta - \delta^{T=0})$ for $\delta \geq \delta^{T=0}$ where $\partial\gamma^{JF}/\partial c^*$ represents $\partial\gamma^{J\Gamma}/\partial c^{*0}$ evaluated at some $c^* \in [c^{*0}, c^0 - \delta^{T=0}]$. Hence $\partial\gamma^{JF}/\partial c^* < 0$ is necessary, but not sufficient for $\gamma^{J\Gamma} - \gamma^J > 0$. Rearranging (A.18) using $\sigma(T) = \sigma(0) + T\sigma'(T)$ where

[49] Although $\phi^{iF}/dc^{*0} > 0$ holding y^J fixed, if an increase in c^{*0} (fall in δ) reduces y^J, ϕ^{iF} may fall, causing more parts to be imported (T increases). Hence there may be more than one value of δ at which $T = 0$.

$\sigma''(i) \equiv c''(i)/C(N) = 0$ from (3.1), it follows, letting $\psi \equiv r^T\sigma(0) - \delta\sigma(T)$ and $\hat{a} \equiv N/(N+\psi)$, that for $\psi > 0$ and $\alpha > \hat{a}, dy^{JF}/dc^{*0} = N - \alpha[N + \psi/r^T\sigma'(T)] < 0$. □

Proposition 8. *Assume* $\theta > \theta^{Z=E}$ *If* $\gamma^{JF} \leq \gamma^A$ *and* $\alpha > 0$, *then* $d(y^J/Y)/d\theta > 0$ *and* $dW/d\theta > 0$.

Proof: (i) From $(y^J/Y)/d\theta = [y^A(dy^J/d\theta) - y^{JF}(dy^A/d\theta)]/(Y)^2$, using (5.4), (A.14), (A.13), and (2.16) it then follows, independently of the sign of π^A_{AJ}, that for $\alpha > 0$ and $y^J \geq y^A$ (which holds for $y^{JF} \leq \gamma^A$) that

$$d(y^J/Y)/d\theta = [y^A(3p' + Yp + (y^J - y^A)p'](\partial\gamma^{JF}/d\theta)/(Y)^2 H > 0. \tag{A.19}$$

Next, we express W in the form $W = u(Y) - \overline{\gamma}Y + \Phi^F$ where $\overline{\gamma} \equiv \gamma^A(y^A/Y) + \gamma^{JF}(y^J/Y)$ represents the average world cost of production of Y. For $\alpha > 0$ and $\gamma^{JF} \leq \gamma^A$, it then follows that $d\overline{\gamma}/d\theta = (\gamma^{JF} - \gamma^A)(d(y^J/Y)/d\theta) + (y^J/Y)(d\gamma^{JF}/d\theta) < 0$ from $\gamma^{JF} - \gamma^A \leq 0$, (A.19), and (A.13) and hence, using $u^f(Y) = F$, that $dW/d\theta = (P - \overline{\gamma})(dY/d\theta) - Y(d\overline{\gamma}/d\theta) + d\Phi/d\theta > 0$. □

References

Aoki, M., *Information, Incentives, and Bargaining in the Japanese Economy* (Cambridge: Cambridge University Press, 1988).

Asanuma, B., "The Organization of Parts Purchases in the Japanese Automotive Industry," *Japanese Economic Studies*, 13 (1985), 32–53.

—, "Manufacturer-Supplier Relationships in Japan and the Concept of Relation-Specific Skill," *Journal of the Japanese and International Economies* 3 (1989), 1–30.

Binmore, K., A. Rubinstein, and A. Wolinsky, "The Nash Bargaining Solution in Economic Modelling," *Journal of Economics* 17 (1986), 176–88.

Branstetter, L., "Vertical Keiretsu and Knowledge Spillovers in Japanese Manufacturing: An Empirical Assessment," *Journal of the Japanese and International Economies*, 14 (2000), 73–104.

Cheng, L. K., and M.E. Krenin, "Supplier Preference and Dumping: An Analysis of Japanese Corporate Groups," *Southern Economic Journal* 63 (1996), 51–9.

Church, G. J., "Launch of an Economic Cold War," *TIME Domestic* 146 (1995), July 3.

Dyer, J. H., and W. G. Ouchi, "Japanese-Style Partnerships: Giving Companies a Competitive Edge," *Sloan Management Review* 35 (1993), 51–63.

Feenstra, R. C., T.-H. Yang, and G. G. Hamilton, "Business Groups and Product Variety in Trade: Evidence from South Korea, Taiwan and Japan," *Journal of International Economics* 48 (1999), 71–100.

Fung, K. C., "Characteristics of Japanese Industrial Groups and their Potential Impact on U.S.-Japan Trade," in R. Baldwin, ed. *Empirical Studies of Commercial Policy* (Chicago: University of Chicago Press, 1991), pp. 137–68.

—, (1998). "International Trade and Bank Groups: Welfare-Enhancing or Welfare-Reducing?," mimeo, UC Santa Cruz, 1998.

Greaney, T. M., "Manipulating Market Shares: The Indirect Effects of Voluntary Import Expansions (VIEs)," *Japan and the World Economy* 11 (1999), 95–113.

Holmstrom, B., and J. Roberts, "The Boundaries of the Firm Revisited," *Journal of Economic Perspectives* 12 (1998), 73–94.

Krishna, K., and J. Morgan, "Implementing Results Oriented Trade Policies: The Case of the US-Japanese Auto Parts Dispute," *European Economic Review* 42 (1998), 1443–67.

Lachica, E., "Japan's Factories in U.S. Import Parts from Home," *Asian Wall Street Journal* August 28 (1995).

Laffont, J.-J., and J. Tirole, *A Theory of Incentives in Procurement Regulation* (Cambridge and London: MIT Press, 1993).

Lawrence, R. Z., "Efficient or Exclusionist? The Import Behavior of Japanese Corporate Groups," *Brookings Papers on Economic Activity* (1991), 311–30.

—, "Japan's Different Trade Regime: An Analysis with Particular Reference to Keiretsu," *Journal of Economic Perspectives* 7 (1993), 3–19.

Levinsohn, J., "Carwars: Trying to Make Sense of U.S.-Japan Trade Frictions in the Automobile and Automobile Parts Markets," in R. C. Feenstra, ed., *The Effects of US. Trade, Protection and Promotion Policies* (Chicago London: University of Chicago Press, 1997), pp. 11–32.

Marvel, H. P., "Exclusive Dealing," *Journal of Law and Economics* 25 (1982), 1–25.

Mclaren, J., "'Globalization' and Vertical Structure," *American Economic Review*, 90 (2000), 1239–54.

— "Supplier Relations and the Market Context: A Theory of Handshakes," *Journal of International Economics* 48 (1999), 121–138.

— Mcmillan, J., "Why Does Japan Resist Foreign Market-Opening Pressure?" in J. Bhagwati and R. Hudec, eds., *Harmonization and Fair Trade* (Cambridge, MA: MIT Press, 1996), pp. 515–541.

Perry, M. K., "Vertical Integration: Determinants and Effects," in R. Schmalensee and R. Willig, eds., *Handbook of Industrial Organization, Volume 1* (New York: North-Holland, 1989). pp. 135–82.

Oiu, L. D., and B. J. Spencer, "Keiretsu and Relationship-Specific Investment: Implications for Market-Opening Trade Policy NBER," working paper WS279, 2001, *Journal of Economics*, forthcoming.

Saxonhouse, G. R., "Efficient or Exclusionist? The Import Behavior of Japanese Corporate Groups: Comment," *Brookings Papers on Economic Activity* (1991), 331–36.

Spencer, B. J., and R. W. Jones. "Trade and Protection in Vertically Related Markets," *Journal of International Economics* 32 (1992), 31–56.

—, and R. S. Raubitschek, "High-Cost Domestic Joint Ventures and International Competition: Do Domestic Firms Gain?," *International Economic Review* 37 (1996), 315–40.

Taylor, C. R., and S. N. Wiggins, "Competition or Compensation: Supplier Incentives under the American and Japanese Subcontracting Systems" *American Economic Review* 87 (1997), 598–618.

Weinstein, D. E., and Y. Yafeh, "Japan's Corporate Groups: Collusive or Competitive? An Empirical Investigation of Keiretsu Behavior" *The Journal of Industrial Economics* XLIII (1995), 359–76.

Chapter 9

Keiretsu and Relationship-Specific Investment: Implications for Market-Opening Trade Policy*

Abstract

This paper considers the implications of relationship-specific investment within keiretsu for policies aimed at opening the Japanese market for intermediate goods, such as auto-parts. Both VIEs applied to parts and VERs restricting Japanese exports of autos cause the keiretsu to import a wider range of parts, but of a relatively unimportant type, such as seat covers. Since keiretsu investment and output fall, the total value of US parts exports may actually fall. For a given value of these exports, a VIE is less costly for US consumers and Japanese producers, but a VER is preferred by US automakers.

1. Introduction

It is well known that Japanese tariff rates on manufactured goods are lower than rates for most other industrialized countries, but that Japan imports significantly less. This has led to complaints, particularly in the United States, that Japan has very high non-tariff barriers. Since visible and formal non-tariff barriers such as quotas are not evident, one focus of complaint has been that typical

*This chapter is reproduced from *Journal of International Economics*, 58, 49–79, 2002, with permission from Elsevier.

Japanese corporate groups, referred to as keiretsu,[1] have acted as a barrier to imports.[2] These complaints have received some support from empirical studies that find lower imports in industries with a high keiretsu presence.[3] In response, policy makers in the United States, have put pressure on Japan to open its markets to meet quantitative targets such as VIEs (voluntary import expansions) in which a country is forced to agree to a given market share or total value for imports of particular products. Prominent targeted products include semiconductors and auto-parts.[4]

Despite these measures to ensure greater access to the Japanese market, it is debatable whether keiretsu constitutes an 'unfair' barrier to trade. In particular, the long-term supply arrangements within vertical keiretsu have been defended as a means of raising efficiency due to gains from relationship-specific investments by keiretsu suppliers[5]. These are investments directed at making a product more valuable to a particular buyer (in this case, the keiretsu automaker), but not to other potential buyers. There are a number of possible examples,[6] but most important for our purposes are

[1]This would include auto producers such as Toyota and Nissan.

[2]For example, according to Church (1995), the keiretsu "do business mainly with each other, freezing out competing buyers and sellers, both foreign and domestic. This system forms the very fabric of the way the Japanese do business, and it does more than outright trade barriers or even government 'administrative guidance' to keep out foreign products. Especially, it seems, US auto-parts ... such as shock absorbers, mufflers, tailpipes and disk-brake pads ... sell for less than half to only a third the price of made-in-Japan parts of comparable quality. What then limits American parts to around 1.5% of the Japanese market? The keiretsu system, Americans conclude".

[3]Examples include Lawrence (1991) and Fung (1991), but Saxonhouse (1989) has an opposing view.

[4]In the 1991 semiconductor pact, the US demanded a 20% market-share target. The 1995 agreement on Japanese autos and parts demanded (among other things) that Japan's automakers increase annual purchases of parts from the US by $9 billion in three years (Bernier *et al.*, 1995, p. 16).

[5]McMillan (1996) argues persuasively that the favoring of keiretsu suppliers in contract renewals helps solve the 'holdup problem' so as to provide appropriate incentives for these investments, which are financed by the supplier with no guarantee that costs will be covered by the subsequent sale of parts.

[6]Another example might involve investment by suppliers in 'just in time' delivery, such as locating close to the automaker's plant or cooperating with other

investments in modifications that improve the fit or ease of assembly with other parts produced by the keiretsu, but which are not relevant to the particular production processes of other auto manufacturers.

Using the auto-industry as an example, Spencer and Qiu (2001) model the effects of relationship-specific investments[7] by suppliers within a vertical keiretsu on the ability of US auto-parts producers to access the Japanese market. By raising efficiency, these investments increase the range of parts produced in the keiretsu at the expense of imports. However, the rents that these investments create are not easily observable outside the keiretsu and Spencer and Qiu (2001) argue that this, combined with some counterintuitive responses of imports, could create a strong impression of a trade barrier. Thus, even if keiretsu do not 'unfairly' block access to the Japanese market, attempts by the US to impose market opening policies may nevertheless be understood as a natural response to the perception of a trade barrier.

In the present paper, we build on Spencer and Qiu (2001) to develop the implications of relationship-specific investments for various policies aimed at opening the Japanese market for intermediate goods, such as auto-parts. We consider three types of VIEs. The simplest, referred to as a 'content VIE', requires that autos produced in Japan achieve at least some specified US content per auto. We also consider a 'market-share VIE', which forces Japan to meet a market-share target for imported parts, as well as a 'total-value VIE', which requires that Japan import a given total value of US parts. Since there is a continuum of parts, with parts ordered in terms of their contribution to the total cost of an auto, referred to as their 'cost-share', we can address the effects of policy on the range of imported parts as well as on their overall value. In line with US complaints, Spencer and Qiu (2001) argue that keiretsu would tend to import those parts that are least important for production.[8]

---

suppliers to coordinate delivery. For applications within keiretsu, see Aoki (1988); pp. 216–218) and Dyer and Ouchi (1993, p. 55).

[7]Also see McLaren (1999), who argues that less formal bargaining arrangements can dominate formal contracts in encouraging cooperative investments.

[8]For example, Rubenstein (1990, p. 8) observes that "American suppliers primarily provide Japanese carmakers with bulky, low-value, low-skill products such as carpets, glass, tires, exhaust systems, and audio-equipment. High-value,

A natural question is then whether a VIE would be met by the import of just a few additional parts, each making a large contribution to the target because of a high cost-share, or if instead, rather more parts would be imported, but with the parts continuing to be of the more peripheral type. There is some indication that the latter was the case with respect to the 1992 US-Japan auto agreement[9] and, consistent with this, we show that for all three types of VIEs, additional imports would be in the order determined by increasing cost-shares, with lower cost parts first. Higher cost-shares increase the returns from relationship-specific investments, making the automaker more reluctant to replace these parts with imports.

Generally a VIE reduces relationship-specific investment, raising the keiretsu cost of production, which leads to a reduction in Japanese auto output and hence to a reduction in the total Japanese demand for parts. Thus although the US share of the Japanese parts' market rises due to the import of a greater range of parts, it is possible that a content or market-share VIE would be self defeating in the sense that the total value of US parts exported to Japan would fall. For the same reason, it may not be feasible for Japan to achieve a specified increase in the total value of its parts imports, particularly if the demanded increase is large.[10] However, if Japan imports no or very few parts at free trade, which could arise due to a high productivity of relationship-specific investment, then US parts exports would rise.

highly-skilled components such as engines, transaxles, suspension systems, and brakes are made for Japanese carmakers by Japanese-owned suppliers." See also Aoki (1988, pp. 208–209) and Dyer and Ouchi (1993, Fig. 1, p. 52).

[9]For example, in response to the 1992 agreement on autos, "initially simple mechanical parts and such items as carpets and aluminium were purchased, rather than more technologically complicated parts like electronic controls and engines" (see McMillan, 1996).

[10]This may partly explain the $0.6 billion shortfall in meeting the 1994 $3.6 billion target for US exports of auto-parts to Japan, which was part of the 1992 auto-parts agreement with President Bush. As stated in the New York Times (July 14, 1995), Japanese imports fell short because production of vehicles in Japan declined, leading all of Japan's top five automakers to miss their targets for the import of parts.

Consideration is also given to the effects of a VER (voluntary export restraint[11]) and an import tariff which limit US imports of autos from Japan. As we show, these policies can have significant effects in opening the Japanese market for auto-parts. This result may initially appear surprising because in standard models, a restriction in final-good output would reduce the demand for both domestically produced and imported parts. However, in the current framework, the reduced output of Japanese autos makes it less profitable for keiretsu suppliers to undertake relationship-specific investments. This leads to an increase in the range of imported parts and hence raises the US share of the Japanese parts market.

The effects of a VER or tariff are particularly relevant since these policies have been extensively applied against the Japanese auto industry, including being used as threats to gain agreement for a VIE in auto-parts.[12] A main result is then to show that a credible threat of a VER (or tariff) giving rise to the same total value of US parts exports as a VIE applied to parts would always be sufficient to induce the Japanese automaker to comply with the VIE.[13] This follows because the VER causes a greater reduction in keiretsu investment and output. This raises the price of autos and if the aim is to achieve a given target value of US parts exports, US consumers as well as the keiretsu would prefer the VIE. Nevertheless, US profit from auto production is higher under the VER and since the gain in profit can more than offset the consumer loss, we find that the US is not necessarily better off using a VIE than a VER as a policy to expand parts exports.

---

[11]The VER acts as an import quota in which the Japanese manufacturer of autos gains the quota rents.

[12]In the 1995 US/Japan auto-dispute, Japan was threatened with prohibitively high tariffs on Japanese luxury automobiles if it did not agree to market-share targets in its auto-parts industry (see Levinsohn, 1997). Also, VERs have been extensively applied to autos, including by the US in May 1981.

[13]In a model with Cournot competition between a US and Japanese parts' supplier, Krishna and Morgan (1998) show that the threat of a sufficiently high tariff on autos can induce the US firm to increase exports to comply with a market-share target, but a tariff on its own causes a decrease in the export of parts.

Managed trade in general and VIEs in particular are strongly opposed by many economists. In 1993, more than 50 economists sent a letter to President Clinton and Prime Minister Hosokawa asking the two leaders to reject the demands for managed trade.[14] However, significant support for the idea from policy makers has lead to considerable interest in research on the topic. Bhagwati (1987) is among the first to criticize VIEs and much of the literature, including Greaney (1996), Krishna *et al.* (1998) and as well as the current paper, show that, by raising the price of the product concerned, market-share VIEs tend to be anticompetitive.[15] Bjorksten (1994) considers both VIEs and VERs and shows that in a Kreps-Scheinkman duopoly model with price competition and capacity constraints, a VER has similar effects as under Cournot competition, leading to a reduction in profits by the exporting firm as in the present paper. However, as shown by Krishna (1989), this outcome tends to be reversed under Bertrand competition. Also, Cronshaw and Markusen (1995) consider the implications of hidden trade barriers for policy in a simple, but useful, asymmetric information framework, but they do not directly model the effects of VIEs or VERs. The current paper differs from all this literature because of its explicit consideration of the effects of keiretsu.

The rest of the paper is organized as follows. Section 2 lays out the model and develops the main effects of the keiretsu under free trade. Section 3 then considers the types of parts that will be imported in response to a VIE and also the implications for the total value of parts imports. Next, Section 4 concerns the use of a VER or tariff applied to final-good exports as a market-opening policy with respect to the import of parts. Comparisons are then made as to the magnitude of the effects of the VIE versus the VER or tariff, leading to some welfare implications. Finally, Section 5 contains concluding remarks.

[14]As explained in the letter (see FEER, 1993, p. 26), the "principal factor underlying such demands for managed trade has been the crude and simplistic view that Japan is importing too few manufactures owing to 'structural barriers' which make Japan 'special'."

[15]There are some exceptions, particularly when the policy applies to an intermediate good (see Krishna and Morgan, 1998 and Krishna *et al.*, 2001).

2. The Investment Model

This section sets out the model for the base case in which there is free trade. Additional justification and explanation of the model can be found in Spencer and Qiu (2001).

2.1. *Relationship-specific investment and cost of production*

A final good, such as an auto, is produced in both Japan and the United States based on Cournot competition between a Japanese firm, referred to as a J-maker and a US firm, referred to as an A-maker. The J and A makers produce homogeneous outputs, denoted y^J and y^A, respectively. Our basic results also apply to the case in which the J-maker has a world monopoly, but the extension to oligopoly seems appropriate given the institutional reality of oligopolistic competition between US and Japanese auto producers and the importance of US production in motivating US trade policy. In order to consider the effects of US import restrictions applied against Japanese autos, we make the convenient assumption that autos are all sold in the US at a price $P = P(Y)$ where $Y = y^J + y^A$.

The J-maker and its long-term suppliers in Japan, referred to as J-suppliers, are assumed to form a keiretsu[16] in which J-suppliers potentially engage in relationship-specific investments of value to the J-maker, but not to the A-maker. Suppliers in the US, referred to as A-suppliers, produce parts for the A-maker and potentially also export these parts to be used by the J-maker, but they operate based on short-term contracts under pure competition[17] and hence

[16]Our analysis applies to top ranked (or first-tier) firms with technological expertise and long-term supply relationships and not to the more marginal firms that may be used as short term capacity buffers so as to help maintain permanent employment in the core manufacturer (see Asanuma, 1989, pp. 16–18 and Aoki, 1988, pp. 208–209). Keiretsu are very stable. For instance, "member firms of Kyohokai, an association formed by Toyota parts suppliers, numbered 171 in 1984. Of these firms, 153 had been continual members of Kyohokai during the 11 years since 1973" (see Asanuma, 1989, p. 5).

[17]For example, a large number of establishments produce auto-parts in the US, 4856 in 1992 (Office of Automotive Affairs) and the average length of contract was only 2.5 years in 1989, up from 1.3 years in 1984 (see Dyer and Ouchi, 1993).

do not undertake relationship-specific investment. The assumption that A-suppliers do not make relationship-specific investments of value to the J-maker captures the institutional reality that the long-term suppliers of parts for Japanese production of autos are overwhelmingly Japanese.[18]

Rather than unfair exclusion, we would argue that this is most likely due to the severe difficulties faced by non-Japanese firms in gaining access to the flow of technical and other keiretsu information necessary for suitable design of parts in coordination with other keiretsu suppliers.[19] In addition to a knowledge of Japanese language and customs, access to this information requires mutual trust, which first involves the development of a good business relationship, perhaps as a simple manufacturer of outsourced parts sold to Japanese assemblers in the supplier's home country.[20] Proximity also facilitates the exchange of information and due to this and other advantages, such as the ease of 'just in time' delivery, actual production in Japan may be necessary if US firms are to become long-term keiretsu suppliers within Japan.[21] Since any such production does not form

---

[18]See Dodwell Marketing Consultants (1990) which lists the main auto-parts suppliers in Japan. Levinsohn (1997, p. 18) estimates that the US share of sales of parts to Japanese automakers in Japan is only about 1%.

[19]Branstetter (2000) documents the importance of the flow of technical information within keiretsu.

[20]For example, Tenneco made agreements with Unisia-Jecs Corp (a keiretsu supplier to Nissan) and with Futuba (a keiretsu supplier to Toyota) to produce parts (such as shock absorbers) designed by its Japanese partners for sale to Japanese plants in the US. This increased confidence in Tenneco's expertise and now Tenneco hopes to supply Japanese automakers in Japan (see Automotive News, April 27, 1998). Rauch (2002) provides an excellent survey emphasising the importance of business and social networks in facilitating trade due to informational advantages and trust.

[21]In addition to alliances with keiretsu suppliers, the importance of location in Japan for the ability to sell parts in Japan is emphasised by Levinsohn (1997, p. 18). An example is TRW (a US firm), which initially engaged in joint ventures with Japanese firms supplying the US plants of Toyota and Nissan and then began supplying these firms back in Japan, but only by producing most of these parts in Japan. Also, there is evidence that Japanese suppliers tend to follow a main keiretsu assembler in setting up production facilities in other countries, but in addition, parts are often imported from Japan (see for example, Belderbos and Sleuwaegen, 1998 and Head *et al.*, 1995). This supports the idea that a

part of US exports to Japan (and is currently small), it would not change our basic results concerning the effects of trade policy on the volume and pattern of US exports of parts to Japan.[22] As for the lack of relationship-specific investment with respect to the A-maker, this highlights the institutional differences across countries, but is mainly for simplicity of the model.[23]

In modelling investment within the keiretsu, a central role is played by the fact that parts differ with respect to their costs of production and hence their importance for downstream costs. Assuming constant returns to scale in production and letting c^i and c^{*i} denote the respective marginal (and average) costs of production of part i in Japan and the US, we arrange auto-parts in order of increasing average cost of production. This ordering is assumed to be the same in both countries. Exploiting the fact that the number of parts, N, is large, it proves convenient to express marginal costs as differentiable and increasing functions, $c = c(i)$ and $c^{*i} = c^*(i)$ on the interval $i \in [0, N]$, The production of an auto requires parts and labor to be combined in fixed proportion and, without loss of generality, we set the units of output of each part i so that each auto is produced using just *one* part of each type. For the keiretsu, the importance of part i for downstream costs is then captured by the cost-share, $\sigma'(\sigma'$ is Greek s for share), defined as $\sigma^i = \sigma(i) = c(i)/C(N)$ for $C(N) = \int_0^N c(i)di$, where the ordering of parts ensures $\sigma'(i) > 0$. In

presence in Japan is important for gaining access to the information flow within keiretsu, but once the benefits are realized, parts incorporating relationship-specific investments can then be exported to keiretsu assemblers or produced locally in a host country. Suppliers producing just in the US (or Europe) would be at an informational disadvantage.

[22]An interesting possibility suggested by a referee is that a US VIE might put pressure on the J-maker to more easily accept US suppliers into the keiretsu, which (in future work) might be modelled as a reduction in the J-maker's bargaining power, making it more profitable for these suppliers to undertake investments. Because of the importance of access to information from keiretsu suppliers in Japan, this analysis would require consideration of US foreign direct investment as well as exports to Japan.

[23]A more complicated model could be developed with symmetric institutions in which the A and J suppliers make relationship-specific investments of value to the A and J-maker's, respectively, but this would not change the pattern of trade with Japan or the main insights with respect to trade policy.

order to focus on the export of parts to Japan, we assume that parts can be produced more cheaply in the US. Since we also assume (for simplicity) that $\sigma^i = \sigma(i)$ and $c^{*1} = c * (i)$ are linear in i with equal slopes, it follows that the efficiency gap, denoted $S = c^l - c^{*1} > 0$ between Japan and the US is constant.[24]

For each part i, a J-supplier, namely supplier i, potentially makes a relationship-specific investment, denoted k^l. This creates rent for the J-maker (but not the A-maker) in the form of a reduction in the cost of the process of assembly for each auto using the part from supplier i. For example, the investment might improve the fit of part i with the other parts that the J-maker uses to produce autos. The magnitude, denoted r^i, of the rent created per auto, is assumed to be proportional to the initial value, denoted w°, of the cost of the assembly process per auto in the absence of relationship-specific investments and also to the relative contribution of part i to cost, as measured by the cost-share, $a(i)$. This last condition reflects the idea that the greater the proportion of costs associated with the part, the greater the potential for cost reduction. For example, a given amount of investment is likely to be more effective in reducing costs when it applies to engines rather than to seat covers. Also, using the cost-share has the reasonable feature that the level of rent is invariant to an inflation in the costs of all parts.

Consequently, letting 9 denote the productivity of investment, we assume:

$$r^i = w^o \sigma(i) \theta h(k^i) for\, 0 < \theta \leq \theta^{\max} \tag{1}$$

where $\theta^{\max} = \min\{l, C(N)/w^o\}$ and $h(k^i)$ satisfies:

$$h(0) = 0, h'(k^i) > 0, \quad h\text{"}(k^i) < 0 \,\text{and}\, h(k^i) < 1. \tag{2}$$

From (1) and (2), higher levels of investment create more rent for the J-maker, but at a decreasing rate.[25] Also, the restrictions on the magnitude of the rent, due to $\theta \leq \theta^{\max}$ and $h(k^i) < 1$ ensure that

---

[24]These assumptions can be relaxed as in Spencer and Qiu (2001) to allow for some parts to be produced at lower cost in Japan and also to allow for δ to depend on i with $\delta'(i) \leq 0$.

[25]That is, $\frac{\partial r^i}{\partial k^i} = w^o \sigma(i) \theta h'(k^i) > 0$ and $\frac{\partial^2 r^i}{(\partial k^i)^2} = w^o \sigma(i) h''(k^i) < 0$.

there is no "free lunch" from assembly or from the production and use of keiretsu parts.[26]

Letting p^i represent the price paid to supplier i, the J-maker's marginal cost for part i is given by $\gamma^i \equiv p^i - r^i$ if the part is purchased from within the keiretsu and by c^{*1} if the part is imported. The J-maker's overall marginal cost, denoted y, is then equal to the total cost of parts plus w°. In the US, the A-maker obtains each part from the A-suppliers at a price c^{*i} giving rise to a marginal cost, denoted by γ^*, which we assume to be constant. The J-maker, supplier i and the A-maker, respectively, earn profits:

$$\pi^J = y^J(P(Y) - \gamma),\ \varphi^i = y^J(p^i - c^i) - k^i, \pi^A = y^A(P(Y) - \gamma^*). \tag{3}$$

2.2. *Order of moves and bargaining over parts' prices*

An important aspect of relationship-specific investment is that it is sunk prior to purchase of the part and the supplier cannot be guaranteed a return based on a contract that is conditional on the amount of investment. This is due to the difficulty of actually observing k^i, which would include non-observable costs, such as the costs of obtaining the information and coordination with other suppliers. Consequently, as in Spencer and Qiu (2001), we assume that the investment, k^i, is sunk prior to bargaining over the price, p^i with the J-maker and also that p^i can be based on the rent, r^i but not k^i.

In the free trade setting, the order of moves is as follows. At stage 1, each supplier i commits to its investment $k^i > 0$, and simultaneously, the J-maker and A-maker both specify their respective outputs, y^J and y^A. Since each firm sets its choice variable to maximize own profit taking the other choice variables as given, this gives rise to a Nash equilibrium in k^i, y^J and y^A. Anticipating the outcome of the stage 2 bargaining process over the prices, p^i the two automakers are assumed to earn strictly positive profits, but for some J-suppliers, investment at stage 1 could cause a loss. If $\Phi^i < 0$ for all $k^i > 0$ or if bargaining would break down at stage 2, then supplier i

[26]These conditions imply $r^i < \sigma^i C(N) = c^i$ and $r^i < w^\circ\sigma(i)$, which implies $w^J \equiv w^\circ - \int_0^N r^i di > 0$.

sets $k^i = 0$ and exits the market at stage 1. At stage 2, the J-maker engages in simultaneous Nash bargaining over the price of part i with each remaining supplier. If an agreement is reached with supplier i, the J-maker orders the y^J parts needed to produce output y^J. Otherwise, the J-maker imports the part from the lower cost US producers.

Considering stage 2 first, in bargaining with supplier i, the J-maker aims to minimize its marginal cost, $\gamma^i = p^i - r^i$ due to part i with a disagreement or "threat point" of importing the part at a price, c^{*i} if bargaining breaks down. Thus for the Nash bargaining problem, the J-maker can be viewed as maximizing its payoff from agreement, as represented by $y^J(c^{*i} - \gamma^i)$, where y^J is given from stage 1. Correspondingly, since investment, k^l, is sunk, supplier i maximizes its variable profit, $y^J(p^i - \gamma^i)$, with a threat point of no production and zero variable profit. Letting $\alpha \in [0, 1)$ represent the bargaining power of the J-maker and $l - \alpha$ the bargaining power of each supplier, it follows,[27] using $\gamma^i = p^i - r^i$ and $\delta = c^i - c^{*i}$ that at the Nash bargaining equilibrium:

$$p^i - c^i = (1 - \alpha)(r^i - 8) \quad \text{and} \quad \gamma^i = c^{*i} - \alpha(r^i - \delta) > 0. \tag{4}$$

From (4) and $\alpha < 1$, supplier i gains a share, $1 - \alpha > 0$, of the net rent, $r^i - \delta$, that it creates due to relationship-specific investment. We assume $\alpha < 1$, since otherwise there is no incentive for investment. The J-maker's share, a, of net rent is reflected in a reduction in the marginal cost, y^1, of part i below the cost c^{*1} of an imported part, but y^1 remains strictly positive. The respective payoffs to the J-maker and supplier i (relative to the disagreement point) are: $y^J\alpha(r^i - \delta)$ and $\varphi^i + k^i = y^J(1 - \alpha)(r^i - \delta)$. It follows that once k^i is sunk, agreement would be reached for supplier i to produce the part if and only if the rent created from investment is sufficiently large to make $r^i - \delta \geq 0$. This requires that supplier i set $k^i > 0$, which from (3) and (4) implies a stage 2 profit for supplier i, given by:

$$\varphi^i = y^J(1 - \alpha)(r^i - \delta) - k^i, \quad \text{if } r^i - \delta \geq 0$$
$$\varphi^i = -k^i, \quad \text{if } r^i - \delta < 0. \tag{5}$$

[27] Setting p^i to maximize $G^i = (c^{*i} - \gamma^i)^\alpha (p^i - c^i)^{1-\alpha} y^J$, we obtain d In $G^i/dp^i = (1 - \alpha)/(p^i - c^i) - \alpha/(c^{*i} - \gamma^i) = 0$. Using $c^i - r^i > 0$ in (4), we obtain $\gamma^i = (1 - \alpha)c^{*i} + \alpha(c^i - r^i) > 0$.

2.3. *Stage 1: Relationship-specific investments and output*

At the Cournot–Nash equilibrium at stage 1, the J and A-makers set their outputs and J-suppliers simultaneously set their investment levels to maximize their respective profits. Considering investment decisions first, at stage 1, supplier i determines the optimal value of k^l in the event that it would produce the part by maximizing φ^i as in (5), taking y^J, y^A and the investments k^J for $j \neq i$ of the other suppliers as given.[28] Using $r^i = w^o \sigma^i \theta h'(k^i)$, this gives rise to the Kuhn-Tucker first order conditions:[29]

$$\frac{\partial \varphi^i}{\partial k^i} = y^J(1-\alpha)w^o\sigma^i\theta h'(k^i) - 1 \leq 0; \left(\frac{\partial \varphi^i}{\partial k^i}\right) k^i = 0 \qquad (6)$$

which define $k^i = k(\sigma^i,\, y^J)$ where $\frac{\partial \varphi^i}{\partial k^i} = 0$ if $k^i > 0$ and $k^i = 0$ if $\frac{\partial \varphi^i}{\partial k^i} < 0$ (parameters *0* and *a* are omitted for convenience). However, even if $k^l > 0$ from (6), it is possible that revenue (due to $r^i - \delta > 0$) would not be sufficient to cover k^l and hence would lead to a loss. In this case supplier i would set $k^i = 0$ and not produce the part. Setting $k^i = k(\sigma^i, y^J)$ in (5) it follows that with free trade in parts, supplier i would produce the part if and only if $\varphi^i > 0$.

From the ordering of parts from low to high cost-shares, investment, k^l, and rent, r^i are increasing in i for $k^i > 0$ (see (A.2) of Appendix A). Supposing that suppliers i and j for $i > j$ make the same level of investment, then since $\alpha > \alpha^i$, part i generates a higher level of rent, which is partly captured by each supplier based on the share $1 - \alpha$. This translates into a higher incentive to invest with the result that $k^i > k^J$ and $\varphi^i > \varphi^j$. Thus from (5), using $\frac{\partial \varphi^i}{\partial k^i} = 0$ and $\frac{\partial r^i}{\partial \sigma^i} = \frac{r^i}{\sigma^i}$, we obtain:

$$\frac{d\varphi^i}{di} = y^J(1-\alpha)r^i\frac{\sigma'(i)}{\sigma(i)} > 0 \text{ for } k^i > 0. \qquad (7)$$

---

[28]The investments k^j for $j \neq i$ and output y^A influence k^i only through their effects on y^J.

[29]For $a < 1, < p^l$ is strictly concave in k^l, since, from (6), $\partial^2\varphi^i/(\partial k^i)^2 = y^J(1-\alpha)w^o\sigma(i)\theta h''(k^i) < 0$.

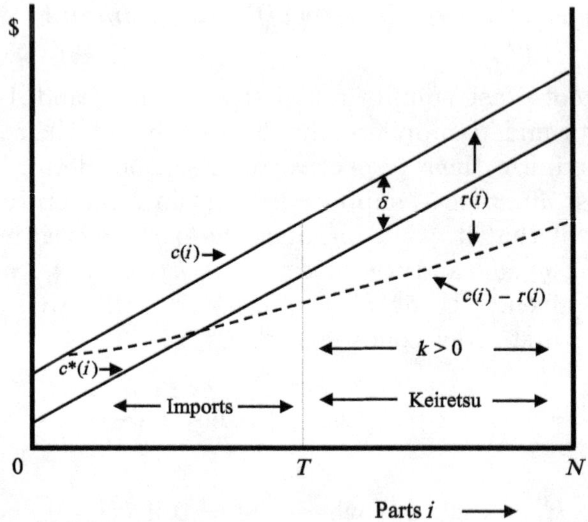

Figure 9.1. Costs and range of imported parts.

Expressing $\varphi^i = \varphi(i,\, y^J; \theta)$ at the stage 1 equilibrium and supposing that part $i = T(T$ for trade) satisfies:

$$\varphi^T = \varphi(T, y^J; \theta) = y^J(1-\alpha)(r^T - \delta) - k(\sigma^T, y; \theta) = 0, \qquad (8)$$

it then follows that T represents the marginal or lowest cost-share part produced by the keiretsu. If $\varphi^0 = \varphi(0, y^J; \theta) \geq 0$, then all parts are produced in the keiretsu.[30]

As illustrated in Fig. 9.1, parts i with equal or higher cost-shares (i.e. for $i > T$) are produced within the keiretsu and parts i with lower cost-shares (i.e. for $i < T$) are imported. Production and investment take place in the keiretsu only if this raises efficiency relative to importing. Thus, for $i > T$, the rent from investment k shown as the difference between $c(i)$ and the dashed line, $c(i) - r(i)$, more than offsets the efficiency gap so as to at least cover the investment cost. For $i < T$, the difference between these lines is the rent that would have been created if the part had been produced in the keiretsu.

From (8), using (7), since y^J varies exogenously due to a VER, it is useful to express the marginal part T as a function $T = T(y^J; \theta)$, where $dT/dy^J < 0$ from (A.4) of Appendix A. The increase in profit

[30]If $\varphi^0 > 0$, then since (7) implies $\varphi^i > 0$ for all $i \in [0, N]$, T is not defined.

associated with an increase in y^J allows more J-suppliers to remain in business and hence reduces the range of imported parts. Also, since T varies due to a VIE (see next section), we express the J-maker's marginal cost as $\gamma = \gamma(T, y^J; \theta)$, where $\gamma = \int_0^T c^{*i}di + \int_0^T c^{*i}di + w^o$. Letting $C^*(N) = \int_0^N c^{*i}di$ denote the total cost of parts if all parts are imported and using $\gamma^i = c^{*i} - \alpha(r^i - \delta)$ from (4), γ can be rearranged into the form:

$$\gamma = \gamma(Ty^J; \theta) = C^*(N) - \int_T^N \alpha(r^i - \delta)di + w^o. \tag{9}$$

As (9) shows, if $\alpha > 0$, then the rents from relationship-specific investment reduce marginal cost below the level, $C^*(N) + w^o$, achieved when all parts are imported, but if $a = 0$, then y is constant whether or not parts are imported. Since this latter possibility would prevent a determinate outcome as to the set of imported parts under a VIE (see Proposition 2 below), we assume $a > 0$ and hence that a 6 (0,1), giving all parties some bargaining power. It is true that if J-suppliers had all the bargaining power (i.e. if $a = 0$), they would set k^l at an efficient level for a fixed level of y^J, but this is not optimal since, as shown by Spencer and Qiu (2001), a small increase in a would reduce the J-maker's marginal cost, leading to an increase in output and aggregate J-supplier (and keiretsu) profit.[31]

Now considering the determination of output, since at the Nash equilibrium in y^J, y^A and k^i the J-maker sets y^J treating k^i (and y^A) as fixed, it follows (see (9)) that the J-maker takes r^i and hence γ as fixed. Thus, there is no strategic role for output in influencing the prices paid for parts at the second stage bargaining game. Since the A-maker sets y^A to maximize π^A as in (3) taking y^J (and k^i) as given, final-good outputs, y^J and y^A satisfy the standard Cournot first order conditions:

$$\begin{aligned} \pi_J^J &\equiv \frac{\partial \pi^J}{\partial y^J} = P + y^J P' - \gamma = 0 \\ \pi_A^A &\equiv \frac{\partial \pi^A}{\partial y^A} = P + y^A P' - \gamma^* = 0 \end{aligned} \tag{10}$$

[31] J-suppliers benefit due to $p^i - c^i > 0$, but the J-maker would prefer a higher value of a.

where subscripts J and A represent partial derivatives with respect to y and y, respectively. Assuming that the following second order and stability conditions:

$$\begin{aligned}\pi^J_{JJ} = 2P' + y^J P'' < 0 \pi^A_{AA} = 2P' + y^A P'' < 0 \\ H^O \equiv \pi^J_{JJ}\pi^A_{AA} - \pi^J_{JA}\pi^A_{AJ} = p'(3p' + Yp'') > 0\end{aligned} \tag{11}$$

hold globally, conditions (10) define equilibrium output levels, $y = y(y)$ and $y^A = y^A(y)$ where the constant y^* is omitted for convenience. However, the dependence of $k^i = k(\sigma^i, y^J)$ on y^J means that $\gamma = \gamma(T, y^J)$ is also dependent on y^J and hence we require the additional (global) stability conditions:

$$\pi^J_{JJ} - \frac{d\gamma}{dy^J} < 0 \quad H \equiv H^O - \pi^A_{AA}\left(\frac{d\gamma}{dy^J}\right) > 0 \tag{12}$$

where $d\gamma/dy^J = (d\gamma/dT)(dT/dy^J) + d\gamma/dy^J < 0$ from $\alpha > 0$, (A.4) and (A.5) of Appendix A. From (10), treating y as a constant with respect to y^J, we first obtain the standard result that an increase in y reduces y^J and then, using (12) to take account of the effect of y^J on y, we obtain:

$$\frac{dy^J}{d\gamma} = \pi^A_{AA}/H^O < 0 \quad 1 - \left(\frac{dy^J}{d\gamma}\right)\left(\frac{d\gamma}{dy^J}\right) = \frac{H}{H^o} \tag{13}$$

In the event that T is fixed due to a VIE, we require $1 - (\frac{dy^J}{d\gamma})(\frac{d\gamma}{dy^J}) > 0$, but since $(\frac{dy^J}{d\gamma}) < (\frac{d\gamma}{dy^J}) < 0$, this condition is implied by (13). Also, for consideration of trade policy, it is useful to assume that outputs are strategic substitutes (i.e. $\pi^i_{ij} = p' + y^i p'' < 0$ for $i \neq j$) and hence that:

$$dy^A/dy^J = -\pi^A_{AJ}/\pi^A_{AA} < 0 \quad dy^J/dy^A = -\pi^J_{JA}/\pi^J_{JJ} < 0. \tag{14}$$

Finally, taking into account the endogenous determination of output and investment and letting a superscript F denote values at free trade, the set of imported parts is given by $\Delta^F \equiv \{i : i < T^F\}$, where:

$$T^F = T(y^{JF}; \theta) \text{ for } y^{JF} = y^J(\gamma^F) \quad \text{and} \quad \gamma^F = \gamma(T^F, y^J(\gamma^F); \theta) \tag{15}$$

Letting $\theta^{T=N}$ represent the value of θ at which supplier A just breaks even (i.e. $\varphi(N, y^J; \theta^{T=N})$, then $T^F = N$ and all other parts are imported. Similarly, letting $\theta^{T=0}$ satisfy $\varphi(0, y^J; \theta^{T=0}) = 0$, then $T^F = 0$ and all parts are produced in the keiretsu. Since, as shown in (A.8) of Appendix A, an increase in *6* causes a reduction in 7^{-1}, parts are fully supplied by imports for $\theta \epsilon [0, \theta^{T=N})$ and by the keiretsu for[32] $\theta \epsilon [\theta^{T=0}, \theta^{\max})$. To ensure some possibility of production by J-suppliers, we assume $\theta \geq \theta^{T=N}$.

3. Voluntary Import Expansion: VIE

This section concerns the effects of VIEs designed to open the Japanese market for imported parts. Three types of VIEs are considered: a content VIE, a market-share VIE and a total-value VIE. A content VIE specifies a minimum level of US content per auto produced in Japan, whereas the market-share target under a market-share VIE depends on US content per auto, but also on the way Japanese parts are valued. A natural possibility, which we focus on here, is that Japanese parts are valued at their marginal cost, c, of production.[33] This reflects the idea that the rents enjoyed by the J-maker from the purchase of keiretsu produced parts and also the prices of these parts as obtained through bargaining would be hard for outsiders to observe, particularly if the observers are foreign, such as the US government. Marginal cost, c, is more easily observable, since c^l is the price that supplier i would quote if it were to sell to outside firms, such as the US automaker. The third possibility, a total-value VIE, also depends on US content per auto, but in addition, induced changes in Japanese production of autos play a central role in achievement of the target.

---

[32] We assume that $\theta^{\max}$ is sufficiently large that $\varphi(0, y^J; \theta^{\max}) > 0$ and hence that $\theta^{T=0} > \theta^{\max}$.

[33] As shown in an earlier working paper, Qiu and Spencer (2000), our results also apply if Japanese parts are valued at the J-maker's net marginal cost, $\gamma^i = p^i - r^i$. The valuation method for parts is important for Proposition 2 (below), showing that the VIE is satisfied by importing parts in the order of lowest to highest cost-share, but given this result, the particular method used does not affect the further insights.

As argued by Krishna *et al.* (1998), the effects of a VIE can depend crucially on how it is implemented. In the current setting, it seems most natural to suppose that the J-maker is responsible for achieving compliance with the policy. One possibility, developed in the next section, is that the J-maker's actions are motivated by a threat of a VER or tariff. However, our results also apply if compliance by the automaker to the VIE is aided by direct pressure from the Japanese government as was the case in the 1986 semiconductor agreement (see Irwin, 1996, pp. 11–12). Pressure to make buying firms responsible is understandable, particularly since the complaints leading to VIEs commonly involve beliefs of unfair procedures by buying firms. For example, with respect to auto-parts, US firms complained that they had difficulty in obtaining the necessary information for bids (see Levinsohn, 1997, pp. 15–16).

With respect to the order of moves, we assume that governments commit to trade policy, such as a VIE, a VER or a tariff, prior to any actions by firms. In response to a VIE, the J-maker makes a commitment at stage 0 to import at least the set of parts denoted by A. The quantity of these imports is subsequently determined by the J-maker's need for parts arising from its equilibrium level of output. Since the J-maker sees through to the outcome of the game, the set A is chosen to ensure compliance with the VIE (if feasible). There are no other changes in the order of moves. Decisions as to investments, k^l, and final-good outputs, y and y^A, are made at stage 1, with bargaining over the prices for parts within the keiretsu at stage 2.

It is important to emphasis that at stage 0, the J-maker makes no commitment as to the set of parts to be purchased from J-suppliers. These parts are endogenously determined as before, leaving open the possibility that further parts in addition to A will be imported. Thus, while compliance with the VIE requires some commitment by the J-maker as to a minimum set of imports, the model maintains the feature that the J-suppliers do not get an advance contract before making relationship-specific investments.[34] It is also important that

[34]A commitment by the J-maker at stage 0 not to import a particular part would change the threat point at the bargaining equilibrium, affecting the incentives for investment and the prices paid for parts.

the modification of the model to allow for a first mover capability of the J-maker at stage 0 confers no strategic advantage and has no effect on the outcome of the model under free trade. To show this, recalling that $\Delta^F \equiv \{i : i < T^F\} <$ represents the set of parts that would be imported at free trade, since J-suppliers for $i \in \Delta^F$ would anyway make losses from production, an up-front commitment to import parts in Δ^F does not change the outcome. Secondly, as we show in Proposition 1, the import of any additional part $j \notin \Delta^F$ serves to raise the J-maker's marginal cost due to a loss of relationship-specific investment. Thus the J-maker's output and profit falls (and the A-maker's profit rises). Consequently the J-maker would not use its commitment ability to import additional parts under free trade and any difference in outcome under the VIE is due to the effects of the VIE and not to a change in the strategic behavior of firms.

To further explain Proposition 1, suppose that at stage 0, the J-maker announces the import of part $j \notin \Delta^F$. Since $r^j - \delta > 0$, the J-maker's marginal cost, $\gamma^j \equiv c^{*i} - \alpha(r^j - \delta)$, for part $j \in [T^F, N]$ from supplier j is strictly less than the import price, c^{*j}, giving rise to a *direct* increase in the J-maker's marginal cost of:

$$m^j \equiv c^{*j} - \gamma^j = \alpha(r^j - \delta) > 0 \text{ for } j \in [T^F, N] \qquad (16)$$

At stage 1, the increase in the direct cost due to $k^J = 0$ will cause a reduction in y^J and a reduction in k^i and r^i for $i \neq j$ and $i \in [T^F, N]$, reinforcing the fall in the J-maker's profit. The A-maker's profit increases since outputs are strategic substitutes. The proofs of all propositions, including Proposition 1, are in Appendix A.

Proposition 1. *For $a \in (0, 1)$, commitment by the J-maker to an import set A that includes at least one part $j \notin \Delta^F$ will result in (i) an increase in marginal cost for part j, (ii) higher y and lower k^i, i^i, y^J and π^J and (iii) higher π^A compared with free trade.*

Proposition 1 reflects the fact that the use of keiretsu suppliers raises efficiency. However, this conclusion is quite different from common beliefs arising without consideration of the keiretsu structure. Part of the impetus for the US/Japan Auto Agreement arose from complaints that keiretsu "unfairly" purchase more expensive Japanese auto-parts rather than cheaper US imports. Thus, a VIE directed at opening the Japanese parts market was expected to reduce Japanese production costs (lower y) and raise Japanese output of autos (larger y^J). As a result, in addition to an increase in US market share, a VIE was expected to increase the total Japanese demand for parts, further raising the value of US parts exports. Since, taking into account the endogenous determination of relationship-specific investment within keiretsu, a VIE would reduce Japanese production of autos, our results suggest that a VIE requiring a given market share for parts could be significantly less effective than expected in raising the value of US parts exports.

Now turning to the question as to the types of parts that will be imported in response to the VIE, in making this choice (at stage 0) the J-maker is assumed to maximize profit subject to satisfying the VIE. Suppose that the J-maker announces the import of just one part $j \notin \Delta^F$ at stage 0. To the extent that part j has a higher cost-share, there is a greater loss of rent from investment, which causes the direct cost, m^1, incurred by the J-maker to rise.[35] This suggests, as shown in Proposition 2, that to satisfy a VIE, additional parts $j \in [T^F, N]$ will be imported in the order from lowest to highest cost-share. However, to prove this result,[36] it is necessary to also take into account the contribution, c^{*1}, of each additional imported part towards achieving an increase in US content. Consequently, it is the effect of a higher cost-share on m^j/c^{*J} that is important, and since the use of higher cost parts will allow the VIE target to be met with a smaller range of imported parts (c^{*J} is also increasing in j), this complicates the proof and the result is not obvious.

Proposition 2. *Assume $a \in (0,1)$. To satisfy (i) a content VIE, (ii) a market-share VIE or (iii) for linear demand, a total-value VIE, additional parts, $j \in [T^F, N]$, above the free trade level will be imported in the order determined by increasing cost-shares (i.e. import lower σ^j).*

As a result of Proposition 2, a (feasible) VIE target for any of the three forms of VIE is implemented by the import of the set of

[35] From (16) and (A.2) of Appendix A, we obtain $dm^J/dj = \alpha(dr^J/d\sigma^j)\sigma'(j) > 0$ for $\alpha > 0$.

[36] Linear demand simplifies the proof of Proposition 2(iii) for the total-value VIE by making dy^J/dy constant. The result generalizes to other demand structures if $d^2y^J/(d\gamma)^2 < 0$ so the effect of an increase in γ in reducing output is magnified as y increases or, alternatively, if $d^2y^J/(d\gamma)^2 > 0$ but sufficiently small.

parts denoted $\Delta^{\bar{T}} \equiv \{i : i < \bar{T}\}$ where $T \in (T^F, N]$ is the smallest value of T at which the particular target is satisfied. To see this, letting $v^*(T) = \int_0^T c^{*i} di$ represent US content per auto from all parts $i < T$, then, since $v^{*\prime}(T) = c^{*T} > 0$, for any target content, $\bar{v}^*$, there is a unique value of $T = T$ satisfying $v^*(\bar{T}) = v^*$ and, as $\bar{v}^*$ increases, the required import set, $\Delta^{\bar{T}}$, expands though an increase in $\bar{T}$. Similarly, letting $v(T) = \int_T^N c^i di$ i represent Japanese content, then the US market share is given by $S * (T) = v^*(T)/(v^*(T) + v(T))$ and any required market share, $\bar{S}^*$, is achieved at the unique value[37] of $T = \bar{T}$ satisfying $S^*(\bar{T}) = \bar{S}^*$. In addition, letting γ^T and V^{*T}, respectively, represent the J-maker's marginal cost and the total value of US exports of parts at $T = \bar{T}$, then $V^{*T} = v^*(\bar{T})y^J(\gamma^T)$, where $\gamma^T \equiv \gamma(T, y^J(\gamma^T); \theta)$. Since the import of additional parts raises US content per auto, but reduces the J-maker's output, it is possible that a greater range of imported parts can actually lower the total value of imports[38] (making $dV^{*T}/dT < 0$) and hence that there may be more than one value of T at which some total-value target, $\bar{V}^*$, is satisfied. However, the J-maker will set T equal to the smallest value of $T \in (T^F, \theta]$ satisfying $V^{*T} = \bar{V}^*$ so as to minimize the increase in marginal cost due to the loss of relationship-specific investment.

As illustrated in Fig. 9.2, we can gain some insights as to the pattern of response in the total value of US parts exports based on the size or restrictiveness of the VIE target as well as on the magnitude of the productivity, θ, of relationship-specific investment. If 6 is sufficiently large that there are no imports at free trade (i.e. if $\theta = \theta^{T=0}$ and hence $T^F = 0$), then any VIE, even a drastic VIE which forces Japan to use only imported parts, must result in an increase in the value of US exports. Thus, as shown by the solid line from the origin at $T^F = 0$, corresponding to $\theta = \theta^{T=0}$, V^{*T} is positive for any $\bar{T} > 0$, reaching a value of V^{*N} under a drastic, content or market share VIE, which is satisfied only at $\bar{T} = N$. However, it is quite possible that the value of US exports is not maximized at $\bar{T} = N$.

[37]Since an increase in T (and US content) reduces Japanese content (i.e. $v'(T) = -c^T < 0$), we obtain $S^{*\prime}(X) > 0$, which implies that T satisfying $S(T) = S^*$ is unique and that $d\bar{T}/d\bar{S}^* > 0$.

[38]We have $dV^{*T}/dT = y^J c^*(T) + v^*(T)(\frac{dy^J}{dT})$ and $dy^J/dT < 0$ from (A.9) in Appendix A.

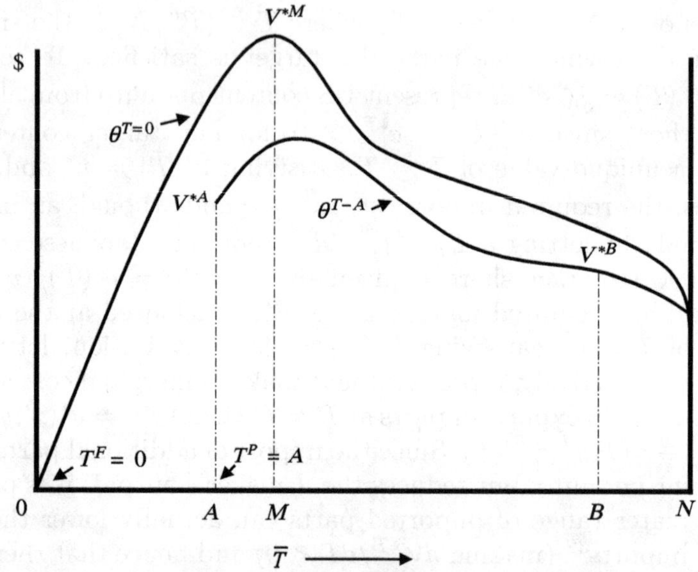

Figure 9.2. Value of US parts exports.

As Fig. 9.2 indicates, V^{*T} initially increases with $\bar{T}$, but, as the VIE becomes more restrictive, the reduction in the J-maker's output may eventually cause V^{*T} to fall, leading to an internal maximum,[39] shown at $\bar{T} = M$, in which the keiretsu continues to produce parts $i \geq M$. Obviously, in this case, a drastic VIE, or indeed any content or market-share VIE that requires $\bar{T} > M$, would not maximize the value of US exports.

As this possibility suggests, a content or market-share VIE, particularly if it is highly restrictive, may actually be counterproductive as a means of raising the total value of US parts exports. By contrast, a total-value VIE has the advantage of retaining more flexibility for the J-maker as to the range of parts to be imported. Consequently, faced with a total-value VIE requiring the same total value of US exports as would be achieved from a content or market-share VIE at

[39] A sufficient condition for an internal maximum is $dV^{*T}/d\bar{T} < 0$ at $\bar{T} = N$. Since an increase in US content per auto magnifies the reduction in the value of US exports from any given fall in y^3, it becomes more likely that $dV^{*T}/d\bar{T} < 0$ as $\bar{T}$ is increased.

some $\bar{T} > M$, the J-maker would import fewer parts (with $\bar{T} < M$) so as to satisfy the VIE based on a lower US content per auto, but a higher level of production. However, a less restrictive content or market-share VIE that can be satisfied for some $\bar{T} \leq M$ would have exactly the same effects as a total-value VIE with the same total value of US exports.

Since the J-maker's loss of output tends to be larger the greater the productivity, 8, an internal maximum for US exports is most likely if $\theta = \theta^{T=0}$ (see Fig. 9.2) and there are no (or very few) exports at free trade. However, an internal maximum is also possible for lower productivity settings in which a significant range of US parts are exported at free trade. As illustrated by the line from V^{*A} to V^{*N}, corresponding to $\theta^{T=A}$ and $T^F = A$, a lower productivity *8* results in a positive value of exports, V^{*A}, at free trade, but, the value of exports for any given T (below N) is reduced.[40] For $\theta = \theta^{T=A}$, a small VIE (of any type) at free trade would increase the value of US exports, but imposition of a more restrictive VIE, such as a content or market-share VIE at $\bar{T} = B$ or a drastic VIE at $\bar{T} = N$ would reduce the value of these exports below the level, V^{*A}, achieved at free trade. Moreover, at an even lower productivity (and higher free trade level of imports), it is possible that the value of US exports is maximized at free trade and hence would be reduced by any market-share VIE, small or large. As this last possibility indicates, a total-value VIE with any target above the free-trade level may actually not be feasible.

4. Voluntary Export Restraint (VER) or Tariff

This section develops the effects of a VER, or alternatively a tariff, applied to US imports of Japanese autos as they work through the vertically connected markets, taking into account the further linkages to relationship-specific investment within the keiretsu. This is of interest in itself since VERs and tariffs have commonly been applied to Japanese auto exports, but the main objective is to

[40]Since $(dV^{*T}/d\theta)\backslash_T = v^*(\bar{T})((dy^J/d\theta)_T) > 0$ (see (A.9)), V^{*T} is increasing in θ for any given $\bar{T} < N$. For a drastic VIE at $\bar{T} = N$, there is no effect of θ, since there is no J-supplier production or investment.

provide comparisons with the effects of VIEs so as to gain a better understanding of the implications of both types of policies for access to the Japanese market for imported parts.

A VER specifies a maximum value of imports of a particular good from a particular country. Since we have assumed that all of the final good is consumed in the US, a binding VER would limit keiretsu production and exports of autos to a given level, denoted by $\bar{y}^J$ where $\bar{y}^J < \bar{y}^J(\gamma)$. Since there is no change in the free trade relationships involving parts suppliers, similar to (17), the VER gives rise to a set of imported parts, $\Delta^y \equiv \{i : i < T^F \text{ for } T^F = T(\bar{y}^J; \theta)\}$ and a marginal cost $\gamma^y \equiv \gamma(T(\bar{y}^J; \theta)\bar{y}^J; \theta)$ for the J-maker where the superscript y represents equilibrium values under a VER. This analysis is easily adapted to apply to a tariff. Given Cournot behavior in the final-good market, a VER differs from a tariff only because the J-maker rather than the US government receives the quota rents. Thus if a specific tariff, denoted t, restricts the J-maker's output to y^{Jt}, then the J-maker's marginal cost is given by $\tau \equiv \gamma(T(y^{Jt}; \theta), y^{Jt}; \theta) + t$. Setting $y^{Jt} = \bar{y}^J$, then, since $\tau = \gamma^y + t$, the J-maker's marginal cost is higher by the amount of the tariff, but the import set, A^v, is unchanged and the tariff is otherwise equivalent to the VER.

We first show, in Proposition 3, that a VER (or tariff) applied to final-good exports has a market opening effect with respect to the range and market share of imported parts. This is due to the endogenous response of relationship-specific investment. By reducing the J-maker's output, the VER (or tariff) causes this investment to fall and, since production by some J-suppliers becomes unprofitable, $T(\bar{y}^J)$ and hence the range of imported parts, Δ^y, is increased. This increases US content per auto and hence US suppliers gain a larger share of the Japanese parts market. Not surprisingly, keiretsu investment is crucially important for this result. In standard models without relationship-specific investments, a reduction in a country's final-good output would reduce that country's demand for intermediate- goods, including the demand for imports with no systematic effect on the share of imported parts. However, just as for a content or market-share VIE, it is not necessarily the case that a VER would raise the total value of US exports of parts. If relationship-specific investment is sufficiently productive that there are no or very few exports of parts at free trade (i.e. if θ is close to

$\theta^{T=0}$, then the effect of the VER in causing some parts to be exported would dominate the effect of the VER in reducing the demand for any given part and the value of US parts exports would rise. By contrast, if the free-trade value of parts exports is large (due to low θ), the effect of the VER in reducing the overall demand for parts could dominate.

Proposition 3. *A VER (or tariff) reduces the J-maker's output, $\bar{y}^J$, and relationship-specific investment, k^J, but raises $T(\bar{y}^J)$, enlarging the set Δ^y of imported parts and the US share of the Japanese parts market.*

Although a VER (tariff) and a VIE (all three types) both enlarge the range of imported parts and reduce keiretsu output, comparing the magnitudes of these effects, we show in Proposition 4((i) and (ii)) that the VIE is more effective in raising the range of imported parts (for a given level of the J-maker's output) and the VER is more effective in reducing the J-maker's output (for a given range of imported parts). Consequently, for both comparisons, the VIE is more effective than the VER in raising the total value of US parts exports. Letting $V^{*y} = v^*(T)\bar{y}^J$ for $T = T(\bar{y}^J, \theta)$ represent the total value of US parts exports under the VER and comparing the policies for the same value of these exports (i.e. for $\overset{*y}{V} = y^{*T})_s$ i$_t$ follows, as set out in Proposition 4(iii), that the import set is larger and the J-maker's output is smaller under the VER than the VIE. For this last result, we assume that the policies raise the value of US exports in the relevant range, i.e. that:

$$dV^{*T}/dT > 0 \text{ for } T \in [T^F, \bar{T}] \quad \text{and} \quad dV^{*y}/dy^J < 0 \quad \text{for } y^J \in [y^J(\gamma^F), \bar{y}^J]. \tag{17}$$

Proposition 4. *(i) For $y^J(\gamma^F) = \bar{y}^J$ the VIE enlarges the import set by more than the VER or tariff (i.e. $\bar{T} > \bar{T}(\bar{y}^J)$). (ii) For $\bar{T} = \bar{T}(\bar{y}^J)$, the VER (tariff) restricts the J-maker's output by more than the VIE {i.e.$\bar{y}^J < y^J(\gamma^F)$). (iii) Assume* (17)*. If $V^{*y} = V^{*T}$, then the import set is larger and the J-maker's output is smaller under the VER (tariff) than the VIE} i.e. $T(\bar{y}^J) > \bar{T}$ and $\bar{y}^J < y^J(\gamma^F)$.*

The basic insight is that a direct reduction in the range of keiretsu produced parts has less of an effect in reducing relationship-specific investment and hence less of an effect in reducing output than the same reduction in keiretsu produced parts achieved by a direct cut in output. Consequently, for the same total value of US parts exports, the VER has more of an effect in reducing output and less of an effect in raising the range of imported parts than would a VIE. These results are not surprising based on the idea that the more direct policy should have more of an effect on the variable of interest (other things equal). Nevertheless, since the results depend on the relative strength of effects on investment decisions by many firms in response to policies applied at different stages of the vertical market, they are also not immediately obvious.

Both types of policies reduce the J-maker's profit due to the loss of output and relationship-specific investment. However, as Proposition 4(iii) suggests, for the same total value of US exports, a VER would reduce the J-maker's profit by more than the VIE and, as set out in Proposition 5, it follows that a credible threat of such a VER is sufficient to induce the J-maker to comply with the VIE without the need for further pressure from the Japanese government.[41]

Proposition 5. *Assume* (17). *If* $V^{*y} = V^{*T}$, *then the* J*-maker's profit is lower under the VER* (*tariff*), *making the credible threat of such a VER* (*tariff*) *sufficient to induce the* J*-maker to comply with the VIE.*

In Fig. 9.3, starting from free trade (at point F), the path of T (the import set) and output, y as a VIE or a VER become more restrictive is shown by the solid lines FH and FG, respectively. Each contour V^{*I}, V^{*II} or V^{*M} represents the combination of the range of imported parts and the J-maker's output required to produce a constant total value of US parts exports. The value of these exports

[41]There is empirical evidence that the US 1981 VER on autos raised the profits of Japanese automakers (see Ries, 1993). If our model were relaxed to allow for more keiretsu automakers or for autos to be strategic complements, then Japanese automakers could also benefit from the VER. However, the effects of a tariff are robust and Propositions 3 and 4 are a consequence of the reduction in investment as output falls and do not depend on the assumption of strategic substitutes or whether J-maker profit rises or falls.

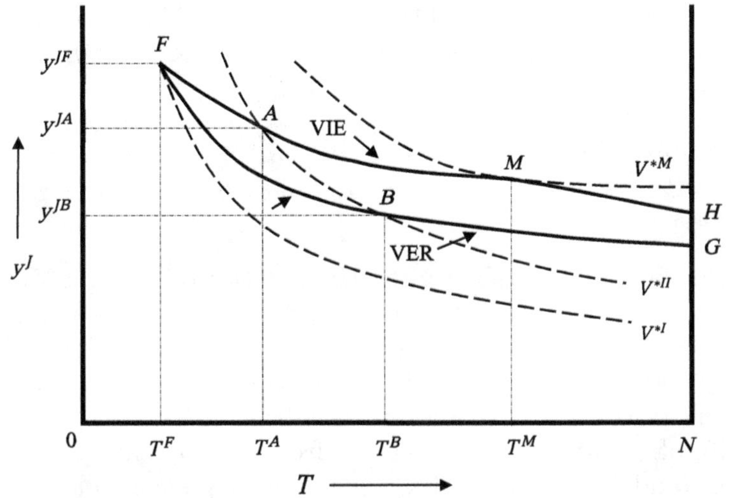

Figure 9.3. VIE vs. VER for a constant value of US parts exports.

ranges from V^{*I} at free trade to the maximum value, V^{*M}, achievable under a VIE at $\bar{T} = T^M$. The value, V^{*II}, is reached with either a VIE at $\bar{T} = T^A$ or with a VER at $\bar{y}^J = y^{JB}$. Since $y^{JA} >> y^{JB}$, and $T^A < T^B$, this illustrates Proposition 4(iii). Since points H and G at $T = N$ are above V^{*I} (and V^{*II}), Fig. 9.3 illustrates a case in which both a drastic VIE and VER would raise the value of exports above the free trade level. However, the value of US parts exports is maximized at an internal VIE corresponding to $\bar{T} = T^M$.

Finally, Proposition 6 examines the welfare implications of the VIE and VER policies. Consumer welfare is represented by the additively separable utility function, $u(Y) + Z$, where $u(Y)$ is the utility from autos and Z is the utility from a tradeable numeraire good produced under pure competition using labor alone. Supposing that all income is spent and that trade is balanced with all autos sold in the US, it follows, letting $\Phi = \Phi(T, y^J) \equiv \int_T^N \varphi(i, y^J)di$ denote the total profit of J-suppliers, that welfare in the US and Japan is, respectively, given by:

$$W^A \equiv u(Y) - P(Y)Y + \pi^A \quad \text{and} \quad W^J = \pi^J + \Phi. \qquad (18)$$

where $Y = y^A + y^J$ and $u'(Y) = P(Y)$. Aggregate or world welfare is $W = W^A + W^J$.

Proposition 6. *Assume* (17). *If a VIE and VER would achieve the same value of US parts exports, then,* (*i*) *US welfare is higher under the VIE than under the VER if* $dW^A/dy^J > 0$, *and lower if* $dW^A/dy^J < 0$. (*ii*) *Japanese welfare falls, but the reduction is less under the VIE than under the VER.* (*iii*) *If* $\gamma^* \geq \gamma$, *then world welfare falls, but the reduction is less under the VIE than under the VER.*

As Proposition 6(i) shows, the US is better off using a VIE than a VER to achieve a target value of US parts exports if and only if the reduction in auto imports would lower US welfare (i.e. iff $dW^A/dy^J > 0$). The import of fewer autos reduces consumer welfare by raising prices, but there is potentially an offsetting gain due to the shift of profits to the A-maker from the J-maker. Consumer interests tend to dominate if y^A is sufficiently small relative to y^J (which occurs if the A-maker has significantly higher costs)[42] and in this case, the VIE is preferred to the VER, but both policies reduce US welfare. For example, for the case of linear demand, the VIE dominates[43] if and only if $y^J > 2y^A$. By contrast, if the A-maker is an equal or lower cost producer at free trade (i.e. if $\gamma^* \leq \gamma$) then $y^J \leq y^A$ under free trade and the VER would dominate. Japanese welfare is reduced by both policies, but as shown in Proposition 6(ii), the VIE is the better policy for Japan, since it involves less of a reduction in Japanese output and relationship- specific investment due to a smaller increase in the range of imported parts. Finally, Proposition 6(iii) shows that if the J-maker is an equal or lower cost producer (i.e. if $\gamma^* \geq \gamma$ for y evaluated under the VIE or VER) then average world production costs are increased by a reduction in y^J, making the VIE the preferred policy from the point of view of world welfare.

From a more general perspective, the welfare results are related to the theory of non-economic objectives developed by Bhagwati and

[42]This could be due to higher US assembly costs. Dyer and Ouchi (1993, p. 53) state that for 1984, US assembly costs were higher than in Japan, both as a proportion of costs (23.1 vs. 15.7%) and in total.

[43]Using $\pi_A^A = 0$, we obtain $\frac{dW^A}{dy^J} = -YP'(dY/dy^J) + y^A P' = -YP'(dY^A/dy^J) - y^J P'$. For $P'' = 0$, it follows using (11) and (14) that $\frac{dW^A}{dy^J} = -P'(y^J - 2y^A)/2 > 0$ iff $y^J > 2y^A$.

Srinivasan (1969) and Bhagwati (1971) in a setting of pure competition. This is the idea that when variables are restricted to certain ranges by non-economic objectives, then the least cost way to achieve these objectives is to choose the policy intervention that directly affects the constrained variable. Although our results broadly satisfy this insight, there are significant differences caused by the presence of other distortions in the economy due to imperfect competition and incomplete contracts for relationship-specific investment. Thus from the US viewpoint, a VIE is only more cost effective than a VER in raising the total value of parts exports from the US if the secondary effects in other markets, such as the reduction in Japanese auto output due to the reduction in relationship-specific investment are actually undesirable.

5. Concluding Remarks

Although a number of studies have addressed the effects of market opening policies such as VIEs directed at Japan (see the Introduction), this literature has not considered how the response to such policies is affected by the special nature of keiretsu. In this paper we develop the effects of such policies in the context of the Spencer and Qiu (2001) model, which captures some important features of long-term keiretsu supply relationships,[44] including relationship-specific investments and bargaining over parts' prices. There are at least three reasons for examining market opening policies in a framework that explicitly incorporates keiretsu. First, keiretsu form a large part of the manufacturing base of the Japanese economy and are responsible for a substantial share of both imports and exports.[45] Secondly, much of the political pressure to impose market opening policies with respect to Japan arises from complaints that trade barriers are created by keiretsu practices and forms of organization.

[44]Some other important features, such as cross-share holding, are not directly modelled. However, provided asymmetric information continues to make relationship-specific investment non-contractible, cross shareholding or even full vertical integration would not fundamentally change the nature of results.

[45]In 1985, the keiretsu share of Japanese net income was around 32%, accounting for about 25% of annual sales, about 44% of exports and about 68% of imports in Japan (Lawrence, 1991, p. 313).

Finally, consideration of the keiretsu structure gives rise to some richer predictions as to the effects of trade policies directed at opening the Japanese market.

In keeping with the perception of a trade barrier, relationship-specific investment causes some parts not to be imported by Japan, despite lower production costs in the US. However, in contrast with the beliefs of those pushing for intervention, the model predicts that if Japan is forced to import more parts due to a VIE, this will reduce keiretsu efficiency (due to a loss of relationship-specific investment), causing a fall in production levels and in Japanese demand for parts. It is even possible that a VIE might reduce the total value of US parts exports. The model also predicts that any additional parts imported by Japan in response to market opening measures such as VIEs will tend to be the least important for production, such as tail pipes and seat covers. Finally, consideration of the keiretsu form of organization has significant implications for trade policies, such as VERs or tariffs, which restrict the exports of final goods from Japan. Since relationship-specific investment is reduced together with output, causing some keiretsu suppliers to be replaced by imports, a VER or a tariff has a market-opening effect with respect to the range of parts imported by Japan. Nevertheless, for any given value of US parts exported to Japan, the VIE proves to be less costly than the VER or tariff in terms of the loss of output and consumer welfare and also with respect to the loss of Japanese profit. If the increase in consumer welfare dominates the loss of US profit from greater imports of autos, then the VIE would also reduce US welfare, but by less than the VER or tariff.

Acknowledgements

This paper has benefited from presentation at Columbia University (Economics), New York University (Economics) and at the University of British Columbia (Commerce). We thank the participants and also an anonymous referee for helpful suggestions and comments. An earlier version of this paper was titled, 'Keiretsu and Relational Quasi Rents: Implications for VIEs and VERs'. Financial support was provided by the Social Sciences and Humanities Research Council of Canada.

Appendix A

A.1. *Comparative statics*

First, using (2) to sign the terms, a useful expression for the comparative statics is:

$$\lambda^i \equiv -\frac{(h'(k^i))^2}{h(k^i)} h''(k^i) > 0 \text{ for } k^i > 0 \qquad \text{(A.1)}$$

From differentiation of $d\varphi^i/dk^i = 0$ as in (6), we obtain $dk^i/d\sigma^i = -h'(k^i)/\sigma^i h"(k^i)$ and since $dr^i/d\sigma^1 = w^\circ \theta h(k^i)[l + \sigma^i h(k^i) dk^i/d\sigma^i)/h(k^i)$ from (1), it follows, using (A.l) and (2), that for $k^i > 0$,

$$dk^i/d\sigma^i = -h'(k^i)/\sigma^i h"(k^i) > 0 \text{ and } dr^i/d\sigma^i = r^i(1+\lambda^i)/\sigma^i > 0 \qquad \text{(A.2)}$$

Similarly from (6) for $k^i > 0$, using $\mathrm{d}r^i/dk^i = r^i h'(k^i)/h''(k^i)$ and (A.l), we obtain:

$$dk^i/dy^J = -h'(k^i)/y^J h"(k^i) > 0 \text{ and } dr^i/dy^J = r^i\lambda^i/y^J > 0 \qquad \text{(A.3)}$$

Also, since $\alpha \in (0,1)$, supposing that $T = T(y^J;\theta)$ satisfying (8) exists (i.e. $\varphi^0 = \varphi(0, y^J;\theta) \leq 0$), it follows from (8) using $\frac{\partial \varphi^T}{\partial y^J} = (1-\alpha)(r^T - \delta) > 0$ and (7) that:

$$dT/dy^J = -(r^T - \delta)\sigma^T/y^J r^T \sigma'^T < 0. \qquad \text{(A.4)}$$

In addition, it follows, using $\alpha > 0$ and $T < N$, that $\gamma = \gamma(T, y^J\theta)$ as in (9) has partial derivatives:

$$\frac{\partial \gamma}{\partial T} = \alpha(r^T - \delta) > 0, \frac{\partial \gamma}{\partial y^J} = -\alpha \int_T^N \left(\frac{dr^i}{dy^J}\right) di < 0. \qquad \text{(A.5)}$$

Next examining changes in θ, since $\frac{\partial \varphi^{TF}}{\partial \theta} = y^J(1-\alpha)r^T/\theta > 0$ (from (8) using $\frac{\partial \varphi^{TF}}{\partial k^T} = 0$), it follows using (7) that, for y^J held fixed and $\theta \in [\theta^{T=N}, \theta^{T=0}]$:

$$\frac{\partial T}{\partial \theta} = -\sigma(T)/\theta\sigma'(T) < 0. \tag{A.6}$$

Since $\frac{\partial k^i}{\partial \theta} = -h'(k^i)/\theta h''(k^i) > 0$ for $k^i > 0$ from (6) using λ^i as in (A.1), we also obtain $\frac{\partial r^i}{\partial \theta} = w^o \sigma^i h(k^i)[1 + \frac{\theta^i h'(k^i)(\frac{\partial k^i}{\partial \theta})}{h(k^i)}] = r^i(1+\lambda^i)/\theta > 0$ for $k^i > 0$. From (9), $\alpha > 0$ and $T < N$, this implies:

$$\frac{\partial \gamma}{\partial \theta} = -\alpha \int_T^N \left(\frac{\partial r^i}{\partial \theta}\right) di < 0. \tag{A.7}$$

From $\gamma^F = \gamma(T^F, y^{JF}; \theta), T^F = T(y^{JF}, \theta), y^{JF} = y^J(\gamma^F)$ and (13), using (A.5), (A.6) and (A.7) to sign expressions, we obtain $\frac{d\gamma^F}{d\theta} = \left[\left(\frac{\partial \gamma}{\partial T}\right)\left(\frac{\partial T}{\partial \theta}\right) + \frac{\partial \gamma}{\partial \theta}\right] H^O/H < 0$. Using (A.4), (A.6), (A.7) and (13), it follows that:

$$dT^F/d\theta = (dT/dy^J)(dy^J/d\gamma)(d\gamma^F/d\theta) + \frac{\partial T}{\partial \theta} < 0. \tag{A.8}$$

Finally, using $\gamma = \gamma(\bar{T}, y^J(\gamma); \theta)$, (13), (A.5) and (A.7), it follows that for $\alpha < 0$ and $T < N$:

$$\frac{dy^J}{d\bar{T}} = (dy^J/d\gamma)\left(\frac{\partial \gamma}{\partial \bar{T}}\right) / \left[1 - (dy^J/d\gamma)\left(\frac{\partial \gamma}{\partial yJ}\right)\right] < 0$$

$$\left(\frac{dy^J}{d\theta}\right)\Big|_{\bar{T}} = (dy^J/d\gamma)\left(\frac{\partial \gamma}{\partial \theta}\right) / \left[1 - (dy^J/d\gamma)(\frac{\partial \gamma}{\partial yJ})\right] > 0. \tag{A.9}$$

A.2. *A VIE and the order of parts' imports*

Since Propositions 1 and 2 involve consideration of the import of one additional part, we use the discrete version of the model. The proofs could be adapted for the continuous model, but to have a finite impact on marginal cost, this would require consideration of the import of a range of contiguous parts.

Proof of Proposition 1. Assume $\alpha > 0$. Letting $m^i = \alpha(r^i - \delta)$, for the discrete version of the model, parts $i = 1, 2.T^F - 1$ are imported at free trade and marginal cost at free trade is given (analogously to (9)) by:

$$\gamma^F = \gamma(T^F, y^{JF}, \theta) = C^*(N) - \sum_{T}^{fN} m^i + w^\circ. \tag{A.10}$$

Supposing the J-maker imports an additional part $j \in [T^F, N]$, then, taking stage 1 levels of k^i, y^J and y^A as given, this causes a direct increase, $m^j = c^{*J} - \gamma^J = \alpha(r^J - \delta) > 0$, in marginal cost (see (16)). Letting y^{J-j} denote equilibrium output when part j is imported and taking into account induced changes in k^i for $i \neq j$, the J-maker's marginal cost, denoted γ^{-j}, becomes:

$$\gamma^{-j} \equiv \gamma(T^F, y^{J-j}, \theta) + m^j \text{ where } y^{J-j} \equiv y^J(\gamma^{-j}). \tag{A.11}$$

Next, from (A.10) and (A.11), evaluating $\partial\gamma/\partial y^J$ for a given T^F at some y^J between y^{J-j} and y^{JF}, evaluating dy^J/dy^j at some γ between γ^{-j} and γ^F and applying the mean value theorem, we can express $\gamma(T^F, y^{J-j}, \theta) - \gamma(T^F, y^{JF}, \theta) = (\partial\gamma/\partial y^J)(y^{J-j} - y^{JF})$ for $y^{J-j} - y^{JF} = dy^J/d\gamma(\gamma^{-j} - \gamma^F)$. Since $\frac{d\gamma}{dy^J} < \frac{\partial\gamma}{\partial y^J} < 0$, we obtain $1 - (\frac{\partial\gamma}{\partial y^J})(\frac{\partial y^J}{\partial\gamma}) > 0$ from (13) and using (A.10) and (A.11), it follows that for $a > 0$, a commitment at stage 0 to import part $j \in [T^F, N]$ causes the following increase in the J-maker's marginal cost at stage 1:

$$\gamma^{-j} - \gamma^F = m^j / \left[1 - \left(\frac{\partial\gamma}{\partial y^J}\right)\left(\frac{\partial y^J}{\partial\gamma}\right)\right] > 0. \tag{A.12}$$

Since $\frac{\partial y^J}{\partial\gamma} < 0, y^J$ falls causing k^i and r^i to fall. Also, from (3), using (11), (13) and (14), we obtain, $\frac{d\pi^J}{d\gamma} = -y^J\left[1 - p'\left(\frac{dy^A}{dy^J}\right)\left(\frac{\partial y^J}{\partial\gamma}\right)\right] = -\frac{y^J p'(2p' + y^J p'')}{H^\circ} < 0$ and $\frac{d\pi^A}{d\gamma} = y^A p'\left(\frac{\partial y^J}{\partial\gamma}\right) > 0$

The proof of Proposition 2 uses the following result, which we refer to as Lemma 1.

Lemma 1. *The direct increase m^j/c^{*j} in the J-maker's marginal cost per unit of the increase in US value added from the import of part j is strictly increasing in j for all $j \in [T^F, N]$.*

Proof: Letting $\sigma^s > \sigma^j$ for parts $js \in [T^F, N]$ it follows using $m^j = \alpha(r^j - c^j)$ from (16), that $m^s/c^{*s} - m^j/c^{*j} = \alpha\Omega/c^{*j}c^{*s} > 0$ iff $\Omega = c^{*j}(r^s - \delta) - c^{*s}(r^j - \delta) = (c^{*s} - c^{*j})\delta + c^{*j}r^s - c^{*s}r^j > 0$. Adding and subtracting $c^{*j}r^jc^s/c^j$, we obtain $c^{*j}r^s - c^{*s}r^j = c^{*j}(r^s - r^jc^s/c^j) - (c^{*s}c^j - c^{*j}c^s)(r^j/c^j)$. Since $\delta = c^j - c^{*j} = c^s - c^{*s}$, it follows that $c^{*s}c^j - c^{*j}c^s = (c^{*s} - c^j)\delta$ and hence that:

$$\Omega = \{c^{*s} - c^{*j})\delta(1 - r^i/c^i) + c^{*j}r^s(r^s - r^jc^s/c^j). \qquad \text{(A.13)}$$

Using $r^i = w^\circ\sigma^i\theta h(k^i)$ and $\sigma^i = c^i/C(N)$, we have $r^s - r^jc^s/c^j = w^\circ\sigma^s\theta h(k^s) - h(k^j)) > 0$ for $\sigma^s > \sigma^j$ and since $c^i - r^i > 0$ (no free lunch from (1)), we obtain $\Omega > 0$ from (A.13). □

Proof of Proposition 2. Since profit, $\pi^J = \pi^J(\gamma) = y^J(P(y) - \gamma)$ for $y^J = y^J(\gamma)$, depends only on γ and $d\pi^J/d\gamma < 0$, the J-maker imports additional parts to minimize the increase in γ subject to achieving the VIE target. Thus the first additional imported part $j \in [T^F, N]$ is chosen to minimize the increase in marginal cost, $\gamma^{-j} - \gamma^F$, per unit of the contribution of part j to achieving the VIE target.

(i) For a content VIE, since part $j \in [T^F, N]$ contributes c^{*j} towards the target, it follows, using (A. 12), that part j is chosen to minimize:

$$\begin{aligned} M^j &\equiv (\gamma^{-j} - \gamma^F)/c^{*j} \\ &= (m^j/c^{*j})/[1 - (\partial\gamma/\partial y^J)(dy^j/d\gamma)] \qquad \text{(A.14)} \end{aligned}$$

where $\partial\gamma/\partial y^J$ is evaluated holding $T = T^F$ fixed. Since from Lemma 1 and (A.14), M^J is strictly increasing in /, the first part imported is $j = T^F$, which has the lowest cost-share in $[T^F, V]$. If the VIE is not satisfied, the same argument can be repeated with respect to a second part, $j \in [T^{F+1}, N]$, but with part $j = T^F$ now included in the initial import set. In (A.14), $\partial\gamma/\partial y^J$ is then evaluated holding T fixed at $T^F + 1$.

(ii) For market-share VIEs, denoting the free trade levels of US and Japanese content (at marginal cost) by $v^{*F} = v^*(T^F) = \sum_1^{T^F-1} c^{*i}$ and $v^F \equiv v(T^F) \equiv \sum_T^{FN} c^i$ respectively, the corresponding US market share is $S^F \equiv v^{*F}/\omega^F$ where $\omega^F \equiv v^{*F} + v^F$. If just one part $j \notin \Delta^F$ is imported in addition to Δ^F, the US market share becomes $S^{F+j} \equiv (v^{*F} + c^{*J})/(w^F - \delta)$

and the contribution towards satisfying the VIE is $S^{F+J} - S^F$. Consequently, part $j \in [T^F, N]$ is chosen so as to minimize:

$$M^{Sj} \equiv (\gamma^{-j} - \gamma^F)/(S^{F+j} - S^F). \tag{A.15}$$

Using $M^j \equiv (\gamma^{-j} - \gamma^F)/c^{*j}$ from (A.14), we can express (A.15) in the form $M^{Sj} = M^j X^{Sj}$ for $X^{Sj} \equiv c^{*J}/(S^{F+j} - S^F)$ and since $S^{F+J} - S^F = (v^{*F} + c^{*j})/(\omega^F - \delta) - v^{*F}/\omega^F = (c^{*J}\omega^F + v^{*F}\delta)/\omega^F(\omega^F - \delta)$, we obtain:

$$X^{Sj} = \omega^F(\omega^F - \delta)/[\omega^F + v^{*F}(\delta/c^{*j})] > 0. \tag{A.16}$$

Next, letting part s satisfy $\sigma^s > \sigma^j$ for $j, s \in [T^F, N]$, it follows that the J-maker will choose parts j in increasing order of cost-share on $j \in [T^F, N]$ if and only if $M^{Ss} - M^{Sj} = (M^s - M^j)X^{Ss} + M^j(X^{Ss} - X^{Sj}) > 0$. Since $X^{Sj} - X^{Ss} > 0$ from (A.16) and $c^{*s} > c^{*j}$ for $s > j$ and $M^s - M^j > 0$ from the proof of (i), the result follows.

(iii) For total-value VIEs, letting $V^{*F} \equiv v^{*F} y^J(\gamma^F)$ denote the total value of US exports at free trade, if part $j \notin \Delta^F$ is imported in addition to A^F, the total value of US exports becomes $V^{*F+j} = (v^{*F} + c^{*j})y^J(y^{-j})$ and the contribution towards satisfying the VIE is $V^{*F+J} - V^{*F}$. Hence part $j \in [T^F, N]$ is chosen to minimize $M^{Vj} \equiv (\gamma^{-j} - \gamma^F)/(V^{*F+J} - V^{*F})$. Using $d^2y^J/(d\gamma)^2 = 0$ from (13) and (11) for $P''(Y) = 0$ (linear demand), we have $y^J(\gamma^{-j}) - y^J(\gamma^F) = (dy^J/d\gamma)(\gamma^{-j} - \gamma^F)$ and, using (18A), we obtain $M^{Vj} = (\gamma^{-j} - \gamma^F)/(V^{*F+J} - V^{*F}) = 1/[v^{*F}(dy^J/d\gamma) + y^J(\gamma^{-j})/M^j]$, Since $M^s > M^J$ from the proof of (i) and $y^J(\gamma^{-s}) < y^J(\gamma^{-j})$, it follows that $y^J(\gamma^{-s})/M^S < y^J(\gamma^{-j})/M^j$ and hence $M^{Vs} > M^{Vj}$, proving the result.

A.3. *Effects of trade policies*

Proof of Proposition 3. Since trade in parts is not restricted by a VER or tariff, parts are imported in the same order (i.e. increasing cost-share) as under free trade. Since $dk^i/d\bar{y}^J > 0$ for $k^i > 0$ from (A.3) and $dT(\bar{y}^J)/d\bar{y}^J < 0$ from (A.4), a reduction in $\bar{y}^J$ due to a VER reduces k^i and increases Δ^y leading to a rise in US content per auto and market-share in the same way as for a VIE. For the tariff, from $\tau = \gamma(T, y^J; \theta) + t$ for $y^J = y^J(\tau)$ and $T = T(y^J(\tau), \theta)$, it follows, using (13) that $d\tau/dt = 1/[1 - (d\gamma/dy^J)(dy^J/dy)] > 0$

and $dy^J/dt = (dy^J/d\tau)(d\tau/dt) < 0$. Setting $y^J(\tau) = \bar{y}^J$, the results follow for the tariff as for the VER. □

Proof of Proposition 4. We first show that if the VIE is binding at free trade (i.e. if $\bar{T} > T^F = T(y^J(\gamma^F))$, then the marginal supplier producing part $i = \bar{T}$, earns a strictly positive profit. This requires that $\bar{T} < T(y^J(\gamma^T))$ for $y^T = \gamma(y^J(\gamma^T), \bar{T})$, which is not obvious since the loss of investment makes $y^J(\gamma^T) < y^J(\gamma^F)$ and $T(y^J(\gamma^T) > T^F$. Since $dT/d\bar{T} = (dT/dy^J)(dy^J/d\gamma)(d\gamma^T/d\bar{T})$ using $d\gamma^T/d\bar{T} = (\partial\gamma/\partial y^J)/[1 - (\partial\gamma/\partial y^J)(dy^J/dy)]$, we obtain $\bar{T} < T(y^J(\gamma^T))$ if $dT(y^J(\gamma^T)/dT < 1$, which holds if $(dT/dy^J)(dy^J/d\gamma)(d\gamma/d\bar{T}) < 1 - (\partial\gamma/\partial y^J)(dy^J/dy)$. This last expression reduces to $1 - (\partial\gamma/\partial y^J)(dy^J/dy) > 0$, which is the stability condition (13). Since for a VER (or tariff with $y^J(\tau) = y^{-J}$, the parts market is not constrained, we obtain:

$$\varphi(\bar{T}, y^J(\gamma^T)) > 0 \text{ and } \varphi(T(\bar{y}^J), \bar{y}^J) = 0. \tag{A.17}$$

(i) To show $\bar{T} > T(\bar{y}^J)$ for $y^J(\gamma^T) = \bar{y}^J$, since $dy^J/d\bar{T} < 0$ from (A.9), it follows that for any $\bar{y}^J < y^J(\gamma^F))$, part $i = \bar{T}$, satisfying $\bar{y}^{J=}y^J(\gamma^T)$, is unique. Since $d\varphi(i, y^J)/\text{di} > 0$ from (7), it follows, setting $\bar{y}^J = \text{y}^J(\gamma^T)$ in (A. 17), that $\bar{T} > T(\bar{y}^J)$.

(ii) To show $y^J(\gamma^T) > \bar{y}^J$ if $\bar{T} = T(\bar{y}^J)$, since $dT(\bar{y}^J)/d\bar{y}^J < 0$ for $\bar{y}^J > y(\gamma^F)$ from Proposition 3, it follows that for any $T \in [T^F, N]$, there exists a unique value of $\bar{y}^J$ such that $\bar{T} = T(\bar{y}^J)$. Since $d\varphi(iy^J)/dy^J > 0$, it follows, setting $T(\bar{y}^J) = \bar{T}$ in (A.17) that $y^J(\gamma^T) > \bar{y}^J$. (iii) To show that $T(\bar{y}^J) > \bar{T}$ and $\bar{y}^J < y^J(\gamma^T)$ for $V^{*y} = V^{*T}$, we have $T(\bar{y}^J) < \bar{T}$ since if $T(\bar{y}^J) = T$, then $V^{*y} < V^{*T}$ from Proposition 4(ii). To rule out $T(\bar{y}^J) < \bar{T}$, suppose initially that $T(\bar{y}^J) = T$. Since $dT/d\bar{y}^J < 0$ from (A.4), we must raise either $\bar{T}$ or $\bar{y}^J$ to obtain $T(\bar{y}^J) < T$, which, using $dV^{*T}/d\bar{T} < 0$ and $dV^{*y}/d\bar{y}^J < 0$ from (17), again implies $V^{*y} < V^{*T}$. Letting $V^*(T, y^J) = v^*(T)y^J$, it follows using the mean value theorem, that $V^{*T} - V^{*y} = (dV^*/dT)(\bar{T} - T(\bar{y}^J)) + (dV^*/dy^J)(y^J(\gamma^T) - y^J)$, where $dV^*/dT = c^*(T)y^J > 0$ and $dV^*/dy^J = v^*(T) > 0$ for intermediate values of y^J and T. Since $\bar{T} - T(\bar{y}^J) < 0$ at $V^{*T} = V^{*y}$, this implies $\text{y}^J(\gamma^T) > \bar{y}^J$.

Proof of Proposition 5. Letting $\pi^{Jy} = \pi^J(\bar{y}^J T(\bar{y}^J))$ and $\pi^{JT} = \pi^J(y^J(\gamma^T)\bar{T})$ represent J-maker profit under the VER and VIE, respectively, and using the mean value theorem, it follows that $\pi^{Jy} - \pi^{JT} = (\frac{\partial \pi^J}{\partial y^J})(\bar{y}^J - y^J(\gamma^T)) + (\partial \pi^J/\partial T)(T(\bar{y}^J) - \bar{T}$, where, using $\pi^J_J > 0$ (from (10) and $\bar{y}^J < \bar{y}^J(\gamma)$), we obtain $\frac{\partial \pi^J}{\partial y^J} = \pi^J_J + y^J[p'(dy^A/dy^J) - (d\gamma/dy^J)] > 0$ for strategic substitutes. Since $\partial \pi^J/\partial T = -y^J(d\gamma/dT) < 0$, it follows using Proposition 4(iii) that $\pi^{Jy} - \pi^{JT} < 0$ for $V^{*T} = V^{*y}$. A tariff would reduce π^J by more than a VER.

Proof of Proposition 6. (i) Since $W^A = W^A(\bar{y}^J)$ for a VER and $W^A = W^A(y^J(\gamma^T))$ for a VIE, using the mean value theorem, we obtain $W^A(y^J) - W^A(y^J(\gamma^T)) = (dW^A/dy^J)(y^J - y^J(\gamma^T))$, where dW^A/dy^J is evaluated at some y^3 between $\bar{y}^J$ and $y^J(\gamma^T)$. Since $\bar{y}^J - y^J(\gamma^T) < 0$ for $V^{*y} = V^{*T}$ from Proposition 4(iii), we obtain $W^A(\bar{y}^J) - W^A(y^J(\gamma^T) < 0$ if $dW^A/dy^J > 0$ and $W^A(\bar{y}^J) - W^A(y^J(\gamma^T) > 0$ if $dW^A/dy^J < 0$. (ii). To show that $W^J = \pi^J + \Phi$ is lower under a VER than a VIE for $V^{*y} = V^{*T}$, since π^J is lower from Proposition 5, it remains to show that Φ is lower. Since $d\Phi/dy^J = \int_T^N (\frac{\partial \varphi^i}{\partial y^J})di$ and $d\Phi/dT = -\varphi^T < 0$ the result follows using Proposition 4(iii). (iii) From (18) and (3), world welfare, $W \equiv W^A + W^J$, can be expressed as $W(y^J, T) = u(Y) - \gamma^w Y + \Phi$ where $\gamma^w \equiv y^*(y^A/Y) + \gamma(y^J/Y)$ represents the average world cost of production. Since $dy^A/dy^J < 0$ from (14), we obtain $d(y^J/Y)/dy^J > 0$ and, using (A.5), it follows that for $\gamma^* \geq \gamma$, $\frac{\partial \gamma^w}{\partial y^J} = -(\gamma * - \gamma)d(\frac{y^J}{Y})/dy^J > 0$. Since $dY/dy^J > 0$ and $d\Phi/dy^J > 0$, this implies $dW/dy^J = (P - \gamma^w)(dY/dy^J) - Y(d\gamma^w/dy^J) + d\Phi/dy^J > 0$ for $\gamma * > \gamma$. Also, using $d\gamma^w/dT = (y^J/Y)(d\gamma/dT) > 0$, we obtain $dW/dT = -Y(d\gamma^w/dT) - \varphi^T < 0$. Using the mean value theorem and Proposition 4(iii), it then follows that $W(\bar{y}^J, T(\bar{y}^J)) - W(y^J(\gamma^w), \bar{T}) = (dW/dy^J)(\bar{y}^J - y^J(\gamma^T)) + (dW/dT)(T(\bar{y}^J) - \bar{T}) < 0$ for $\gamma * \geq \gamma$.

References

Aoki, M., 1988. Information, Incentives and Bargaining in the Japanese Economy. Cambridge University Press, Cambridge, UK.

Asanuma, B., 1989. Manufacturer-supplier relationships in Japan and the concept of relation-specific skill. Journal of the Japanese and International Economies 3, 1–30.

Belderbos, R., Sleuwaegen, L., 1998. Tariff jumping DFI and export substitution: Japanese electronic firms in Europe. International Journal of Industrial Organization 16 (5), 601–638.

Bernier, L., Borrus, A., Bremner, B., Holstein, W.J., 1995. Rougher trade: The US-Japan chasm widens. Business Week 17 (July), 16–18.

Bhagwati, J.N., Srinivasan, T.N., 1969. Optimal intervention to achieve non-economic objectives. Review of Economic Studies 36 (1), 27–38.

Bhagwati, J.N., 1971. Generalized theory of distortions and welfare. In: Bhagwati, J.N., Mundell, R.A., Jones, R.W., Vanek, J. (Eds.), Trade, Balance of Payments and Growth. Papers in International Economics in Honor of Charles C. Kindleberger. North-Holland, Amsterdam, pp. 69–90, Chapter 4.

Bhagwati, J.N., 1987. VERs, quid pro quo DFI and VIEs: Political-economy-theoretic analysis. International Economic Journal, 1–14.

Bjorksten, N., 1994. Voluntary import expansions and voluntary export restraints in an oligopoly model with capacity constraints. Canadian Journal of Economics 1, 446–457.

Branstetter, L., 2000. Vertical keiretsu and knowledge spillovers in Japanese manufacturing: An empirical assessment. Journal of the Japanese and International Economies 14, 73–104.

Church, G.J., 1995. Launch of an economic cold war. TIME Domestic 146 (July 3), 1.

Cronshaw, M.B., Markusen, J.R., 1995. The theory and consequences of results-oriented trade policy. In: Deardorff, A.V., Levinsohn, J., Stern, R.M. (Eds.), New Directions in Trade Theory. University of Michigan Press, Ann Arbor, MI, pp. 295–326.

Dodwell Marketing Consultants, 1990. The Structure of the Japanese Auto Parts Industry. Dodwell Marketing Consultants, Tokyo.

Dyer, J.H., Ouchi, W.G., 1993. Japanese-style partnerships: Giving companies a competitive edge. Sloan Management Review 35 (1), 51–63.

PEER, 1993. Reject managed trade. Far Eastern Economic Review 4 (November), 2.

Fung, K.C., 1991. Characteristics of Japanese industrial groups and their potential impact on US-Japan trade. In: Baldwin, R. (Ed.), Empirical Studies of Commercial Policy. University of Chicago Press, Chicago, pp. 137–168.

Greaney, T.M., 1996. Import now! An analysis of market-share voluntary import expansions (VIEs). Journal of International Economics 40 (1–2), 149–163.

Head, K., Ries, J., Swenson, D., 1995. Agglomeration benefits and location choice: Evidence from Japanese manufacturing investments in the United States. Journal of International Economics 38, 223–247.

Irwin, D.A., 1996. The US-Japan semiconductor trade conflict. In: Krueger, A.O. (Ed.), The Political Economy of Trade Protection. University of Chicago Press, Chicago, Chapter 1.

Krishna, K., 1989. Trade restrictions as facilitating practices. Journal of International Economics 26, 251–270.

Krishna, K., Morgan, J., 1998. Implementing results-oriented trade policies: The case of the US-Japanese auto-parts dispute. European Economic Review 42 (5), 1443–1467.

Krishna, K., Roy, S., Thursby, M., 1998. Implementing market access. Review of International Economics 6 (4), 529–544.

Krishna, K., Roy, S., Thursby, M., 2001. Can subsidies for MARs be procompetitive. Canadian Journal of Economics 34 (1), 212–224.

Lawrence, R.Z., 1991. Efficient or exclusionist? The import behavior of Japanese corporate groups. Brookings Papers on Economic Activity 1, 311–330.

Levinsohn, J., 1997. Carwars: Trying to make sense of US-Japan trade frictions in the automobile and automobile parts markets. In: Feenstra, R.C. (Ed.), The Effects of US Trade, Protection and Promotion Policies. University of Chicago Press, Chicago, pp. 11–32.

McLaren, J., 1999. Supplier relations and the market context: A theory of handshakes. Journal of International Economics 48 (1), 121–138.

McMillan, J., 1996. Why does Japan resist foreign market-opening pressure. In: Bhagwati, J., Hudec, R. (Eds.), Harmonization and Fair Trade. MIT Press, Cambridge, MA, pp. 515–541.

New York Times, 1995. Japan buys more US auto-parts. New York Times (National Edition) CXCLIV (50), 122, July 14.

Qiu, L.D., Spencer, B.J., 2000. Keiretsu and relationship-specific investment: Implications for marketopening trade policy. IBTF working paper 00–04.

Rauch, J.E., 2002. Business and social networks in international trade. Journal of Economic Literature, forthcoming.

Ries, J.C., 1993. Windfall profits and vertical relationships: Who gained in the Japanese auto industry from VERs. Journal of Industrial Economics XLI (2), 259–276.

Rubenstein, J.M., 1990. Japanese motor vehicle producers in the USA: Where and why. Focus 1 (Summer), 7–11.

Saxonhouse, G.C., 1989. Differentiated products, economies of scale and access to the Japanese market. In: Feenstra, R.C. (Ed.), Trade Policies for International Competitiveness. University of Chicago Press, Chicago, pp. 145–174.

Spencer, B.J., Qiu, L.D., 2001. Keiretsu and relationship-specific investment: A barrier to trade? International Economic Review 42 (4), 871–901.

Chapter 10

How Do Technical Barriers to Trade Influence Trade?*

Abstract

This paper empirically estimates the trade effects of technical barriers to trade (TBT) based on all TBT notifications from 105 World Trade Organization (WTO) countries during 1995–2008. The paper adopts a modified two-stage gravity model to control for both sample selection bias and firm heterogeneity bias. It was found that a country's TBT notifications decrease other countries' probability of exporting, but increase their export volumes. The result can be explained by the TBT's differential effects on the fixed and variable cost of export, and consumer confidence. It was further found that (i) a developing country's TBT have significant effects on other developing countries' exports, but no significant effects on the developed countries' exports, (ii) a developed country's TBT have significant effects on the exports from both types of countries, and (iii) exports from developed countries are affected by a developed country's TBT more seriously than a developing country's TBT.

1. Introduction

The multilateral negotiations under the World Trade Organization (WTO) have successfully liberalized trade, especially with the large scale and widespread tariff reductions. However, non-tariff

*This chapter is reproduced from *Review of International Economics*, 20(4), 691–706, 2012, with permission from Wiley.

barriers (NTBs) have arisen to substitute the traditional trade protection, namely tariffs. Among various forms of NTBs, the so-called technical barriers to trade (TBT), which mainly include standards and technical regulations, are relatively new, but have become more and more important.[1] TBT are introduced for a range of reasons (for example, for environmental protection, safety, national security and consumer information), and they vary from country to country in terms of their magnitude and product coverage. If TBT are set properly, they can promote trade, but they can also be used as an excuse for protection when they are set at a high level. The WTO's TBT Agreement tries to ensure that the imposed standards and technical regulations "do not create unnecessary obstacles to trade."[2]

The first objective of this paper is to empirically examine how TBT affect trade at the global level. All WTO members are required to keep each other informed of their new or changed regulations each year through the WTO. Table 10.1 shows the TBT notifications made by WTO members every year from 1995 to 2008. There are several observations.

First, TBT are widespread and significant. A total of 105 WTO members made 9,913 TBT notifications to the WTO during that period. Second, although TBT are in general rising, there exists a large variation (yearly changes) even at the aggregate level. The total number of TBT notifications reached an earlier peak at the number 794 in 1997, but then dropped to 538 in 2001, and finally rose to the new height at 1,251 in 2008. Third, developed countries were the main users of TBT in the earlier years, but in recent years developing countries introduced roughly equal number of TBT as the developed countries. The TBT introduced by these two groups of countries could be different and these two groups of countries

[1]Technical regulations arise from the norms that are set by policymakers and so are compulsory while standards are only optional. These two types of TBT may have different effects on trade. While some existing studies focus on standards and some focus on technical regulations, we consider all types of TBT. For the definitional differences between these two types of TBT, see "Difference between a technical regulation and a standard" at http://www.wto.org/english/tratop-e/tbt_e/tbtinfo-e.htm.

[2]See http://www.wto.org/english/docs_-e/1egal_-e/17-tbt.pdf.

Table 10.1. TBT notifications by country groups.

Year	1995	1996	1997	1998	1999	2000	2001	2002	2003	2004	2005	2006	2007	2008	Total
Developed Countries' Share(%)	0.87	0.73	0.75	0.68	0.58	0.58	0.52	0.50	0.49	0.50	0.47	0.44	0.47	0.51	0.56
Developing Countries' Share(%)	0.13	0.27	0.25	0.32	0.42	0.42	0.48	0.50	0.51	0.50	0.53	0.56	0.53	0.49	0.44
Total No.	365	479	794	648	669	611	538	576	695	611	771	875	1030	1251	9913

Sources: Calculated based on the WTO TBT notification database.

could be affected by the same TBT differently in their exports to the TBT-adopting countries. The second objective of this paper is to empirically examine the differential effects of TBT on the developing and developed countries.

Given the increasing importance and the complexity of TBT, researchers have started to pay attention to understanding the effects of TBT on trade. Most studies ask *whether* TBT promote or restrict trade, and find that TBT generally restrict trade flows.[3] Unlike those studies, the main focus of the present paper is on *how* TBT affect trade and whether there is any *difference* in their effects on the developing and developed countries. To this end, the heterogeneous-firm approach of Melitz (2003) and Helpman *et al.* (2004) is used to empirically investigate and understand the TBT impacts on bilateral trade. When Country A imposes TBT, it raises both the fixed cost and variable cost to exporters of other countries who want to sell their goods to Country A because, for example, exporters have to improve their product quality to meet the new standards, which raises the variable production costs. In addition, exporters have to make material investment in inspection equipment, quarantine process, and the coordination of technique experts to pass the examination, imposing a high fixed cost for exporting to the TBT imposing country.[4] Hence, the cost-raising aspect of TBT reduces both the export extensive margin (i.e. the number of exporting countries) and intensive margin (i.e. the export volume or value of each exporting country). However, TBT inform the consumers that the imported products have met specific standards (health, safety, and others) and have passed the regulations, which promotes imports because consumers become more confident about the products. In this case, TBT help correct market failure because of incomplete information. This information-revealing aspect of TBT raises consumers' demand, thereby raising both the extensive and intensive margins. Therefore, how trade is affected by TBT becomes an empirical issue.

[3]Bao and *Oiu* (2010) have a review of the empirical studies of TBT's impacts on trade. While most studies find TBT trade restricting, some find it trade promoting in some sectors in some countries.

[4]See Baldwin (2001), Fischer and Serra (2000), Ganslandt and Markusen (2001), and Maskus and Wilson (2001) for more explanations.

Conducting such an empirical study at the global scale, however, seems implausible because the Melitz (2003) model is based on firm-level export decisions, whereas the available trade data in most countries are at country level (or industry level at most).[5] Fortunately, Helpman *et al.* (2008) have developed a methodology that makes the mission of the present paper possible. Sufficiently abundant bilateral trade data have the capacity to capture heterogeneous firms' decisions. Because of the existence of fixed cost of export, only a subset of firms finds it profitable to serve foreign markets. Some find it profitable to serve all markets, whereas others find it profitable to serve only some export markets. Therefore, one can infer the characteristics of a firm from its market behavior. Technically, this is done using a two-stage gravity model. Following such a procedure, predicting the impact of TBT on firms' export decisions (extensive margin) through the changes in their international trade value (intensive margin) becomes possible. The present study is based on TBT notifications of all countries to the WTO and bilateral trade data from 1995 to 2008. TBT are found to reduce the export extensive margin (i.e. the export probability), but raise the export intensive margin. Furthermore, developed and developing countries are found to be different with regard to their TBT effects on other countries, as well as how they are affected by TBT of other countries. Specifically, TBT of a developed country reduce the imports from all countries. In contrast, TBT of a developing country reduce the imports from other developing countries, but have insignificant effects on the imports from developed countries. TBT of a developed country reduce the extensive margin of all other countries, but increase their intensive margin. In contrast, TBT of a developing country have no significant

[5]A direct way to estimate the TBT effects on trade using heterogeneous-firm models is of course to use firm level datasets. However, firm-level data are available at much smaller scale and only for some special analysis. The World Bank has surveyed 619 firms in 17 developing countries and collected data on the impact of product standards on their production costs and export ability; however, such a dataset is too small and narrow for the present study. Chen *et al.* (2008) used the World Bank's survey data, which provide firm level data but only from a small sample of countries, to examine the impact of adapting to foreign standards on export decision and export market diversity.

effects on either the extensive margin or intensive margin of exports from developed countries.

This present paper has four distinguishing features. First, TBT represent one of the most difficult non-tariff measures to quantify, as argued by Deardorff and Stern (1998). The present paper is the first to use all TBT notifications of individual countries to the WTO to measure the degree of TBT and analyze the TBT effects on trade at the global level.[6] This complements the existing studies that focus on some firms, some industries, or some countries. Second, the TBT effects are compared based on whether the TBT-imposing country is a developed or developing country and whether the exporting countries are developed or developing countries. Third, a modified two-stage gravity model is used to estimate the TBT effects on trade, correcting the potential selection bias and firm heterogeneity bias. As a result, how TBT affect trade through extensive and intensive margins can be explained. Fourth, we use country-level TBT data to examine TBT effects on a country's total imports, as compared with TBT and trade at industry-level. Different industries are affected by TBT differently; thus, investigating how a specific industry's TBT affect the industry's trade is important. However, country-level TBT and country-level trade are chosen in the current study for two important reasons. On the one hand, from 1995 to 2008, approximately 70% TBT notifications fail to specify the coverage of the harmonized commodity description and coding system (HS) products. Thus, using TBT notifications with industry information would result in loss of many data. On the other hand, although TBT of one industry affect the industry's trade, they also affect trade of other industries if they are substitutes or complements. Therefore, exploring the effects of all TBT on a country's total trade is important.

The current study fits in the growing literature on TBT and trade. The above description regarding the features of the present paper provides a clear distinction between this paper and other papers in the literature, as mentioned below. Using the World

---

[6]Similar to the current study, Disdier *et al.* (2008) made use of all TBT notifications to the WTO. However, they focus on the agricultural product trade, only consider exporters to the OECD, and construct the TBT variable differently.

Bank survey data (firm-level in some developing countries), Maskus *et al.* (2005) estimated the cost increase in developing countries for complying with the stricter developed countries' product standards. Chen *et al.* (2008) used the same survey data to examine the impact of adapting to foreign standards on export decision and export market diversity. These two papers study the TBT impacts on trade using firm-level data from a small sample of countries with focus on the standards. Unlike these papers, the present study uses country-level bilateral trade data on all TBT in all WTO member countries.

Without the availability of firm-level data, some researchers use bilateral trade data of some industries in some countries to examine the marginal effects of some types of TBT on exports. For example, Chevassus-Lozza *et al.* (2005) investigated the impact of EU's import qualification on trade of agricultural products between the new and old EU members. With the similar empirical strategy as Chevassus-Lozza *et al.* (2005), Essaji (2008) examined the effects of the US technical regulations in agriculture, mining industry, and manufacture industry on the US trade pattern. Some other papers use the firm-heterogeneity model more explicitly and completely. Czubala *et al.* (2009) studied the impact of the EU standards on African exports of textiles, clothing, and footwear. Portugal-Perez *et al.* (2009) extended the above analysis to study electrical products. Shepherd (2007) studied the impact of EU product standards on their import of textiles, clothing, and footwear sectors. All these papers model the export decisions of a firm (positive or zero value) using the Heckman procedure (Stage 1 in our model), and so correct for sample selection bias, but do not follow Helpman *et al.* (2008) to correct firm heterogeneity bias (Stage 2 in our model).

Baller (2007) analyzed the effects of regional TBT liberalization agreements in electronic communication and medical machinery industries between the Organisation for Economic Co-operation and Development (OECD) members and non-members on trade from countries in and outside the agreements. Xiong and Beghin (2011) studied the influence of the EU aflatoxin maximum residue limit (MRL) on African exports of groundnut products. Similar to the current paper (in methodology), these two studies also use the Helpman *et al.* (2008) model in their heterogeneous firm framework; however, they examine only the trade effect of some special TBT in a small number of countries, as opposed to the general TBT at the global level used in the present paper. Chen and Mattoo (2008) extended Baller's (2007) analysis by using a larger dataset covering trade of 42 countries at the SITC 3-digit level of manufacturing industries from 1986 to 2001.[7]

All aforementioned studies found evidence on the negative (or insignificant, in one case) effects of both the extensive and intensive margins. In contrast, the present paper finds positive effects on the intensive margin. There are two possible reasons for the difference in the findings between the current study and theirs. One is the coverage: those studies covered only a small set of countries for some sets of products, whereas the current study includes (almost) all countries and all products. The second possible reason is the methodology: the current study follows Helpman *et al.* (2008) in using the two-stage estimation procedure, whereas most of other studies did not.

2. The Impacts of TBT on Trade

2.1. *The gravity model and data*

Gravity models are widely used to estimate trade volumes. It is generally agreed that bilateral trade volumes (or values) are determined by the economic size of the trading countries and the multilateral resistance, which includes trade policies, bilateral geographical distance, common borders, the proximity of language, the membership of free trade zones, and others (Anderson and van Wincoop, 2003). Accordingly, we use the following gravity model to estimate the effect of TBT on bilateral trade flows.

$$\begin{aligned}\ln(EX_{iit}) = \alpha_i + \alpha_j + \alpha_t + \beta\ln(1 + TBT_{jt-1}) + \gamma_1 \ln gdp_{it} \\ + \gamma_2 \ln gdp_{it} + \gamma_3 \ln dist_{ij} + \gamma_4 contig_{ij} \\ + \gamma_5 comlang_{ij} + \gamma_6 colony_{ij} + \gamma_7 smctry_{ij} + \mu_{ijt}. \quad (1)\end{aligned}$$

[7]Though Chen and Mattoo (2008) explicitly mentioned that they adopted the Helpman *et al.* (2008) procedure, they did not implement it exactly. Specifically, they did not correct for firm heterogeneity in the second stage, which is the important feature that differentiates the Helpman *et al.* two-stage model from a standard Heckman model.

In equation (1), the dependent variable is EX_{ijt}, which is the value of country i's export to country j in year t. Our key explanatory variable is TBT_{jt-1}, which represents the importing country's (country j) introduction of TBT in year $t - 1$. We also include a set of control variables: gdp_{it} and gdp_{jt} are the gross domestic production level of country i and country j in year t, respectively; $dist_{ij}$ is the geographical distance between the two countries; $contig_{ij}$, $comlang_{ij}$, $colony_{ij}$, and $smctry_{ij}$ are dummies, representing respectively the existence of common borders, common official language, colonial history (i.e. whether countries i and j had colonial ties in the past), and whether the trading partners have belonged to the same country group.[8] Since our analysis is based on panel data, we use the year fixed effect (α_t) to control for the determinants of trade values that only change with time. In addition, we use the importing country fixed effect (α_j) and exporting country fixed effect (α_i) to control for those time-invariant country characteristics.

There are a number of issues that require a discussion. The first issue is how to measure TBT. Bora *et al.* (2002) provided a review of various approaches to quantify non-tariff measures, including TBT. Conventionally, there are two approaches, which are the frequency index and coverage ratio. In Bao and Oiu (2010), we have applied those approaches to the study of China's TBT impacts on China's imports.[9] Different from those approaches, in the present paper, we use a country's total number of TBT notifications to the WTO in every single year as the quantitative measures of the country's TBT.

The second issue is the use of multilateral resistance variable. As pointed out by Anderson and van Wincoop (2003, 2004), a correct specification of a gravity model should include the multilateral resistance variable. In our setting with panel data, the multilateral

[8]This variable equals one if countries used to or do belong to the same state or the same administrative entity for a long period and zero otherwise. Examples include countries that belonged to the same empire (Austro-Hungarian, Persian, Turkish), countries that have been divided (Czechoslovakia and Yugoslavia), and countries that belonged to the same administrative colonial area.

[9]Disdier *et al.* (2008) used three approaches: a dummy to indicate whether a country has TBT notification to the WTO, the frequency index, and the tariff equivalent.

resistance can be captured by the importer–year and exporter–year fixed effects. However, inclusion of these fixed effects will result in the drop of all time-variant country variables such as GDP and only bilateral, time-invariant variables will remain. Unfortunately, our TBT variable is not a bilateral time-invariant variable, but a country specific general variable and time variant. Thus, the TBT variable will also be dropped automatically if we introduce the multilateral resistance variable. For this reason, we use exporter fixed effect, importer fixed effect, and year fixed effect, instead of exporter—year and importer–year fixed effects. Many existing studies in the literature avoid using such multilateral resistance variables; and we are no exception. For example, Helpman *et al.* (2008) also used country fixed effect and year fixed effect instead of country-year fixed effects in their estimation of trade flows.

The third issue is that TBT_{jt} may take the value zero for some countries in some years. Hence, we use $\ln(1 + TBT_{jt-1})$ instead of $\ln(TBT_{jt-1})$ in our model.

Finally, an importing country may introduce more TBT when it faces more import competition. This will result in the reverse causality problem when we try to analyze the effects of TBT on trade. To partly solve this possible reverse causality problem, we use the lagged TBT (one year before t) rather than TBT in the same year as trade flows.

With regard to the data sources, we obtain bilateral trade data from United Nations Commodity Trade Statistics Database (Comtrade database), which is available from http://comtrade.un.org/*db*/, and the TBT notification data from the WTO's *TBT Annual Reviews of the Implementation and Operation of the Agreement.* For the control variables, the GDP data can be found from the US Department of Agriculture Economic Research Services International Macroeconomic Data Set, and other bilateral relationship data can be obtained from the CEPII database (the Centre d'Etudes Prospectives et d'Informations Internationales in France database). In model (1), the unit of EX_{ijt} is current year US dollar, the unit of GDP is billion US dollars of the year 2005, and the unit of distance is kilometer. Note that we do not use constant year dollar for EX_{ijt} because Comtrade provide current dollar value of trade statistics and we control for year fixed effect in our model which can partly control for inflation.

Table 10.2. Descriptive statistics of the key variables.

Variables	Mean	Std Dev.	Min	Max
ln EX	16.0269	3.8371	0.0000	26.6303
ln gdp	3.8714	2.2105	−1.2958	9.5853
ln dist	8.7465	0.8476	4.0877	9.9010
ln(1+TBT)	1.0506	1.3035	0.0000	5.6560
contig	0.0190	0.1367	0.0000	1.0000
comlang	0.1360	0.3428	0.0000	1.0000
colony	0.0161	0.1259	0.0000	1.0000
smctry	0.0099	0.0990	0.0000	1.0000

Our study covers 105 countries and regions from 1995 to 2008. These 105 countries are those available in the WTO's TBT notification database, which includes 41 developed countries and 64 developing countries.[10] They represent 85% of the global trade and in this sense our study largely exhibits the TBT effects on global trade. The 14-year, 105-country sample gives us 152, 880 observations ($105 \times 104 \times 14$).

Table 10.2 presents the descriptive statistics of the relevant variables, and Table 10.3 gives the Pearson coefficients between different variables. In Table 10.3 (and also Tables 10.4 and 10.5), $\ln gdp\_ex$ and $\ln gdp\_im$ are the log value of the exporting country's GDP and the importing country's GDP, respectively. We observe that there is no significant correlation between the TBT notifications and the other control variables in column (1), which, together with the large sample characteristics of the dataset, indicates that there is no multicolinearity to bias our estimation.

There are 47,317 zero observations, amounting to 30.95% of the sample data, as some countries do not trade with some others in some

[10]In fact, there are 106 countries in the WTO TBT report database, but only 105 of them have data available. The data for Qatar are unavailable and therefore dropped. According to the World Bank's standards in 2008, countries can be classified to three groups depending on income per capita. We treat the high income group as the developed countries, and the middle income and low income groups as the developing countries. By this definition, among our 105 countries in the dataset, 41 are developed countries and 64 are developing countries.

Table 10.3. Pearson coefficients between each pair of variables.

	(1)	(2)	(3)	(4)	(5)	(6)	(7)	(8)	(9)
(1) ln *EX*	1								
(2) ln *gdp_ex*	0.5890	1							
(3) ln *gdp_im*	0.3896	−0.1412	1						
(4) ln *dist*	−0.2555	0.0603	0.0122	1					
(5) ln(1 + *TBT*)	0.1891	−0.0635	0.4816	0.0714	1				
(6) *contig*	0.1821	0.0193	0.0392	−0.3755	0.0069	1			
(7) *comlang*	0.0362	−0.0976	−0.0778	−0.1383	−0.0078	0.1375	1		
(8) *colong*	0.1325	0.0734	0.0764	−0.0344	0.0064	0.0517	0.2103	1	
(9) *smctry*	0.0904	−0.0475	−0.0331	−0.3048	−0.005	0.4158	0.1621	0.0565	1

Table 10.4. Effects of TBT on trade.

	Country level data			Industry level data	
	(1)	(2)	(3)	(4)	(5)
	EX_dummy	ln *EX*	ln *EX*	*EX_dummy*	ln *EX*
	Probit	NLS	Polynomial	Probit	Polynomial
ln *gdp_ex*	0.028	1.0795***	1.036***	0.707***	0.267***
	(0.0714)	(0.0904)	(0.0897)	(0.0108)	(0.0245)
ln *gdp_im*	0.803***	0.0342	−0.142	0.505***	0.656***
	(0.0773)	(0.154)	(0.152)	(0.0102)	(0.0240)
ln *dist*	−0.414***	−0.746***	−0.701***	−0.634***	−0.509***
	(0.0178)	(0.0742)	(0.0717)	(0.00122)	(0.00946)
contig	−0.501***	0.935***	1.107***	0.228***	0.123***
	(0.103)	(0.168)	(0.151)	(0.00606)	(0.00983)
comlang	0.362***			0.470***	
	(0.0279)			(0.00292)	
colony	−0.141	1.014***	0.926***	0.254***	0.183***
	(0.121)	(0.110)	(0.0996)	(0.00757)	(0.0125)
smctry	0.170	0.677***	0.501***	0.528***	0.301***
	(0.127)	(0.189)	(0.173)	(0.00690)	(0.0148)
ln(1+*TBT*)	−0.0216***	0.0303***	0.0279***		
	(0.0061)	(0.00754)	(0.00759)		
CR				−0.0000176	0.000368**
				(0.0000808)	(0.000163)
$\hat{\eta}^*_{ijt}$		−1.442***	0.135		1.980***
		(0.183)	(0.218)		(0.0180)
δ		1.973***			
		(0.160)			
$\hat{z}^*_{ijt}$			6.305***		7.176***
			(0.466)		(0.0435)
$\hat{z}^{*2}_{ijt}$			−1.010***		−1.530***
			(0.166)		(0.0153)
$\hat{z}^{*3}_{ijt}$			0.0474**		0.118***
			(0.0202)		(0.00174)

(*Continued*)

Table 10.4. (*Continued*)

	Country level data			Industry level data	
	(1)	(2)	(3)	(4)	(5)
	EX_dummy	ln *EX*	ln *EX*	*EX_dummy*	ln *EX*
	Probit	NLS	Polynomial	Probit	Polynomial
N	152,880	105,563	105,563	5,658,510	2,112,584
Pseudo or adj. R^2	0.453	0.988	0.776	0.499	0.523

Notes: Exporter, importer and year fixed effect. The *Comlang* variable is excluded variable in all second stage specifications; Robust standard errors in parentheses (clustered by country pairs). $^{*}p < 0.10$; $^{**}p < 0.05$; $^{***}p < 0.01$. CR is the coverage ratio (%) of TBT. Industry fixed effect in columns (4) and (5) are added.

years. This large number of null data could make the ordinary least squares (OLS) estimation inconsistent. Simply abandoning the zero trade data will cause sample selection bias and will over estimate the impact of TBT on trade values. Helpman *et al.* (2008) attributed the absence of trade to exporting firms' self selection behavior. They developed a model of international trade with heterogeneous firms to predict positive as well as zero trade flows across pairs of countries. Their model yields a generalized gravity equation that accounts for asymmetric trade flows, zero trade observations, and the overlooked extensive margin from new firms entering export markets. The estimation of their generalized gravity model does not require firm-level data and can be implemented via a two-stage modified Heckman procedure. We adopt this method to estimate the TBT effects on trade.

The two-stage model is captured by the two regression equations (2) and (3) given below.

Stage 1: The sample selection model for export probability (Probit estimation)

$$\begin{aligned} EXdummy_{ijt} &= \alpha_i + \alpha_j + \alpha_t + \beta \ln(1 + TBT_{jt-1}) \\ &\quad + \gamma GravityControls_{ijt} + \mu_{ijt} \end{aligned} \tag{2}$$

Table 10.5. Differential effects of TBT on trade by country groups.

	Stage 1 (Probit estimation)			Stage 2 (NLS estimation)		
	All	Developed	Developing	All	Developed	Developing
	(1)	(2)	(3)	(4)	(5)	(6)
Exporting countries	*ex_dummy*	*ex_dummy*	*ex_dummy*	ln *EX*	ln *EX*	ln *EX*
ln *gdp_ex*	0.0284	−0.854***	0.437***	1.080***	10.51***	0.556***
	(0.0714)	(0.157)	(0.0813)	(0.0904)	(1.881)	(0.147)
ln *gdp_im*	0.803***	0.700***	0.897***	0.0315	−6.305***	−0.352*
	(0.0774)	(0.146)	(0.0956)	(0.153)	(1.536)	(0.202)
ln *dist*	−0.414***	−0.221***	−0.558***	−0.746***	1.005**	−0.446***
	(0.0178)	(0.0317)	(0.0180)	(0.0742)	(0.493)	(0.102)
contig	−0.501***	−0.568***	−0.443***	0.934***	5.927***	1.398***
	(0.103)	(0.123)	(0.124)	(0.168)	(1.226)	(0.190)
comlang	0.362***	0.0398	0.449***			
	(0.0279)	(0.0617)	(0.0313)			
colony	−0.141	0.00787	−0.263*	1.014***	0.598***	1.343***
	(0.121)	(0.165)	(0.141)	(0.110)	(0.149)	(0.184)

(*Continued*)

Table 10.5. (*Continued*)

	Stage 1 (Probit estimation)			Stage 2 (NLS estimation)		
	All	Developed	Developing	All	Developed	Developing
	(1)	(2)	(3)	(4)	(5)	(6)
Exporting countries	*ex_dummy*	*ex_dummy*	*ex_dummy*	ln *EX*	ln *EX*	ln *EX*
smctry	0.170	0.240	−0.0211	0.677***	−1.796***	0.831***
	(0.127)	(0.194)	(0.145)	(0.189)	(0.544)	(0.233)
ln(1 + *TBT*)	−0.0130*	−0.00108	−0.0148*	0.0290***	0.00935	0.0392***
	(0.00720)	(0.0132)	(0.00894)	(0.00851)	(0.00961)	(0.0130)
im_devped	−1.482***	−0.930***	−7.786***	−1.888***	−68.98***	32.98***
	(0.184)	(0.320)	(1.017)	(0.629)	(17.14)	(1.246)
ln(1 + *TBT*)* *im_devped*	−0.0258**	−0.0542**	−0.0154	0.00774	0.578***	−0.00758
	(0.0126)	(0.0225)	(0.0153)	(0.0142)	(0.121)	(0.0201)
$\hat{\bar{\eta}}^*_{ijt}$				−1.440***	−11.40***	−1.181***
				(0.183)	(2.196)	(0.189)
δ				1.972***	11.43***	2.371***
				(0.160)	(2.190)	(0.162)
Observations	152,880	59,696	93,184	105,563	47,409	58,154
Pseudo or adjusted R^2	0.453	0.507	0.427	0.988	0.827	0.707

Notes: Exporter, importer, and year fixed effect. The *Comlang* variable is excluded variable in all second stage specifications; Robust standard errors in parentheses (clustered by country pairs). $^{*}p < 0.10$; $^{**}p < 0.05$; $^{***}p < 0.01$.

Stage 2: The trade flow equation [non-linear least squares (NLS) estimation]

$$\begin{aligned}\ln(EX_{ijt}) = {} & \alpha_i + \alpha_j + \alpha_t + \beta \ln\left(1 + TBT_{jt-1}\right) \\ & + \gamma GravityControls_{ijt} + \theta \hat{\bar{\eta}}^*_{ijt} \\ & + \ln\left\{\exp\left[\delta\left(\hat{z}^*_{ijt} + \hat{\bar{\eta}}^*_{ijt}\right)\right] - 1\right\} + \varepsilon_{ijt}, \end{aligned} \tag{3}$$

where γ is a vector of coefficients, $\hat{\bar{\eta}}^*_{ijt} = \varphi(\hat{z})/\Phi(\hat{z})$ is the inverse Mills ratio, and $\hat{z} = \Phi^{-1}(\hat{p})$, in which $\hat{p}$ are the estimates from the Probit regression in stage 1.

The first stage, equation (2), is the sample selection model, whereby the dependent variable is a dummy variable representing the existence of country i's exports to country j in year t, and the independent variables are the same as those in regression equation (1), which consist of the TBT notification variable and the standard control variables in any gravity model, all together denoted by vector $GravityControls_{ijt}$. Since the dependent variable is a 0-1 dummy, we can identify the probability of one country's export to another and the effects of TBT on the extensive margin of trade. The second stage, equation (3), is the trade flow equation, whereby the dependent variable is the log value of country i's exports to country j in year t. There are two important points to make. On the one hand, the vector $GravityControls_{iit}$ in equation (3) is obtained from that in equation (2) by excluding one variable, $Comlang_{ii}$ (common language), for the exclusion restriction purpose.[11] On the other hand, we construct two variables using the estimates of the Probit model as additional regressors in the second-stage estimation. One is the inverse Mills

[11] Helpman *et al.* (2008) controlled for the trade effect of the fraction of exporting firms in the second stage, which can be consistently estimated from the first stage of the Heckman two-stage procedure. The parameter identification requires that at least one explanatory variable included in the selection equation be excluded from the outcome equation. A variable that affects the probability of observing a non-zero flow between two countries, but not the value, would qualify. Helpman *et al.* (2008) used two variables, the regulation cost of firm entry and common religion, to achieve this objective. They also tried to use the common language variable as the excluded variable and obtain identical results. We let the common language dummy variable serve this role.

ratio, which will be used to correct for the sample selection bias in the standard Heckman procedure, and the other is an expression that controls for unobserved firm heterogeneity, that is, the effect of trade frictions and country characteristics on the proportion of exporters. This allows us to estimate the TBT effect on the intensive margin using the sample of all country-pairs with positive trade flows.

Helpman *et al.* (2008) show that a transformation of equation (3) that will give consistent estimates is

$$\ln\left(EX_{ij^t}\right) = \alpha_i + \alpha_j + \alpha_t + \beta \ln\left(1 + TBT_it - 1\right) + \gamma GravityControls_{ij}t + \theta\bar{\eta}^*_{ijt} + \overline{\overline{z}}^*_{ijt} + \overline{\overline{z}}^{*2}_{ijt} + \overline{\overline{z}}^{*3}_{ijt} + \varepsilon_{ijt} \quad (4)$$

where the polynomial in $\hat{\overline{z}}^*_{ijt} = \hat{z}^*_{ijt} + \hat{\overline{\eta}}^*_{ijt}$ is an approximation of an arbitrary and increasing function of the latent variable z_{ijt}.

2.2. *Regression results*

We follow Helpman *et al.* (2008) to estimate the above TBT models through a two-stage procedure. The first column in Table 10.4 reports Probit estimates of equation (2) using the Maximum Likelihood method. The second column reports the estimates of equation (3) using NLS and the third column provides the polynomial results of equation (3) using OLS.

In our second-stage estimation, the magnitude and significance of the coefficients obtained in polynomial specification in column (3) are very similar to that of the NLS estimation in column (2), indicating that our estimation is not very sensitive to the functional form specifications. Most control variables are significant and have the signs consistent with the existing studies and theories. The supply ability of exporting countries measured by their respective GDP has a positive and significant effect on bilateral trade value. The importing country's GDP has a positive effect on trade (although it is not significant when the estimation is done using NLS and polynomial). If the trading partners are closer to each other, share a common border, have colonial history, or belong to the same country group, their bilateral trade is larger. The variables that impact export value (intensive margin) are not exactly the variables that impact export probability (extensive margin). As we can see from column (2), higher demand capacity of the importer, shorter distance, common language will increase the probability of country i's export to country j. However, common border reduces the probability of trade, which is also found by Helpman *et al.* (2008), who attribute this to the effect of territorial border conflicts that suppresses trade between neighbors. Whether the two countries have a colonial tie with each other and whether they belong to the same country group does not have significant impact on trade probability.

We now turn to our core variable, i.e. TBT. In the presence of fixed export costs, firms make two decisions with regard to international entry, whether to enter the foreign market (via exports) and if yes, how much to export. As Helpman *et al.* (2008) pointed out, despite the fact that the theoretical model has firm heterogeneity, we do not need firm-level data to estimate the gravity equation. This stems from the fact that the features of marginal exporters can be identified from the variation in the characteristics of the destination countries. That is, for every country i, its exports to different countries vary according to the characteristics of the importing countries. As a result, there exist sufficient statistics, which can be computed from aggregate data, to predict the value of exports of heterogeneous firms. Since TBT raise both fixed costs and variable costs of exports, they reduce both the number of exporters entering the international market (extensive margin) and the total value of export by each exporter (intensive margin). However, TBT also have the information revelation or quality assurance feature, which raises consumers' confidence and hence boosts demand. This tends to have a positive effect on the intensive margin. As we can see in Table 10.4, in general TBT significantly reduce the probability of exporting in stage 1 owing to the fixed compliance cost as we expected [column (1)]. However, TBT significantly raise the export value in stage 2 [columns (2) and (3)]. This finding implies that the negative cost-raising effect is dominated by the positive information-revealing effect.[12] It is also possible that TBT raise the fixed costs

[12]In Bao and Oiu (2010), we found that TBT is more likely to have a trade promotion effect for products that are more sophisticated and the quality of which is less known to consumers. In these products, the information-revealing effect is more likely to offset the cost-raising effect.

of export relatively more than the variable costs. In any case, we will expect that the exporting countries experience a reallocation of resources towards the remaining exporters.

We summarize the above analysis in Result 1 below.

Result 1. An increase in *a country's TBT notifications to the WTO reduces other countries' export extensive margins to this country (i.e. the probability of exporting), but raises other countries' export intensive margins to this country (i.e., the export values).*

2.3. *Robustness checks*

In this subsection, we discuss the robustness of our results established in the previous subsections. Generally, we find that Result 1 is robust.

First, we try different periods of lagged TBT. TBT are importing country specific. It is very unlikely that an importing country's TBT, which apply to imports from all other countries, are set in response to unexpected large bilateral imports from a particular exporting trade partner. Therefore, we do not expect any serious endogeneity problem and so in the previous subsections we use 1-year lagged TBT to correct for any potential inverse causality between TBT and trade. Using lagged independent variable to circumvent the endogeneity problem is common, although not perfect, in the literature. For example, Fernandes (2007) examined whether increased exposure to foreign competition generates productivity gains for manufacturing plants, and she used lagged tariff to address the issue that the government may raise current protection in response to lobbying by firms in less productive industries. Following Fernandes (2007), Njikam and Cockburn (2011) examined whether trade liberalization fosters total factor productivity growth in the manufacturing sector in Cameroon and they control for the endogeneity of trade policy using one-period lagged liberalization variables. Topalova and Khandelwal (2011) adopted the same approach in examining the Indian case.

As one-period lagged TBT may not completely solve the endogeneity problem, it is useful, as a robustness check, to try to use more-period lagged TBT as they are less likely to be affected by current trade flows. Using two-period lagged TBT, we obtain the same qualitative result stated in Result 1: TBT have negative (−0.0174) and significant effects on extensive margins, and positive (0.0201) and significant effects on intensive margins.

Second, we try industry level data. Recall that Result 1 is obtained based on the country-level TBT data and country-level bilateral trade flows. Obviously, TBT are defined at industry or product level in any country. An industry's TBT affect imports of the industry and some related industries, but not necessarily all other industries. Therefore, it might be more accurate to use industry-level TBT and industry-level trade data in our regression analysis. We did not do this in the previous subsections mainly because of the lack of data. In the period of 1995-2008, about 70% of TBT notifications did not specify their coverage of HS products.[13] Hence, running a regression based on the remaining 30% of the data is likely to result in severe bias. Nevertheless, it is still interesting to have a robustness check with industry-level data based on this small sample. To this end, following the literature (see Bao and Qiu, 2010), we first use TBT notifications at HS4 product level to construct and calculate the TBT coverage ratios at HS2 product level and then regress the industrial-level bilateral trade flows on this coverage ratio.[14] The empirical analysis shows that TBT coverage ratio has a negative, but not significant, effect on export extensive margins (the first stage result, as shown in column 4 in Table 10.4), and positive and significant effect on export intensive margins (the second stage result, as shown in column (5) in Table 10.4). This basically confirms Result 1.

3. The Differential Effects of TBT on Trade: Developing vs Developed Countries

We have just shown the TBT effects on trade in all countries on average. However, different countries may have different TBT and their trade may be affected by other countries' TBT differently. Consumers in developed countries may be more concerned about the

[13] Only 67 WTO TBT-notifying countries have provided some product-level TBT information for the period of 1995–2008.

[14] Details about the construction of the TBT coverage ratios are available upon request from the authors.

health standard of food products while consumers from developing countries may be more sensitive to prices. Producers from developed countries may have better technologies and resources to adjust their products to meet the new TBT from the importing countries than producers from developing countries. Products from developed countries may have already met the new standards imposed by importing countries and so are not affected.

To explore whether there are such differential effects, we run three regressions, respectively, following the same two-stage procedure as in Section 2. First, we introduce a dummy variable $im_{\_devped}$ which equals 1 when the importing country is a developed country and 0 otherwise. We include this dummy variable and its interaction with the TBT variable in our regression. The coefficient of the interaction term, $\ln(1 + TBT) * im_{\_devped}$, would enable us to test whether or not the effects of TBT from developing countries and from developed countries are significantly different. The results of the two-stage estimation are reported in columns (1) and (4) in Table 10.5. We observe that in stage 1 [column (1)], TBT from both developing and developed countries reduce the probability (extensive margin) of all other countries' exporting [the sign of $\ln(1 + TBT)$ is negative and the sign of $\ln(1+ TBT) * im_{\_devped}$ is also negative], but TBT from a developed country reduce other countries probability of exporting more than TBT from a developing country [the sign of $\ln(1 + TBT) * im_{\_devped}$ is negative].

In stage 2 [column (4)], we find that the trade value effects (intensive margin) of TBT from developing countries and those of TBT from developed countries are both positive and significant [the sign of $\ln(1+TBT)$ is positive and the sign of $\ln(1+TBT)*im_{\_devped}$ is also positive], but these two effects are not significantly different [the estimate of $\ln(1 + TBT) * im_{\_devped}$ is not significant].

Next, we further divide all exporting countries into two groups, developed and developing countries, and run the regression using data of exporting countries from each group separately. The regression results for developed countries are reported in columns (2) and (5) in Table 10.5, and those for developing countries are in columns (3) and (6) in Table 10.5.

When we focus on exporters from developed countries, we observe that they are affected by TBT from a developing country and TBT from a developed country differently. On the one hand, from column (2), a developing country's TBT do not significantly reduce the developed countries' export probability [the sign of $\ln(1+TBT)$ is not significant although negative]; on the other hand, from column (5), a developing country's TBT do not raise the developed countries' export value either [the sign of $\ln(1+TBT)$ is not significant although positive]. In contrast, from column (2), a developed country's TBT significantly reduce the export probability of other developed countries [the coefficient of $\ln(1+TBT)*im\_{devped}$ is negative and significant while the sign of $\ln(1+TBT)$ is negative]; and, from column (5), a developed country's TBT significantly raise the export value of other developed countries [the coefficient of $\ln(1+TBT)*im\_{devped}$ is positive and significant while the sign of $\ln(1+TBT)$ is positive]. Thus, the effect of a developing country's TBT and that of a developed country's TBT on developed countries' exports are different significantly in statistic sense, in both stages.

When we focus on exporters from developing countries, we find that they are affected by TBT from a developing country and TBT from a developed country similarly. Based on column (2), we observe that a developing country's TBT significantly reduce other developing countries' export probability; and based on column (6), we observe that a developing country's TBT raise other developing countries export value. As the interaction term is not statistically significant in columns (2) and (6), we know that the corresponding effects of a developed country's TBT on developing countries' export probability and export values are not significantly different from those of a developing country's TBT.

We can summarize the above discussions in Table 10.6 and in the following two results.

RESULT 2. *A developing country's TBT notification to the WTO does not have significant effects on developed countries' exports (both extensive and intensive margins). In all other cases, a country's TBT notification to the WTO reduces the other countries' probability of exporting (extensive margin), but raises the export value of the exporting countries (intensive margin).*

RESULT 3. *A developed country's TBT notification to the WTO has stronger effects on other developed countries' exports (both extensive and intensive margins) than a developing country's TBT*

Table 10.6. Summary of the effects of TBT on trade.

	Exporting countries		
Importing countries	Developing	Developed	All
Developing	(−, +)	(0, 0)	(−, +)
Developed	(−, +)	(−, +)	(−, +)

Notes: The first sign in the bracket is the effect on extensive margin while the second sign is the effect on intensive margin. 0 represents no significant effect.

notification to the WTO. The TBT effects from developed and developing countries on developing countries' exports are not significantly different.

Here is a possible explanation for the above comparisons results. On the one hand, TBT raise the costs to all exporters, from developed and developing countries, because the exporters have to meet the higher standards and go through the technical examination procedure; but TBT raise the costs of the developing countries' exporters more than those of the developed countries, because producers from developed countries have already produced high standard products and therefore the cost for upgrading them is not high, but it will take a lot more effort for the producers from developing countries to bring their products up to the standard. On the other hand, developing countries' technical standards are relatively lower than the developed countries, so TBT imposed by a developing country might influence other developing countries but not the developed countries, and so TBT imposed by developed countries has stronger effects than TBT imposed by developing countries. However, since the TBT from developing or developed countries are already a big cost to developing countries' exporters, whether the TBT are from a developed or a developing country makes no significant difference with regards to their impacts on developing countries' exports.

4. Conclusions

The present study analyzes the TBT effects on trade based on all countries' TBT notifications to the WTO in the period of 1995–2008.

Using a two-stage gravity model, we find that generally TBT reduce the export extensive margins, but raise the export intensive margins. We further find that the TBT effects are different depending on the country's economic development level. Specifically, TBT of a developed country reduce extensive margins of all other countries, but increase their intensive margins. In contrast, a developing country's TBT have no significant effects on either the extensive or intensive margins of exports from developed countries although they reduce the extensive margins and raise the intensive margins of export from other developing countries. We hope that more research studies along this line will be conducted to offer us a better understanding of the trade effects of TBT necessary for trade negotiations in the WTO.

References

Anderson, James E and Eric van Wincoop, "Gravity with Gravitas: A Solution to the Border Puzzle," *American Economic Review* 93 (2003): 170–92.

Anderson, James E. and Eric van Wincoop, "Trade Costs," *Journal of Economic Literature* 42 (2004): 691–751.

Baldwin, Richard, "Regulatory Protectionism, Developing Nations and a Two-tier World Trade System," CEPR discussion paper 2574 (2001).

Baller, Silja, "Trade Effects of Regional TBT Liberalization: A Heterogeneous Firms Approach World Bank policy research working paper 4124 (2007).

Bao, Xiaohua and Larry D. Oiu, "Do Technical Barriers to Trade Promote or Restrict Trade? Evidence from China," *Asia-Pacific Journal of Accounting & Economics* 17 (2010): 253–80.

Bora, Bijit, Aki Kuwahara and Sam Laird, "Quantification of Non-tariff Barriers United Nations Conference of Trade and Development (UNCTAD), Policy Issues in International Trade and Commodities (*UNCTAD/ ITCD/TAB*/19)," Study Series No. 18, UNCTA, New York (2002).

Chen, M. X. and A. Mattoo, "Regionalism in Standards: Good or Bad for Trade?" *Canadian Journal of Economics* 41 (2008): 838–63.

Chen, M. X., T. Otsuki, and J. S. Wilson, "Standards and Export Decisions: Firm-level Evidence from Developing Countries," *Journal of International Trade and Economic Development* 17 (2008): 501–23.

Chevassus-Lozza, E., D. Majkovic, V. Persillet, and M. Unguru, "Technical Barriers to Trade in the EU: Importance for the New EU members." An Assessment for Agricultural and Food Products Paper presented at the 11th EAAE Congress, 24–27 August, Copenhagen, Denmark (2005).

Czubala, Witold, Ben Shepherd, and John S. Wilson, "Help or Hindrance? The Impact of Harmonized Standards on African Exports," *Journal of African Economies* 18 (2009): 711–44.

Deardorff, Alan V. and Robert Stern, "The Measurement of Non-tariff Barriers," OECD working paper 179 (1998).

Disdier, A., L. Fontagne, and M. Mimouni, "The Impact of Regulations on Agricultural Trade: Evidence from the SPS and TBT Agreements," *American Journal of Agricultural Economics* 90 (2008): 336–50.

Essaji, Azim, "Technical Regulations and Specialization in International Trade," *Journal of International Economics* 76 (2008): 166–76.

Fernandes, Ana, "Trade Policy, Trade Volumes and Plant Level Productivity in Colombian Manufacturing Industries," *Journal of International Economics* 71 (2007): 52–71.

Fischer, Ronald, and Pablo Serra, "Standards and Protection," *Journal of International Economics* 52 (2000): 377–400.

Ganslandt, M. and J. R. Markusen, "Standards and Related Regulations in International Trade: A Modeling Approach," NBER working paper WS346 (2001).

Helpman, Elhanan, M. Melitz, and S. R. Yeaple, "Exports versus FDI with Heterogeneous Firms," *American Economic Review* 91 (2004): 300–16.

Helpman, Elhanan, M. Melitz, and Y. Rubinstein, "Estimating Trade Flows: Trading Partners and Trading Volumes," *Quarterly Journal of Economics* 123 (2008): 441–87.

Maskus, K. E. and J. S. Wilson, "Quantifying the Impact of Technical Barriers to Trade: A Review of Past Attempts and the New Policy Context," in K. E. Maskus and J. S. Wilson (eds), *Quantifying the Impact of Technical Barriers to Trade*, Ann Arbor, MI: The University of Michigan Press (2001).

Maskus, K. E., T. Otsuki, and J.S. Wilson, "The Cost of Compliance with Product Standards for Firms in Developing Countries: An Econometric Study," World Bank policy research working paper series 3590 (2005).

Melitz, Marc J., "The Impact of Trade on Intra-industry Reallocations and Aggregate Industry Productivity," *Econometrica* 71 (2003): 1695–725.

Njikam, Ousmanou and John Cockburn, "Trade Liberalization and Productivity Growth: Firm-level Evidence from Cameroon," *The Journal of Developing Areas* 44 (2011): 279–302.

Portugal-Perez, A., J.-D. Reyes, and J. S. Wilson, "Beyond the Information Technology Agreement: Harmonization of Standards and Trade in Electronics," World Bank policy research working paper 4916 (2009).

Shepherd, Ben, "Product Standards, Harmonization, and Trade: Evidence from the Extensive Margin," World Bank policy research working paper 4390 (2007).

Topalova, Petia and Amit Khandelwal, "Trade Liberalization and Firm Productivity: The Case of India," *The Review of Economics and Statistics* 93 (2011): 995–1009.

Xiong, Bo and John Beghin, "Aflatoxin Redux: Does European Aflatoxin Regulation Hurt Groundnut Exporters from Africa?" *European Review of Agricultural Economics*, First published online: November 22 (2011).

Chapter 11

Do Technical Barriers to Trade Promote or Restrict Trade? Evidence from China*

Abstract

The use of technical barriers to trade (TBT) is widespread and has increasing impact on international trade. In contrast to most other trade measures, TBT have both trade promotion and trade restriction effects. Due to their theoretical complexity and their scarcity, TBT have been considered as one of the most difficult non-tariff barriers (NTBs) to quantify. In this paper, we construct a TBT database from 1998–2006 to examine the influence of TBT imposed by China on the country's imports. When using the frequency index, we find that TBT are trade restrictive: a one unit increase in TBT will decrease import value by about 0.8%. However, when the coverage ratio is used, we find that the negative effects of TBT are not statistically significant based on the entire period. However, if the focus is shifted to data from 1998–2001, we find that TBT have trade promotion effects. A one unit increase in TBT will increase import value by about 0.2%. Finally, China's TBT (measured by both frequency index and coverage ratio) are trade restricting for agriculture goods but trade promoting for manufacturing goods.

*This chapter is reproduced from *Asia Pacific Journal of Accounting & Economics*, 17, 253–280, 2010, with permission from Taylor & Francis.

1. Introduction

Technical barriers to trade (TBT) are widely utilized government administrative measures for environmental protection, safety, national security, and consumer interests, which have increasing impact on international trade. The wide use of TBT is for a variety of reasons. First, TBT are legitimate. World Trade Organisation (WTO) members are authorized by WTO TBT/SPS Agreement to take such measures to protect human health as well as animal and plant health, provided that the enforced measures are not disguised protectionism. Second, the increasing income of an importing country and consumer preference may result in a higher demand for product quality, safety, and environment protection. Third, as trade liberalization becomes more complex, it has become more difficult to use traditional trade protectionist measures to protect domestic industries. Thus, TBT have been used (or misused) to substitute for tariffs and other non-tariff barriers to trade.[1]

Unlike tariffs and other non-tariff barriers (NTBs), TBT can promote trade or restrict trade. TBT promote trade by providing consumers of importing countries with confidence on the quality, safety, and other health related concerns of the imported products. On the other hand, governments of importing countries can use TBT to restrict imports even if the import products are safe and meet the standard imposed. Facing potential examination harassment under TBT, importers and exporters are discouraged to carry out their trade. Given the proliferation of TBT and their theoretical complexity, the OECD (2001) has suggested more empirical research on TBT with a view that quantitative analysis is an important step in the regulatory reform process and can help inform governments in defining more efficient regulations. However, due to their theoretical complexity and data scarcity, TBT have been considered as one of the most difficult NTBs to quantify (Deardorff and Stern, 1997). Some attempts have been made in this direction, but there is still

[1]As Baldwin (1970) puts it, "The lowering of tariffs has, in effect, been like draining a swamp. The lower water level has revealed all the snags and stumps of non-tariff barriers that still have to be cleared away." Wallner (1998) considered this phenomenon a "law of constant protection," referring to perfect substitutability between tariff and none-tariff barriers in maintaining a degree of desired domestic protection.

no preferred quantification strategy and consensus on "whether such restrictions tend to reduce trade by virtue of raising compliance costs or expand trade by increasing consumer confidence in the safety and quality of imported goods" (Maskus and Wilson, 2001). Our paper attempts to make a contribution to this research agenda by examining the trade promotion or restriction aspects of TBT adopted by China.

In this study, we analyze how TBT, along with other trade barriers, affect China's imports during the period between 1998 and 2006. To this end, we first need to construct a database in which we quantify all NTBs, including TBT, import license, and import quota. We use both frequency index and coverage ratio approaches to measure non-tariff barriers. Although the final measures are obtained for all industries defined at the Harmonized System (HS) two-digit level, data on HS four-digit level and even eight-digit level are required to obtain measures for HS2-digit-level industries. We find that most of the TBT-rocked (i.e., the severely affected) product categories are in the agriculture sector.

We then use the extended gravity model to estimate the degrees of the impacts of NTBs on China's imports. Upon using the frequency index, we find that tariff, TBT, and quota all have a negative impact on China's imports, but license had a positive impact. The results are different using coverage ratio. Based on the entire period of 1998–2006, the negative effects of TBT are not statistically significant. Moreover, focusing on 1998–2001 (the pre-WTO period), we find that TBT have a trade promotion effect: a one unit increase in TBT will increase import value by about 0.2%.

The impact of TBT on agriculture and manufacturing goods imports is different. We find that TBT (measured by both frequency index and coverage ratio) are trade reducing for agriculture goods but trade promoting for manufacturing goods.

Our paper contributes to the current literature in a number of ways. First, in contrast to existing empirical studies that focus almost exclusively on TBT of developed countries, this paper analyzes a developing country, that is, China. Second, this paper has a self-constructed non-tariff measures database that is constructed based on highly disaggregated data to produce HS2-product-level non-tariff measures. It also allows us to explore sectoral differences of the TBT impacts. Third, while most studies in the literature rely on cross-section data[2], our paper covers a nine-year time period that allows us to examine also the different impacts of TBT before and after China's entry into the WTO.

The rest of the paper is organized as follows. In Section 2, we review the related literature and further explain the contributions of our paper. In Section 3, we construct a TBT database from 1998-2006 and use the inventory approach (frequency index and coverage ratio) to quantify the stringency of technical measures in China. In Section 4, we present our regression model, discuss all the variables, and describe the data. In Section 5, we discuss our findings. We present our concluding remarks in Section 6. The main findings are reported in Table 11.5 and Table 11.6.

2. Related Literature Review

Beghin and Bureau (2001), Ferrantino (2006) and Korinek, Melatos and Rau (2008), Maskus, Otsuki, and Wilson (2001), and Maskus and Wilson (2001) all provide comprehensive reviews on key economic issues related to TBT modeling and measurement. Quantification techniques can be broadly grouped into two categories: ex post approach and ex ante approach. The *ex ante* approach includes simulations with the calculation of tariff equivalents and is usually employed to predict unobserved welfare impact. On the other hand, the *ex post* approach includes gravity-based econometric models used to estimate the observed trade impacts of TBT. Both approaches have their respective advantages and drawbacks depending on the nature of the specific TBT, availability of data, and objective of the measurement, among others (Popper, *et al.*, 2004).

As our paper uses the *ex post* approach, we focus our discussion on studies that used the *ex post* approach. Although a unified methodology does not exist for examining the trade effects of TBT, the most commonly used methodology is the gravity model.

[2]There are a few exceptions: Moenius (2004, 2006) tried to determine the impact of standard using a 10-year panel that includes frequency data on standards. Metha and Nambiar (2005) accounted for the changing maximum residue levels for only four years. Cao and Johnson (2006) examined the effect of HACCP (denoted by a dummy variable) implemented in New Zealand for nine years.

To employ the gravity model, the TBT should first be measured or quantified. Beghin and Bureau (2001) summarize three sources of information that could be used to assess the importance of domestic regulations as trade barriers: data on regulations, such as the number of regulations and number of pages in the regulations; data on frequency of detentions, including the number of restrictions, frequency index, and import coverage ratio; and data on complaints from the industry against discriminatory regulatory practices and notifications to international bodies about such practices.

Swann, Temple, and Shurmer (1996) use counts of voluntary national and international standards recognized by the UK and Germany as indicators of standard over the period of 1985–1991. They find that shared standards influence exports positively but have little influence on imports; unilateral standards have positive influence on imports but have negative influence on exports. Moenius (2004, 2006) examines the trade effects of country-specific and bilaterally shared standards over the period of 1985–1995. Both papers used the counts of binding standards in a given industry as a measure of stringency of standards. In particular, Moenius (2004) focuses on 12 OECD countries and finds that at the aggregate level, bilaterally shared and country-specific standards implemented by the importing or exporting countries are both trade promoting on average; at the industry level, however, the importer-specific standards have a negative trade effect on non-manufacturing sectors. Moenius (2006) confirms that bilateral standards in the European Union (EU) have very strong trade promotion effects on the trade between EU and non-EU members, but harmonization decreases the internal trade within EU.

Fontagné, Mimouni, and Pasteels (2005) and Disdier, Fontagné, and Mimouni (2008) use a frequency index based on notification directly extracted from the TRAINS database. Fontagné, Mimouni, and Pasteels (2005) collect data on 61 product groups, including agri-food products, in 2001. Their paper generalized the findings of Moenius (2004) and indicated that non-tariff measures, including standards, have a negative impact on agri-food trade but have an insignificant or even positive impact on the majority of manufactured products. Based on data covering 61 exporting countries and 114 importing countries, they find that over the entire product range, least developed countries (LDCs), developing countries, and OECD countries seem to be similarly affected. However, OECD agri-food exporters tend to benefit from non-tariff measures at the expense of exporters from other developing countries and LDCs.

Disdier, Fontagné, and Mimouni (2008) estimate the trade effect of standards and other non-tariff measures on 690 agri-food products (HS6-digit level). Their data cover the bilateral trade between the OECD as importing countries and 114 others as exporting countries in 2004. When they consider different groups of exporting countries, they show that OECD exporters are not significantly affected by TBT in their exports to other OECD countries, whereas the exports of developing countries and LDCs are negatively and significantly affected.

A number of studies are supportive of the use of maximum residue levels to measure directly the severity of food safety standards within a gravity model. These studies include Otsuki, Wilson, and Sewadeh (2001*a* and 2001*b*), Wilson and Otsuki (2004*b* and 2004*c*), Wilson, Otsuki, and Majumdsar (2003), Lacovone (2003), and Metha and Nambiar (2005). These studies tend to focus on specifc types of standards for specifc products and countries. For example, Otsuki, Wilson, and Sewadeh (2001*a* and 2001*b*) and Wilson and Otsuki (2004b) examine the trade effect of aflatoxin standards in groundnuts and other agricultural products (e.g., vegetables, fruits, and cereals) adopted by many importing countries. Lacovone (2003) focuses on the effects of European aflatoxin standards on imports from Latin America. Wilson, Otsuki, and Majumdsar (2003) analyze the effects of standards for tetracycline residues on beef trade. Wilson and Otsuki (2004c) study the effects on chlorpyrifos exports. By and large, these studies indicate that imports are reduced when the importing countries impose more stringent standards on foreign products (trade restricting).

The literature review clearly indicates that our study is not only related to those studies but also makes a unique contribution. Our study focuses on a single large developing country (China) for a long period of time, and it distinguishes the development levels of exporting countries. Moreover, our study examines sectoral differences of TBT and considers and compares the pre-WTO and post-WTO period. Some of the above-mentioned studies have some of these features, but our paper is the only one that includes all these aspects into one study.

3. Quantification of TBT and China's TBT

In this section, we first describe the two methods of quantifying TBT to be used in this study and then apply them to China to obtain our database of China's TBT and other NTBs, namely, import license and quota.

3.1. *Quantification of TBT*

Bora, *et al.* (2002) review various approaches to quantify non-tariff measures. We adopt two of these approaches in our study, namely, coverage ratio and frequency index. The coverage ratio captures the extent of trade covered by TBT. Specifically, the coverage ratio of TBT in China for product category j in a particular year is the percentage of import values by China in product category j that is affected by China's TBT in that year:

$$CR_j = \frac{\sum_i D_i V_i}{\sum_i V_i} \tag{1}$$

where i is a product item contained in product category j. If TBT is applied to product i, the dummy variable D_i takes the value of one and zero otherwise. V is the value of product i's imports by China. Thus, the coverage ratio of product category j is higher if more of its products are subject to TBT scrutiny and/or the products under TBT have larger import values. However, there is a problem associated with the coverage ratio: the endogeneity of the weights in import value. At the extreme, if TBT is so restrictive in product i, it will preclude all imports of product i, and consequently the weight V will be zero. Thus, the coverage ratio is downward biased. One way to solve this problem is to use the counterfactual free trade weights, but it is not available to us. Alternatively, we also use another approach in our study, the frequency index, which does not suffer from this problem.

The frequency index considers only the presence or absence of TBT in a product without indicating the value of the imports covered. It shows the percentage of import transactions affected by TBT. Specifically, the frequency index of TBT in China for product category j in a particular year is the percentage of import products by China in product category j affected by China's TBT in that year:

$$FI_j = \frac{\sum_i D_i M_i}{\sum_i M_i} \quad (2)$$

where i is a product item contained in product category j. If TBT is applied to product i, the dummy variable D_i takes the value of one and zero otherwise. M_i is a dummy variable equal to one if there is import of product i and zero otherwise. Unlike the coverage index, however, the frequency index does not reflect the relative value of the affected products and thus cannot provide any indication of the relative importance of the TBT among all product items in product category j.

The frequency index measures the number of product items subject to TBT as a percentage of the total number of product items in a product category, whereas the coverage ratio measures the value of imports of TBT-affected product items as a percentage of total imports of a product category. In the former case, the occurrence of TBT is not weighted by the import value, whereas in the latter case, it is. As both measures have their respective advantages and disadvantages, we use both in our study below.

Formulas (1) and (2) describe two distinct approaches in quantifying TBT. The same measures can be used to quantify other types of NTBs, such as import license and quota.

3.2. *China's NTB database: Data description and methodology*

Based on the inventory approach discussed above, we construct a Chinese NTB database that covers 96 agricultural and manufacturing products at the HS2-digit level from 1998–2006.[3] To obtain the import coverage ratio of each HS2 product, we calculate the frequency index at HS4-digit level and aggregate them. Data on Chinese tariffs and NTBs (i.e., TBT, license, and import quota) are mainly from the *Administrative Measures Regarding Import & Export Trade of the People's Republic of China* (Ministry of Commerce and

[3]TBT data was first available in China in 1998.

Custom General Administration of China), which provides detailed information at the HS8-digit level on tariff and non-tariff measures.

Every year, the Chinese government provides a code list of supporting documents subject to customs control, based on which we identify the tariff line products subject to NTBs. Within those NTBs, the technical measures include government administrative measures for environmental protection, safety, national security, and consumer interests. The codes slightly change over the years, undergoing a major revision in 2002. In Annex 1, we provide a code list for 2002–2006 as an example. The code subject to TBT control remains almost the same during 1998–2001.

Specifically, the frequency index of TBT (FI-TBT) measures the proportion of product items (e.g., HS8) covered by TBT within a product category (e.g., HS4), which varies between 0 (no coverage) and 100% (all product items are covered). First, for every HS4 product category, we count the number of HS8 product items (of the corresponding HS4 product category) covered by TBT and divide it by the total number of product items belonging to the HS4 product category. This gives us the frequency ratios of TBT at the HS4-digit level. For example, regarding HS2402 (i.e., cigars, cheroots, cigarillos, and cigarettes of tobacco or of tobacco substitutes), there are three product items [i.e., HS24021000 (cigars, cheroots, and cigarillos containing tobacco), HS24022000 (cigarettes containing tobacco), and HS24029000 (other)], with only one of them (i.e., HS24022000) covered by TBT. Hence, the corresponding FI-TBT is equal to 33.33% (1/3). We apply the same method to obtain FI-TBT for HS2 products.

On the other hand, the import coverage ratio of TBT (CR-TBT) measures the proportion of TBT-affected import within a product category. Let us take HS17 (i.e., sugars and sugar confectionery) for example. It has four product items, HS1701, HS1702, HS1703, and HS1704, with a total import value of USD182.244 million. Three product items (except for HS1703) are covered by TBT, with a total import value of USD111.216 million. Hence, the CR-TBT of HS17 is equal to 66.46% ($= 111.216/182.244$). However, the FI-TBT of HS17 is equal to 75%($= 3/4$).

Similarly, we also calculate the frequency index of license (FI-L), import coverage ratio of license (CR-L), frequency index of quota (FI-Q), and import coverage ratio of quota (CR-Q).

3.3. *TBT-rocked products in China*

Tables 11.1 and 11.2 provide information on all products affected by trade measures (i.e., tariffs and non-tariff measures). Around 80% of imported product lines (FI) and more than 90% of import value (CR), except in 2001 (77.29%), in China are subject to TBT. However, different products are affected differently.

By calculating the frequency index and/or import CR-TBT, we can examine which products are more seriously affected. According to the definition of UNCTAD (1997), those with a frequency and coverage ratio *both* above 50% are called TBT-rocked products. In Annex 2, we provide a list of TBT-rocked products in China. There are 31 products that are TBT rocked in every single year from 1998-2006, both years inclusive. Eight other products are TBT-rocked in some of the years during the same period. Most of the TBT-rocked products, especially those rocked in the entire period, are agricultural products and processed foods (i.e., HSOI to HS24). Indeed, all HS2-digit level agriculture products and processed foods are TBT rocked.

As there are a total of 96 products at the HS2-digit level, these TBT-rocked products account for about $1/3(= 31/96)$ of all products. The total import value of these TBT-rocked products as the share of China's total import value of all products ranges from 10–16%.

4. Model, Methodology and Data

Following the literature, we use the gravity model to study a country's trade. In particular, we introduce our constructed TBT variable to examine how TBT in China influences the country's import. As in most gravity models, we include GDP, distance, and common language as independent variables. GDP captures the effect of the country's size. We use the real GDP of an exporting country to proxy its supply capacity and the real GDP of an importing country to proxy its demand capacity.[4] The bilateral distance between the importing and exporting countries captures the transportation costs.

[4]Real GDP data are taken directly from the US Department of Agriculture database. We also tried to use nominal GDP, with no change in the qualitative results.

Table 11.1. Restrictiveness of trade measures by frequency index (HS2).

Type of measure	Year	No. of affected products (1)	Restrictiveness = (1) / Total no. of products	Affected imports (thousand US$) (2)	Restrictiveness = (2) / Total imports (thousand US$)
Tariff	1998	96	100.00%	136,698,089	100.00%
	1999	95	98.96%	164,039,379	99.00%
	2000	95	98.96%	208,724,085	98.73%
	2001	95	98.96%	276,491,273	99.02%
	2002	95	98.96%	279,654,465	98.97%
	2003	95	98.96%	407,605,638	99.05%
	2004	95	98.96%	554,406,001	99.05%
	2005	95	98.96%	651,765,484	99.06%
	2006	95	98.96%	782,291,262	99.10%
TBT	1998	70	72.92%	125,641,672	91.91%
	1999	65	67.71%	152,705,419	92.16%
	2000	74	77.08%	200,023,143	94.62%
	2001	73	76.04%	215,806,053	77.29%
	2002	76	79.17%	267,412,019	94.64%
	2003	81	84.38%	399,786,552	97.15%
	2004	82	85.42%	547,067,690	97.74%
	2005	83	86.46%	642,031,520	97.58%
	2006	83	86.46%	768,634,084	97.37%
License	1998	21	21.88%	89,549,798	65.51%
	1999	22	22.92%	114,601,204	69.16%
	2000	22	22.92%	149,079,530	70.52%
	2001	25	26.04%	175,663,852	62.91%
	2002	30	31.25%	234,498,993	82.99%
	2003	37	38.54%	371,968,600	90.39%
	2004	36	37.50%	503,444,064	89.95%
	2005	35	36.46%	570,994,948	86.78%
	2006	35	36.46%	719,767,331	91.18%
Quota	1998	15	15.63%	83,212,840	60.97%
	1999	16	16.67%	106,109,004	64.04%
	2000	12	12.50%	126,286,133	59.74%
	2001	16	16.67%	149,452,821	53.52%
	2002	7	7.29%	9,015,966	3.19%
	2003	7	7.29%	11,816,213	2.87%
	2004	8	8.33%	18,645,068	3.33%
	2005	7	7.29%	17,617,835	2.68%
	2006	6	6.25%	15,419,738	1.95%

Source: Based on the authors' calculation.

Table 11.2. Restrictiveness of trade measures by coverage ratio (HS2).

Type of measure	Year	No. of affected products (1)	Restrictiveness = (1) / Total No. of products	Affected imports (thousand US$) (2)	Restrictiveness = (2) / Total imports (thousand US$)
Tariff	1998	96	100.00%	136,698,089	100.00%
	1999	95	98.96%	164,039,379	99.00%
	2000	95	98.96%	208,724,085	98.73%
	2001	95	98.96%	276,491,273	99.02%
	2002	95	98.96%	279,654,465	98.97%
	2003	95	98.96%	407,605,638	99.05%
	2004	95	98.96%	554,406,001	99.05%
	2005	95	98.96%	651,765,484	99.06%
	2006	95	98.96%	782,291,262	99.10%
TBT	1998	69	71.88%	125,359,645	91.71%
	1999	65	67.71%	146,455,222	91.85%
	2000	74	77.08%	200,023,143	94.62%
	2001	73	76.04%	215,806,053	77.29%
	2002	76	79.17%	264,458,262	94.24%
	2003	81	84.38%	402,145,549	97.17%
	2004	81	84.38%	545,402,498	97.50%
	2005	82	85.42%	639,854815	97.25%
	2006	83	86.46%	768,634,084	97.37%
Licence	1998	20	20.83%	86,869,156	63.55%
	1999	22	22.92%	109,836,855	68.89%
	2000	21	21.86%	149,010,983	70.49%
	2001	25	26.04%	175,663,852	62.91%
	2002	30	31.25%	234,498,993	83.56%
	2003	38	39.58%	372,493,219	90.01%
	2004	36	37.50%	503,102,069	89.94%
	2005	36	37.50%	571,701,832	86.89%
	2006	35	36.46%	712,482,707	90.25%
Quota	1998	15	15.63%	83,212,840	60.87%
	1999	16	16.67%	101,407,700	64.04%
	2000	12	12.50%	126,286,133	59.74%
	2001	16	16.67%	149,452,821	53.52%
	2002	7	7.29%	9,015,966	3.21%
	2003	7	7.29%	11,816,215	2.86%
	2004	8	8.33%	18,645,070	3.33%
	2005	7	7.29%	17,617,835	2.68%
	2006	6	6.25%	15,419,738	1.95%

Source: Based on the authors' calculation.

Common language is often conducive to bilateral trade because it results in easy communication and captures culture proximity. Aside from the usual gravity model variables, we also introduce our key variables, tariff and non-tariff trade measures, including our TBT variables.

Our basic regression model takes the following form:

$$\begin{aligned}\log IM_{jt}^{k} = {} & \alpha_0 + \alpha_1 \log GDP_t + \alpha_2 \log GDP_{jt} + \alpha_3 \log Dist_j \\ & + \alpha_4 Contig_j + \alpha_5 Comlang_j + cx_6 \log Tariff_t^k \\ & + \alpha_7 TBT_t^k + \alpha_8 L_t^k + \alpha_9 Q_t^k + \varepsilon, \end{aligned} \tag{3}$$

where the variables are defined as follows:

IM_{jt}^{k} is the value of China's import of product k from country j in year t;
GDP_t and GDP_{jt} are China's and country j's real GDP in year t, respectively;
$Dist_j$ is the geographical distance between China and country j;
$Contig_j$ is the dummy variable indicating whether China and country j are contiguous; $Comlang_j$ is the dummy variable indicating whether China and country j share a common language;
$Tariff_t^k$ is China's average preferential tariff applied to product k in year t;
TBT_t^k is the frequency index or import coverage ratio of China's TBT applied to product k in year t;
L_t^k is the frequency index or import coverage ratio of China's import license applied to product k in year t; and
Q_t^k is the frequency index or import coverage ratio of China's import quota applied to product k in year t.

We also include other variables to examine their impacts and check for robustness of the results from the basic model. These variables include *Developing* (dummy indicating the exporting country is a developing country) and *Agriculture* (dummy indicating the product k is a agricultural product). China entered the WTO in 2002. We also want to see if there is any systematic difference between the effects of trade measures before and after China's entry into the WTO.

In our sample, China is the only importing country, whereas there are 43 exporting countries/economies, including Burma (Myanmar), Hong Kong, India, Indonesia, Iran, Japan, Macau, Malaysia, Pakistan, Philippines, Kazakhstan, Saudi Arabia, Singapore, Korea, Thailand, Turkey, Vietnam, United Arab Emirates, Taiwan, South Africa, Belgium, Denmark, UK, Germany, France, Italy, Netherland, Spain, Austria, Finland, Romania, Sweden, Switzerland, Russian Federation, Ukraine, Argentina, Brazil, Chile, Canada, US, Australia, New Zealand, and the EU. The time span covers 1998–2006. With these 43 exporters and nine years at HS2-digit level products, we have a panel of about 37,000 observations. When running the regression based on (2), we also include the year dummy to control for the time fixed effect.

China's import values from the 43 individual exporters are gathered from *China Custom Statistic Year Book*. Each country's GDP (in billion US dollars in 2005) are obtained from the US Department of Agriculture Economic Research Services International Macroeconomic Data Set. Data for the geographical distance are collected based on the average distance between the capitals of the two countries and the distances as well as the data of Comlang and Contig, which are all extracted from the Centre d'Etudes Prospectives et d'Informations Internationales in France database.

5. Empirical Results

5.1. *All products*

Table 11.3 shows the summary statistics of the key variables. Table 11.4 reports the Pearson coefficients of the trade control measure variables and other variables. FI-L, CR-TBT, and CR-L have a negative correlation with tariff. All other import control policies are positively correlated with each other. In general, different kinds of import control measures in China seem to be complementary to each other. Among these measures, import license and import quota have the highest positive coefficient, which is in accordance with fact that these two measures are sometimes combined together in use. Normally, a country will distribute import quotas to import license holders. TBT, import license and quota measured by frequency index and coverage ratio are highly correlated with the Pearson coefficient

Table 11.3. Summary statistics of the key variable.

Variable	Obs	Mean	Std. Dev.	Min	Max
im	37152	5.872	4.208	0	19.94
gdp	37152	5.706	1.538	1.74	9.49
contig	37152	0.186	0.389	0	1
comlang	37152	0.116	0.321	0	1
dist	37152	8.679	0.666	6.86	9.87
tariff	37152	2.582	0.634	0	4.1
fi-tbt	37152	42.844	39.665	0	100
fi-l	37152	7.845	18.406	0	100
fi-q	37152	2.295	9.836	0	90
cr-tbt	37152	54.133	42.294	0	100
cr-l	37152	15.439	29.803	0	100
cr-q	37152	4.351	16.201	0	100

all above 0.8, which proves that frequency index and coverage ratio are alternative measures to quantify the non-tariff barriers.

China has zero import in many products from many countries. Accordingly, we use Tobit estimation to deal with the censorship problem because of the many zero import observations.[5] We first run the regressions based on the whole sample period and then on 1998–2001 and 2002–2006 sub-periods respectively to capture the possible structural changes due to China's accession to the WTO. In all regressions, we control for the year fixed effect. Regression results based on all HS2 products are reported in Table 11.5 for the frequency ratio and in Table 11.6 for the coverage ratio. Column 1 of Table 11.5 for the period 1998–2006 shows the results from the basic model (3). All estimates are statistically significant. Most of the explanatory variables in the standard gravity model have the expected signs. The GDP of an exporting country has a positive effect on China's import (1% increase in the exporting country's GDP raises China's imports from that country by 1.564%). The distance between exporting country and China has negative effects on trade between the two countries (1% increase in distance reduces China's

[5]Among the 37,152 observations, 7,529 observations have zero trade and account for about 20% of the whole sample.

Table 11.4. Pearson coefficient between the variables.

	im	gdp	contig	comlang	dist	tariff	fi-tbt	fi-l	fi-q	cr-tbt	cr-l	cr-q
im	1.000											
gdp	0.456	1.000										
contig	−0.156	−0.398	1.000									
comlang	0.098	−0.306	0.199	1.000								
dist	−0.085	0.290	−0.464	−0.433	1.000							
tariff	−0.126	0.017	0.000	0.000	0.000	1.000						
fi-tbt	−0.066	0.006	0.000	0.000	0.000	0.128	1.000					
fi-l	0.170	0.008	0.000	0.000	0.000	−0.027	0.013	1.000				
fi-q	−0.007	−0.004	0.000	0.000	0.000	0.133	0.132	0.309	1.000			
cr-tbt	0.037	0.009	0.000	0.000	0.000	−0.007	0.870	0.144	0.136	1.000		
cr-l	0.207	0.011	0.000	0.000	0.000	−0.066	−0.002	0.824	0.224	0.154	1.000	
cr-q	0.026	−0.003	0.000	0.000	0.000	0.128	0.127	0.260	0.846	0.156	0.229	1.000

Table 11.5. Tobit regression results by using frequency index.

	1998–2006			1998–2001			2002–2006		
	(1)	(2)	(3)	(1)	(2)	(3)	(1)	(2)	(3)
gdp	1.564	1.564	1.564	1.569	1.568	1.568	1.562	1.561	1.561
	(83.58)[a]	(83.96)[a]	(83.96)[a]	(55.78)[a]	(56.19)[a]	(56.19)[a]	(62.50)[a]	(62.77)[a]	(62.77)[a]
dist	−1.466	−1.465	−1.465	−1.620	−1.618	−1.618	−1.345	−1.345	−1.345
	(36.09)[a]	(36.25)[a]	(36.25)[a]	(26.32)[a]	(26.51)[a]	(26.51)[a]	(24.99)[a]	(25.09)[a]	(25.09)[a]
contig	−0.748	−0.746	−0.746	−0.629	−0.628	−0.628	−0.837	−0.834	−0.834
	(11.01)[a]	(11.04)[a]	(11.04)[a]	(6.10)[a]	(6.14)[a]	(6.14)[a]	(9.31)[a]	(9.33)[a]	(9.33)[a]
comlang	3.219	3.215	3.215	3.752	3.745	3.745	2.793	2.790	2.790
	(41.69)[a]	(41.86)[a]	(41.86)[a]	(32.22)[a]	(32.43)[a]	(32.43)[a]	(27.19)[a]	(27.29)[a]	(27.29)[a]
developing	−1.112	−1.111	−1.111	−1.343	−1.339	−1.339	−0.933	−0.932	−0.932
	(18.79)[a]	(18.86)[a]	(18.86)[a]	(14.86)[a]	(14.95)[a]	(14.95)[a]	(11.94)[a]	(11.98)[a]	(11.98)[a]
tariff	−0.648	−0.498	−0.155	−0.311	−0.163	−0.000	−0.863	−0.816	0.271
	(17.77)[a]	(11.27)[a]	(1.67)[c]	(5.84)[a]	(2.55)*b*	(0.00)	(16.48)[a]	(13.22)[a]	(1.69)[c]
-tbt	−0.008	0.005	−0.046	−0.007	0.009	−0.024	−0.007	0.002	−0.133
	(13.53)[a]	(4.70)[a]	(5.53)[a]	(8.32)[a]	(5.73)[a]	(2.63)[a]	(8.65)[a]	(1.40)	(6.97)[a]
-l	0.044	0.043	0.036	0.009	0.015	0.010	0.045	0.043	0.017
	(35.16)[a]	(28.32)[a]	(12.16)[a]	(1.82)[c]	(1.36)	(1.68)[c]	(32.81)[a]	(27.63)[a]	(3.80)[a]
-q	−0.019	−0.033	−0.005	0.019	−0.007	0.048	−0.027	−0.036	−0.032
	(7.83)[a]	(9.87)[a]	(1.52)	(3.59)[a]	(0.63)	(6.89)[a]	(6.19)[a]	(2.70)[a]	(6.46)[a]
agriculture		2.482			0.833			9.368	
		(2.94)[a]			(0.87)			(4.79)[a]	
tariff_agri		0.343			0.163			1.088	
		(3.38)[a]			(1.13)			(6.34)[a]	

(*Continued*)

Table 11.5. (*Continued*)

	1998–2006			1998–2001			2002–2006		
	(1)	(2)	(3)	(1)	(2)	(3)	(1)	(2)	(3)
-tbt_agri		−0.050			−0.033			−0.135	
		(6.05)[a]			(3.54)[a]			(7.05)[a]	
-l_agri		−0.007			−0.005			−0.026	
		(2.17)[b]			(0.39)			(5.56)[a]	
-q_agri		0.028			0.055			0.004	
		(5.72)[a]			(4.14)[a]			(0.28)	
manufacture			−2.482			−0.833			−9.368
			(2.94)[a]			(0.87)			(4.79)[a]
tariff_manu			−0.343			−0.163			−1.088
			(3.38)[a]			(1.13)			(6.34)[a]
-tbt_manu			0.050			0.033			0.135
			(6.05)[a]			(3.54)[a]			(7.05)[a]
-l_manu			0.007			0.005			0.026
			(2.17)[b]			(0.39)			(5.56)[a]
-q_manu			−0.028			−0.055			−0.004
			(5.72)[a]			(4.14)[a]			(0.28)
Observations	37152	37152	37152	16512	16512	16512	20640	20640	20640
Censored ob.	7529	7529	7529	3753	3753	3753	3776	3776	3776

Notes: Absolute values of t statistics are in parentheses. a, b and c denotes significant at 1%, 5% and 10% level, respectively. Year fixed effects are controlled for.

imports from that country by 1.466%). Countries/economies sharing the same language with China have more exports to China (with a 3.219% difference); however, sharing the same border reduces export to China (by 74.8%). This result can be understood by realizing that the most important exporting countries, such as the US, Japan, and EU members, are not contiguous with the Chinese mainland. And DCs generally have less export to China than developed countries.

Turning to the impacts of trade measures, we note that tariff, TBT, and quota have negative impacts on China's imports. A 1% increase in the MFN tariff will decrease import value by about 0.648%. A 1 unit increase in TBT will decrease import value by about 0.8%. A 1 unit increase in quota will decrease import value by 1.9%. However, import license has a positive impact. A 1 unit increase in license will increase import value by 4.4%. This surprising result can be explained partly by the positive correlation between license and quota (see Table 11.4). The trade restriction effects of license have been captured by quota. The key result from this regression is that when measured in frequency index, TBT has net trade reducing effects.[6]

China entered the WTO in 2002. To determine whether there are any systematic changes in the effects of China's trade measures on its imports after the WTO accession, we run separate regressions for two time periods, 1998–2001 and 2002–2006. By comparing the results from these two periods in column 1 of Table 11.5, we observe one important difference: import quota has positive effects on China's trade in the pre-WTO period but has negative effects in the post-WTO period.[7] However, it is worth

---

[6]As suggested by Chris Milner, we also try to drop other trade policy variables (i.e., tariff, license, and quota) from the regression to allow TBT to capture all policy impacts on imports. It is not surprising that in this case, the negative impact of TBT becomes stronger: −0.010 (as opposed to −0.008 in Table 11.5) for the whole sample period, −0.007 (same in Table 11.5) for the pre-WTO period, and −0.013 (as opposed to −0.007 in Table 11.5) for the post-WTO period. However, our regression (including tariffs and other NTBs) allows TBT to capture its net effect.

[7]This may be due to the fact that quota has stronger negative effects on agriculture goods imports and China had more agriculture products subject to quota after its WTO entry. Note that although the number of quota-affected

pointing out that the TBT effects on trade are not different before and after entry to WTO.

We also run the same regressions using coverage ratios of NTBs. The results are reported in column 1 of Table 11.6. While most of the estimates have the same sign in Table 11.6 as their counterparts in Table 11.5, we observe one important difference in our key variable, TBT. Running the regression on the entire period, we obtain a negative estimate that is statistically insignificant. However, in running the regressions on the two sub-periods, we obtain significant estimates with opposite signs: positive in 1998–2001 and negative in 2002–2006. The CR-TBT has trade promotion effects on China's imports in 1998–2001 but has trade restriction effects in 2002–2006.

5.2. *Agriculture products vs. manufacturing products*

Trade barriers, especially TBT, may have different impacts on a country's imports depending on the nature of the products. To observe this, we interact the individual terms of trade measures with the product classification dummy at the HS2-digit level: *agriculture* (indicating that product k belongs to the agricultural products: HS01 −24) or *manufacture* (indicating that product k belongs to the manufacturing products: HS25-97). Note that the products in the first product group are all TBT-rocked products, whereas only part of the products in the second group is TBT rocked. Column 2 (column 3) of Table 11.5 reports the results after adding the agriculture (manufacture) dummy and the dummy's interaction with each of the trade control measures in terms of frequency index. The estimating results for coverage ratio are reported in columns 2 and 3 of Tables 11.6.

Based on Tables 11.5 and 11.6, we summarize the key results in Table 11.7. Since the standard gravity model variables (*GDP Contig, Dist, Comlang*) show the same pattern in Table 11.5 and 11.6, we only focus on the trade control measures. Notice that to obtain some

products declined after the WTO accession (see Table 11.1), the quota-affected agriculture products increased. Before 2002, there were only one to two agriculture products covered by the quota (i.e., HS 17 and HS24), but after 2002, there were three to four agricultural products covered by the quota (i.e., HS10, HSII, HS15, and HS17).

Table 11.6. Tobit regression results by using coverage ratio.

	1998–2006			1998–2001			2002–2006		
	(1)	(2)	(3)	(1)	(2)	(3)	(1)	(2)	(3)
gdp	1.563	1.562	1.562	1.567	1.565	1.565	1.560	1.559	1.559
	(83.90)[a]	(84.89)[a]	(84.89)[a]	(56.09)[a]	(57.13)[a]	(57.13)[a]	(62.64)[a]	(63.24)[a]	(63.24)[a]
dist	−1.468	−1.465	−1.465	−1.623	−1.619	−1.619	−1.347	−1.345	−1.345
	(36.31)[a]	(36.70)[a]	(36.70)[a]	(26.54)[a]	(27.01)[a]	(27.01)[a]	(25.09)[a]	(25.31)[a]	(25.31)[a]
contig	−0.749	−0.744	−0.744	−0.631	−0.625	−0.625	−0.838	−0.832	−0.832
	(11.08)[a]	(11.14)[a]	(11.14)[a]	(6.16)[a]	(6.23)[a]	(6.23)[a]	(9.35)[a]	(9.38)[a]	(9.38)[a]
comlang	3.220	3.212	3.212	3.751	3.738	3.738	2.795	2.790	2.790
	(41.91)[a]	(42.33)[a]	(42.33)[a]	(32.43)[a]	(32.96)[a]	(32.96)[a]	(27.30)[a]	(27.52)[a]	(27.52)[a]
developing	−1.115	−1.111	−1.111	−1.347	−1.339	−1.339	−0.935	−0.933	−0.933
	(18.93)[a]	(19.08)[a]	(19.08)[a]	(15.00)[a]	(15.21)[a]	(15.21)[a]	(12.01)[a]	(12.10)[a]	(12.10)[a]
tariff	−0.715	−0.279	0.037	−0.446	0.139	−0.013	−0.909	−0.628	0.434
	(19.91)[a]	(6.31)[a]	(0.43)	(8.69)[a]	(2.16)[b]	(0.11)	(17.67)[a]	(10.20)[a]	(3.01)[a]
cr-tbt	−0.000	0.013	−0.005	0.002	0.022	0.017	−0.002	0.007	−1.273
	(0.40)	(17.37)[a]	(0.26)	(2.74)[a]	(19.02)[a]	(0.89)	(2.57)[b]	(7.04)[a]	(4.59)[a]
cr-l	0.031	0.031	0.018	0.016	0.029	0.013	0.032	0.032	0.014
	(40.33)[a]	(34.25)[a]	(11.66)[a]	(7.28)[a]	(9.20)[a]	(3.99)[a]	(36.60)[a]	(32.48)[a]	(6.76)[a]
cr-q	−0.001	−0.011	0.006	0.015	−0.013	0.024	−0.003	−0.011	−0.008
	(0.68)	(5.57)[a]	(2.91)[a]	(5.38)[a]	(3.52)[a]	(5.77)[a]	(1.29)	(2.98)[a]	(2.95)[a]

(*Continued*)

Table 11.6. (*Continued*)

	1998–2006			1998–2001			2002–2006		
	(1)	(2)	(3)	(1)	(2)	(3)	(1)	(2)	(3)
agriculture		−1.038			−1.817			123.823	
		(0.55)			(0.94)			(4.47)[a]	
tariff_agri		0.316			−0.151			1.062	
		(3.32)[a]			(1.14)			(6.79)[a]	
cr-tbt_agri		−0.017			−0.005			−1.280	
		(0.93)			(0.24)			(4.62)[a]	
cr-l_agri		−0.013			−0.016			−0.018	
		(7.11)[a]			(3.63)[a]			(7.95)[a]	
cr-q_agri		0.017			0.037			0.003	
		(5.97)[a]			(6.64)[a]			(0.67)	
manufacture			1.038			1.817			−123.823
			(0.55)			(0.94)			(4.47)[a]
tariff_manu			−0.316			0.151			−1.062
			(3.32)[a]			(1.14)			(6.79)[a]
cr-tbt_manu			0.017			0.005			1.280
			(0.93)			(0.24)			(4.62)[a]
cr-l_manu			0.013			0.016			0.018
			(7.11)[a]			(3.63)[a]			(7.95)[a]
cr-q_manu			−0.017			−0.037			−0.003
			(5.97)[a]			(6.64)[a]			(0.67)
Observations	37152	37152	37152	16512	16512	16512	20640	20640	20640
Censored ob.	7529	7529	7529	3753	3753	3753	3776	3776	3776

Notes: Absolute values of t statistics are in parentheses. a, b and c denotes significant at 1%, 5% and 10% level respectively. Year fixed effects are controlled for.

Table 11.7. Summary and comparison of the results.

HS2	Whole sample				Agriculture				Manufacture			
Frequency index	Tariff	TBT	L	Q	Tariff	TBT	L	Q	Tariff	TBT	L	Q
98 – 06	–	–	+	–	–	–	+	ns	–	+	+	–
98 – 01	–	–	+	+	ns	–	+	+	–	+	ns	ns
02 – 06	–	–	+	–	+	–	+	–	–	ns	+	–
Coverage ratio	Tariff	TBT	L	Q	Tariff	TBT	L	Q	Tariff	TBT	L	Q
98 – 06	–	ns	+	ns	ns	ns	+	+	–	+	+	–
98 – 01	–	+	+	+	ns	ns	+	+	+	+	+	–
02 – 06	–	–	+	ns	+	–	+	–	–	+	+	–

Note: +, –, and ns, stand for positively significant, negatively significant, not significant, respectively.

general conclusions, there are three-dimensional comparisons to be made with a focus on the impacts of trade measures. Let us take FI-TBT in agriculture products for example. We compare its impacts on China's import to those obtained from the all products, those obtained from agricultural products but with CR-TBT, and those from manufacturing products with FI-TBT. In all the comparisons, our discussion focuses on their differences rather than similarities.

We first compare columns 1 and 3 of Table 11.5. We find that tariff has the expected negative and significant impacts on imports in column 1, but the impact is statistically positive in column 3 for the period 2002–2006. This finding indicates that agriculture product imports are more responsive to changes in non-tariff measures than tariffs. Despite these differences, we do not find any qualitative differences between the TBT effects in columns 1 and 3 of Table 11.5, even for the two sub-periods. Hence, *FI-TBT has negative and significant impacts on China's imports for all products and for agriculture products during the pre-WTO and the post-WTO periods.*

Second, we compare the effects of frequency index non-tariff measures and coverage ratio non-tariff measures for agricultural products in column 3 of Tables 11.5 and 11.6. Tariff has significant negative impacts for the entire period, but has significant positive impacts in the post-WTO period. This result is unexpected because it does not make economic sense. One explanation is that the large negative impacts on agricultural product imports have been taken up by the CR-TBT. This is shown in the CR-TBT effect in the post-WTO period, which is −1.273 in Table 11.6, compared with the FI-TBT effect, which is −0.133 in Table 11.5. Therefore, we tend to think the difference is due to measurement differences. Another possible explanation may be the fact that the positive tariff effect for agricultural products from developed countries in the post-WTO period dominates the tariff effect during the whole sample period. It is not surprising because China cut down on the tariff for agricultural products after accession to the WTO; thus, developed countries can still export despite the tariff if their agriculture products are competitive enough.

Quota has different impacts depending on its measurement type for the whole period. As shown in Table 11.6, coverage ratio quota has positive and significant impacts on imports, whereas frequency index quota has negative (but insignificant) impacts on imports in Table 11.5. The two types of measures have qualitatively similar effects: positive in 1998–2001 and negative in 2002–2006. The main reason for the difference during the whole period is the much stronger negative impacts of frequency index quota, which is −0.032 in Table 11.5, than the coverage ratio quota, which is −0.008 in Table 11.6.

More importantly, CR-TBT's negative impacts on imports are insignificant (see column 3 of period 1998–2006 in Table 11.6). This is affected by the positive (insignificant) impacts of CR-TBT in the period 1998-2001. The same difference between FI-TBT and CR-TBT has been identified from the all-product regression. Thus, agricultural products retain the same pattern, or perhaps the pattern from agricultural products dominates in all products.

Third, the impacts of FI-TBT in agricultural products are compared with those in manufacturing products. Based on the results in columns 2 and 3 in Table 11.5, it is interesting to find that the FI-TBT has contradictory impacts on agricultural and manufacturing imports. Although TBT has negative and significant impacts on agricultural imports, it has positive and significant impacts on manufacturing imports. Thus, *FI-TBT is trade restricting for agriculture goods but is trade promoting for manufacturing goods.* This property appears in both the pre-WTO and the post-WTO period. We do not find this difference surprising because TBT is more likely to have a trade promotion effect for products that consumers lack information about the quality of the imports, and manufacturing products suffer from more such informational asymmetry problem than agriculture products.[8]

Finally, we compare the impacts of coverage ratio non-tariff trade measures on agricultural (column 3 of Table 11.6) and on manufacturing imports (column 2 of Table 11.6). The interesting result with regard to TBT obtained for the FI-TBT above also holds: *CR-TBT is trade reducing for agriculture goods but is trade promoting for manufacturing goods.* This can be observed from the negative (insignificant) estimate for the whole period for agriculture products, which is −0.005 in column 3, and the positive (significant) estimate for the whole period for manufacturing products, which is 0.013 in column 2. This difference is much clearer and stronger for the post-WTO period: −1.273 (significant) for agricultural goods and 0.007 (significant) for manufacturing goods.

The impacts of tariff and other non-tariff measures on the two groups of imports are also different. For agricultural goods imports, tariff has positive (insignificant) impacts and coverage ratio quota has positive (significant) impacts; in contrast, for manufacturing goods imports, their impacts are both negative and significant. The impacts of coverage ratio license for both agricultural and manufacturing goods are qualitatively the same.

5.3. *Marginal effects of trade measures*

From a pure economic point of view, the estimated raw coefficients reported in Tables 11.5 and 11.6 are simply the effects of the

[8] Our result is consistent with that of Moenius (2004) on standards. He explains his results using the transaction cost argument based on incomplete information: although standards impose high compliance costs, standards lower information costs on trade partners. As agrifood products are relatively homogeneous, information requirements are comparatively low. Hence, lower information costs arising from importer standards are unlikely to be sufficient to compensate producers for compliance costs. Therefore, TBT tends to negatively impact agrifood trade. However, manufacturing industries are more technologically sophisticated. If the costs of adapting products to foreign markets are small relative to information costs, a positive effect might occur.

independent variables on the "latent" variable underlying the Tobit model. In particular, we examine how China's trade measures affect imports of a product from a foreign country *given* that the product is imported to China from that foreign country. However, analyzing the *marginal effects* of the trade measures is also important, that is, the effects on the margin. Following Alberto (2006), we calculate three types of marginal effects based on the basic gravity model (3). First, the "unconditional expected value" provides a marginal effect of a one-unit change in a trade measure on the unconditional expected value of trade flow. It estimates the overall impacts of the trade measure, considering that there is zero trade for some products from some exporting countries. Second, the "conditional marginal effect" picks up the marginal effect on the expected value of trade flow conditional on being uncensored. It captures the impact of the trade measure on the positive trade volume, that is, the trade already taking place. Third, the "probability uncensored" measures the marginal effect on the probability of being uncensored. It estimates the impact of trade measure on the probability of observing positive trade.

Table 11.8 shows the marginal effects of trade measures during the whole sample period using frequency index. Based on the whole product sample results, a 1% increase in tariff will result in about 0.586% decrease in import value. This includes about a 0.466% decrease of the positive trade volume and a $0.12(= 0.586 - 0.466)\%$ decrease of potential trade as well. This potential loss is caused by the tariff decreasing the probability of foreign countries in accessing China's import market by 2.7%. Tariff does not have significant restrictive impacts on agricultural products. As for manufacturing products, a 1% increase in tariff will result in about 0.467% decrease in import value, which includes about 0.381% decrease of the positive trade volume and $0.086(= 0.467-0.381)\%$ decrease of potential trade as well due to the lower probability of exporting to the Chinese market for some products by some foreign countries.

Turning to the frequency index non-tariff measures, license has positive impacts, whereas quota has negative impacts, all of which are statistically significant. If the FI-L increases by 1%, our imports will increase by 4% due to a 3.2% increase in the trade value from the existing import products and some new products, which

Table 11.8. Marginal effects of trade control measures: Frequency index.

	Whole sample (HS01-96)			Agriculture (HS01-24)			Manufacture (HS25-96)		
98 – 06	(1)	(2)	(3)	(1)	(2)	(3)	(1)	(2)	(3)
tariff	−0.586	−0.466	−0.027	−0.107	−0.081	−0.007	−0.467	−0.381	−0.018
	(17.77)[a]	(17.74)[a]	(17.59)[a]	(1.27)	(1.27)	(1.27)	(11.58)[a]	(11.57)[a]	(11.50)[a]
fi-tbt	−0.007	−0.006	−0.0003	−0.038	−0.029	−0.002	0.0043	0.0035	0.0002
	(13.54)[a]	(13.53)[a]	(13.43)[a]	(5.21)[a]	(5.21)[a]	(5.20)[a]	(4.84)[a]	(4.84)[a]	(4.83)[a]
fi-l	0.040	0.032	0.002	0.031	0.023	0.002	0.040	0.033	0.002
	(35.15)[a]	(35.01)[a]	(33.66)[a]	(11.83)[a]	(11.81)[a]	(11.71)[a]	(28.74)[a]	(28.64)[a]	(27.37)[a]
fi-q	−0.017	−0.014	−0.0008	−0.005	−0.004	−0.0003	−0.031	−0.026	−0.001
	(7.83)[a]	(7.82)[a]	(7.81)[a]	(1.68)*c*	(1.68)*c*	(1.68)*c*	(10.17)[a]	(10.16)[a]	(10.10)[a]

Note: Column (1) for "unconditional expected value"; column (2) for "conditional marginal effect"; and column (3) for "probability uncensored". Absolute value of z statistics in parentheses; a, significant at 1%; b, significant at 5%; c, significant at 10%.

Table 11.9. Marginal effects of trade control measures: Coverage ratio.

	Whole sample (HS01-96)			Agriculture (HS01-24)			Manufacture (HS25-96)		
98 – 06	(1)	(2)	(3)	(1)	(2)	(3)	(1)	(2)	(3)
tariff	−0.647	−0.516	−0.0293	0.0747	0.0562	0.0049	−0.270	−0.2215	−0.0102
	(19.90)[a]	(19.87)[a]	(19.63)[a]	(0.94)	(0.94)	(0.94)	(6.70)[a]	(6.70)[a]	(6.68)[a]
cr-tbt	−.00019	−0.00015	−0.000008	−0.0047	−0.0035	−0.0003	0.0117	0.0095	0.0004
	(0.40)	(0.40)	(0.40)	(0.28)	(0.28)	(0.28)	(17.86)[a]	(17.84)[a]	(17.46)[a]
cr-l	0.0279	0.0222	0.0013	0.0154	0.0116	0.0010	0.0288	0.0236	0.0011
	(40.31)[a]	(40.11)[a]	(38.08)[a]	(11.07)[a]	(11.06)[a]	(10.97)[a]	(35.01)[a]	(34.84)[a]	(32.44)[a]
cr-q	−0.00087	−0.00069	−.000039	0.0046	0.0035	0.0003	−0.0107	−0.0088	−0.0004
	(0.68)	(0.68)	(0.68)	(2.59)[a]	(2.59)[a]	(2.59)[a]	(5.90)[a]	(5.90)[a]	(5.89)[a]

Note: Column (1) for "unconditional expected value"; column (2) for "conditional marginal effect"; and column (3) for "probability uncensored". Absolute value of z statistics in parentheses; a, significant at 1%; b, significant at 5%; c, significant at 10%.

become available because of the increased probability of market access (0.2%). Similar changes can be observed for both agricultural and manufacturing goods.

In contrast, if the FI-Q increases by 1%, import will decrease by 1.7% on average, which includes a decrease of the positive trade (1.4%) and a decrease of the potential trade. Similar changes can also be observed for both agricultural and manufacturing goods.

Let us next turn to the TBT effects. For all products, a 1% increase in the FI-TBT will decrease imports by 0.7%, which includes a 0.6% decrease in the imports of existing products and a decrease in the potential imports due to the falling probability of market access. These trade-reducing impacts of FI-TBT are also observed for agricultural imports. However, trade promoting impacts are observed for manufacturing imports. A 1% increase in the FI-TBT will increase imports by 0.43%, which includes a 0.35% increase in the imports of existing products and an increase in the potential imports due to the higher probability of market access.

Finally, Table 11.9 shows the marginal effects of trade measures during the whole sample period using coverage ratio. Focusing on the TBT effects, we observe that TBT has negative effects on agriculture imports, but the effects are not statistically significant. However, TBT has significant trade promoting effects on manufacturing products. A 1% increase in the coverage ratio TBT will increase manufacturing products imports by 1.17%, which includes a 0.95% increase in the imports of existing products and a 0.04% increase in the potential imports due to the increased probability of market access.

6. Conclusion

This paper contributes to the literature of empirical studies on TBT effects on imports. In particular, we analyze how TBT, together with other trade barriers, affect China's imports during 1998 and 2006. We use both frequency index and coverage ratio approaches to measure TBT. When using the frequency index, we find that TBT has a negative impact on China's imports. The results are different when coverage ratio is used. Based on the entire period of 1998–2006, the negative effects of TBT are not statistically significant. Focusing on the period 1998–2001 (the pre-WTO period), we find the TBT has trade promotion effect. The impacts of TBT on agricultural and manufacturing goods imports are different. We find that TBT (measured by both frequency index and coverage ratio) are trade reducing for agricultural goods but are trade promoting for manufacturing goods.

TBT become more influential when traditional trade barriers, both tariff and non-tariff, are phased out gradually through multilateral negotiations. However, concluding whether TBT in general promote or restrict trade is still premature. The literature, including the present study, has reached different conclusions depending on the type of country,[9] the type of industry, and time periods. Further studies on this area are encouraged to reach general conclusions, which are important and necessary for policy designs.

Acknowledgement

We would like to thank the referee for the valuable comments and suggestions. We are grateful for the presentations at the Canadian Economic Association Annual Meeting, Asia-Pacific Trade Seminars, the first IEFS China Conference, and especially the 2010 APJAE Symposium on International Trade and China Economy. We wish to acknowledge the financial support from the Hong Kong Government's Competitive Earmarked Research Grant 2008-2010 ($HKU643108H$), the Mrs. Li Ka Shing Fund of the University of Hong Kong, National Nature Science Foundation of China (NSFC project No.70703021), Ministry of Education of China (NCET-10-0537) and Shanghai Education Committee ($10ZS49$).

[9]We have also run regressions using China's import from developing countries and developed countries separately. We find some different effects of China's TBT on the exports by these two groups of countries to China.

Annex 11.1. Code list of supporting documents subject to customs control of PRC.

Code	Name of licences or instruments of ratification	Authorized institution that issue the documents
1	Import licence	Quota & Licence Administrative Bureau Ministry of Commence or its authorized institution
2	Import licence for dual-use item and technologies	Ministry of Commerce
3	Export licence for dual-use item and technologies	Ministry of Commerce
4	Export licence	Quota & Licence Administrative Bureau Ministry of Commence or its authorized institution
5	Textile products for interim export licence	Ministry of Commerce
6	Used machinery and electrical products are on the list of prohibited import goods	The importing of used electro-mechanical products with this code at the end of its code of goods is prohibited
7	Automatic import goods	Ministry of Commerce
8	Articles on the list of prohibited export goods	Products with this code are prohibited to be exported
9	Articles on the list of prohibited import goods	Products with this code are prohibited to be import
A	Certificate of inspection for goods inward	The administration of quality supervision
B	Certificate of inspection for goods outward	The administration of quality supervision
D	Certificate of inspection for goods inward/outward (for semi-finished diamonds)	The administration of quality supervision
E	Export licencing certificate for endangered species	The administrative bureau of the Import and species Export of Endangered Wild Animal or by other relevant administrative

(*Continued*)

Annex 11.1. (*Continued*)

Code	Name of licences or instruments of ratification	Authorized institution that issue the documents
F	Import licencing certificate for endangered species	The administrative bureau of the Import and species Export of Endangered Wild Animal or by other relevant administrative
G	Export licence for dual-use item and technologies	Ministry of Commerce
H	Hongkong and Macao OPA textile certificate	(1) Hongkong Trade and Industry Department releases OPA certificate of Textile Processing in Mainland China; (2) Macao Ministry of Economy releases certificate of Textile Processing in Mainland China
I	Import or export permit for psychotropic drugs	State food and drug administration
J	Import or export permit for gold products	The People's Bank of China
K	Application form of transfer between factories during further processing	Local custom
L	Import or export of medicines permit licence	State food and drug administration and its authorized in institution
O	Automatic import licence (machinery and electrical products, whether used or not)	Business Department, local institutions in charge of foreign trade or department of Electrical and Mechanical Services
P	Import permit for waste and scraps	State environmental protection administration of China
Q	Report of inspection of soundness on import medicines	State food and drug administration and its authorized institution

Annex 11.1. (*Continued*)

Code	Name of licences or instruments of ratification	Authorized institution that issue the documents
R	Clearance form for import veterinary drugs	Ministry of Agriculture of the People's Republic
S	Import or export registration certificate for pesticides	Ministry of Agriculture of the People's Republic
T	Entry or exit permit for foreign currency cash transfer and reallocation between banks	(1) "License for banks to transfer foreign currencies" released by state Administration of Foreign Exchange is required for the entry and exist of foreign currency; (2) Sanction from the Silver, Cold & Currency Department of People's Bank of China is required for the entry and exit of RMB
W	Import or export permit for narcolic drugs	State food and drug Administration
X	Environment control release notice for poisonous chemicals	State environmental protection administration of China
Y	Certificate of origin	State environmental protection administration of China
Z	Issuance permit for audio/or video products, release for prototype tape	License for Importing and Exporting Visual Product released by the Department of Academy and Culture; List of Imported Movies and Television Programs released by the State Association of Broadcasting, Films & Television
a	Certificate of examination and approval signed and sealed before-hand	Business association
c	Domestic sales collect tax contact sheet	Local Custom

(*Continued*)

Annex 11.1. (*Continued*)

Code	Name of licences or instruments of ratification	Authorized institution that issue the documents
e	Quota certificate for importing cotton beyond the tariff quota at a preferential rate	Quota & License Administrative Bureau Ministry of Commerce or its authorized institution
q	Country-specific tariff quota certificates	National development and Reform commission
r	Pre-classified signs	
s	Relative certificate for ITA products issued by information industry ministry	Local Custom duty department
t	Certificate of customs quota	Quota & License Administrative Bureau Ministry of Commerce or its authorized institution

Annex 11.2. TBT-rocked products.

Chapter	Description	98	99	00	01	02	03	04	05	06
01	Live animals	√	√	√	√	√	√	√	√	√
02	Meat and edible meat offal	√	√	√	√	√	√	√	√	√
03	Fish, crustaceans, molluscs, aquatic invertebrates	√	√	√	√	√	√	√	√	√
04	Dairy products, eggs, honey, edible animal product	√	√	√	√	√	√	√	√	√
05	Products of animal origin	√	√	√	√	√	√	√	√	√
06	Live trees, plants, bulbs, roots, cut flowers etc	√	√	√	√	√	√	√	√	√
07	Edible vegetables and certain roots and tubers	√	√	√	√	√	√	√	√	√
08	Edible fruit, nuts, peel of citrus fruit, melons	√	√	√	√	√	√	√	√	√
09	Coffee, tea, mate and spices	√	√	√	√	√	√	√	√	√
10	Cereals	√	√	√	√	√	√	√	√	√
11	Milling products, malt, starches, inulin, wheat glute	√	√	√	√	√	√	√	√	√
12	Oil seed, oleagic fruits, grain, seed, fruit, etc, ne	√	√	√	√	√	√	√	√	√
13	Lac, gums, resins, vegetable saps and extracts	√	√	√	√	√	√	√	√	√
14	Vegetable plaiting materials, vegetable products	√	√	√	√	√	√	√	√	√

(*Continued*)

Annex 11.2. (*Continued*)

Chapter	Description	98	99	00	01	02	03	04	05	06
15	Animal, vegetable fats and oils, cleavage products, etc	√	√	√	√	√	√	√	√	√
16	Meat, fish and seafood food preparations	√	√	√	√	√	√	√	√	√
17	Sugars and sugar confectionery	√	√	√	√	√	√	√	√	√
18	Cocoa and cocoa preparations	√	√	√	√	√	√	√	√	√
19	Cereal, our, starch, milk preparations and products	√	√	√	√	√	√	√	√	√
20	Vegetable, fruit, nut, etc food preparations	√	√	√	√	√	√	√	√	√
21	Miscellaneous edible preparations	√	√	√	√	√	√	√	√	√
22	Beverages, spirits and vinegar	√	√	√	√	√	√	√	√	√
23	Residues, wastes of food industry, animal fodder	√	√	√	√	√	√	√	√	√
24	Tobacco and manufactured tobacco substitutes	√	√	√	√	√	√	√	√	√
30	Pharmaceutical products	√								
31	Fertilizers		√	√	√	√	√	√	√	√
33	Essential oils, perfumes, cosmetics, toiletries		√	√	√	√	√	√	√	√

Annex 11.2. (*Continued*)

Chapter	Description	98	99	00	01	02	03	04	05	06
41	Raw hides and skins (other than furskins) and leather	√	√	√	√	√	√	√	√	√
42	Articles of leather, animal gut, harness, travel good						√	√	√	√
43	Furskins and artificial fur, manufactures thereof						√	√	√	√
44	Wood and articles of wood, wood charcoal	√	√	√	√	√	√	√	√	√
45	Cork and articles of cork	√	√	√	√	√	√	√	√	√
46	Manufactures of plaiting material, basketwork, etc	√	√	√	√	√	√	√	√	√
47	Pulp of wood, fibrous cellulosic material, waste etc	√	√	√	√	√	√	√	√	√
50	Silk							√		
51	Wool, animal hair, horsehair yarn and fabric thereof	√	√	√	√	√	√	√	√	√
72	Iron and steel	√	√	√	√	√	√	√	√	√
76	Aluminum and articles thereof								√	√
80	Tin and articles thereof							√	√	√

References

Abbott, Frederick L., 1997, "The Intersection of Law and Trade in the WTO. System Economics and the Transition to a Hard Law System", in: David Orden and Donna Roberts, eds., *Understanding Technical Barriers to Agricultural Trade* (St. Paul: Minnesota).

Baldwin, Richard, 2000, "Regulatory Protectionism, Developing Nations and a Two-Tier. World Trade System", CEPR Discussion Paper No. 2574.

Beghin, John C. and Jean-Christophe Bureau., 2001, "Quantification of Sanitary, Phytosanitary, and Technical Barriers to Trade for Trade Policy Analysis", Center for Agricultural and Rural Development, Working Paper 01-WP 291.

Bora, Bijit Aki Kuwahara and Sam Laird, 2002, "Quantification of Non-tariff Barriers", United Nations Conference of Trade and Development, Policy Issues in International Trade and Commodities, Study Series No.18.

Cao, K. and R. Johnson, 2006, "Impacts of mandatory meat hygiene regulations on the New. Zealand meat trade", *Australasian Agribusiness Review* 14, paper 3.

Cipollina, M. and L. Salvatici, 2006, "Measuring protection: mission impossible?" Trade AG, Working Paper No. 06/07.

Deardorff, Alan V. and Robert Stern, 1998, "The Measurement of Non-Tariff Barriers", OECD Economics Department, Working Paper No. 179.

Disdier, Anne-Celia., Lionel Fontagne, Mondher Mimouni, 2008, "The Impact of Regulations. on Agricultural Trade: Evidence from the SPS and TBT Agreements", *American Journal of Agricultural Economics* 90(2), 336–350.

Ferrantino, Michael, 2006, "Quantifying the Trade and Economic Effects of Non-Tariff. Measures", OECD Trade Policy Working Papers, No. 28, Paris: OECD.

Jayasuriya, S., D. MacLaren, and R. Metha, 2006, "Meeting Food Safety Standards in Export. Markets: Issues and Challenges facing Firms Exporting from Developing Countries", Paper presented at the IATRC Summer Symposium, Food Regulation and Trade: Institutional Framework, Concepts of Analysis and Empirical Evidence, Bonn, Germany, 28–30 May 2006.

Korinek, Jane, Mark Melatos and Marie-Luise Rau, 2008, "A Review of Methods for. Quantifying the Trade Effects of Standards in The Agri-food Sector", OECD Trade Policy Working Paper No. 79.

Lacovone, L., 2003, "Analysis and Impact of Sanitary and Phytosanitary Measures", Available at http://www.cid.harvard.edu/cidtrade/Papers/iacovone.pdf.

Maskus, K.E. and John S. Wilson, 2000, "Quantifying the Impact of Technical Barriers to. Trade: A Review of Past Attempts and the New Policy Context", Paper prepared for the World Bank Workshop on "Quantifying the Trade Effects of Standard and Technical Barriers: Is it Possible?" World Bank, 2000.

Metha, R. and R.G. Nambiar, 2005, "International food safety standards and processed food. exports: India", report within project "International food safety standards and processed food exports from developing countries:

a comparative study of India and Thailand", The Australian National University, unpublished.

Moenius, J., 2004, "Information versus product adaptation: The role of standards in trade", Kellogg School of Management Working Paper, Northwestern University.

Moenius, J., 2006, "The Good, the Bad and the Ambiguous: Standards and Trade in. Agricultural Products", IATRC Summer Symposium, May 28–30, Bonn, Germany.

OECD, 2001, *Measurement of sanitary, phytosanitary and technical barriers to trade*, Paris.

Otsuki, T., Wilson, J.S. and M. Sewadeh, 2001a, "Saving two in a billion: Quantifying the trade effects of European food safety standards on African exports", *Food Policy* 26(5), 495–514.

Otsuki, T., Wilson, J.S. and M. Sewadeh, 2001b, "What price precaution? European. harmonization of afatoxin regulations and African groundnuts", *European Review of Agricultural Economics* 28(3), 263–283.

Thornsbury, Suzanne, 1998, "Technical Regulations As Barriers to Agriculture Trade", Phd. Dissertation of Virginia Polytechnic Institute and State University.

UNCTAD, 1997, Indicators of Tariff and Non-tariff Barriers on CD-ROM.

Wallner, K., 1998, "Mutual Recognition and the Strategic Use of International Standard", SSE/EFI Working Paper No.254, Stockholm School of Economics.

Wilson, J.S. and T. Otsuki, 2004a, "Standards and Technical Regulations and Firms in. Developing Countries: New Evidence from a World Bank Technical Barrier to Trade Survey", World Bank, Washington DC.

Wilson, J.S. and T. Otsuki, 2004b, "Global trade and food safety: winner and losers in a non-harmonized world", *Journal of Economic Integration* 18(2), 266–287.

Wilson, J.S. and T. Otsuki, 2004c, "To spray or not to spray: pesticides, banana exports and. food safety", *Food Policy* 29, 131–145.

Wilson, J.S., T. Otsuki, and B. Majumdsar, 2003, "Balancing food safety and risk: do drug residue limits affect international trade?" *Journal of International Trade and Development* 12(4), 377–402.

Index

CPSIA information can be obtained
at www.ICGtesting.com
Printed in the USA
LVHW022327040920
664999LV00006B/23

9 789811 203985